Frommer's®

Caribbean Hideaways

ELEVENTH EDITION

by Ian Keown

WILEY

Wiley Publishing, Inc.

Published by:

Wiley Publishing, Inc.

111 River St.
Hoboken, NJ 07030
www.frommers.com

First published by Harmony Books, a division of Crown Publishers, Inc., and represented in Canada by the Canadian MANDA Group.

ISBN 0-7645-3922-1
ISSN 1069-580X

Editor: Billy Fox
Production Editor: Bethany André
Cartographer: Roberta Stockwell
Design by: Nick Anderson
Production by: Wiley Indianapolis Composition Services

For information on our other products and services or to obtain technical support, please contact our Customer Care Department within the U.S. at 800-762-2974, outside the U.S. at 317-572-3993 or fax 317-572-4002.

Wiley also publishes its books in a variety of electronic formats. Some content that appears in print may not be available in electronic formats.

Manufactured in the United States of America

5 4 3 2 1

Contents

Acknowledgments   *xi*
Introduction   *xiii*
The Rates — How to Figure Them Out   *xxxv*

THE TURKS & CAICOS   1
Pine Cay
The Meridian Club   2

Parrot Cay
Parrot Cay   5

Providenciales
Grace Bay Club   7
Point Grace   9

OTHER CHOICES: *Caribbean Paradise Inn, Sibonné Boutique Hotel (Providenciales), Windmills Plantation (Salt Cay)*   *11*

THE CAYMAN ISLANDS   15
Grand Cayman
Hyatt Regency Grand Cayman   16

JAMAICA   21
Montego Bay
Round Hill Hotel & Villas   22
The Tryall Club   26
Half Moon Golf, Tennis & Beach Club   28

Ocho Rios
Jamaica Inn   31

Oracabessa
   Goldeneye   33
Port Antonio
   Trident Villas & Hotel   36
   Hotel Mocking Bird Hill   37
Irish Town
   Strawberry Hill   39
Treasure Beach
   Jake's   42
Negril
   The Caves   43
   OTHER CHOICES: *The Jamaica Palace Hotel (Port Antonio); Coyaba Beach Resort & Club (Montego Bay); Tensing Pen Village, Rockhouse, Idle Awhile (Negril)*   45

THE DOMINICAN REPUBLIC   49
La Romana
   Casa de Campo   50

THE U.S. VIRGIN ISLANDS & PUERTO RICO   55
Puerto Rico
   Hyatt Dorado Beach Resort & Country Club
      (Dorado)   58
   The Horned Dorset Primavera (Rincón)   60
   The Water Club (San Juan)   63
   Hotel El Convento (Old San Juan)   65
   Las Casitas Village (Las Croabas)   67
   Wyndham Martineau Bay Resort & Spa (Vieques)   68
St. John
   Caneel Bay   71
St. Thomas
   Point Pleasant Resort   75
   Pavilions & Pools   78
   The Ritz-Carlton, St. Thomas   79
St. Croix
   The Buccaneer   81
   OTHER CHOICES: *Hibiscus Beach Hotel (St. Croix)*   84

THE BRITISH VIRGIN ISLANDS 85

Tortola

Long Bay Beach Resort 86

The Sugar Mill 89

Peter Island Resort 91

Guana Island

Guana Island 94

Virgin Gorda

Little Dix Bay 96

Biras Creek Resort 98

The Bitter End Yacht Club 101

OTHER CHOICES: *Anegada Reef Hotel (Anegada); Sandcastle Hotel (Jost Van Dyke); Frenchman's Cay Resort Hotel (Tortola) 103*

THE DUTCH WINDWARDS 107

St. Martin

La Samanna 110

Le Meridien 112

Le Mississippi 114

Hotel La Plantation 115

Saba

Willard's of Saba 117

Queen's Gardens Resort 119

OTHER CHOICES: *Hotel L'Esplanade Caraïbe, Le Petit Hotel (St. Martin); The Cottage Club (Saba) 121*

THE QUEEN'S LEEWARDS 123

Anguilla

Malliouhana Hotel 125

Cap Juluca 129

La Sirena Hotel 131

CoveCastles Villa Resort 133

CuisinArt Resort & Spa 134

St. Kitts

The Golden Lemon 136

Rawlins Plantation 139

Ottley's Plantation Inn 141

Nevis
Nisbet Plantation Beach Club 143
Four Seasons Nevis Resort 144
Montpelier Plantation Inn 148
Golden Rock 150
Hermitage Plantation Inn 151
Old Manor Estate & Hotel 153

Antigua
Jumby Bay Resort 154
Curtain Bluff 157
The Inn at English Harbour 159
The Admiral's Inn 160
Siboney Beach Club 162
Galley Bay 163
Blue Waters 165

Barbuda
K Club 166

OTHER CHOICES: *Hurricane Cove Bungalows, The Mount Nevis Hotel & Beach Club (Nevis); Ocean Terrace Inn (St. Kitts); The Copper & Lumber Store Hotel, Cocobay, Harmony Hall (Antigua)* 169

THE FRENCH WEST INDIES 173

St. Barthélemy
François Plantation 175
Hôtel Carl Gustaf 177
Hôtel St. Barth Isle de France 179
Hôtel Le Toiny 181
Hôtel Manapany Cottages 183
Filao Beach Hotel 184
Hôtel Eden Rock 186
Tom Beach Hotel 188
Hôtel Guanahani 189
Village St. Jean Hotel Cottages 191

Guadeloupe
Le Jardin Malanga 192
Hôtel Saint-Georges 195
Hôtel La Cohoba (Marie–Galante) 196

Martinique

    Habitation Lagrange 197

    Le Plein Soleil 200

OTHER CHOICES: *Tropical Hotel, Hôtel Emeraude Plage, Résidence les Lataniers (St. Barthélemy); Frégate Bleue Inn, Hôtel Cap Est Lagoon Resort, Hôtel Plantation Leyritz (Martinique); Auberge Les Petits Saints (Terre-de-Haut)* 201

THE QUEEN'S WINDWARDS 207

St. Lucia

    Windjammer Landing Beach Resort 209

    East Winds Inn 211

    Ti Kaye Village 213

    Anse Chastanet Beach Hotel 214

    Ladera Resort 217

    Jalousie Hilton Resort & Spa 219

Barbados

    Coral Reef Club 221

    Fairmont Glitter Bay 224

    Fairmont Royal Pavilion 226

    Cobblers Cove 228

    The Sandpiper 230

    Sandy Lane 231

    The House 233

    Villa Nova Hotel 235

    Hotel Little Good Harbour 238

Tobago

    Mount Irvine Bay Hotel & Golf Club 239

    Blue Haven Hotel 241

OTHER CHOICES: *Exotica, Fort Young (Dominica); The Royal St. Lucian Hotel (St. Lucia); The Savannah, Lone Star (Barbados)* 243

ST. VINCENT-GRENADINES & GRENADA 247

St. Vincent

    Young Island 251

    Grand View Beach Hotel 253

Bequia
    Spring on Bequia 254
    Plantation House Hotel 256
    The Frangipani 257
Mustique
    The Cotton House Hotel 259
    Firefly 262
Mayreau
    Saltwhistle Bay Club 263
Petit St. Vincent
    Petit St. Vincent Resort 266
Grenada
    The Calabash Hotel 269
    Secret Harbour Resort 270
    Spice Island Beach Resort 271
    Laluna 273
OTHER CHOICES: *Twelve Degrees North, Blue Horizons Cottage Hotel, (Grenada); Canouan Beach Hotel, Tamarind Beach Hotel, Palm Island (St. Vincent–Grenadines)* 275

THE DUTCH LEEWARDS 279
Curaçao
    Hotel Kurá Hulanda 281
    Avila Beach Hotel 284
    Floris Suite Hotel 286
    Curaçao Marriott Beach Resort & Emerald Casino 287
Bonaire
    Harbour Village Beach Resort 289
    Captain Don's Habitat 292
OTHER CHOICES: *Bellafonte Chateau de la Mer (Bonaire)* 293

ALL-INCLUSIVE RESORTS 295

RESERVATIONS & TOURIST INFORMATION 299

INDEX 303

List of Maps

The Caribbean Islands xiv

The Turks & Caicos 3

The Cayman Islands 17

Jamaica 23

The Dominican Republic 51

Puerto Rico 57

St. John 73

St. Thomas 77

St. Croix 83

The British Virgin Islands 87

St. Martin/St. Maarten 109

Saba 117

Anguilla 127

St. Kitts 137

Nevis 145

Antigua 155

Barbuda 167

St. Barthélemy 177

Guadeloupe 193

Martinique	199
St. Lucia	211
Barbados	223
Tobago	241
Dominica	245
St. Vincent–Grenadines & Grenada	249
Curaçao	281
Bonaire	291

Acknowledgments

As they say in Bonaire, *masha danki* (thank you) to scores of friends and colleagues for tips and suggestions; to readers who took the trouble to send me their critiques and comments (pro and con), and to those others who bumped into me in resorts and airports and told me to my face what they thought of my recommendations; to innkeepers who took time to show me rooms and facilities, reconfirm flights, and get me to the airport on time.

They are too numerous to name individually, but for special efforts beyond the call of duty, I'd like to offer a special *masha danki* to the following (in alphabetical order, of course): Rob Barrett, Mark Carter, Janine Cifeli, Myron Clement, Laura Davidson, Bernadette Davis, Dwiennel Dennis, Arhlene Flowers, Martine Gerard, Hilari Graff, Virginia Haynes, Andrea Hutchinson, Steve Johnson, Tony Johnson, Richard Kahn, Bill Keen, Ralph Locke, Marcella Martinez, Marilyn Marx, Joe Petrocik, Allison Ross, Dianelle Taylor, Valerie Vulcain, Lynn Weber, and Julie Wilson.

An Invitation to the Reader

In researching this book, we discovered many wonderful places — hotels, restaurants, shops, and more. We're sure you'll find others. Please tell us about them so we can share the information with your fellow travelers in upcoming editions. If you were disappointed with a recommendation, we'd love to know that, too. Please write to:

Caribbean Hideaways, 11th Edition
Wiley Publishing, Inc.
111 River St.
Hoboken, NJ 07030

An Additional Note

Please be advised that travel information is subject to change at any time — and this is especially true of prices. We therefore suggest that you write or call ahead for confirmation when making your travel plans. The authors, editors, and publisher cannot be held responsible for the experiences of readers while traveling. Your safety is important to us, however, so we encourage you to stay alert and be aware of your surroundings. Keep a close eye on cameras, purses, and wallets, all favorite targets of thieves and pickpockets.

Introduction

Here is a guide for lovers of all kinds and inclinations — Romeo and Juliet, Romeo and Romeo, Juliet and Juliet, rich lovers, poor lovers, newlyweds and newly unwedded, actresses and bodyguards, and moms and dads who would still be lovers if only they could get the kids out of their hair for a few days. In other words, it's for anyone who has a yen to slip off for a few days and be alone in the sun with someone he or she fancies, likes, loves, has the hots for, or simply wants to do something nice for.

Whatever your tastes or inclinations, you'll probably find something that appeals to you in these pages. This is a fairly eclectic selection: Some of the resorts are on the beach and others are in the mountains; some are on big islands and some are on islands so small you won't find them on a map; some large resorts are included because there are lovers who prefer the anonymity a large resort affords (but none of them so vast as to be tourist-processing factories); some have nightlife of sorts but most of them don't even have a tape recorder; some are for lovers who want to dress up in the evening and others are for lovers with cutoff jeans and beat-up sandals. These hotels and resorts all have something special going for them. It may be seclusion (Spring on Bequia or Petit St. Vincent Resort, both in the Grenadines), it may be spaciousness (Caneel Bay on St. John, Casa de Campo in the Dominican Republic); charm (Golden Rock on Nevis, Rawlins Plantation on St. Kitts); a sense of the past (The Admiral's Inn on Antigua); or luxury (Malliouhana and Cap Juluca on Anguilla, Jumby Bay on Antigua). They may be here because they have some of these qualities and are, in the bargain, moderately priced (The Frangipani on Bequia, the Hotel Mocking Bird Hill on Jamaica, Hotel Saint-Georges on Guadeloupe, for example).

In most cases, they're a combination of one or more of these characteristics; in almost every case they're places where you can avoid neon, plastic, piped music, air-conditioning, casinos, conventions, swarms of children, and that peculiar blight of the Caribbean — masses of cruise-ship passengers.

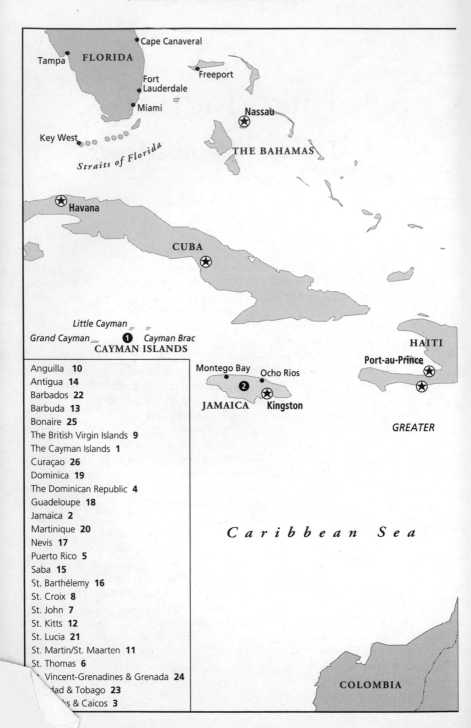

Cape Canaveral

Tampa FLORIDA

Fort
Lauderdale
Miami

Freeport

Key West

Straits of Florida

Nassau

THE BAHAMAS

Havana

CUBA

Little Cayman

Grand Cayman ❶ Cayman Brac
CAYMAN ISLANDS

HAITI

Port-au-Prince

Montego Bay   Ocho Rios
❷
JAMAICA   Kingston

GREATER

Anguilla **10**
Antigua **14**
Barbados **22**
Barbuda **13**
Bonaire **25**
The British Virgin Islands **9**
The Cayman Islands **1**
Curaçao **26**
Dominica **19**
The Dominican Republic **4**
Guadeloupe **18**
Jamaica **2**
Martinique **20**
Nevis **17**
Puerto Rico **5**
Saba **15**
St. Barthélemy **16**
St. Croix **8**
St. John **7**
St. Kitts **12**
St. Lucia **21**
St. Martin/St. Maarten **11**
St. Thomas **6**
Vincent-Grenadines & Grenada **24**
dad & Tobago **23**
s & Caicos **3**

Caribbean   Sea

COLOMBIA

The Caribbean Islands

ATLANTIC OCEAN

③ THE TURKS AND CAICOS

④ DOMINICAN REPUBLIC

Santo Domingo

ANTILLES

VIRGIN ISLANDS

LEEWARD ISLANDS

PUERTO RICO Tortola ⑨ Anegada

San Juan Virgin Gorda

Anguilla ⑩ St. Maarten/ St. Martin

⑪

⑥ ⑬ Barbuda

St. Thomas ⑫ St. Kitts ⑭

⑦ Saba ⑮ Antigua

St. John ⑯

⑧ St. Barthélemy Montserrat

St. Croix St. Eustatius ⑰

Nevis

⑱

Guadeloupe ⑲

Dominica **WINDWARD ISLANDS**

Martinique ⑳

St. Lucia ㉑

㉒

St. Vincent **BARBADOS**

㉔ THE GRENADINES

LESSER ANTILLES Grenada

DUTCH LEEWARD ISLANDS

Aruba Curaçao Tobago ㉓

Bonaire Port of Spain **TRINIDAD AND TOBAGO**

㉖ ㉕

Caracas *Trinidad*

VENEZUELA

SOUTH AMERICA

Above all, none of these hotels tries to disguise the fact that it's in the Caribbean; none of them tries, the minute you arrive, to transport you instantly to back-street Hong Kong or Ye Olde Pubbe in Ye Olde Englande (well, one or two of them maybe, but you'll read about their follies so that you won't be too startled when you get there). These hotels don't make you line up for breakfast in an air-conditioned dining room and then line up immediately afterward to make a reservation for the first or second seating at dinner. They're not the sort of hotels (well, most of them anyway) that entice you with promises of soft air and trade winds, then seal you into a box where you're not allowed to leave the balcony door open to let in the promised soft air and trade winds.

PET PEEVES

Curmudgeons of the world unite! There are innkeepers who also believe in some of the standards you try to uphold. I quote: "Please do not let your wife wear those ghastly hair curlers out of your room"; or "Tennis whites does mean wearing a shirt on court"; or "Transistor radios can be very disturbing to other people. Guests are requested not to play them in public areas"; or "No jeans and tank tops in the dining room"; or "No cellphones around the pool, please."

AIR-CONDITIONING   For me, and I'm sure for a lot of you, louvers and ceiling fans are more romantic than whirring, dripping, throbbing, rusting, shuddering, grinding air-conditioning units, so many of the hotels in this guide either do not have air-conditioning or use it only as a backup system. There is, of course, another side to the air-conditioning debate: In some hotels, the device is necessary to block out such extraneous noises as stray dogs, roosters, and roisterers, and on occasion you may welcome the background hum to keep your own noises in; moreover, one of my colleagues, who shall remain nameless, claims air-conditioning is a necessity for after-lunch lovemaking in the tropics. And I have been reminded by more than one innkeeper that given the locations of their hotels (i.e., close to a beach or former swamp), there could be no hotel without air-conditioning. Nevertheless, it is inexcusable not to give people the option to choose between fresh air or processed air. It's not enough to say you can always open the windows or doors because that's not always a smart move, especially after dark. Therefore, when a hotel has air-conditioning as a backup system, the fact is noted in the listings — but please don't take this as a commendation at the expense of hotels without air-conditioning. (**Note:** Except for a few weeks in summer, air-conditioning is not as necessary in the Caribbean as a lot of vacationers — and travel agents — think it is.)

CRUISE SHIP PASSENGERS   Presumably you're going to the Caribbean to find a quiet, secluded beach that won't remind you of Coney Island on the Fourth of July, but you can forget that idea if a few hundred old salts arrive in ankle socks and T-shirts. Some hotels encourage these visits because they represent instant profit; others ban them unequivocally; and still others are beginning to learn that after they've cleared up the litter and tallied up the missing souvenirs, cruise-ship passengers aren't worth the trouble. ("They buy one Coke, then use the toilet, and the profit on the Coke is less than what I pay for the water.") Most of the hotels in this guide ban cruise-ship passengers — or at least limit the numbers.

RECORDED MUSIC If you take the trouble to search out a hideaway, as opposed to a big swinging resort, you probably don't want your peace and quiet to be disturbed by piped-in noise, especially when it's music that has no connection, harmonic or otherwise, with the setting — such as dining by candlelight on the veranda of a centuries-old inn and having to listen to a record of a contemporary chanteuse belting out, "It's so-o goo-oo-ood."

OTHER MUSIC Piped-in noise is not the same thing as discreet background music carefully selected by the management to match the mood of the guests or the setting; but any kind of music, recorded or live, combo or steel band, should be avoidable (that is, if you don't want to listen, you should be able to go to another lounge or patio where you can't hear it), and it should never keep guests from their sleep. Another ubiquitous blight these days is Bartender's Radio. He's bored, standing around all day serving drinks to a bunch of frolicking foreigners, and he wants his music — usually noisy with an insensate beat. It's a pain for owners, too: "I can see the bartender scurrying to turn down the radio every time he sees me approaching; I agree with you, guests shouldn't have to listen to the bartender's music." The "all" in "getting away from it all" includes other people's radios, and that wish should be respected. Worst offense of all, of course, is amplified music — singer, combo, native band, or, horror of horrors, steel band. Quite apart from the fact that the music is often so loud you can't hear yourselves whisper sweet nothings, the sound systems usually distort the music itself — too much kaBOOM-kaBOOM, not enough trala-trala. Too often, I suspect, loud music is managerial camouflage to distract guests' attention from wishy-washy food. Earlier editions of this guidebook noted that any resort that plays "Island in the Sun" more than six times an evening should lose a star; I'm now almost persuaded it should be the other way round — most amplified pop music is such repetitive drivel that I'd be grateful for "Island in the Sun" six times an evening.

In this guidebook, loud music is tolerated (but with the greatest reluctance) only if the hotel offers alternative facilities for imbibing and dining away from the noise; but if the *kabooming* follows guests all the way to their beds or balconies, or lasts beyond, say, 11pm, that place loses points. Hotel people often boast about the days when their guests were entertained by impromptu performances by a Noel Coward or a Cole Porter; Coward and Porter never went kaBOOM-kaBOOM, yet presumably people still managed to enjoy their vacations back in the days before combos carted around their own power stations.

Please, please: When you resent the music or the volume of the music, take the manager aside and explain that you paid all that money and took that long journey to get some peace and quiet. Remind him or her, gently, that it's considered bad manners to talk so loudly that people at the next table can't enjoy their own conversation. Ditto a band that plays too loudly. Remind him/her also that when a brochure promises peace and serenity and relief from the hubbub of the everyday world, you'd prefer the sound of tree frogs or surf to the intrusive efforts of Madonna or Eminem.

TELEVISION   In the following pages, you will come across several references to television that may at first seem befuddling. The reason is that many innkeepers and thousands of their guests (this one included) feel that television is not compatible with an escapist vacation, and the whole point of a vacation is to get away from television and telephones. For many years, of course, there was no point in TV because no one wanted to watch the local programs. But now, with cable and satellite facilities available on most islands, vacationers and islanders can tune in to their daily dose of Today, Tonight, and CNN. Several innkeepers have mentioned that when they considered installing sets they were overruled by their guests, a typical response being, "This is the one time in the year when I can enjoy his company without competing with baseball/her company without dragging her away from Oprah." Et cetera.

Moreover, many resorts are designed to enjoy a natural flow of breezes, encouraging guests to open windows, louvers, and doors and leave the cooling to the ceiling fans. The air of tranquillity would be instantly destroyed if the neighbors on the left were watching car chases with sirens and the neighbors on the right were watching the shoot-out at the O.K. (or any other) corral. Television tends to be noisy; hideaways are supposed to be quiet. Hooray, then, for those inns and resorts that put in a device ensuring that the sets can never be too loud.

But what about major sporting events? What about the Super Bowl? Most anti-TV resorts get around this by setting aside special rooms for TV and video (and now, in many cases, DVD), a much better arrangement because major sports events are more enjoyable when watched in the company of fellow enthusiasts rather than sulking companions.

PAGING SYSTEMS & CELLULAR PHONES   Even worse than intrusive music is the paging system around the swimming pool and bar; if you're trying to escape telephones and reminders of the office, it doesn't do much for your spirits to know that the people around you are wanted on the phone. Anyone who tips a telephone operator to be paged at the pool should be sealed in a phone booth! I can think of only one hotel in this guide with a paging system, and even then it's used sparingly.

Now some resorts are beginning to take steps to control the profligate use of cellphones or, in the case of the Meridian Club in the Turks & Caicos, banning them altogether. The message from Firefly on Mustique is "We don't want your cellphones or your computers here. We don't want you receiving or sending a constant stream of telephone calls, faxes, or e-mails." When the local phone company told one manager he couldn't expect cellphone service in his hilly Eden for another year, he responded, "Could you make that three years?"

CHILDREN Some hotels ban them completely, as they do cruise-ship passengers; others shunt kids off in a far corner of the property and feed them separately. It's not really the children who are the problem. It may be the parents, who are trying to have a vacation themselves and have allowed family discipline to break down until it reaches the point where it can be restored only by a public shouting match — usually on the beach or around the pool. As one innkeeper puts it, "Kids around pools mean noise — so we don't allow them at the pool." In any case, many couples in hideaways are parents trying to get away from their own families for a day or two, so they're hardly enchanted to be surrounded by other people's youngsters. Rowdy families are less of a bother in the Caribbean than they are back home because parents can't just pile everyone into a car and drive off to the islands. (Sometimes there's a lot to be said for stiff airfares.) However, in recent years, many resorts — even such traditional holdouts as Little Dix Bay in the British Virgins, Caneel Bay in St. John, and Malliouhana in Anguilla — have created special facilities for kids that serve a double of purpose of keeping kids under control and keeping them amused in the company of their peers, rather than boring old adults.

CONVENTIONS The object of a convention or sales conference is to whip people into a frenzy of enthusiasm, but frenzied enthusiasm is something you don't need when you're trying to escape the business or urban world. Very few of the hotels in this guide accept conventions. If they do, the groups are either small enough to be absorbed without a trace, or so large that they have to rent the entire hotel. However, most of the hotels in this guide will accept small, seminar-type groups in the off-season, and in many cases they have to do so to stay in business; but that kind of group shouldn't interfere with your privacy and pleasure. In some cases, it's an advantage: While the group is cooped up studying or discussing its specialty, you have the beach, sailboards, and tennis courts all to yourselves.

SIGNING IN

Some managers prefer that you sign in with your real names, even if they don't match; others prefer you to sign as a couple because it's simpler for the staff. Unless you have strong views one way or another, the simplest procedure is to write the noncommittal M/M — that is, M/M John Smith, M/M Ian Keown, and so on.

However, at least one of you should use your real name. If it's absolutely imperative that you both travel incognito, then at some point you'd better take the manager aside and explain that "Mr. John Smith" will be paying the bill with checks or credit cards in the name of whatever your name is.

Note: If you want to be totally anonymous and don't want anyone to find out in December where you were staying in July, ask the manager to make sure your name does not appear on any mailing lists for Christmas cards, newsletters, and such. Even the noncommittal M/M won't save your skin if the wrong person gets the newsletter.

RESERVATIONS

It's nice to pack a bag and just go on the spur of the moment, and if the moment happens to spur in the off-season, you may be able to drop in on some of these hotels and get the best room without a reservation.

But is it worth the risk? Think of it: You fly down there and take a long, costly taxi ride to the other side of the island, only to discover that by some fluke this happens to be the weekend when a bunch of people have come over from an adjoining island and have filled every room, or that the owners decided to close down for a few weeks because they have some maintenance that needs attention. At least call ahead. In any case, at peak season it's imperative that you also reserve your flight weeks in advance.

For lovers who think ahead, there are several alternatives:

1. **Travel Agent** They're still (next to this guide) the best source of information because the best agencies make sure that their staffers get out to visit the places they're recommending — and make sure that they keep up with changes of owners, managers, chefs, and so on. Above all, he or she will also attend to the business of deposits and confirmations. However, some travel agents often have their own favorite islands and resorts, sometimes places that eliminate complications (for them) in terms of flights or reservations or paperwork. If your agent tries to sell you a bigger island or resort, by all means consider it, but if you feel strongly about your own choice, dig in your heels. I have often heard of instances where an agent will try to steer people to an all-inclusive resort rather than the room-only resort or inn of their choice, for the simple reason that an all-inclusive pays the agent a bigger commission. Do not be persuaded. Get a new agent.

2. **Hotel Representative** You pick up the telephone, call someone such as WIMCO or Ralph Locke Islands, tell them where you want to stay, and they can let you know (often right there and then) if your hotel is full or otherwise; they'll make your reservation and, if there's time, send you confirmation — at no extra charge, unless they have to make lots of telephone calls. You'll find a list of the leading hotel reps (who handle two or more of the hotels) at the end of this guide;

individual hotel representatives and phone numbers are listed under the hotel itself.

3. **Fax** This is usually an efficient way to make a reservation directly, since you will receive your confirmation quickly — and in writing on the resort's stationery.

4. **Letter** This is the least efficient way of making a reservation. Although mail services have improved significantly in the islands, you could be senile by the time you get a reply.

5. **E-mail/websites** The tiniest inns on the tiniest islands, places that didn't even have a telephone just a few years ago, now have e-mail addresses and their own websites, just like the big guys. They represent two more options for people who want to make their own arrangements and make them fast. I have included websites in this edition, but I should point out that not all of them can handle reservations and many of those that can are infuriatingly inefficient because they've been compiled by people who never took a geography class in school. Moreover, although a few are genuinely informative (like Young Islands in St. Vincent, which includes useful floor plans of the cottages), most of them are simply hype and hogwash.

Whatever method you choose to make your reservation, you should be specific: List the number of people in your party; date and time of arrival; flight number if possible (in peak season, some resorts may not even consider your reservation unless you already have airline seats); number of nights you plan to stay; date of departure; whether you want king, queen, double, or twin beds, a bathtub or a shower, the least expensive room or most expensive suite, a sea or garden view, or whatever; and whether you want the EP, MAP, or FAP rate (these terms are explained on p. xxxv). Finally, don't forget your return address and telephone number.

DEPOSITS

Once you get a reply to your request for a reservation, assuming there's time, you'll be expected to make a deposit (usually based on the cost of 1, 2, or 3 days, depending on the length of your stay). Of course it's a nuisance — what if you want to change your mind? That's just the point. The smaller hotels can't afford to have reservations for a full house and turn down other reservations in the meantime, only to have half of their expected clientele cancel at the last minute.

From your point of view, the deposit guarantees your reservation. People sometimes make mistakes, especially with reservations, but if you have a written, confirmed reservation in your hand with proof of a deposit, you're not going to be turned away from your hotel.

If you're going in the peak season, you should always allow yourself time to send a deposit and get a written confirmed reservation.

HOW TO LICK HIGH COSTS

As long as people insist on scuttling south to the sun at the first hint of frost or snow, hotel rates will remain astronomical in the Caribbean during the winter months. The period from December to April is the island inns' chance to make a profit, and they grab the chance with a vengeance (remember, the owners may have to pay wages and overhead in spring, summer, and fall, too — even if you're in Maine or Europe).

Here are a few ways to keep your budget within bounds:

1. **Avoid the Peak Season:** Obviously, it's great to get some Caribbean sun when the frost is nipping up north; but March and April are not so hot in northern climes either, and it's often very pleasant to escape to the islands in October, November, and early December. Some people head south in May and June to get an early start on a sun-tan. Even during summer, the Caribbean has its attractions, and more and more people are discovering them. Oddly enough, summer in the Caribbean islands can be cooler than summer in stifling, stateside cities, even up north. While northern beaches and facilities are overcrowded in summer, the beaches in the Caribbean are often half empty, and while the northern resorts are charging peak-season rates, the Caribbean is available at bargain rates. So remember that the peak season lasts only 4 months (usually Dec 15 through Apr 15), and for 8 months of the year rates are one-quarter to one-half less.

2. **Choose Your Resort Carefully:** Some resorts throw in everything with the rate — sailing, water-skiing, tennis, snorkeling, and so on; others charge extra for almost everything. Compare, for example, Curtain Bluff and St. James's Club on Antigua — free scuba diving and water-skiing at the former; you pay for scuba at the latter. Obviously, if you don't want to scuba dive or water-ski, you may be better off at St. James's Club. But this sort of situation also occurs with tennis, wind-surfing, and even with snorkeling gear.

3. **Dodge Taxes:** Some islands have no tax on tourists; others, such as the Dominican Republic, have taxes as high as 23%. On a 2-week vacation, that can add up to a few hundred dollars. Read these details carefully, for they can save you a small bundle, not simply because some service charges are 10% and others are 15%, but because in many cases the service charge relieves you of the need to tip.

4. **Drink Rum:** On rum-producing islands, rum is less expensive than scotch or bourbon, and in a thirst-building climate, this can make a noticeable difference when the tab is tallied at the end of your stay.

However, some island governments clamp such enormous duties on soda or tonic that your rum may cost less than its mixer. In that case, drink the local beer or locally produced mixers. The best way around big bar tabs is to buy a tax-free bottle of your favorite liquor at the airport before you leave. This may be frowned on in smaller hotels; in any case you should never drink from your bottle in public rooms. Several of the hideaways in this guide have a complimentary bottle of rum and mixers waiting for you in your room.

5. **Kitchens:** No one wants to go off on vacation and spend time cooking, but a small kitchen is useful for preparing between-meal snacks, lunches, and drinks without running up room-service charges. Several of the hotels listed in this guide have refrigerators and/or kitchenettes and/or fully equipped kitchens, and a few of them have mini-markets on the premises. They can save a lot of dollars without a lot of extra effort. In any case, a refrigerator is often more convenient — and much less expensive — than a stocked minibar.

6. **Double Up:** Consider the possibility of trotting off to the islands with your favorite couple and sharing a suite, bungalow, cottage, or villa. If you do this in a place such as, say, Siboney Beach Club on Antigua or The Sandpiper on Barbados, you can trot around to the nearest general store, pick up a few items and save yourself a few dollars on breakfast, lunches, or between-meal snacks. You'll find many more examples of such cost-cutting options in this guide.

7. **Packages:** These are special rates built around the themes of honeymoons, watersports, tennis, or golf. "We have people coming back every year for five or six years on the honeymoon package," sighs one hotelkeeper. In fact, some couples have arrived on a honeymoon package with all their children in tow, looking for reduced rates for them, too. Honeymoon packages usually include such frills as a bottle of champagne, flowers for the lady, or a half-day sail up the coast. Check them carefully — you may be better off with a regular rate. Sports packages usually are a good deal (the Four Seasons on Nevis is an especially good example of this). They will probably include free court time (carefully specified) for tennis players, or X number of free rounds for golfers. If you're a sports enthusiast, check with the hotel rep or your travel agent for the nitty-gritty details — especially if only one of you is a participant (no point in two of you paying for golf if only one of you plays). Before settling on a price, ask the resort if it's offering any special packages at the time of your proposed stay.

8. **Tour Packages:** These are dirty words to some people, but they needn't be. A tour package is not the same thing as an escorted tour: It can mean simply that 10 or 20 people will be booked on the same flight to take advantage of a special fare. They may be given their choice of two or three hotels on the island, so you may never see them

again until you get to the airport for your return flight. Local sightseeing is sometimes included, and sometimes it's an option; some packages
include boat trips and barbecues. If you don't feel like taking part in
these activities, you may still be ahead of the game, because the special
rates you will be paying for hotels and flights may be such good deals.
The advantages of package tours are that you may qualify for lower airfares (always with conditions, but you can probably live with them),
and the tour operator may have negotiated lower hotel rates.

Most important, in winter, tour operators may have "blocked off" a
group of hotel rooms and seats on jets, and package tours may be your
only hope of finding flight or hotel reservations.

Few of the hotels in this guide are likely to be overrun with package tours, but some of them do accept small tour or meeting groups, a
fact that is noted under the "PS" at the end of each hotel listing. Look
into the tour brochures of some of the airlines, say, American or Air
Jamaica, and you may find special packages built around some of these
hotels, such as the Half Moon Golf, Tennis & Beach Club in Jamaica;
Glitter Bay in Barbados; Casa de Campo in the Dominican Republic;
The Ritz-Carlton and Point Pleasant on St. Thomas — even the tony
Little Dix Bay on Virgin Gorda.

9. **Air Fares:**   In addition to scouring the web for the cheapest possible
fare, look into special airline offers like Air Jamaica's "Caribbean
Hopper Program" — one special fare lets you visit two, three, or five
islands. As of spring 2003, the fares are $550 economy class and $900
first class, which could well be what you have to pay to visit just one
island.

THE RATINGS

All the hotels and resorts in this guide are above average in one way or
another, but some obviously are more special than others. To make choosing
simpler, I've rated the hotels (using symbols) for romantic atmosphere (stars),
food and service (goblets), sports facilities (beach balls), and cost (dollar signs).
The ratings are highly personal and subjective — the fun part of compiling
the guide, my reward to myself for scurrying around from island to island and
hotel to hotel when I could just as easily have been lying on the beach.

Stars represent the romantic atmosphere of a hotel or resort more than
the quality or luxury or facilities. Of course, the two go together, and here
we're also talking about the setting, decor, size, efficiency, location, and
personality — the intangibles.

Goblets evaluate not just the quality of the food but the overall emphasis and attitude toward dining, the competence of the waiters, and the way the food is placed before you. This is a specifically Caribbean evaluation — it takes into consideration the special circumstances in the islands. In other words, any hotel that promises "the finest in gourmet dining" or "the ultimate in continental cuisine" almost certainly gets a low score because this is a vain promise: "The finest Continental cuisine" is something you find at a three-star restaurant in France; Caribbean islands just don't have access to the market gardens and meat markets to match those standards. There are times, in fact, when you get the impression that all the meals in the Caribbean (even the fish) are coming from some giant commissary in Miami; so hotels that list local dishes, such as conch pie, *keshi yena,* or *colombo de poulet riz* on their menus, even if only occasionally, stand a better chance of getting a higher rating than most hotels trying to emulate Continental cuisine (unless they do it really well).

Any hotel that forces you to dine indoors in an air-conditioned restaurant ranks badly (there are only two or three of them in this guide, and although one of them is Hyatt Dorado Beach Resort & Casino, which gets a three-goblet rating, at least there you're given the option of dining alfresco in a second restaurant or on your room balcony). It seems to me that one of the great pleasures of dining in the Caribbean is being in the open air, surrounded by the sounds of the tropical night or the sea, in an atmosphere of palms and stars — not in some interior designer's concept of an English pub or a Manhattan night spot. Wine does not enter into consideration in this guide. The conditions, usually, are all wrong for storing and caring for wine, and by the time it has been shipped three times, it's overpriced. Most of the hotels that rate highly for food have passable-to-good wine lists; otherwise, it's a hit-and-miss affair (except, perhaps, on the French islands, or in special cases such as Curtain Bluff in Antigua, Malliouhana on Anguilla, and Cobblers Cove on Barbados).

While on the subject of dining, please note that under each hotel listing, I spell out the evening dress code. I've seen too many hapless vacationers laden with wardrobes they have no opportunity to show off, or, conversely, men who have to borrow ties or jackets to get into the dining room. Although most of these hideaways set their dress code as casual or informal, this does not mean sloppy — and for most places that means no shorts, tank tops or T-shirts, no jeans and, in some cases, hotels require collared shirts and enclosed shoes rather than sandals in the evening; wet swimsuits are usually taboo at lunchtime but, wet or dry, cover-ups are usually worn. My personal preference is to have the option of dressing up or not, depending on my mood. However, most hotels have been relaxing their dress codes in recent years, and while I used to include some places that expected guests to dress up every evening (that is, jacket and tie for men) provided they either had alternative dining areas or would arrange for you to have dinner on your private patio or balcony, this is less of an issue than in the past. The problem for many hoteliers is that having relaxed the dress code, how do they prevent things from getting out of hand? No jackets today, no shirts tomorrow. That's why some of their rules seem slightly quixotic — e.g., the collared shirts and long trousers but no jeans sort of thing. And I guess there's nothing the manager can do if someone observes the dress code, as happened a few years ago at Little Dix Bay, but the guest turns up with spiky green hair. Anyway, there are enough hotels and enough dress codes in this guide to please all but the scruffiest — if you don't like the rules (or lack thereof) at A, choose B, where you'll be more comfortable.

Beach Balls offer you a quick idea of the availability of sporting facilities, and you'll also find the actual facilities spelled out at the end of each hotel listing. I tried originally to include prices for each activity, but this became too cumbersome; however, you will learn from the listings whether a particular sport is free or whether you have to pay an additional fee.

Remember, no matter how well endowed the hotel, sports facilities are less crowded in the non-winter months.

Dollar Signs should be used as a rough guide only, primarily for comparing one resort with another. The $ symbols are based on winter rates for two people; since the most accessible rate for comparison between hotels is

---

RATINGS

☆	*A port of call*
☆ ☆	*A long weekend*
☆ ☆ ☆	*Time for a suntan*
☆ ☆ ☆ ☆	*A place to linger*
☆ ☆ ☆ ☆ ☆	*Happily ever after*
Y	*Sustenance*
Y Y	*Good food*
Y Y Y	*Something to look forward to*
Y Y Y Y	*As close to* haute cuisine *as you can get in the Caribbean*
❻	*Some diversions*
❻ ❻	*Lots of things to keep your mind off sex*
❻ ❻ ❻	*More diversions than you'll have stamina for*
❻ ❻ ❻ ❻	*All that and a spa or horseback riding, too*
$	*$300 or under, MAP for two*
$ $	*$300 to $400, MAP for two*
$ $ $	*$400 to $500, MAP for two*
$ $ $ $	*$500 to $600, MAP for two*
$ $ $ $ $	*$600 and above, MAP for two*

the MAP rate, this is the one that is used (that is, for a room, breakfast, and dinner).

Each symbol represents roughly $100 increments; where a hotel overflows into more than one category, I've used the lower category, assuming that this represents a reasonable proportion of the available rooms. For a quick guide to summer rates, you will not be far off the mark if you reduce the higher ratings by one.

OTHER CHOICES

A special feature in this guide is the "Other Choices" section at the end of the listings for some islands. These are, for the most part, hotels, inns, and resorts that we visited as possibilities, but that didn't quite measure up. In some cases, they are hotels that are on the brink of opening or they opened too late to be seriously reviewed, or, again, they are hotels that were rated in earlier editions of the guide but have since lost some of their appeal or changed management or ownership. They may help fill a few gaps for you, especially because several of them are relatively inexpensive. If you visit any of them and think they deserve to be featured and rated, please let me know.

DOUBLE BEDS

Some Caribbean hoteliers seem to have installed twin beds in most of their rooms. However, most hotels of any size have some rooms with double, queen-, or king-size beds, and all but the tiniest hideaways can arrange to push two twins together to make a double — if you give them advance notice. If this is the case, however, check before using the bed like a trampoline, because if the beds are pushed together and sheeted lengthwise rather than crosswise, they may part like the Red Sea, and you may end up in a voluptuous heap on the floor. This is particularly true on the French islands.

CREEPY-CRAWLIES & OTHER HAZARDS

Snakes, spiders, and tarantulas are not a problem. Mosquitoes, no-see-ums, and sand flies have been sprayed almost to oblivion on most islands; however, they do sometimes appear in certain types of weather, so if you have the sort of skin that can rouse a dying mosquito to deeds of heroism, take along a repellent (or check into a hotel with air-conditioning).

Sea urchins are a hazard on some islands, depending on tides or seasons or something I just don't understand. Every hotel seems to have a solution, but, for what it's worth, here is the traditional remedy from the island of Saba: "Count the number of spines sticking in you; then swallow one mouthful of seawater for each spine." Sea urchin stings are painful, so check with the hotel staff before venturing into the sea.

Drinking water is not a problem on most islands, but it is chemically different from what you're accustomed to; so if your system is touchy about such things, ask for bottled water.

Sun is something else altogether. Naturally, you want to get a quick tan, and of course you love lying on the beach — but remember, your reason for slipping off together is love, and love can be a painful affair if you both look like lobsters and feel like you've been barbecued.

Remember, too, the Caribbean sun is particularly intense; 1 hour a day is enough, unless you already have a hint of tan. Some enthusiasts forget they can get a sunburn while in the water; if you plan to do a lot of snorkeling, wear a T-shirt. If you do get a burn, stand in a lukewarm shower. Some people recommend compresses of really strong tea; one of the beach boys on St. Maarten has quite a sideline going — he rubs on the leaf of the aloe plant; the Greeks recommend rubbing on yogurt. For heat prostration, Sabans again seem to have the endearing answer: "Rub the body with rum, particularly around the stomach."

MUGGINGS & OTHER VEXATIONS

Each time I set out to research this guide, friends keep cautioning me about the horrible things that might happen to me in the Caribbean — robbery, mugging, assault, battery, anti-Americanism, fascism, racism, and other everyday hassles.

Nothing has happened so far. There are probably plenty of statistics around to prove that things can be unpleasant in the Caribbean, but it has never been immediately obvious to me. Nevertheless, travelers should always be alert and follow a few obvious precautions: Keep valuables in a safe place; don't flash jewelry and expensive watches; keep your camcorder around your neck; listen to any warnings given by hotel personnel or local people; never walk along public beaches by yourselves after dark; and wear clothing that will not send the wrong signals to locals (people who walk around in skimpy, show-all bathing attire shouldn't be flirted with — they deserve to be laughed off the island).

I recall one occasion when I arrived on Barbados, checked out the local newspaper, and read that the U.S. State Department had imposed one of its dreaded travel advisories for the island. I chided a local friend about the islanders' criminal propensities. "Where have you been the past few days — in the Grenadines? Haven't you been reading about what's happening in Los Angeles?" I hadn't, and when I did, I learned that L.A. had been suffering through more unrest than Barbados has seen since the Caribs tossed out the Arawaks. The moral: Although you're on a dreamy Caribbean island, when you're out in public areas, think like you're in L.A. or Cincinnati. If in doubt, check with the State Department's website before you leave.

PIRACY ON THE HIGH ROADS

Caribbean taxi drivers. Now there's a motley bunch! They begin hectoring you, if they can, through customs and immigration, and before they take time to welcome you to their lovely island in the sun, they're already trying to make you "reserve" them for sightseeing tours and the trip back to the airport. (There are, of course, exceptions, and I hereby apologize to Mr. Johnson, Leroy, Shalom, Williams, and those other taxi drivers who are unfailingly pleasant, courteous, punctual, and honest.)

To avoid problems, ask your hotel to assign one of its pool of "approved" drivers to meet you at the airport. The hotel will send you the driver's name when confirming your reservation, in which case, you simply ask for Williams or Leroy or whomever when you get there. If there's no time to send the name before you arrive, the hotel may post a message for you on the airport notice board, telling you to ask for Sebastian. (This procedure is not the same thing as sending over a hotel limousine, which is rare because it's frowned on by taxi unions; you still have to pay the regular taxi fare, but at least it will be the official rate and not whatever the driver thinks he or she can get away with.) Things are a bit more organized on St. Barths, where most of the hotels send their own minivans to the airport to meet guests.

Taxis can cost you an arm and a leg in the Caribbean, and the driver may go for the shoulder and thigh, too. That's why I've included the cost of the taxi ride from the airport in the list of nitty-gritty details following each hotel. The high cost of taxis also puts a damper on going out to dinner — the fares can easily add $20 to $40 to the cost of the meal, unless you hook up with another couple and share the burden.

The drivers' point of view is that their costs are unusually high — imported cars, imported gas, imported parts, highways that knock the hell out of the cars, stiff insurance rates, and so on. Fine. What's not so understandable is why island governments kowtow to the drivers, who won't allow anyone else to operate a bus or limousine service; the result is that you, the visitors, have to pay perhaps $10 to $12 for a taxi ride, when you could be paying only $2 to $3 for a minibus or limousine. On some islands, authorities quite blatantly post lower rates for residents. In some cases, taxis operate on a "seat available" basis — that is, you pay a share of the cost with other people going in the same direction; but if only six people get off an inter-island flight, they may not be going in your direction, and in any case, by the time the immigration officer has finished stamping your passport, all the "seat available" taxis may have mysteriously left. Your best bet, if you have a long taxi ride, is to ask your hotel to have a taxi and driver waiting for you at the airport. Always make sure that you establish whether you and the driver are talking about US, Jamaican, or any other kind of dollar — it can make a huge difference.

SOME CARIBBEAN COMMENTS

WATER   You'll be constantly reminded of the old Caribbean adage "Water is the gold of the Caribbean," or as it's less eloquently phrased on some signs, "On our island in the sun, we don't flush for number one." In deluxe resorts with their own catchments and reverse osmosis plants, the cost to the hotel for one shower may be $5 — your two showers each per day account for $30 of your rate; hotels that have to import water will have an even higher bill. Be sparing. Shower together.

CARIBBEAN SERVICE   Don't expect the staff to rush around. It's all right for you — you're there for only a few days — but the people who live there don't find the glaring sun so appealing day after day. And you wouldn't want them to serve your drinks in perspiration-stained shirts or blouses. They'll operate at a normal Caribbean pace no matter how much you tip, and at a less than normal pace if you shout and snap your fingers and stamp your feet. You just have to learn a few tricks. For example, always anticipate your thirst: Order your drinks about 10 minutes before you'll be gasping for them. Also, place your order in simple English; the islanders don't want to figure out what you're trying to say — it's too hot to bother.

ESCAPE ROUTES TO THE CARIBBEAN

There are several hundred flights a week from the North American mainland to the Caribbean islands, and it's about time you were on one of them. But which one? You'll find a quick summary of the major services to the various islands, or groups of islands, at the beginning of each chapter in this guide; please note that this information is based on winter schedules and lists only nonstop or direct (that is, with no change of aircraft) flights from major North American departure points.

The major multi-destination carriers to the islands are American Airlines, Air Canada, British West Indies Airways (BWIA), Delta, United (if it manages to stay in business), Continental, Air Jamaica and now US Airways. If you live in or travel via the Northeast, then American, Continental, US Airways, and Air Jamaica are the carriers with the most options to the islands, and they should be your first choice. JetBlue recently introduced its highly acclaimed service and no-nonsense fares to Puerto Rico and I'm not alone in hoping they'll be expanding to other islands in the region.

Overall, however, **American** is now the primary Caribbean carrier, with its major hub at San Juan and inter-island services on its offshoot, American Eagle. It blankets the islands with modern fleets of twin-engine turboprop aircraft and has above-average consideration for matters that other Caribbean carriers seem to find tiresome — such as maintaining on-time schedules and honoring confirmed reservations — but their service can be inconsistent: I was recently required to check a bag which was considered cabin luggage on a connecting American flight, and it had nothing to do with the size of the aircraft, more the size of the clerk's ego. When using regional services, remember (and I've also said this elsewhere because it's important) that the smaller aircraft do not have capacious overhead bins or racks for garment bags, so luggage that would normally be considered carry-on will have to be checked (although you can sometimes have it tagged right at the aircraft). That probably means taking a little more care in packing.

Of the Caribbean-based international airlines, **BWIA** (known affectionately as BeeWee) is a sort of national carrier for the islands of the eastern Caribbean. Although it became a private company a few years ago, it probably still has to serve too many islands and, indirectly, too many masters for its own good — Antigua, St. Lucia, Barbados, Trinidad/Tobago, and Grenada.

Air Jamaica is the clear winner for any awards for "most improved airline in the Caribbean." As an alternative to American Airlines's hub in San Juan, Air Jamaica has been steadily building up a hub in Montego Bay, Jamaica, filtering passengers from New York (JFK and Newark), Philadelphia, Baltimore/Washington, D.C., Atlanta, Tampa, Ft. Lauderdale, Miami, Los Angeles, and Chicago, to connecting flights on Air Jamaica or Air Jamaica Express to Grand Cayman, St. Lucia, Bonaire, Curaçao, Antigua, and Dominican Republic. This is in addition to direct flights to Grenada, St. Lucia, and Barbados. Air Jamaica also has one of the most up-to-date fleets of aircraft anywhere. Into the bargain, Air Jamaica promises two islands for one: If you fly via Montego Bay you can stop off for a few days in Jamaica at no extra cost. This all sounds very ambitious, but since Air Jamaica is now headed by "Butch" Stewart, the seemingly irrepressible entrepreneur who has made Sandals all-inclusive resorts a resounding success, folks in the islands are keeping their fingers crossed that they will no longer be totally dependent on the whims of American Airlines. It probably helps, of course, that Air Jamaica offers champagne on the house to all its passengers — as good a way as any for getting a vacation off to a jolly start.

AIRLINES WITHIN THE CARIBBEAN

Apart from American Eagle, mentioned above, it may be necessary to finish your trip to your chosen hideaway on a local island-hopper.

Windward Island Airways is my favorite interisland carrier. Based on St. Maarten, it shuttles between Juliana Airport and Saba, St. Eustatius, St. Kitts, St. Barthélemy, and Anguilla. This very efficient outfit, which was 40 years old in 2000, operates a complex "bus service" (more than a thousand flights a year to Saba alone) with a few DeHavilland Twin Otters, those short takeoff and landing (STOL) workhorses, the engines of which are washed every morning — inside and out.

The biggest operation in the Caribbean is **Leeward Islands Air Transport** (LIAT). In terms of departures/arrivals per day, it's actually one of the largest airlines in the world. It's always been a sort of laughingstock; in an earlier edition of this guide I quoted some of the scathing comments associated with its acronym — Leave Island Any Time, and so on. Truth is, LIAT too is a much-improved airline and has turned tails on its critics by devising the slogan, Leaves for the Islands Any Time. Serving so many independent islands with the kind of frequency (45,000 takeoffs and landings a year) LIAT has to maintain is a momentous task. LIAT now has a first-rate on-time record (officially), although it's hard to believe when you're on a flight, as I was once, leaving 1 hour early and heading north instead of south. Moreover, the line is now operating nifty DeHavilland Dash 8 50-seater and 37-seater prop jets. Despite the expansion of Air Jamaica Express (above), LIAT is still the warhorse, but a few "island-regional" carriers (that is, private or subsidized airlines created specifically to ensure frequent and dependable service among a small group of islands) now bring travelers a much wider choice of departure times.

Two-year-old **Caribbean Star** has made a favorable impression in a short time. Owned by a wealthy American entrepreneur and run by an airline veteran, its network covers 12 islands, including Puerto Rico in the west and Trinidad in the south, served by the comfy and dependable Dash 8s of DeHavilland. As of March 2003, Star has been joined by a sister airline, **Caribbean Sun,** operating the same kind of aircraft, flying mostly out of Puerto Rico (connecting with flights from mainland USA) and serving St. Kitts, the British Virgins, the Dominican Republic, and ultimately the islands to the west.

Nevis Express is a small, 5-year-old operation that has earned its wings by operating a six-times-a-day shuttle linking the sister islands of St. Kitts and Nevis. In addition, its nine-passenger BN2 Islanders are available for full-plane charters to some 20 other islands, a welcome and popular convenience for European passengers arriving in Antigua, who frequently charter a plane for their connection to Anguilla — $480, one-way. Massachusetts-based **Cape Air** is scoring kudos with its bus-service frequencies between the U.S. and British Virgin Islands (and is doing so well, in fact, it may be expanding into neighboring islands).

The French West Indies have formed a consortium called **Air Caraïbes,** although you may still find yourselves flying on planes sporting the colors of

Air Guadeloupe, Air Martinique, Air St. Martin, and Air St. Barthélemy. Depending on the route, you'll be flying twin-engine seven-seater Islanders, Twin Otters, or the spanking-new ATR 42 turboprops, carrying 46 passengers in pressurized cabins with overhead bins, toilets, and flight attendants.

However, you may also find yourself booking Air Caraïbes and flying aircraft operated by Winair or LIAT because these small regional carriers are trying to consolidate services, maintenance, and overhead. The promise is "to serve the public better" by giving us more options, but last time I noticed, there were two flights a day where there used to be four. So much for better service.

For flights to St. Vincent and its gorgeous Grenadines, you once had a choice between **LIAT** and **Mustique Airways,** but now these Cinderellas have what amounts almost to bus-service convenience with such additional carriers as **Trans Air** and **SVG Air/Grenadine Express.** The aircraft of choice is, again, the BN2 Islander or Twin Otter, but 18-year-old, privately owned, St. Vincent–based Mustique Airways now also flies a Cessna 402C, a Baron, and a 20-passenger EMB100 Bandeirante — and generally has the widest ranging, most professional service. It's the airline the Mustique-bound celebrities and stars have been flying all these years (its U.S. number, by the way, is 800/223-0599).

Not all Caribbean airlines have the sophisticated electronic reservations systems or even the alert staffs of U.S. airlines, so always double-check tickets — date, flight number, check-in times, and so forth.

Even if you're taking a 10-minute flight with only half a dozen passengers to be boarded, you'll be expected to check in 1 hour before departure. I questioned this with one airline executive, and his disarming reply was: "Because the flight may leave early." He wasn't kidding, either. Moreover, to be sure of your seat, get to the check-in desk as early as possible, even if your ticket is reconfirmed — and make sure the check-in attendant sees it. Don't assume that being in line on time is enough to guarantee your seat.

Also, even a reconfirmed ticket doesn't mean a thing until it's in the hands of the ticket agent. You can be standing politely in line, ticket in hand, and still lose your seat. The people huddled around the check-in counter may not have tickets; they may be waiting for someone to not show up — you, for example. Push your way to the front — before the ticket agent's cousin displaces you.

Always reconfirm your flight 24 hours or 48 hours before departure. This is no longer a requirement, except with a few down-island carriers, but is still very important, because some of the airlines have a tendency to overbook, and some passengers have a tendency not to show up; so the airline may simply decide that if you don't reconfirm, you're not going to fly, and they'll give your seat to someone else. Many hotels will handle your re-confirmations, but there's not much they can do if you wait until it's too late.

If you're taking along carry-on luggage, remember that what may qualify as carry-on size on a 747 may have to be checked on smaller island-hopping aircraft, so make sure it is locked and labeled. Also, luggage allowances on U.S. carriers may not be acceptable to local carriers, and you may find yourself paying excess baggage charges on some stretches. If you anticipate problems, see your travel agent before you leave.

BOAT TRAVEL

Several of the islands or groups of islands are linked by seagoing ferries.

In the Virgin Islands, the **M/V Bomba Charger, M/V Native Son,** and **M/V Speedy's Fantasy** operate 90-passenger, air-conditioned multi-hulls between Charlotte Amalie in St. Thomas and West End, Road Town, and Virgin Gorda in the British Virgins. Fares are about $20 per person each way.

There are also regular services, by powerboat, hydrofoil, or catamaran, between St. Maarten/St. Martin and St. Barthélemy, Anguilla and Saba; some depart in the afternoon to connect with flights from New York and other northeastern destinations. Another speedy twin-hulled service, **Caribbean Express,** operates between Guadeloupe, Dominica, Martinique, and St. Lucia and is worth considering if you think you can't face another airport. Some of the most enjoyable boat trips are from Guadeloupe (three locations) to the outlying islands of the Iles des Saintes; and if you have time to spare, you might always want to consider the relatively new ferryboat service between Curaçao and Bonaire.

The Rates —
How to Figure
Them Out

Before you go any further, know this: All the room rates quoted in this guide-book are for two people.

This is the most hazardous chore in putting together a reliable guidebook. When most of the hotels in this new edition were visited, the managers had not yet established their rates for the following winter. I feel that rates are indispensable in a guide like this, so to level the playing field, for all hotels I have opted for the rates in effect during the winter season 2002–03. Add 5% to those numbers and you won't be far off.

To get the best value for your money, read the text for each resort to determine what additional charges you will incur — especially in terms of sports — a small task that could end up saving you a bundle. Even then, to get the complete story you should send off for copies of the hotel's brochures and rate sheets and read them very carefully. Moreover, to give you some quick indication of what you can expect to pay, I've also included with the description of each hotel a **$** symbol for approximate costs.

The dollar symbols (please note this carefully) are based on high-season MAP (Modified American Plan) rates for two people — that is, the cost of the room plus breakfast and dinner. (See below for a full explanation of the rates.) They are high-season rather than summer rates because they happened to be the most reliable figures available when this guidebook was compiled.

Note: Please remember that the symbols would look much less ominous if they represented off-season figures, and if you are considering a summer trip, I suggest that as a rule of thumb you chop off one $ except in the case of the lowest category.

FAP and MAP rates may mean that you order your meals from a fixed menu, rather than from the a la carte menu; in some Caribbean hotels this is a racket because the choice you're offered is so limited or unpromising you're almost obligated to order the items that cost a few dollars more. That happens in only a few of the hotels in this guide; but in some of the smaller inns you will be offered a fixed menu for dinner, served at a fixed hour, often at communal tables.

Which rate should you choose? They all have their advantages. Usually you're better off having the EP or CP rate because those give you the flexibility to eat wherever you want to eat — for instance, to sample an Indonesian *rijstafel* in Curaçao or dine in some of the Creole bistros on Martinique. On the other hand, in many cases the hotel dining room may be the best eating spot on the island (in some cases it's the only spot), and you'd want to eat there anyway; or the nearest restaurant may be a $10 or $15 cab ride away on the other side of the island and not worth the fare.

On some islands, as in Barbados, some hotels have wisely banded together to arrange an exchange program — in other words, you tell your hotel that you want to dine in hotel B, in which case they arrange to have hotel B send the bill to them. On other islands, you may encounter a tiresome attitude among hotel managers in which each one claims to have the best restaurant on the island and therefore "everyone wants to dine in my place anyway."

DIFFERENT TYPES OF RATES

Hotels in the Caribbean quote five types of rates:

EP (European Plan): You pay for the room only. No meals.
CP (Continental Plan): You get the room and breakfast (usually a continental breakfast of juice, rolls, and coffee).
MAP (Modified American Plan): You get the room with breakfast plus one meal — usually dinner.
FAP (Full American Plan): You get everything — room, breakfast, lunch, afternoon tea (where served), and dinner. This is sometimes known as American Plan and abbreviated "AP."
FAP+ (Full American Plan with extras): You get the room, all meals, afternoon tea, and items like table wines, drinks, laundry, and/or postage stamps — virtually all-inclusive resorts.

REBATES ON MEALS

Many hotels allow a rebate on the dinner portion of your MAP or FAP rate — probably not a full rebate, but most of it, and only if you let them know before lunchtime that you're not going to dine there that evening.

The reason why hotels put you through this hassle is that their supplies are limited, and they have to know in advance how many dinners they must prepare (in the case of steaks, for example, how many they have to thaw), without incurring a lot of waste.

In the hotel listings in this guide, I've included the price of dinner where a hotel offers a choice of EP or MAP/FAP rates. Usually, the cost of dinners on a one-shot deal is more expensive (a couple of dollars or so) than the MAP/FAP rates. The cost of dinner is given for two people unless otherwise noted.

TAXES

Most islands entice you to their shores and then clobber you with a tax, sometimes two. These taxes may go under any of several euphemisms — room tax, government tax, airport tax, departure tax, energy tax — but what it boils down to is that you're going to pay more than the advertised hotel rates. Some taxes are as high as 15% on your total bill; some are 3% on your room only. If you're on a tight budget, or if you simply don't feel like being taken for a ride, choose an island with no such tax. In any case, check out such things with each hotel if you're watching your pennies. If you are concerned about your dollars, note that on the French islands, taxes and service charge are almost always included in the rate.

SERVICE CHARGES

Most hotels in the Caribbean now add a service charge to your bill, usually 10%, 12%, or 15%, ostensibly in lieu of tipping. In some hotels you may tip in addition to the service charge; in others it's positively forbidden to tip, and any member of the staff caught taking a *pourboire* is fired on the spot. The system has its pros and cons: From your point of view, it means you can relax and not have to bother about figuring out percentages, sometimes in unfamiliar currencies; on the other hand, a flat fee doesn't reward individual feats of activity, initiative, and personal attention — and without that incentive, service can be lethargic. But the chances are service will be lethargic either way. If tipping is included, don't encourage layabouts who hover around looking for an additional tip — send them on their way; if service overall is so bad it almost ruins your sex life, just refuse to pay the service charge.

For example, this reminder from Antigua's Curtain Bluff: "A service charge of 10% will be added; please, no tipping." (This does not mean that guests cannot express their appreciation: "Curtain Bluff has a fund for the community of Old Road. If you want to donate funds, please see a member of the management.")

ADDITIONAL NOTES
ON RATES

In the listing of rates in this book, please remember that "off-season" is spring, summer, and fall. In other words, these seemingly horrendous peak-season rates are in effect only 4 months of the year, the lower rates the remaining 8 months.

For most hotels, the peak season runs from December 15 through Easter Sunday, but this may vary by a few days; if you check into the matter carefully, you may find that in some hotels the higher rates do not begin until Christmas, or even until late January, and you can grab a few unexpected "peak" season bargains. Still others will give you a reduced rate during the first 2 weeks in January.

REMEMBER

The figures quoted are not the full story, so make a more accurate comparison of rates between hotels. Rates for, say, The Caves in Negril or Curtain Bluff on Antigua may seem beyond your budget but in the case of the former it includes an open bar, in the latter all bar drinks and wines with dinner — good wines at that. You should also check out the paragraph marked "sports" in the individual hotel listings, to determine what activities are included in the rates at no extra charge. For instance, most resorts will charge extra for the use of sailboats or scuba diving, but The Bitter End Yacht Club on Virgin Gorda includes virtually unlimited sailing and Curtain Bluff, again, includes complimentary scuba diving. Even a few rounds of tennis can cost a bundle at some resorts so if you plan to put in a few sets a day, you should scour the listings for resorts that include tennis in the rates.

SPECIAL PACKAGES

As I mentioned in the "Introduction" and remind you here, your wallet may benefit if you look into special packages offered by individual hotels and airlines to independent travelers. For example, Young Island in the Grenadines treats lovers to their own special off-season rate that includes everything but drinks and postage stamps. The summer sports package at the Four Seasons Resort Nevis is an exceptional bargain — if you deduct the cost of all the free court time or rounds of golf, you are basically getting your luxury room at motel prices. Your travel agent can probably help you here, if you don't want to spend the time clicking around a bunch of websites.

The Turks & Caicos

*T*he what? The British Colony

of the Turks & Caicos Islands, to give them their formal
title. Or the TCI, as they're known among friends.

Although they're not strictly in the Caribbean, these
islands lie close enough to Hispaniola (Haiti and the
Dominican Republic) to qualify for this guide. Geologically,
they are the last trickle of oceanic inkblots known as the
Bahamas, a collection of 40 or so islands, islets, and cays that
cover 193 square miles — a landmass slightly larger than
Martha's Vineyard. They lie low in the water without any

scenery that makes you say "Wow!" — except for the water itself, which is of a surpassing beauty that completely outshines the islands. Most important for vacationers, the archipelago is ringed with a 200-mile-long reef system, which in turn shelters mile after mile of soft white sands.

The capital of this charmed Crown colony is a funky hamlet known as Cockburn Town on Grand Turk, but the most populous island is Providenciales (known to islanders as Provo), which is where you'll find most of the resorts, most of the "Belongers," and most of the expatriates who long ago decided that here was a demi-paradise with a great climate, little traffic, hardly any crime, and an international airport just 90 minutes from Miami.

HOW TO GET THERE   It's easier than you might think, given the islands' relative obscurity — American Airlines flies in jets twice a day from Miami, once a week from New York; other options are US Airways via Charlotte, Delta from Atlanta, and Air Jamaica via Montego Bay.

For information on the Turks & Caicos, call 800/241-0824 or visit www.turksandcaicostourism.com.

The Meridian Club

PINE CAY

☆☆☆☆☆	🍸🍸	➏	$ $ $ $
ATMOSPHERE	DINING	SPORTS	RATES

This resort is something of a throwback to the good old days of Caribbean escapes, a sort of sand castle of nostalgia.

Item: For 6 months of the year, the club is on "Pine Cay time" because clocks on the island are not reset to coincide with daylight saving time up north. Item: "In the past 10 years," according to the club directory, "we have had one or two necktie sightings." Item: The resort recently installed a solitary pay phone for guests ("It's hidden in a bush near the tennis court . . . and it doesn't always work unless you kick it"), and cellphones have been banned in perpetuity.

If this is your sort of castaway, no-frills, back-to-nature kind of place, then let me surprise you by saying it doesn't take a day and a half to get there. You fly to Provo, then board a twin-engine plane for a 10-minute flight directly to the island's packed-sand airstrip. But if you're really in the spirit of the place, instead of the short flight you might take a 20-minute taxi ride to Leeward to board the club's 36-foot launch for a 20-minute ride past Grouper Cay and some of the most beckoning beaches you've ever seen,

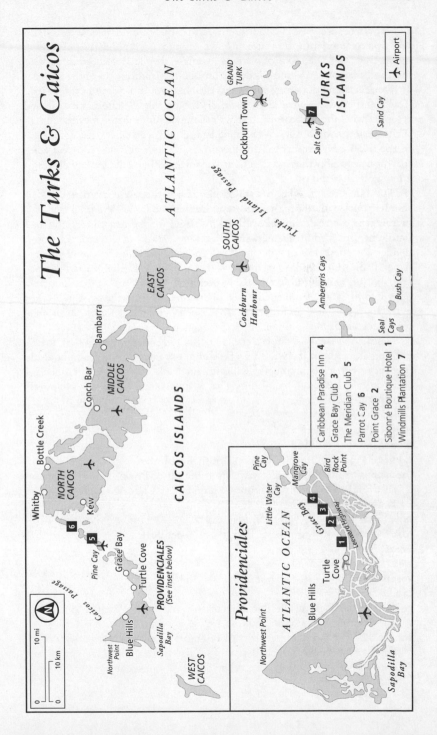

The Turks & Caicos

ATLANTIC OCEAN

Airport ✈

GRAND TURK

Cockburn Town ✈

TURKS ISLANDS

Salt Cay 7

Sand Cay

Turks Island Passage

SOUTH CAICOS ✈

Cockburn Harbour

Ambergris Cays

Bush Cay

Seal Cays

EAST CAICOS

Caribbean Paradise Inn 4
Grace Bay Club 3
The Meridian Club 5
Parrot Cay 6
Point Grace 2
Sibonré Boutique Hotel 1
Windmills Plantation 7

Bambarra

Conch Bar

MIDDLE CAICOS ✈

CAICOS ISLANDS

Bottle Creek

Whitby

NORTH CAICOS ✈

Kew

6

5

Pine Cay

Grace Bay

Turtle Cove

PROVIDENCIALES
(See inset below)

Caicos Passage

Northwest Point

Blue Hills ✈

Sapodilla Bay

WEST CAICOS

N

10 mi
0
10 km
0

Providenciales

Pine Cay

Little Water Cay

Mangrove Cay

Bird Rock Point

4

3

Grace Bay

2

1

Leeward Highway

ATLANTIC OCEAN

Blue Hills

Turtle Cove

Northwest Point

✈

Sapodilla Bay

across waters so crystalline and turquoise that the crew may have to restrain you from leaping into the water and swimming ashore.

The 800-acre pancake of a cay is privately owned by the escapists who built or bought the 35 cottages dotted around the landscape (6 of the cottages are for rent, some of them dating from the creation of the club in the 1970s). The members also own the 12-room clubhouse that welcomes like-minded escapists who are not invited to stay in the cottages. In other words, most of the time you have 2 miles of ravishing beach all to yourselves, to say nothing of the miles of lanes for walkers, joggers, and bikers and the 200-plus acres that are irrevocably preserved in their natural state. The only traffic consists of a few golf carts and bikes.

The guest rooms, like everything else about the place, hearken back to simpler times with decor that has never known the touch of a celebrity decorator, yet nevertheless manages to be just right for the location: double bed with cheerful bedspread, ceramic tile floors, stack of paperbacks, room divider, sofa, desk, lots of colorful island doodads, paintings by the island gardener, bathroom and dressing room with Crabtree & Evelyn toiletries, separate shower, and outdoor rinsing shower (the bathrooms were extensively upgraded in 2000). A screened porch opens directly onto the sea oats and sea grape trees, and here and there along the beach, thatched *bohios* (small shelters) offer shade and solitude.

Despite the fact that this is a real club with long-standing members, there's nothing aloof about it. Twice a week, clubhouse guests mingle at a poolside barbecue with club members — investment bankers, doctors, publishers — and everyone has a jolly good time. That is, unless someone unwisely appears wearing socks or a tie.

Name: The Meridian Club
Managers: Bev and Wally Plachta
Address: Pine Cay, Turks & Caicos, British West Indies
Location: On Pine Cay, a few yards from the tip of Provo, about 10 min. by air from Provo airport or about 40 min. by taxi and launch (let the resort know your flight times)
Telephone: None
Fax: 649/941-7010 (for guests, charges are expensive)
E-mail: pinecay@tciway.com
Web: www.meridianclub.com
Reservations: 866/746-3229 or 770/500-1134
Credit Cards: None
Rates: $850 FAP (Dec 18–Mar 31); tax 10% and service charge 10% extra; off-season 25% less (cottages from $4,300 a week)
Rooms: 12 in the clubhouse, all with ceiling fans, refrigerator, personal safe, kimonos, umbrella, screened porch, separate shower, dressing room, and outdoor rinsing shower; among the rentals, 2 one-bedrooms and 1 two-bedroom cottage

Meals: Breakfast 7:30–9:30am, lunch 1–2pm, afternoon tea 4–5pm, dinner 7–8pm; casual dress; room service for breakfast only; beach barbecue and jump-up every Wed and Sat; there's also a small commissary for in-between noshing or picnic provisions

Entertainment: Library, parlor games, the barbecues; and during the full moon, everyone hops into a launch to watch the mating ritual of the Odontosyllis enopla, or Pine Cay glowworm, which puts on a spectacular phosphorescent underwater show

Sports: More than 2 miles of beach on one side, freshwater pool, tennis (1 court, no lights), bicycles, windsurfing, small boat sailing, snorkeling and bonefishing gear — all free; more elaborate watersports and golf on Provo (you can be teeing off within 30 min. of leaving the island, if everything runs like clockwork)

PS: No children under 12; "no cellphones ever"; closed late June to Nov

Parrot Cay

PARROT CAY

☆☆☆☆☆   ♉♉♉   ❻❻❻ $ $ $ $
ATMOSPHERE   **DINING**   **SPORTS**   **RATES**

At the airport you take the resort's taxi to Leeward Going Through, where you board one of the resort's 48-foot launches for the trip past long ribbons of deserted sand, and past Water Cay, Pine Cay, and Fort George Cay. Dead ahead, another ribbon of white sand, but no sign of a hotel.

Then the launch rounds one final headland, and there, behind yet another sweep of white beach, is your first glimpse of the 5-year-old Parrot Cay resort, a mass of gardens with low-profile, shingle-roofed villas beside the dunes, a poolside dining pavilion, then an estate-like array of white villas atop a knoll set well back from the beach.

The launch makes one final turn into a bayou-like inlet and settles alongside a small wooden dock with a shingle roof and a few golf carts to take you up the hill to reception. Your total elapsed travel time is 45 to 75 minutes from the airport, depending on the baggage carousel and the winds and tides. It's the price you pay for solitude — but you may welcome the ride back at the end of your vacation because it eases you more gently back into the humdrum everyday world.

The main lodge with its white octagonal core sprouted from its hilltop several years ago, but its Mideastern investors never managed to get the place open; in 1998, the "new" but abandoned property was acquired by a second group of investors that includes the family who own the two highly acclaimed Four Seasons Resorts in Bali. If they had started from scratch on Parrot Cay, they might have done things differently, but what they have done is some sort of consolation for you not being able to go all the way to Bali. As it is, you'll discover a level of taste and refinement here you hardly expected to find on an uninhabited, scrub-and-cactus backwater in the Turks and Caicos — custom-designed teak furniture in Oriental-colonial style, original art, and Asian artifacts. Even the bronze-and-teak ashtrays are pleasing to the eye. The bar/lounge, with its 16 French doors opening to a terrace, offers a striking backdrop of wraparound turquoise, and the 5,500-square-foot beachside pool has a sand-colored bottom so that its infinity edge blends more naturally with the patterns of the sea.

The main lodge is flanked by a collection of two-story boxy villas in the island vernacular of white plaster walls, red-clay tile roofs, and gingerbread verandas with white balustrades. Parrot Cay guest-nests come in two basic types: the hilltop rooms for taking in the view, and the brand-new villa suites nestled in the dunes. Stay on the hill and you walk some 260 paces to the beach; stay in the dunes and you walk some 260 paces to dinner. All of them offer a rare sense of privacy and peace. They all have exquisite furnishings in that oriental-colonial style, but the hilltop rooms are predominantly white-on-white with walls, curtains, four-poster netting, bedspreads, and bathroom tiles in as many shades of white as there are greens in the sea beyond the veranda. The beachside lodgings are more wood-plank in style, a contemporary blend of Bali and Cape Cod, built of Alaskan pine with shingle roofs, set back from the beach among the low dunes, each with a spacious patio screened by partitions and foliage from its neighbors. Hilltop, you might find yourself spending much of your time on that ramada-shaded veranda, which has a daybed for two at one end equipped with a deep tray for the drinks you'll find in the refrigerator at the opposite end. Both locations offer sparkling bathrooms and four-poster beds draped in netting (necessary in the dunes, decorative on the hilltop).

The owners haven't cut many corners. The toiletries are custom-blended Invigorate, and breakfast arrives on your balcony with Royal Doulton china. Almost the entire kitchen brigade is Australian and many of the waiters have come over from Malaysia and Bali, adding to the Asian flavor of the place. Many of their culinary creations are light and healthful, in harmony with the acclaimed two-story spa, Shambhala, where guests coax themselves into shape with a Parrot Cay Bath or hatha yoga, or trot off to one of the beachside thatched cabanas where they can purr through Balinese or Thai massage, lulled by the gentle lapping of the surf and the cool flutter of the trade winds. People (and not just any old folks — Bruce Willis, Barbra Streisand, and others) rave about Shambhala (you sometimes almost get the impression there's no resort, just a spa), but my advice is this: Spend the first couple of days flaking out on that marvelous beach and wallowing around in that gorgeous water and see how much better you feel before handing over $240 for a 2-hour Javanese Royal Lulur Bath.

Name: Parrot Cay
Manager: Carl Henderson
Address: P.O. Box 164, Providenciales, Turks & Caicos, British West Indies
Location: On one of the tiny islets to the east of Provo (next cay over, in fact, from the Meridian Club), reachable by taxi and launch — a cinch because the resort has someone to greet you at the airport and someone to return you to the airport, all included in the rate
Telephone: 649/946-7788
Fax: 649/946-7789
E-mail: parrotcay@provo.net
Web: www.parrot-cay.com
Reservations: 877/754-0726, toll-free direct
Credit Cards: American Express, MasterCard, Visa
Rates: $560–$1,830 CP (Dec 17–Apr 28); tax 10% and service charge 10% extra; in summer 30% less
Rooms: 60, including 6 one-bedroom Beach Houses, 3 one-bedroom Ocean-front Villas with plunge pools, and three larger villas with private full-size pools; all with air-conditioning and ceiling fans, tub/shower, direct-dial telephone with modem port, personal safe, minibar, hair dryer, bathrobes, fax, TV/VCR (flat-screen Sony), Bose stereo; the resort now has 5 three-bedroom rental villas in 2 private compounds (one owned by Bruce Willis), about 7 min. by buggy from the lodge, from $3,850 and up in winter
Meals: Breakfast 7–10am, lunch noon–3pm, dinner 7–10pm; casual elegant ("no shorts"); quiet recorded music; room service 7am–10pm, special menu
Entertainment: Talking, reading, stargazing; the library has about 120 DVDs, and once or twice a week there's live music with a guitarist or vocalist
Sports: 3 miles of beach, 5,500-square-foot swimming pool, air-conditioned fitness center, daily yoga, Sunfish sailing, kayaking on the mangrove-ringed pond, snorkeling gear, windsurfing, hiking, mountain bikes, tennis (2 courts, with lights) — all free; water-skiing, scuba diving, fishing, and spa treatments at extra charge; golf on Provo and excursions to the nature reserves on Middle Caicos can be organized in minutes
PS: Some children; no rules regarding cellphones, but they don't work well except on the hill; open all year

Grace Bay Club

PROVIDENCIALES

☆☆☆☆   ΥΥΥ   ❻❻ $ $ $ $ $
ATMOSPHERE   DINING   SPORTS   RATES

The main enticement on Provo is a 12-mile-long stretch of gorgeous sand known as Grace Bay, and the crown jewel along this beach is the Grace Bay

Club. It's the Turks & Caicos's priciest lodging, a deluxe retreat of Spanish-Mediterranean architecture with red-tiled roofs peeking above courtyards and patios.

It has accommodations for only 44 guests, who are all housed in suites decorated in a style that's much more refined than you'd expect on such a laid-back island. Quarry floor tiles are accented with Guatemalan and Turkish rugs, louvered shutters and large windows are set off with Colombian and Mexican pottery, and McGuire rattan furniture graces the rooms. Luxury touches include fully equipped designer kitchens (with microwaves and ice-makers), 33-channel cable TV, washer-dryers — and even the one-bedroom suites come with two full bathrooms. Suites on the third floor, some of them duplexes, are especially popular because of their panoramic views and spacious terraces (one suite has three), but the privacy of the ground-floor patios is protected by the skillful placement of swales and palm trees. The clover-shaped pool is surrounded by greenery, hammocks, and a gazebo for afternoon tea or sundown cocktails; beach towels are stacked on a wrought-iron cart.

One of the loveliest dining rooms on the islands, the Anacaona Restaurant consists of three circular pavilions that rise 35 feet to a *palapa*-thatched roof crafted in the traditional style of the Seminoles by a team of Osceola Indians from Florida, supervised by a chief's daughter and her trusty laptop. Tables are arrayed on three levels so that everyone has a view of the seagrape trees, wispy casuarinas, and, in the evening, the tiki lamps. The menu changes frequently, but Chef Eric Brunel skillfully blends continental classics with island produce, like ceviche of baby Caicos conch with a salad of smoked cucumber with a ginger and teriyaki sauce, braised red snapper in banana leaf with chayote and ginger coulis, or crab cakes with pineapple chutney.

Grace Bay is another boutique resort that has installed a small but versatile spa, The Serenity Spa at Grace Bay, where Dee Dempsey and Megan Bates enhance the regular facials and massages with holistic touches like a warm aromatic compress on arrival and the Cultural Touches of Elemis.

New owners took over Grace Bay in 2001, but the urbane Martein van Wagenberg is still running day-to-day operations, and the service is still efficient and gracious. When you check in, you're seated at an antique desk, handed a chilled towel, and offered complimentary champagne or soda; attendants spritz you with Evian water and bring you homemade sorbets every afternoon.

Name: Grace Bay Club
Manager: Martein van Wagenberg
Address: P.O. Box 128, Providenciales, Turks & Caicos, British West Indies
Location: On Grace Bay, about 15 min. from the airport (transfer included in the room rate)
Telephone: 649/946-5050

Fax: 649/946-5758
E-mail: info@gracebayhotel.com
Web: www.gracebayclub.com
Reservations: 800/946-5757, toll-free direct
Credit Cards: American Express, MasterCard, Visa
Rates: $675–$1,155 EP (Dec 20–Apr 21); service charge 10%; off-season 25% less
Rooms: 22 suites and penthouses, all with terraces or patio, air-conditioning, ceiling fans, satellite TV/VCR, clock/radio, washer-dryer, full kitchen, hair dryer, bathrobes; most rooms have 2 full bathrooms
Meals: Breakfast 7–10:30am, lunch noon–3pm, afternoon tea 4pm, dinner 6:30–10pm (about $100), all served in the open-air Anacaona Restaurant; casual elegant ("collared shirts, long pants — no jeans, please"); room service for all meals at extra charge
Entertainment: Live music three times a week, the manager's weekly cocktail party; casinos nearby
Sports: Miles of uncrowded beach, free-form freshwater pool, Jacuzzi, tennis (2 courts, with lights), bicycles, windsurfing, Sunfish sailing, snorkeling gear, snorkeling trips, temporary membership at nearby fitness center — all free; treatments at the Serenity Spa at Grace Bay extra; other watersports and golf nearby (complimentary shuttle to clubhouse)
PS: No children under 12; check into the status of construction work through 2004; closed Sept

Point Grace

PROVIDENCIALES

☆☆☆☆ ⵞ ⵞ ⵞ ❻ ❻ $ $ $ $ $
ATMOSPHERE   DINING   SPORTS   RATES

The view from your balcony — white glistening sand, water clear as crystal, palm trees nodding in the trade winds — is so picture-perfect you might think it's been electronically enhanced.

Open since spring 2000, this luxury enclave consists of two four-story cupola-topped villas separated by a stunning lipless pool from four large two-story cottages around the garden (even the smallest suite is over 1,000 sq. ft.). Only the beachside lodgings get direct views of that picture-perfect beach, but for my money I prefer the gingerbread-trimmed cottages — they have more of a Caribbean feel to them than the starkly white, less-than-graceful structures on the beach (plantings and vines may soften the contours in time).

Point Grace cocoons guests in comfort well beyond the norm, even for a luxury resort. Guests get two bathrobes — one for the tub, one for the beach. Frette linens cover the canopy beds; the marble bathrooms have eight Frette towels and separate soaking tubs. Each suite comes with elegant custom-made mahogany furniture, a washer-dryer, and $20,000 kitchens with Frigidaire Galley Professional Series refrigerators (you can have a cook sent over from the kitchen if you don't want to prepare your own banquet).

But it's the little grace notes that make Point Grace so appealing — antique Indonesian tea tables, Javanese silk cushions, and Indonesian wicker hampers for your used Frettes. The tiles in the pool are trimmed with gold leaf, the poolside trash cans are tucked away in teak trellis containers, the cabana-chaises on the beach (German-made, a cool $3,000 each) have footrests and holders for your drink and your paperback. In the evening, the turndown maid lights a dainty oil lamp beside your bed.

In the beginning, guests had to hop into taxis and head off for dinner but now the resort has its own restaurant, Grace's Cottage, a 62-seater decorated in tones of coral and lime and trimmed with white gingerbread. Dine outdoors beneath a gazebo or beneath the stars (but not, unfortunately, beachside), indoors beside a mahogany bar against a wall of antiqued yellow — either locale a pleasant setting for Carib-Asian fusion dishes like pumpkin and coconut soup and jerk wahoo with ginger plum sauce. You can now also indulge in spa treatments without leaving Point Grace — its new Thalasso Spa tucks three high-ceilinged cottages into a quiet corner behind the dunes, doors and windows opening to the breezes while you drift off beneath the spell of a micronized marine algae wrap or deep tissue massage.

Tranquility, as much as luxury, is the name of the game here. The "beach boys" not only keep an eye on guests who need drinks or towels but also discourage casual visitors from dropping in for a look around. Even the blender at the poolside bar has been muffled to drown out the usual whirring and grinding — heaven forbid that a dozing guest should be awakened by someone else's piña colada.

Name: Point Grace
Manager: TBA
Address: Box 700, Providenciales, Turks & Caicos Islands, British West Indies
Location: On Grace Bay, about 15 min. from the airport (transfer included in the rate, but you can pay extra and travel in a Rolls-Royce)
Telephone: 649/946-5096
Fax: 649/946-5097
E-mail: pointgrace@tciway.tc
Web: www.pointgrace.tc
Reservations: 866/924-7223, toll-free direct
Credit Cards: American Express, Discover, MasterCard, Visa
Rates: $525–$4,900 CP (Dec 20–Apr 22); 10% tax and 10% service charge extra; off-season 30% less; or, if you want to go whole hog, $6,500 for the owners' duplex four-bedroom penthouse with private elevator
Rooms: 32 suites in beachside villas or garden cottages, all with balconies or verandas, air-conditioning and ceiling fans, full kitchens, DVD/VCR TV,

CD players, direct-dial telephones with dataports, hair dryers, and bathrobes for room, kimonos for beach

Meals: Breakfast 7:30–10am, lunch noon–3pm, dinner 7–10pm (about $110–$120 for 2, indoor or out in Grace's Cottage); casual dress, but you'll feel more comfortable if you're elegantly casual; room service during dining-room hours

Entertainment: Library of DVDs, CDs, and books; casinos and bars nearby

Sports: Miles of beach, lipless pool with swim-up bar, pool table, fitness center, snorkeling gear — all free; watersports, tennis and golf 5 min. away (complimentary shuttle to clubhouse)

PS: Few children; open year-round

OTHER CHOICES

Caribbean Paradise Inn

PROVIDENCIALES

You have to walk 3 minutes to the beach — but what a beach. Grace Bay on "Provo" is one of those ribbons of sand that seem to go on forever, blinding white beside a sea that's startlingly turquoise. The inn's nearest neighbor is the tony Grace Bay Club ($500 a night, see above), but you can check in here for just $157 a night (even less if you sign up for a dive package) — in winter! Just over 5 years old and the handiwork of a computer programmer from Germany, Vern Niebel, Caribbean Paradise nevertheless captures that laid-back, easy-does-it ambience of the old-timers' Caribbean. The architecture is vaguely colonial, with two two-story dormer-windowed wings forming an L around a pool surrounded by lots of shrubbery and flowers. Clumps of oleander and fan palms shut out the neighboring vacant lots waiting to become luxury condos, and the reception/office patio doubles as a bar and breakfast terrace ("our croissants come from the same bakery as Grace Bay Club"). Breakfast conversations, more likely than not, will turn to scuba diving because the inn offers some exceptional values in scuba packages, and it's not unknown to share a table here with dive fanatics who've just flown in on their private jet.

When you're ready to crash, really crash, but you don't want to spend a small fortune on DVD/TVs and designer kitchens, when you want a beach but you don't want to pay a premium for stepping from your room directly onto sand, here's the answer — convenient to restaurants and shops yet only a 5-minute walk to the sea. The guest rooms (with air-conditioning and ceiling fans) are nicely furnished in tropical-rattan style, with shiny bathrooms, balconies or lanais, minibars, and 20-channel non-DVD televisions (with

HBO and The Movie Channel). The suites also have small kitchenettes for anyone who can't be bothered strolling to the nearby restaurants for lunch. And
each room comes equipped (unsurprisingly, given the high-tech background of
Vern Niebel) with a modem jack and Internet access. Niebel spent many years
in the computer business in the U.S.; his English is excellent and he's happy to
sit down and tell you about the best dive sites, restaurants, and sightseeing tours.
Note: Temporarily closed in summer 2003, so double-check status for winter
2003/04. 16 rooms. Doubles: $157–$169 CP, winter 2002–03 (less if you book
by the week). *Caribbean Paradise Inn, P.O. Box 673, Grace Bay, Providenciales, Turks
& Caicos Islands, British West Indies. Telephone: 866/946-5020 (toll-free); fax: 640/
946-5022; e-mail: inn@paradise.tc.*

Sibonné Boutique Hotel

PROVIDENCIALES

It sits among low dunes at one end of Grace Bay Beach, somewhat removed
from the grander hotels but close enough to restaurants and shops that going
out in the evening is not a major undertaking — not that you're likely to
go out often, now that new owners have spiffed up the beachside restaurant
and revamped the menu. For some old TCI hands, the good news is that
Sibonné is now run by The Macleods, Ken and Sandra, who have been managing hotels in these parts for so long and with such enthusiasm, they are now
officially "Belongers" — citizens of the Turks & Caicos. Some of you might
have known this 26-roomer as Le Deck Beach Club and Hotel, a modest but
comfy spot for feet-in-the-sand, sandals-and-shorts vacations; now it has
emerged as the Sibonné Boutique Hotel on world-famous Grace Bay Beach,
with the sophisticated decor and extra trappings that implies. But it is still ideal
for those feet-in-the-sand, laid-back vacations. You'll be bedding down here in
a room of more modest proportions than its luxe compatriots farther along the
beach, but each is charmingly appointed with striped bedspreads and decorative netting; and each has air-conditioning, ceiling fan, unstocked fridge,
coffeemakers, in-room safes, and 33-channel TV. Because of the dunes, most of
the rooms overlook a garden courtyard with shady palms and bursts of hibiscus, but all are just a few paces from that glorious beach. Between trips to the
sea, you can enjoy a freshwater pool. But, for many guests, Sibonné's most
appealing feature (besides its location and refreshingly manageable rates) is the
dune-top restaurant, now known as the Bay Bistro and serving a menu of
remarkable versatility — brie and smoked salmon canapes, conch fritters with
hot rouille sauce, crab and cheese potstickers, grilled layered vegetable with
feta and goat cheese. And that's just the tapas. Main dishes run the gamut from
crispy chicken with ginger and peanut sauce to fresh tuna glazed with balsamic
vinegar and fried capers. Once you've sampled Bay Bistro's chocolate Bailey's

gateau and Key lime pie from North Caicos, you'll understand why the place stays open from 10 to 10:30 just for pastry and dessert: That gives diners from other restaurants a chance to drive over to Sibonné and top off their evenings in true sweet-tooth style. Expect to pay $60 to $70 for two or three courses, without drinks. 28 rooms, including 2 suites and 1 one-bedroom apartment. $200–$375 EP, winter 2003–04. *Sibonné, P.O. Box 144, Grace Bay, Providenciales, Turks & Caicos Islands, British West Indies. Telephone: 649/946-5547; fax: 649/946-5770; e-mail: sibonne@provo.net; Web: www.sibonne.com. (For information on a sister hotel, the moderately priced Turtle Cove Inn located at the marina, check out www.turtlecoveinn.com.)*

Windmills Plantation

SALT CAY

Say you went to the old Caribbean, the Caribbean of unpaved roadways, of donkeys in the garden and cows ambling around in front of your bikes, of islands with less than 100 inhabitants. You have to take an extra hop on a puddle-jumper to get there, but you'll instantly become part of the past on Salt Cay, which used to be the domain of salt barons and is now the secret of escapists — secret, because the largest inn has only eight rooms so, by word of mouth, it might take a century for the word to get out. It's called Windmills Plantation, owned and run by Jim and Sharon Shafer who were excellent hosts during their stint at the Meridian Club. What Windmills has going for it is a 2½-mile white sand beach, peace and solitude, and surpassing tranquility. The eight rooms are decorated in a style befitting the past — four-poster beds; shaded verandas; slow-turning ceiling fans, some with cathedral ceilings, some with lofts; and lots of nice little homey touches. Between leisurely home-baked breakfasts and leisurely gourmet dinners, you can absolutely fill your days with nothing — reading, napping, shell hunting, walking, biking, maybe even bone-fishing if you want something energetic. There's also a small Total Gym so that you don't go totally to pot. And, in fact, getting there is not such a chore — Inter-Island Airways flies between Provo and Salt Cay three times a day, a flight of 10 minutes. Three nights on Provo, three on Salt, sounds like an ideal break to me. 8 rooms. $325–$425 room only, winter 2002–03 (but there's a small-print line on their website that says if you book online, meals are included). *The Windmills Plantation at Salt Cay, Salt Cay, Turks & Caicos Islands, British West Indies. Tel: 649/946-6962; fax: 649/946-6930; e-mail: windmillsplantation@msn.com; Web: www.windmillsplantation.com.*

The Cayman Islands

There are three of them —

Grand Cayman, Little Cayman, and Cayman Brac. Together
they're a British Crown Colony that will probably remain
that way for some time because, as one local taxi driver put
it, "If we got independence we'd only end up with a lot of
politicians."

Otherwise, the Caymans can't seem to make up their
mind what they want to be. On the one hand, the colony
claims it is, as the brochures put it, "as unspoiled as it was
the day Columbus sailed by." On the other hand, a banking
boom has "transformed George Town from a sleepy village

into a dynamic financial capital." At last count there were about 400 banks for a population of fewer than 20,000 people, plus who knows how many megabucks wheeler-dealers skulking among the seagrape trees searching for the perfect offshore bank. The islands are touted as a tax haven, but everyone seems to forget to mention that it's tax-free only for people who live there or buy condominiums; the poor visitors get zapped with a tax on rooms, a departure tax, another fee for a local driver's license, and the aftereffects of an import duty that has sent prices for food and drink soaring alarmingly.

All of this would be easier to take if Grand Cayman, the largest of the trio, were really something special. But this is no lofty, luxuriant Jamaica or St. Lucia. It's flat, swampy, and characterless (what else can you call a place whose prime tourist attraction is a turtle farm?). True, there are lots of beaches, most notably Seven Mile Beach running north from George Town, but they're lined with an uninspired collection of hotels and condos (most of them, it should be noted, no higher than the palm trees, so no one can accuse the authorities of ruining the place).

What the Caymans do have — in abundance — are miles, fathoms, leagues of coral reefs, with water so clear you can spot an angelfish 200 feet away.

HOW TO GET THERE   There are now nonstop flights to Grand Cayman from New York, Charlotte, Orlando, Tampa, Baltimore/Washington, Atlanta, Miami, and Toronto on American, Continental, Delta, US Airways, Cayman Airways, Air Canada and Northwest; Air Jamaica has frequent connections via Montego Bay and Kingston.

For information on the Cayman Islands, call 345/949-0623 or visit www.caymanislands.ky.

Hyatt Regency Grand Cayman

GRAND CAYMAN

☆	ϒ ϒ	❻ ❻ ❻	$ $ $
ATMOSPHERE	DINING	SPORTS	RATES

You won't find many chain hotels represented in these pages, but, like its sister resort at Dorado Beach in Puerto Rico, this multi-million dollar resort eschews the usual Hyatt formula.

The architecture, described as British colonial, is really more birthday-cake colonial, with white iron verandas and decorative trim "icing," a pastel-blue facade accented by flower boxes, and decorative fanlights. After dark, the mise-en-scène becomes positively magical, with a zillion lights gleaming

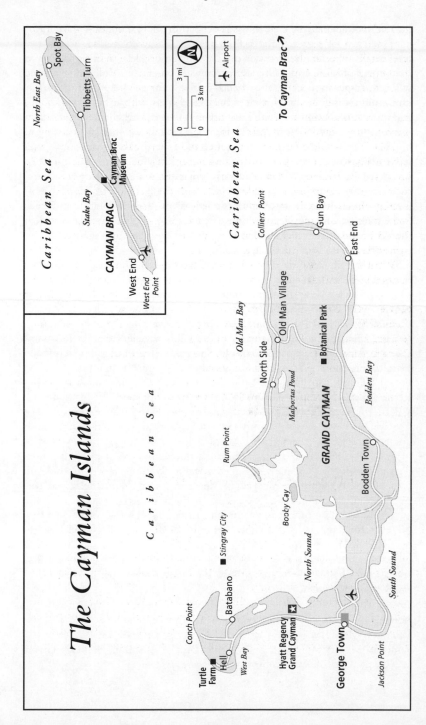

through French windows, bathing the reflecting pools, spotlighting the fountains, and festooning the ficus trees.

The Hyatt is just one corner of a 90-acre resort-development known as Britannia, a tropical conglomerate with one-, two-, three-, and four-bedroom villas; its own beach club and marina; and the current hotel and one-of-a-kind golf course. The hotel itself is composed of a courtyard of lawns, pools, and fountains surrounded by the seven wings of the hotel, the tallest of which is five stories high. At nearly 300 rooms, it is, for my money, 100 rooms too big, but it brings to the Caymans a touch of luxury hitherto found only in a few of the island's condominiums. The solution may be to check into one of the newer beachfront suites — 53 of them with two swimming pools and their own swim-up bar.

The guest rooms are tastefully designed, as you would expect from Hyatt, and equipped with all the trimmings, such as minibars. Color schemes reflect the aquas and corals of sea and sand, with flashes of lilac and pink tossed in; travertine marble layers the foyers, bathrooms, and oval bathtubs; the custom-designed furniture features mostly upholstered rattan and wicker (the only complaint here is that in the standard rooms a two-seat couch crowds the room without adding much in comfort or convenience, unless you plan to watch hours of television).

Generous in all things, the Hyatt people give you a choice of dining spots — the veranda of the Britannia Golf Club & Grille; another restaurant at the beach club called Hemingways; and the Garden Loggia, which is the main dining room, where breakfast is served, and which is stylishly decorated in bleached ash paneling with latticed ceilings and French windows opening to the alfresco garden extension. Menus are hardly predictable Hyatt fare, but a masterly combination of continental, American, and Caribbean dishes — like wahoo ceviche with shaved red onions, and pan-roasted double lamb chops with tropical tuber gratin.

Even Hyatt's watersports facilities are a notch above the usual, with three flagship 65-foot catamarans designed specifically for cruising around the Caymans and equipped with spacious decks, comfortable seating, stereo, bar, two restrooms, and underwater glass panels for fish watching.

But what calls most of the attention to Britannia is its golf course. The Jack Nicklaus Signature people designed not only the nine-hole links-style course, but also the special Cayman Ball, a sphere that claims to do something my own tee shots have been doing for years — going half as far as they should. It may not be St. Andrews, but at least it's another reason besides scuba diving for going to the Caymans.

Name: Hyatt Regency Grand Cayman Resort & Villas
Manager: Mark Bastis
Address: 51 Britannia Dr., Seven Mile Beach, P.O. Box 1588GT, Grand Cayman, British West Indies

Location: On the Britannia resort development, across the main road from Seven Mile Beach, 2 miles outside of George Town, 12 min. and $20 from the airport

Telephone: 345/949-1234

Fax: 345/949-8528

E-mail: quality@cayman.hyatt.com

Web: www.grandcayman.hyatt.com

Reservations: 800/554-9288, Hyatt Worldwide

Credit Cards: All major cards

Rates: $415–$2,100 EP (Dec 20–Apr 15); service charge 10%; off-season 40% less

Rooms: 289, including 53 beachfront suites, 44 Regency Club rooms, 8 Deluxe Suites, 2 Luxury Suites, some with terrace or patio, some with small veranda, all with air-conditioning and ceiling fans, fully stocked minibar (wet bars in suites), satellite TV, clock/radio, direct-dial telephone, in-room safe, coffeemaker, umbrella, and hair dryer; some suites are duplexes with sleeping loft and canopy bed

Meals: Breakfast 7–11:30am, lunch 11:30am–2:30pm (everything from sandwiches to complete meals, at any of 6 indoor/outdoor locations), dinner 6–10pm, June–Nov (in the fan-cooled indoor/outdoor Garden Loggia, $70–$100 for 2); Sun champagne brunch buffet 11:30am–2:30pm; casual resort wear appropriate in all restaurants; nonsmoking area in dining room; 24-hr. room service

Entertainment: 5 bars, live music all nights except Sun

Sports: Beach (a section of the popular Seven Mile Beach across the road), 6 freshwater swimming pools (2 with swim-up bars), Jacuzzi, tennis (3 Plexipave courts, with lights), croquet — all free; snorkeling gear, catamaran and Sunfish sailing, windsurfing, parasailing, paddleboats, scuba diving, and day sails on the resort's private 65-ft. catamaran at extra charge; private 9-hole golf course that can be played 3 ways

PS: At any season you may encounter groups that come perilously close to behaving like conventioneers, and some children; open year round

Jamaica

*I*t's the stuff travel posters are made of — rafting down Jamaica's Rio Grande, frolicking in waterfalls, limbo dancing, reggae, aristocratic plantations, and elegant villas.

Where to go in Jamaica? Most flights from North America touch down in Montego Bay before continuing to Kingston, so MoBay is the place to begin. Once a quiet haven for honeymooners, it's now crowded with tour groups, cruise-ship passengers, and honky-tonks. Since there's still plenty to enjoy in town and in the surrounding areas, begin with a few days at one of the three classy resorts just outside town. Two hours east along the north shore, Ocho Rios is a scaled-down version of MoBay, with oodles of activities, from scrambling up Dunn's River Falls to touring Prospect Plantation to polo — spectating or playing — at not one but two locations. A little farther along the coast, Port Antonio is the least developed of the three resorts, though visitors drive from all over the island to go rafting down the Rio Grande or hiking through the foothills of the Blue Mountains. Then, of course, there's Negril with its celebrated 7-mile beach and sunset watching among the coral coves of West End.

A tip on planning: If you find choosing where to stay as difficult as I do, you might begin with a few days at one of MoBay's top resorts, with a day trip to Negril. Then I suggest you sightsee your way to Kingston — driving along the north shore, spending a night or two in Ocho Rios and/or Port Antonio on your way to the airport in Kingston, where you can board a flight home (although it may stop in MoBay). If you stop over in the capital itself, stay in the mountains at Strawberry Hill, but be sure to visit the crafts boutiques, cafe, and restaurants at Devon House in town.

The selection in these pages begins on the north coast, near Montego Bay, moves east toward Port Antonio, detours to the mountains behind Kingston, then swings along the south coast via Treasure Beach to Negril.

HOW TO GET THERE   Jamaica is now one of the easiest islands to get to from North America. The much improved Air Jamaica has nonstop or direct flights to Montego Bay (some to Kingston) from Atlanta, Baltimore/Washington, Boston, Chicago, Ft. Lauderdale, Houston, Los Angeles, Miami, New York (JFK and Newark), Philadelphia, and Orlando (not all fly daily, but at least frequently); American, Delta, Northwest, Continental, and US Airways have daily direct or nonstop flights from some 20 destinations between them. There's additional service from Toronto, Montréal, and Winnipeg on Air Canada.

Note: You might also want to look into connections from MoBay on Air Jamaica Express to Negril, Boscobel, Kingston, and Port Antonio airstrips.

For information about Jamaica, call 800/223-4582 or visit
www.jamaicatravel.com.

Round Hill Hotel & Villas

NEAR MONTEGO BAY

☆☆☆☆☆	♈♈♈	❻❻❻	$ $ $ $
ATMOSPHERE	DINING	SPORTS	RATES

The sweeping, casuarina-lined driveway says "class." When you get to the crest of the hill and take in the gardens and the view of coves and mountains,

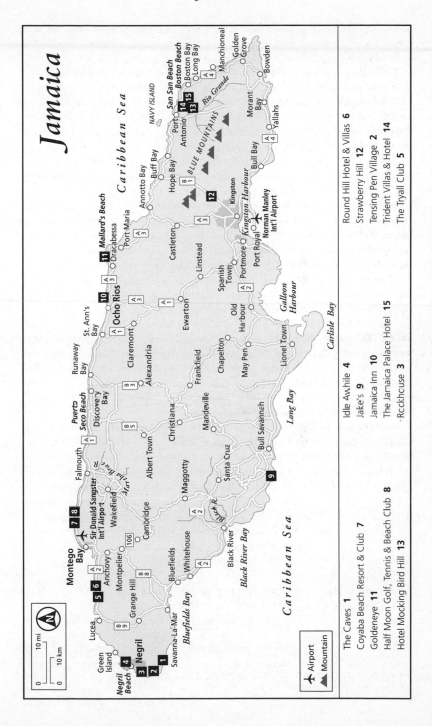

Jamaica

Caribbean Sea

NAVY ISLAND

Rio Grande

BLUE MOUNTAINS

Mallard's Beach

San San Beach
Boston Beach
Boston Bay
Long Bay
Golden Grove
Bowden
Manchioneal

Port Antonio

14 15
13 15
13

Morant Bay
Yallahs

Golden Grove

Buff Bay
Hope Bay
Annotto Bay
Port Maria
Oracabessa 11
Ocho Rios 10
St. Ann's Bay
Runaway Bay
Discovery Bay
Puerto Seco Beach

Kingston
Norman Manley Int'l Airport
Port Royal
Portmore
Spanish Town
Old Harbour
Kingston Harbour
Bull Bay

12

Castleton
Linstead
Ewarton
Claremont
Alexandria
Frankfield
Chapelton
May Pen
Lionel Town
Galleon Harbour
Carlisle Bay
Long Bay

Falmouth
Martha Brae
Sir Donald Sangster Int'l Airport
Montego Bay 7 8
5 6
Anchovy
Montpelier
106
Wakefield
Cambridge
Grange Hill
Lucea
Green Island
Savanna-La-Mar
Bluefields
Whitehouse
Bluefields Bay
Bull Savannah
Santa Cruz
Maggotty
Albert Town
Christiana
Mandeville
Black R.
Black River
Black River Bay

Negril
Negril Beach
3 2 1
4

9

Caribbean Sea

✈ Airport
▲ Mountain

N

0   10 mi
0   10 km

The Caves **1**
Coyaba Beach Resort & Club **7**
Goldeneye **11**
Half Moon Golf, Tennis & Beach Club **8**
Hotel Mocking Bird Hill **13**

Idle Awhile **4**
Jake's **9**
Jamaica Inn **10**
The Jamaica Palace Hotel **15**
Rockhouse **3**

Round Hill Hotel & Villas **6**
Strawberry Hill **12**
Tensing Pen Village **2**
Trident Villas & Hotel **14**
The Tryall Club **5**

it's easy to understand why this elegant resort has been hosting the rich and famous for 45 winters.

Of all the resorts along Jamaica's fabled north shore, this is probably the one that still comes closest to the glory years of everyone's memories. Its villas and servants have beckoned the likes of Oscar Hammerstein, Moss Hart, and, in Villa 25, Adele Astaire. As if that weren't cast enough for one resort, Cole Porter and Noel Coward (Villa 3) used to entertain the entertainers. Ever since, the upper crust of show business, high society, and big business has been chauffeured up that driveway in loyal streams, among them Paul McCartney, Harrison Ford, Diane Sawyer, and Mike Nichols. Designer Ralph Lauren spends every other weekend here at his secluded villa (sorry, it's not for rent) and recently redecorated the terrace bar in Laurenesque blue and white.

Many visitors to Round Hill have to bed down in three two-story wings alongside the beach, once known as the Barracks, but now rechristened Pineapple House after what passes in these conservative parts as a major renovation — pencil-post beds handcrafted from local mahogany; pale, cool, green walls; new clay-tile floors; bigger windows for better views; newly tiled bathrooms; and more space by incorporating the balconies into the rooms. In other resorts, they'd probably be the most desirable rooms because of their beachfront location; but the true Round Hill is found on the bosky bowl rising from the beach in what seems to be 28 acres of tropical garden planted with villas, rather than the other way around. Each whitewashed, shingle-roofed villa is privately owned; 22 of them have private pools; many have been outfitted recently with new kitchens and bathrooms; and each is designed in such a way that it can be rented as an individual suite, with a bedroom with louvered doors opening to a covered outdoor patio framed by bougainvillea and croton and mahogany trees.

Because they're privately owned, all the villas are different. Unless you book now for winters 2 or 3 years down the line, you will almost certainly have to settle for whatever is available; but if I were specifying lodgings, these are some of the villas I'd bid for: number 8 (the owners spent a bundle installing marble floors, silk rugs, walls hand-stenciled by a specially imported Japanese craftsman, and a canopy bed with pink chintz); number 13 (these owners have installed a large deck, pool, and Jacuzzi); number 18 (a particularly attractive high-ceilinged, arched living room, with fabrics to match the anthurium and elephant ear in the garden); number 1 (with an inviting pool at the end of the lawn) and number 16 (which has one of the grandest terrace/decks of them all).

But what sets Round Hill apart is probably the service. The staff numbers 250. When you rouse yourselves in the morning, your maid sets the terrace table and prepares breakfast. Your gardener (there are 40 of them!) has already cleaned the pool and positioned your lounger to catch the morning sun. If you opt for the cove, each time you paddle into the sea, you'll return to find that a beach boy has edged your chaise around to face the sun. At the lunchtime buffet, an army of waiters totes your laden plates to your table, whisks away the empties when you're ready for refills, recharges your water glasses, and holds chairs for the ladies. Laundry? The maid will take care of it. Room service? If you can't be bothered trotting down the hill, the dining room will send your dinner up. There are drivers to get you to and from your rooms when you don't feel like walking, and ball boys to retrieve stray serves on the tennis courts.

Many people have misconceptions about Round Hill, so let me correct three myths: It's not formal, it's not stuffy, and it's not prohibitively expensive. Black tie is requested for some Saturday gala evenings, but only a handful of men actually dress up; other evenings, dress is informal (but stylishly so, of course). These rules (or suggestions) are now in effect year-round. Everyone who wants to mingle, mingles — marquises and marchionesses included, especially at the Monday beach picnic. During the peak season, managing director Josef Forstmayr makes a point of inviting hotel guests to the Tuesday-evening cocktail parties put on by villa owners. Compare rates here (and elsewhere in Jamaica, for that matter) with some other islands; for what some down-island resorts charge for room only, Round Hill throws in a suite and a personal maid.

One minor drawback: On weekends in winter, regular jet services are augmented by charter flights that occasionally might intrude on your sense of seclusion.

But that's no reason to forego the lap of luxury. Once in a lifetime (at least) everyone should sample a week in the villa of, say, an Italian count, English lord, or dot-com whiz. You'll enjoy plush outdoor living rooms, pools shared with only one other couple, a gardener to move your lounger around with the sun, and a personal maid to have your breakfast waiting for you in the morning.

To make life even more pampered, Round Hill has added a new wellness center and spa by taking over a plantation next door, extending the resort's waterfront, and converting its great house into treatment rooms. The wide range of treatments includes hot-and-cold stone therapy, smoothing papaya wrap and yoga — and the spacious lawns have become a quiet area for lounging, with a discreet sign saying, "NO CHILDREN."

In February 2003, Round Hill Hotel celebrated its 50th anniversary with a gala tribute to founder The Honorable John Pringle, who recalled how, as a 22-year-old ex-equerry to the Duke of Windsor, he flew first-class from Montego Bay to New York, found himself seated next to Noel Coward, no less, and launched into a sales pitch for his trendsetting concept. Halfway through the flight, Coward patted him on the knee and said: "Dear boy, if you'll just stop boring me so, I'll buy one of your cottages." He did. And Round Hill has been a glittering getaway ever since.

Name: Round Hill Hotel & Villas
Managing Director: Josef Forstmayr

Address: P.O. Box 64, Montego Bay, Jamaica, West Indies
Location: On a promontory west of Montego Bay, about 10 miles, 25 min., and $28 by taxi from the airport
Telephone: 876/956-7050
Fax: 876/956-7505
E-mail: roundhill@swjamaica.com
Web: www.roundhillhotel.com
Reservations: 800/972-2159, toll-free direct or 800/237-3237, Elegant Resorts International
Credit Cards: All major cards
Rates: $420–$850 EP (Dec 15–Apr 15); service charge and taxes included; off-season 40% less
Rooms: 110, including 36 supreme and deluxe rooms in Pineapple House, plus 74 suites in 27 villas; rooms in Pineapple House have walls of shutters facing the bay, standing fans or ceiling fans, telephones; villas have maids and gardeners, air-conditioning, ceiling fans, balcony or patio, garden or lawn, indoor/outdoor living room, CD players, direct-dial telephones, kitchen (for maids' use), private or shared pool (some also have TV)
Meals: Breakfast 7:30–10:30am, lunch 12:30–2:30pm, dinner 7:30–9:30pm (on the beachside patio beneath the almond trees, about $100); bonfire beach picnic Mon nights; "Jamaica Night" with local cuisine and calypso music Fri; dress informal, except jacket and tie after 7pm (black tie is "requested" on Sat nights in season); room service to 9:30pm at no extra charge; music (amplified until 11pm) for dancing most evenings
Entertainment: Local trio (The Upbeaters) for beach barbecue, resident jazz band, steel band; library, parlor games, TV lounge, art shows
Sports: Private beach (60 or 90 yd., depending on the tides), freshwater pool, 22 villa pools, snorkeling, floats, kayaks, floating trampoline, tennis (5 courts, with lights, pro shop) — all free; water-skiing, scuba diving, windsurfing, Sunfish sailing, paddleboats from newly rehabbed watersports center on the beach, new spa with 6 treatment rooms and fitness center, deep-sea fishing boat charters at extra charge; horseback riding 40 min. away, golf 10 min. away
PS: Some children, some small executive groups; "cellphones don't work here"; open year-round

The Tryall Club

NEAR MONTEGO BAY

☆☆☆☆   ♈♈♈   ➏➏➏ $ $ $ $
ATMOSPHERE   DINING   SPORTS   RATES

Tryall is 2,200 acres of lush Jamaican plantation that long ago switched from sugar to the sweet life. The 160-year-old Estate Great House sits atop a low hill a few hundred yards inland from the beach, surrounded by championship fairways and sumptuous private villas. Golfers know Tryall well — they've seen it often on live telecasts of made-for-TV tournaments (Shell's Wonderful World of Golf, Johnnie Walker World Championship). It's an appealing layout with waterholes lined with coconut palms, lily ponds, and a fairway that skirts a centuries-old sugar mill with a still-turning waterwheel. So many fruit trees line the fairways, the caddies not only are expert in club selection but they'll also tell you the perfect timing for eating the star apples, oranges, breadfruit, and mangos.

Tryall started out decades ago as an exclusive enclave for millionaires, mostly American, mostly Texan. Hence the lavish, sometimes dramatic, villas, most of which are available for rent. The Great House and its adjoining annexes are now run as a hotel, a parade of privately owned Great House Villa Suites (basically, two-floor suites) for fewer than 30 guests.

The shingle-roofed, native-stone Great House, designated a national monument in 1989, has had a face-lift and one surprising addition — an Internet room — but it still has its lovely indoor/outdoor dining terrace overlooking the terraced garden, an inviting pool with swim-up bar, and beyond that the fairways, the beach, and the sea. Most of the rental villas have three, four, or six bedrooms and come with private staff. The new Estate Villa Suites in the Great House take the elegance and gracious lifestyle of the villas and make them available to couples or foursomes who enjoy spacious, sumptuous suites with bedrooms, living rooms, full kitchens, and private patios or veranda; you can rent a personal cook if you fall in love with your suite so much you don't want to leave. Each one is decorated with individual details, but upper levels are set up in such a way that a whirlpool tub separates the bathroom from the bedroom, with louvered shutters to block out the view or open up the entire space — to include the view. The sunset views from the tub (or the patio, for that matter) are a mesmerizing mix of densely forested hills with white walls and gray shingle roofs popping up here and there among the foliage. At sea level, bright green fairways fingered with the shadows of palms weave through the meadow, and beyond them dark headlands scallop the coast all the way to Montego Bay.

Some Tryall guests never leave this hilltop knoll. Why should they? A few paces from their rooms they have nine tennis courts (newly rehabbed with Nova cushion surfaces) and a full-time pro, as well as that spectacular swimming pool with a waterfall and swim-up bar (the first of its kind on Jamaica when it was installed back in the 1960s). The friendly, responsive staff makes you feel almost like you're really staying in one of the big private villas. One small snag has been attended to: the main road from MoBay to Negril. Previously, guests planning to spend time at the beach or tee off on the golf course had to buck the traffic to get to the other side of the road. Now the road has been improved, and in the process, four underpasses have been built to link the two parts of the resort, and the place is abuzz with guests riding around in golf carts.

Name: The Tryall Club
Manager: Edward H. (Ted) Ruddock
Address: P.O. Box 1206, Montego Bay, Jamaica, West Indies
Location: About 12 miles and $30 west of Montego Bay
Telephone: 876/956-5660
Fax: 876/956-5658
E-mail: tryallclub@cwjamaica.com
Web: www.tryallclub.com
Reservations: 800/238-5290, toll-free direct
Credit Cards: American Express, MasterCard, Visa
Rates: $400–$750 EP (Dec 15–Apr 14); service charge 10%; off-season 30% less
Rooms: 8 one-bedroom and 5 two-bedroom Great House Villa Suites, all with air-conditioning, balconies or patios, direct-dial telephones, 2 TVs, king-size beds, hair dryers, whirlpool tubs, bathrobes, full kitchens; also, 65 fully staffed private Estate Villas for rent (they're not as expensive as you might think, if you share with other couples)
Meals: Breakfast 7–10am, lunch 11:30am–3:30pm (at the Beach Café), complimentary afternoon tea 4pm, dinner 7–10pm (about $100, all but lunch served at the Great House); dress country club casual but elegant; room service for breakfast only
Entertainment: Barbecue beach buffet with live music twice a week, manager's cocktail party — and all the nightlife you can handle, oh my, in MoBay or Negril (which you can now get to within an hour, thanks to the new, improved roadway)
Sports: Hilltop swimming pool, more or less private (but not great) lagoon-like beach, kayaks, Hobie Cats, Sunfish sailing, fitness room — all free; tennis (9 Laykold courts, with lights, pro shop), golf (6,920 yd., pro shop, practice facilities) at extra charge; horseback riding, mountain biking nearby
PS: Some children allowed; "no cellphones allowed on golf course"; open year-round

Half Moon Golf, Tennis & Beach Club

NEAR MONTEGO BAY

☆☆☆☆   ♟♟♟   ✿✿✿✿ $ $ $ $
ATMOSPHERE   DINING   SPORTS   RATES

The beach is indeed an almost perfect half moon, shaded by seagrapes onshore, sheltered by a reef offshore, and dotted with tiny black-and-white shells, like the Half Moon's logo in miniature. The first vacationers settled around their half moon in the 1950s in a cluster of private cottages, each one different from its neighbor. Later expansions included undistinguished two-story wings of beachside rooms and suites and the tastefully renovated studios and apartments that were once the neighboring Colony Hotel. The total tally of 213 rooms and suites, plus 32 new five-, six-, and seven-bedroom Royal Villas with private pools, is spread along 11 miles of beach, which in turn is a mere corner of a 400-acre estate that includes riding stables and a Robert Trent Jones golf course.

That lovely half-moon beach may have been the reason people were first lured to this spot, but the resort's sports facilities are the prime draw today. How many resorts that promise free tennis actually give you a chance to get in a game by providing 13 courts? (And seven of them with lights, too.) How many resorts that promise horseback riding have a complete equestrian center with 28 horses? How many resort golf courses also offer a David Leadbetter Academy to sharpen your game beyond recognition?

The club has been through several additions and lots of fine-tuning recently. The original cottages on the bay are now subdivided into suites — Imperial, Royal, and Deluxe — some with private pools (although regular guests such as Eddie Murphy frequently rent an entire complex of suites and pools for family and entourage). The new complex of Royal Villas, with five to seven bedrooms and butler, cook, and maid, has been installed in an extension to the eastern end of the estate, alongside a brand-new, island-style shopping complex called Half Moon Shopping Village, complete with coffee shop, English pub, gourmet takeout, Japanese restaurants, and a new Bob Marley museum. Even the resort's regular dining facilities have been upgraded: The beachside Seagrape Terrace looks lovelier than ever and is still the most popular choice for dinner, despite the air-conditioning in the mostly Italian Il Giardino.

As if that weren't enough in the way of choices for a single resort, Half Moon just happens to have one of the best specialty restaurants on the island, the famed Sugar Mill, across the roadway at the golf course and the still-turning waterwheel of the original mill. Its menu is an intriguing blend of continental and West Indian dishes, served on a bosky terrace beneath trees trimmed with wicker-shaded lights.

Despite the rambling nature of the place, it all seems to hold together architecturally and stylistically; even with all the additional guests and distractions, the Half Moon staff still manages to offer service in the old Jamaica tradition. Chances are the maitre d's and waiters will have your name down pat on your second visit to their breeze-cooled domain, even if it's not George Bush (as in former president), Itzhak Perlman, Kiri Te Kanawa, Prince Philip, Prince Rainier, Whitney Houston, or Spike Lee, to name just a few guests in the past decade. This obvious commitment to service comes, of course, right from the top — Heinz Simonitsch, the part owner and cosmopolite who recently retired as managing director after 40 years; he knows, I suspect, every flower in the garden, which wins oodles of environmental awards. He'll still be a major influence although he has now turned over the day-to-day running of the resort to Richard Whitfield.

Which of Half Moon's varied accommodations you stay in may depend less on the rates than on how you want to fill your days. If you want to step directly from your room into the sea, check into one of the original cottages; the two-story wings of junior and superior suites are closest to the tennis courts (but they may be closed for major refurnishing in the next 2 years); the neo-Georgian villas have private maid service and kitchens, which can be stocked from the commissary across the driveway.

Name: Half Moon Golf, Tennis & Beach Club
Managing Director: Richard Whitfield
Address: Half Moon Post Office, Rose Hall, Montego Bay, Jamaica, West Indies
Location: 7 miles from town; 5 miles from the airport; 10 min. and $15 by taxi
Telephone: 876/953-2211
Fax: 876/953-2731
E-mail: reservations@halfmoonclub.com
Web: www.halfmoonjamaica.com
Reservations: 800/237-3237, Elegant Resorts International
Credit Cards: All major cards
Rates: $390–$1,140 EP (Dec 15–Apr 15); service charge included; off-season 30% less
Rooms: 419, in 8 categories including 36 villas, all with air-conditioning (some with air-conditioning and ceiling fans), satellite TV, balconies or patios, refrigerators or minibars, and direct-dial telephones; some with kitchens, some with private or semiprivate pools, some with high-speed Internet access
Meals: Buffet breakfast 7:30–10am, continental breakfast 6:30am–noon (in La Baguette snack bar), lunch noon–6pm, dinner 7–10pm (on the open beachside Seagrape Terrace, in Il Giardino restaurant, at Half Moon Shopping Village, or the Sugar Mill at the golf course, $60–$100); long-sleeved shirts after 6pm in the winter; jacket and tie requested on Sat, otherwise informal (however, "shorts, T-shirts, and jeans are not allowed" in the evening in the hotel proper or Sugar Mill, but more casual attire is acceptable in the Village eateries); room service 7am–11:30pm at extra charge; some soft background music in some of the restaurants
Entertainment: Bar/lounge/terrace, live music after dinner every evening for dancing (resident band, calypso, steel band), floor shows, crab races (the profits from the betting go to local charities), beach barbecue every Mon and Fri with manager's rum punch party; shopping village with 40 stores and 5 restaurants
Sports: Beach, 53 freshwater pools including a lap pool, tennis (13 courts, 9 with lights, pro shop), croquet, putting green, nature reserve, fitness center, sauna, Jacuzzi, squash (4 courts) — all free; golf (18 holes, pro shop, $100 for 18 holes, David Leadbetter Golf Academy), windsurfing, Sunfish

sailing, scuba, snorkeling, bicycles, horseback riding (with guide), spa (14 treatment rooms for massage, double massage with champagne, aromatherapy, beauty treatments, yoga, aerobics) at extra charge

PS: Children have their own playground and castle, teens have their own program of activities; some seminar groups up to 120; open year-round

Jamaica Inn

OCHO RIOS

☆☆☆☆☆ ΥΥΥΥ ❻❻❻ $ $ $ $
ATMOSPHERE   **DINING**   **SPORTS**   **RATES**

The loggias alone are larger than rooms in most hotels — better furnished, too, with padded armchairs, ottomans and overstuffed sofas, breakfast tables, desks, desk lamps, fresh flowers, and drying racks for soggy swimsuits and beach towels. Have a swim before lunch and you'll find a fresh supply of big, bulky beach towels waiting for you in your room; have a nap or something after lunch, then a dip, and, sure enough, the maid has straightened out your mussed-up bed by the time you get back. Your nap may take place in a romantic pencil-post bed, in a tropical boudoir of cool pastel blues, the sunlight filtered by sheer drapes, the breezes filtered by louvered windows and doors, the terrazzo floors softened by white rugs. The owners are currently in the process of redecorating, which, in the case of Jamaica Inn, probably means going from off-white to white or cerulean to eggshell blue. Few rooms anywhere are as welcoming or as comfortable — like a favorite bathrobe.

The West Wing is best — with your loggia right on the edge of the water, your front door facing the beach and garden. If you want to be right on the beach, choose the Beach Wing, and you can step from your patio over a shin-high balustrade right onto the sand. If you can afford the best, ask for the Blue Cottage, a self-contained cottage right on the beach; if the very best, then ask for the White Suite, where Winston Churchill stayed in the 1950s — it has its own small pool with a circular ramp, and a path over a private promontory to a very private sun terrace right above the sea.

The inn, once the private hideaway of a Texas millionaire, has two one-story and two two-story wings, all a pretty periwinkle blue, strung out along a private 700-foot beach on 6 acres of lawns, wild banana, seagrapes, hibiscus, bougainvillea, and very tall coconut palms. The cove-like beach (one of the most beautiful on the island), the clear water (as cool and inviting as the bedrooms), and the placid tempo and elegance of the place have been attracting devoted fans for more than 40 years. Service is exemplary, mainly because one of the Morrow family, the owners, or a manager is sitting right there in a sort of Captain's Seat on the terrace, with an uninterrupted view of reception, lounge, bar, dining terrace, and beach.

The latest piece of fine-tuning is the KiYara Ocean Spa, in a seaside cottage next door, where dexterous fingers work their magic in a bamboo-encased terrace above the soothing sea or in its own tropical version of a Swiss shower. An outdoor terrace beside the sea becomes the setting for moonlight massages for twosomes, surrounded by scented candles and fragrant flowers, lulled by the lapping of the sea below.

But ask fans of this resort what they like most about Jamaica Inn and they may well answer "dinner." For a start, it's served in a grand setting like something out of a Busby Berkeley musical — a broad, lamp-lit terrace with a white ornate balustrade, beside the sea, beneath the palms.

All that and Chef Kai Bechinger's refined, light but flavor-rich cuisine — crispy dasheen-coated chicken breast on green papaya curry with coconut-fried mini banana, or brown-sugar-seared yellow fin tuna brushed with a marinade of sake snaps and black bean. A musical combo (native or restrained reggae, jazz, or classic pop) entices diners from their Jamaica coconut pie and zabaglione to boogie beneath the stars. Although the inn's dress code has been loosened in recent years, some of the old-timers still slip into their tuxedos to add an extra ritzy touch to the setting. Some non–foxtrotters mosey over to the croquet lawn for a moonlight duel, while lovers and romantics who forgot to book a moonlight massage slip off arm in arm to those tempting loggias with the big, comfy sofas sheltered by wild banana and serenaded by the surf.

Name: Jamaica Inn
Manager: Mary Phillips
Address: P.O. Box 1, Ocho Rios, Jamaica, West Indies
Location: On the eastern edge of town, $100 by taxi from Montego Bay (if you alert the hotel, they will have a reliable driver there to meet you with an air-conditioned minibus stocked with chilled beverages)
Telephone: 876/974-2514
Fax: 876/974-2449
E-mail: jaminn@cwjamaica.com
Web: www.jamaicainn.com
Reservations: 800/837-4608 or 877/470-6975, toll-free direct
Credit Cards: American Express, MasterCard, Visa
Rates: $440–$1,400 EP (Dec 16–Mar 15); service charge and tax included; off-season 60% less
Rooms: 45 in 7 categories, all facing the sea, all with air-conditioning plus fans and breezes, large furnished loggia, direct-dial telephone with Internet access, bathrobes, hair dryer; there is also a small compound of cottages (2 and 3 bedrooms) next door to the inn, available for rent
Meals: Breakfast 8–10am, lunch 1–2:30pm, dinner 7:30–9pm (beneath the stars; about $80; jackets (and often, by preference of the guests, black tie) in winter, "long trousers and shirts with collars" in off-season; room service at no extra charge

Entertainment: Dancing every evening to a moderately amplified four-piece combo (who recently — cringe — added a keyboard), library/lounge with masses of jigsaw puzzles

Sports: Beach (good swimming and snorkeling), freshwater pool, Sunfish sailing, croquet, snorkeling gear, sea kayaks, exercise room, tennis (nearby) — all free; spa treatments extra; scuba, boat trips, golf, horseback riding, polo (for players, learners — sometimes your hosts cart all the guests off to a match for a jolly afternoon of spectating) nearby at extra charge

PS: No conventions, no children under 14; open year-round

Goldeneye

ORACABESSA

☆☆☆☆☆　　ＹＹＹ　　🕏　　$ $ $ $ $
ATMOSPHERE　　**DINING**　　**SPORTS**　　**RATES**

You'll find resorts in these pages that have showers on the patio, but how about a hideaway where the entire garden is the bathroom? Or, if you prefer, where the bathroom is the garden?

Step from your bedroom through the louvered door. Ahead of you is a 12 × 15 flagstone patio screened by a wall of head-high bamboo. In the far corner, a green claw-foot bathtub with gilded fixtures sits atop a wooden platform. To the right, a large showerhead tops a wooden pole. Opposite stands a wrought-iron table and chairs and, leaning against one wall, a full-length antique mirror. Next to the door is a polished concrete counter, wherein a washbasin and dainty toiletries rest. Beyond, birds flutter between the mahoe and ebony and logwood trees. It's a complete alfresco bathroom sans john, which is inside with a second, more conventional shower and washbasin.

If that were the only thing that sets this place apart, it would still be worth the effort to get there; but this is Goldeneye, the villa of Ian Fleming, and I write these words on the very desk where he penned his James Bond novels. His house was modest, a squat, almost-minimalist block (this was way back in the 1950s, mind you) with 8-foot glassless windows facing the sea.

The luxuriant 15-acre estate is now the fiefdom of Jamaican impresario Chris Blackwell (see also Strawberry Hill hotel, later in this chapter), who has restored the house and generally turned it into the house of 1,001 delights: The king-size bed in the master bedroom is placed inside a "tent" formed by four stout bamboo poles draped in white muslin; the living room is dominated by a bamboo daybed and an oversized, overstuffed ottoman for a twosome; the open bar on the sideboard is complete down to a fresh lime and knife resting on their own small cutting board; windows and doors close at night with louvers of Brazilian hardwood. There are Balinese stools, African prints, carved wooden statuettes, and original paintings. And then there are the Fleming artifacts — his desk, family photographs, picture books, and biographies. What looks like an island-style guest cottage in the garden is actually the TV pavilion, with another enormous daybed, self-service bar, two oversized trays for drinks, big-screen TV, and roll-down screen for DVD movies. At the edge of the lawn, where two seagrape trees form a natural arbor, a wooden table and bench seats are ideal for breakfast and lunch. Down a flight of coral stone steps you come to a bikini-size patch of white sand with stone terraces that harbor loungers, a barbecue grill, a thatched shade for a wooden table, and a rinsing shower in its own little grotto.

Fleming spent 18 winters at this serene retreat and entertained frequently. His chums — Elizabeth Taylor, Noel Coward, Graham Greene, Truman Capote, the Blackwells (who had a country home nearby) — have been superseded by Harry Belafonte, Jim Carrey, Martha Stewart, Naomi Campbell, and a galaxy of celebrities, many of whom can afford the few hundred dollars (which go to one of Blackwell's local charities) to have a tree planted in their honor, as well as pay the stiff price for the rental.

Which brings me to the bad news: The villa has three bedrooms and costs $3,500 a night (with full staff, of course, and all meals and drinks, but the price is beyond the range of most couples, even though it's been reduced substantially since the last edition of this guide). On the other hand, team up with two other pairs of lovers and you can have this unique hideaway for just over $1,000 a night apiece and still have lots of privacy — unless you all sing in the bathtub.

Now the good news: The Goldeneye "village" has six more enchanting, birdcage cottages designed more or less in the local vernacular — wooden walls, pitched roofs, lots of louvered windows, painted in dry-brush, crack-and-peel renditions of pink poui and rose apple. (If you've seen Blackwell's Compass Point in Nassau, you'll have an idea of what to expect here.) They're set by the edge of a 30-foot-high limestone bluff (breezes aplenty to augment the ceiling fans if you don't want the air-conditioning), decorated with whimsy and taste, some with pedestal beds, most with outdoor shower stalls, but all with stereo players and stacks of CDs. They can be rented as bedrooms, suites, or two or three units together, as a "village." There's a separate terrace-dining pavilion overlooking an inlet and featuring home-style Jamaican meals (ackee and codfish, chicken curry with mango chutney, the sort of dishes the staff might eat at home). To get to the beach from these rooms, you walk down a flight of steps, hop on the glass-bottom boat or paddle a kayak across an inlet to a beach on an artificial island. Or, you can have one of the staff drive you a couple of blocks to James Bond Beach, where you'll find public watersports facilities. On the grounds, there's also a tennis court that must be one of the prettiest (and most fragrant) anywhere, its walls draped with purple plumbago.

It all sounds kind of idyllic. And it is, more or less. Beside the tub in the jungly master patio there's a small pedestal and a basket for stacking your toiletries so that you don't have to reach for your peppermint bath salts and vanilla coconut soap. And there's a wooden hook protruding from the bamboo to hold your kimono — a precise arm's length from the tub. But, if you take a shower, there's no pedestal, no hook — you have to bend down for the soap and walk four whole paces to get your robe. Bond, James Bond, wouldn't put up with that kind of nonsense.

Name: Goldeneye
Manager: Jenny Wood
Address: Oracabessa, St. Mary, Jamaica, West Indies
Location: 25 min. beyond Ocho Rios and just beyond the village of Oracabessa, 2 hr. from Montego Bay, about $150 by taxi, but for about the same price you can fly from MoBay on Air Jamaica Express or Timair to the local airfield (Boscobel), which is 10 min. from the estate
Telephone: 876/975-3354
Fax: 876/975-3620
E-mail: goldeneye@islandoutpost.com
Web: www.islandoutpost.com
Reservations: 800/688-7678, Island Outposts
Credit Cards: All major cards
Rates: $795–$3,500 FAP+ (the latter for the 3 rooms in the Fleming House); tax and service charge included (but tips are in order); off-season 30% less
Rooms: 12 rooms and suites in 5 cottages; each "village," a group of cottages, has indoor/outdoor dining, kitchen, entertainment/TV room; each room/suite has ceiling fans and air-conditioning, direct-dial telephones, selection of drinks, outdoor showers, batik bathrobes; and the $3,500, three-bedroom Fleming House has air-conditioning in the bedrooms, unique garden bathrooms, four-poster beds, dining room, party-size lounge, and a separate home-theater cottage with DVD TV and bar
Meals: In the Fleming House, meals are prepared more or less when you want them; otherwise, meals are served in the new beachside pavilion; some recorded background music; limited room service; fairly casual dress; there are also several fine restaurants 25 min. away in Ocho Rios
Entertainment: The TV rooms, oodles of CDs and videocassettes
Sports: Small pool at main house, series of small beaches, tennis court, snorkeling, kayaks — all free; massage, jet skis, scuba diving and other watersports nearby
PS: Few children; open year-round

Trident Villas & Hotel

PORT ANTONIO

☆	☩	❻❻	$ $ $ $
ATMOSPHERE	DINING	SPORTS	RATES

White breakers come plunging through, under, and over the craggy coral. A winding pathway leads to a gazebo for two that seems to float in the middle of the sea spray. Farther along the coast, scores of waves spume and fume, the Blue Mountains crowd the shore, and the narrow road winds among coves dotted with villas and lush green headlands. This is one of the more dramatic corners of Jamaica, and Trident makes the most of its setting. Of all the small luxury hideaways along Jamaica's north shore, this is the one that most magically puts you into another world. Screened from the roadway by garden walls, it's a whitewashed, shingle-roofed enclave of gardens and courtyards, with most of its villas strung out along the edge of the shore, cuddled in bougainvillea and allamanda. At one end of the garden, a big circular swimming pool sits atop the coral; at the other, a columned doorway leads to a secluded cove with private beach and lagoon.

The main lodge has something of the look of one of those whitewashed, black-trimmed, staging-post inns in England's Lake District. Even the interiors are more English country house than Antillean resort, the drawing room decked with striped fabrics and wingback armchairs, the dining room with Oriental rugs and French flambeaux. The villas and rooms display many of the grace notes associated with their Jamaican architect, Earl Levy — peaked shingle roofs, roughcast stucco, lattice window grills and ornamentation, gazebos, and clay-tile patios.

Furnishings vary from suite to suite, with no un-tropical intrusions like carpeting or air-conditioning.

Dinners indoors in an air-conditioned, chandeliered salon are nicely paced, with small portions, classic cuisine accented with local variations such as ackee paté, smoked blue marlin with capers, and red-snapper patties.

Because of its relative remoteness, Port Antonio has been harder hit than other parts of Jamaica by recent world events, and, truth to tell, Trident is looking a tad frayed these days. New villas (in the same basic style) are on the drawing board, and there may be a link up with a Canadian company that specializes in all-inclusive vacations. Let's hope things pick up in the near future because this can be a truly magical place.

Name: Trident Villas & Hotel
Manager: Suzanne Levy
Address: P.O. Box 119, Port Antonio, Jamaica, West Indies
Location: A few miles east of Port Antonio, 2 hr. and $120 by taxi from Kingston, or 20 min. on Air Jamaica Express from Montego Bay, $150 for two, one-way

Telephone: 876/993-2602 or 876/993-2705
Fax: 876/993-2590
E-mail: trident@infochan.com
Web: www.tridentjamaica.com
Reservations: 876/993-2692, direct
Credit Cards: All major cards
Rates: $340–$800 MAP (Dec 15–Apr 15); service charge 10%; off-season 40% less
Rooms: 30 rooms, including 15 villas, 13 Junior Suites, and 2 Deluxe Suites, all with ceiling fans and louvers, some with air-conditioning, balcony or patio, telephones; all villas have refrigerator and wet bar
Meals: Breakfast 7:30-10am, lunch 12-2:30pm, afternoon tea 4:30–5:30pm (all served on the awning-covered terrace), dinner 8–10pm (about $80 for two, in the main dining room); jackets required, jacket and tie preferred; room service for breakfast and lunch only at no extra charge
Entertainment: Bar/lounge, piano player, calypso trio every evening, occasional folklore shows, parlor games in drawing room
Sports: Small beach, freshwater pool, snorkeling gear, Sunfish sailing, croquet, tennis (2 courts, no lights) — all free; massage, windsurfing, scuba diving, and river rafting can be arranged
PS: "Children any age, any time," but the place is not really suitable for young children; open year-round

Hotel Mocking Bird Hill

PORT ANTONIO

☆☆   Y Y   ✸ $
ATMOSPHERE   **DINING**   **SPORTS**   **RATES**

Take your favorite small, family-owned, family-run inn in New England, set it down on a lush hillside in Jamaica, and you have some idea of the charms of Mocking Bird Hill. Most hotels around here have a view of the sea, but here's one that, with one fell swoop, combines the sea and the Blue Mountains — rolling ranges of lush greenery striding upward to forested peaks. Mocking Bird Hill, in a quiet residential quarter 600 feet above town, is basically a split-level villa converted, with the addition of a new bungalow (and another still to come), into a 10-room inn.

You're greeted in the open lobby-lounge and living room (newly renovated with bright pastel colors). Note the original art and a figurine of a seated lady crafted from wire and newspapers — they're the work of co-owner Barbara Walker, a Jamaican artist who lived in Germany for several years and established a reputation for her works in places like Düsseldorf and Cologne. Her partner, Shireen Aga, is an Indian woman who enjoyed an earlier career as an executive with InterContinental Hotels and now finds herself adapting the methods of big-city hotels to a 10-roomer in the back woods of a Caribbean island — fairly successfully, I might add. The staff is young and eager, creating a place of warmth and tranquility.

The guest rooms come with pretty white-on-white decor, ceramic-tile floors, bamboo furniture, and jaunty blue-and-white striped curtains that match the bedspreads and upholstery. There are no frills, other than coffee-makers and magnifying makeup mirrors, but the rooms are very attractive. Committed environmentalists (and winners of no fewer than 14 environ-mental awards), the owners have banished oversize soaps, paper napkins, and plastic laundry bags, and almost all the furniture and fabrics were produced on the island.

Public areas of the Mocking Bird include a spacious sunset-viewing deck, the perfect place for a panoramic view of the Blue Mountains, and the 36-seater Mille Fleurs Restaurant, another aptly named terrace with views across the flowers and trees to the sea. Meals focus on island produce, and you may find your evening coasting along with a delicious sweet-potato-and-tomato soup, citrus salad with freshly made plantain fritters, plantain stuffed with callaloo, grilled filet of snapper with lime butter in a white-wine sauce, stuffed papaw with minced beef, or local "rundown" in coconut sauce. All but six of the drinks in the bar are produced locally.

Obviously, there's no need for a daily activities bulletin here. That's the attraction. A few steps down from the pool terrace, there's a wooden bench beneath the trees, and a couple of hammocks. Then there's a pathway leading off through the trees. Frenchman's Cove Beach is only 5 minutes away by car, but I suspect that guests will likely spend most of their sojourn grabbing a book from the library, settling into a hammock, and idling a few hours away until it's time for the next piece of coconut pie with mango ice cream.

Name: Hotel Mocking Bird Hill
Owners/Managers: Barbara Walker and Shireen Aga
Address: P.O. Box 254, Port Antonio, Jamaica, West Indies
Location: A few minutes by car from the center of Port Antonio, or 2 hr. and $90 by taxi from Kingston, or by Air Jamaica Express from Montego Bay, $94 for two, one-way
Telephone: 876/993-7267 or 876/993-7134
Fax: 876/993-7133
E-mail: mockbird@cwjamaica.com
Web: www.hotelmockingbirdhill.com
Reservations: birdees@mail.infochan.com
Credit Cards: American Express, MasterCard, Visa
Rates: $180–$230 (Dec 15–Apr 30); tax included, service charge optional; off-season 25% less

Rooms: 10 rooms, with ceiling fans, balcony or patio (some with a hammock), tiled bathroom (some with shower only), private safe; superior rooms with coffeemakers, bathrobes, and hair dryers

Meals: Breakfast 8:30–10am, lunch noon–2:30pm, dinner 7–9:30pm ($70–$80 for two); casual dress; limited room room service; no intrusive music

Entertainment: Satellite TV in lounge, but mostly listening to tree frogs or enjoying the artwork, occasional evenings of folklore by a local "mento" band, art workshops

Sports: Pool, walking trails on the grounds, beaches 5 min. away; massage in the bamboo gazebo, guided hiking treks in the nearby rain forest at extra charge; tennis and watersports nearby

PS: Few children; no rules regarding cellphones because even global cellphones don't work without costly modifications; open year-round

Stawberry Hill

IRISH TOWN

☆☆☆☆☆	ＹＹ	❽❽	$ $ $
ATMOSPHERE	DINING	SPORTS	RATES

Take the best of native Jamaican architecture; mold it into a collection of little birdhouses; drape them around the crest of a hilltop high above Kingston; add a garden, a sophisticated restaurant, a spa, and a few contemporary frills; and you end up with one of the most picturesque and romantic of the Caribbean's hideaways. All of Kingston at your feet (when the lights twinkle, it could almost be Monte Carlo), the sweep of the great estuary, the causeway to Fort Royal, the forested slopes and glens of the Blue Mountains surround you on three sides.

Each of the 12 cottages (with a total of just 18 rooms) is designed by one of the island's leading conservation architects, Ann Hodges, who had a chance to apply old island theories to the creation of a brand-new inn that appeals to contemporary tastes: peaked roofs with cedar shake shingles, white clinkerboard walls with jalousie louvers where most architects would put glass, lowslung eaves shading wraparound porches, broad plank floors of mahogany covered with khus khus rugs, fretwork panels set high in the walls to surprise the eye (each one has a different theme) and keep the breezes flowing.

The interiors (by Tanya Melica) are designed with a minimalist elegance — white-on-white walls and doors accented with period sideboards, cane chairs, sofas, and exotic objects — a coffee table from Indonesia, perhaps, or South American earthenware pots and figurines, or wrought-iron lamps crafted specially for the hotel. Some cottages have complete kitchens with yellow-and-green patterned china, toasters, blenders, microwaves, coffeemakers, and family-size refrigerators.

Many of the bedrooms have four-posters draped with wispy mosquito netting and louvered French doors opening to wood-plank verandas with mahogany planters' armchairs. The attractive bathrooms have nice touches, such as multi-head showers and recessed lighting. Closets have heating rods, and beds have heated mattress pads. Guest rooms are identified by fanciful names like Timbuc Two, Timbuc Three, and Mountain View. I ended up in Birds Hill, a one-bedroom suite with a gazebo at the end of the path. A hot tub sat in the gazebo, screened from the view of every creature except the birds. But 59 Steps is another favorite, a studio almost swallowed up by banana plants and ferns, and Mountain View's panorama takes a sweep of the valley to what looks like a romantic little Italian hill town but is, in reality, a boot camp for the Jamaica Defense Force. Don't get bogged down in the subtleties of views and amenities — any of these rooms, studios, or suites is a winner.

The flat top of the 26-acre estate is given over to a lawn that occasionally doubles (but, fortunately, only very occasionally) as a heliport for people who can't wait to get there from the airport, about 50 minutes away by car. Tables and chairs sit beneath eucalyptus and cedar trees. Wooden walkways link three pavilions: the bar (with a fireplace that can be most welcome at this elevation), a library/lounge with big-screen TV and an eclectic collection of reading material, and a dining pavilion that must rank as one of the prettiest in the Caribbean, with its double row of fretwork panels, polished mahogany tables and chairs, sparkling crystal and candles, and four ceiling fans topping off the tropical ambience.

Even the cuisine gets a local touch. Strawberry Hill's signature Jamaican-accented dishes keep the palate whetted meal after meal with such delicious offerings as steamed callaloo with boiled green bananas and warm grilled jerk chicken salad in a honey mustard ginger dressing. As if this weren't enough in the way of gratification for one vacation, you can also submit yourselves to Himalayan Rejuvenation, one of several nature-based treatments offered by the inn's Aveda Concept Spa. The fresh mountain air is probably all you need, but a little patting here and a little kneading there never did anyone any harm.

This hilltop has led a charmed life. Back in the 1950s, a prominent local family, the Blackwells, whose ancestors came over from the United Kingdom generations ago, used to come here for afternoon tea every weekend. Young Chris Blackwell fell in love with the spot. Years later, after he was the enormously successful founder-impresario of Island Records (Bob Marley, U2, The Cranberries, and others of that ilk), he decided he would like to live on Strawberry Hill; so he bought the entire hilltop, revamped the Great House, added a few cottages for friends, then later created his small hotel, having caught the innkeeping bug at his famed Deco hotels in South Beach.

Not only did he decide to build in the island style, but he also used local crafters wherever possible. Thus, you sit on cane chairs woven by people at the School for the Blind in Kingston, the frames themselves made according to traditional plantation designs and antiqued with shoe polish; the fabrics were sewn by a sewing bee in Irish Town, just up the road; the beautifully framed black-and-white photographs in the rooms were all taken by local photographers.

Blackwell has done at last what scores of other hoteliers should have done years ago: take the vernacular architecture and adapt it to a contemporary inn. Keep this up, Blackwell, and I may have to stop griping about recorded music in restaurants and lounges.

Name: Strawberry Hill
Manager: Mara Bouvier
Address: Irish Town P.A., St. Andrew, Jamaica, West Indies
Location: 3,100 ft. up in the Blue Mountains, near the village of Irish Town, about 20 min. from downtown Kingston, 50–60 min. from the airport (let them know when your plane arrives, and they'll pick you up for $40, up to 4 passengers); if you're driving yourself, better call for directions and write down every word
Telephone: 876/944-8400
Fax: 876/944-8408
E-mail: strawberry@cwjamaica.com
Web: www.islandoutpost.com
Reservations: 800/688-7678 or 305/534-2135, Island Outpost in Miami
Credit Cards: American Express, MasterCard, Visa
Rates: $315–$775 CP (year-round); service charge 10%
Rooms: 18 rooms, studios, and suites in 12 villas, all with period furniture, direct-dial telephone, radio, CD player (with Island Records CDs), makeup mirror, hair dryer, bathrobes, room safe, veranda; some with full kitchen; one with private hot tub; satellite TV/VCRs and cassettes on request
Meals: Breakfast 8–10am, lunch 11:30am–2:30pm, afternoon tea 4pm, dinner 6–10pm (about $70–$80 for two); all in the hilltop dining pavilion; casual but stylish dress; limited room service 8am to 10pm
Entertainment: TV lounge, bar lounge, and chatting beside the big wood-burning fire
Sports: Lipless pool, fitness center — all free; Aveda spa treatments, guided hikes through the mountains at extra charge
PS: Not really suitable for children; cellphones for rent, open year-round;

Jake's

TREASURE BEACH

☆☆	♈	◑	$
ATMOSPHERE	DINING	SPORTS	RATES

Ever seen one of those Island Primitive paintings of colorful gardens dotted with native houses with pitched roofs, with seashore in the background and white combers breaking over reefs? Now pass a magic wand across the picture, bring it to life, add a free-form swimming pool, and you end up with something that might look very much like Jake's.

Everything here is designed to blend with the natural surroundings. Even the wispy cassia tree that separates the dining terrace from the pool gets into the act with a wood plank installed as a bench between its two gnarled trunks. Rustic, russet-colored Adirondack armchairs ring the pool, two more chairs huddle beneath a lignum vitae tree over by the edge of the shore, the doors and window frames of one of the cottages are made from bleached driftwood. This is clearly a place designed for kicking back, chilling out, and letting the sun and the sea take over your life.

Owner Sally Henzell is a local theater designer and decorator, and what she has conjured up here could be a setting for an Antillean-style ballet — Giselle meets Bob Marley. The 10 cottages are dinky, finished in an imaginative crack-and-peel palette of tropical colors. The rooms are deliciously rustic and trimmed down to the bare essentials (if you can call a mini-fridge, and CD player essentials). Some have outdoor showers (the newest, Cockles Upstairs, is especially inviting, with a stall of bamboo accented with seashells on two sides and a third side facing the open sea beyond a "wall" of foliage); Abalone #1 sports romantic Moroccan-style windows and doors beneath overhanging ramada screens to shade the patio and veranda. Most of them have decorative fretwork that echoes their sea-creature names — Abalone, Sea Puss, Conch, and Sea Horse — all done on the premises.

Two dining spots — one, the six-table terrace beside the pool, the other, a six-table gallery on the garden side of the lilac office-cum-lounge-cum-cybercafe — zero in on seafood (Treasure Beach is, after all, one of that endangered species known as unspoiled fishing village), vegetarian, and Jamaican. The menu will hardly break the bank (traditional chicken fricassee for $6, banana flambee $4), but if you want a change of pace, you can walk a few yards toward the beach and sample the seafood and pizzas at the Henzell's Jack Sprat's Café. But the focal point of Jake's (named, by the way, for a local parrot) is the bamboo-and-thatch bar beside the pool, where Duggie mixes killer drinks while chatting up the guests and making sure everyone knows everyone else. If you stay up beyond 9:00, blame Duggie.

Make no mistake, Jake's is rustic. There are few refinements and the rooms are quite small, but what it lacks in size and amenities it more than makes up for in charm and personality. And look at the rates: you don't find prices like that these days in places where you're liable to rub shoulders with such a worldly bunch of escapists. And escapists they are: Jake's is on the far side of Jamaica, the untrampled (for now, at least) southern coast, but there are lots of interesting sightseeing excursions and natural attractions to fill your mornings or afternoons — and, if things get to be too quiet, naughty Negril is less than 2 hours away to the west.

Name: Jake's
Manager: Jason Henzell
Address: Treasure Beach, Jamaica West Indies
Location: On the south coast, 2 hours from Montego Bay, over narrow, winding mountain roads, so ask the hotel to have a trusty driver waiting for you at the airport ($90 each way)
Telephone: 876/965-3145
Fax: 876/965-0552
E-mail: jakes@cwjamaica.com
Web: www.islandoutpost.com
Credit Cards: American Express, Visa, Mastercard, Discover
Rates: $115–$295 (Dec 20-Apr 20); tax included, service charge 10% extra; off-season 10% less
Rooms: 15 rooms, each with ceiling fans (a few with air-conditioning); safe, small fridge, hair dryer, CD player and library of CDs; also, a couple of cottages next door are now available for rent
Meals: Breakfast 7:30–11am, lunch noon–4pm, dinner 6–9:30pm (approx. $50 for two); recorded mood music; no room service; dress code is more or less whatever you're wearing; additional meals at the Jack Sprat's Café, just beyond the garden
Entertainment: Library of CDs, media room with TV and about 40 DVDs, board games, complimentary Internet service, poolside bar
Sports: Saltwater pool, nearby beach (swimming not advised at the hotel), yoga/meditation room — free; Cannondale Terra mountain bikes, snorkeling gear, kayaks, and massage at extra charge
PS: Some children; open year-round

The Caves

NEGRIL

☆☆☆☆	⊻ ⊻	❻	$ $ $
ATMOSPHERE	DINING	SPORTS	RATES

First thing on check-in, book the Sunset Hot Tub, if not today, tomorrow. Next, book the dining grotto for a candlelit, flower-festooned dinner for two, if not today, then tomorrow. Then, once you've changed into swimwear, dive into the swimming hole (it really is a hole) and swim *under* the hotel to the clear waters of a cove ringed by low coral bluffs.

In other words, this is not your run-of-the-mill hotel. Actually, there may come a stage on your drive to The Caves when you think the place doesn't even exist. It's all the way past Negril Beach, past the jerk stands and Rick's Cafe, almost all the way to the lighthouse, a preserved national monument, which makes the location of The Caves one of the quietest in these partying parts.

The Caves is a member of Chris Blackwell's Island Outpost fraternity of one-of-a-kind hideaways (see Goldeneye, Strawberry Hill, and Jake's in this section), although it was the dream of two Negril residents — owners Greer-Ann and Bertram Saulter, designer/decorator/innkeeper and architect respectively. It's another of those remarkable hideaways that fit themselves neatly into and around the natural contours of the coral caves and coves of West End, with walkways and stone steps leading to light-stoned terraces and miradors set like ramparts into various levels of the cliffs.

You enter via heavy wooden doors into a high-walled garden where narrow stone paths lead through shoulder-caressing tropical foliage to a 2-acre colony of cottages painted in the subtlest of pastel colors and secluded by flowers. All but two of the 10 peak-ceilinged, wood-and-stone cottages are one story. Some are sequestered among the foliage, a few almost submerged beneath thatching, like something out of Hansel and Gretel. One Drop is an A-frame topped with thatch and outfitted with a queen-size bed swathed in netting; Bird's Nest is on the second floor with a very private veranda and a custom-crafted bamboo king-size bed with netting. The cottages eschew air-conditioning and TV — the only distraction from birdsong or the sea slapping on the coral is a CD player and a small library of mood-setting CDs. Furniture is custom-designed by the Saulters and handcrafted locally, interspersed with a few Jamaican heirlooms and a lot of whimsy.

Breakfast and lunch are served on the breeze-cooled terrace at one end of the garden (meals are mostly Jamaican at lunchtime), dinner in a two-story cottage or on the large deck with hand-painted tables, a rustic setting that belies the caliber and sophistication of the (mostly international) menu. All meals are included in the rate, which raises a point: At first glance The Caves might seem pricey, but since the rates include all meals *and* drinks (if there's no bartender around, just help yourselves), the place is really quite moderate. Take the basic $462 for the off-season months, deduct the cost of meals (say, $20 each for breakfast, $30 for lunch, $50 for dinner), then deduct the cost of drinks per day (mimosas for breakfast, white wine for lunch, piña coladas at sunset, a merlot with dinner, maybe aged Appleton's rum for nightcaps), and you find that the cost of the room can't be much more than what you'd pay for a cookie-cutter resort on Negril Beach.

And how many of those cookie-cutters will reserve a Sunset Hot Tub for two, fill the grotto with scented candles and fresh flowers, and ice the champagne? Throw open the blue shutters, and, from your tub, you're looking directly to the setting sun from what is, give or take a cove or two, the most westerly point of Jamaica.

Name: The Caves
Owner/Manager: Greer-Ann Saulter
Address: P.O. Box 3113 Negril, Jamaica West Indies
Location: On Lighthouse road at West End, the last resort before the landmark lighthouse; 20 min. from Negril Aerodrome (transfers included in rate), 75 min. and $75 from Montego Bay (about $100 by taxi)
Telephone: 876/957-0270
Fax: 876/957-4930
E-mail: thecaves@cwjamaica.com
Web: www.islandoutpost.com
Credit Cards: American Express, Visa, Mastercard
Rates: $575–$925 FAP+; taxes included, 10% service charge extra; off-season 20% less
Rooms: 12 rooms in 10 cottages, some with tub and shower, others with outdoor patio showers, all with ceiling fans, pre-stocked refrigerators, direct-dial telephones with dataports, bathrobes, hair dryers, safes, tea/coffemakers, CD players and CDs (TV/VCR on request)
Meals: Breakfast 7:30–10:30am, lunch 12:30–3pm on the small dining terrace, dinner 7:30–10pm in the main dining room (both for hotel guests only); room service on request; recorded background music; casual but tidy attire after 6:00pm
Entertainment: Sunsets, other guests
Sports: Small pool, kayaks, snorkeling gear, mountain bikes — all free; Aveda Mini-Spa (treatments extra, on the terrace or in your room); watersports nearby
PS: No children under 16; open year-round (although it may close during September)

OTHER CHOICES

The Jamaica Palace Hotel

PORT ANTONIO

It sounds grand, and it looks grand at first sight. But then it turns kind of pompous. The white palatial facade with its porte-cochère and two matching faux portes-cochères lead to a spacious lobby replete with marble floors and white pillars, chandeliers, and gilt-framed portraits. Jamaica, particularly tumble- down Port Antonio, could be on another planet — until you step out onto the big play terrace and discover that the 118-foot swimming pool is shaped to duplicate the coastline of Jamaica. The original intention of the European aristocrat who built the place seems to have been a grande luxe hotel to outshine Trident Villas & Hotel, just down the road (see review earlier in this chapter), so the guest rooms are quite posh, with lots of marble and ormolu, teardrop chandeliers, and antiques; but somewhere along the way, dreams turned into reality and the rates and aspirations were toned down. Lucky you — what we have here is exceptional value.

There's a downside to all this: The service is lackluster, the restaurant is gloomy, and the beds consist of circular or semicircular mattresses on concrete bases (not the last word in comfort).

Although the rates are reasonable, many of the rooms are located off an open passageway that may remind you of a shopping mall. These guest rooms are like tiny boutiques with big windows, with everyone looking into some-one else's window. Check out your room before you unpack — or splurge on one of the Junior Suites, which are $30 more. 80 air-conditioned rooms and suites. Doubles: $190–$274, winter 2002–03. *The Jamaica Palace Hotel, P.O. Box 277, Port Antonio, Jamaica, West Indies. Telephone: 800/472-1149 (reservations only) or 876/993-2020; fax: 876/993-3459; Web: www.jamaicapalace.com.*

Coyaba Beach Resort & Club

MONTEGO BAY

Coyaba, according to the brochure, is the Arawak word for a place of peace and rest. That about sums up this friendly, laid-back but stylish beachfront hotel. Three three-story buildings cluster around a verdant courtyard, with views of the garden, the ocean, or the parking lot (not recommended). No shortcuts were taken on the 52 tasteful rooms: The tile floors, classy fabrics, and hand-carved furniture actually look Jamaican Colonial, not vaguely European, and the best of them have large sitting areas or bright breakfast nooks and roomy terraces. Rates include the use of the tennis court (charge for lights), fitness room, Sunfish sailboats, and kayaks. And although there are just 52 rooms, Coyaba pampers its guests with a choice of three restaurants, indoors and alfresco, serving cuisine that ranges from the Caribbean to Provence. 52 rooms. Doubles: $290–$390, winter 2002–03. *Coyaba Beach Resort & Club, Little River, Montego Bay, Jamaica, West Indies. Telephone: 876/ 953-9150 (toll-free 877/269-2228); fax: 876/953-2244; e-mail: coyaba@n5. com.jm; Web: www.coyabaresortjamaica.com.*

Tensing Pen Village

NEGRIL

Two words best describe Tensing Pen: rustic and romantic. Imagine staying in a circular thatched-roof tree house that rises above a jungle of dense island foliage and looks out over a small cove cut out of the cliffs. On a promontory stretching into the ocean, two hammocks (usually occupied) sway in a gazebo. A narrow wooden unfenced gangplank spans one of the rocky coves to challenge your equilibrium. Thirteen cottages and huts (newly refurbished) are scattered along 1,700 feet of oceanfront, reached by footpaths that twist throughout the property (additional rooms may be added, "but never too many to take away from the tranquil feelings . . . "). The rooms are open to the breezes, with louvered doors and windows, ceiling fans, tile floors, carved furniture, refrigerators, bathrooms, and, in some cases, outdoor showers. The new SeaSong Hut gives you a chance to slip off to a secluded cliff-top gazebo for a salt scrub or relaxing facial. There's a common kitchen for preparing meals, but four times a week the inn's in-house cooks prepare meals. Most guests seem to prefer to immerse themselves in total privacy — no phones, no TVs, no distractions — and the feeling of seclusion is reinforced by the fact that Tensing Pen is almost as far west as the West End of Negril will allow; next door (although not within stereo range) is the famous Rick's Beach Bar. 10 rooms. Doubles: $110–$240, including continental breakfast, winter 2002–03. *Tensing Pen Village, P.O. Box 3013, Negril, Jamaica, West Indies. Telephone: 876/957-0387; fax: 876/957-0161; e-mail: tensingpen@cwjamaica. com; Web: www.tensingpen.com.*

Rockhouse

NEGRIL

This is one of those back-to-nature resorts that lured flower children to the rocky shores of Negril all those moons ago, but this is a new Rockhouse. It's been taken over by a trio of energetic Australians — a Wall Street arbitrageur, an anthropologist, and a restaurateur — one of whom is always there to keep an eye on things. It's been spruced up with such niceties as a new cliffside lipless pool, poolside bar, and Polynesian-style dining pavilion. All the rooms are timber and stone with tilted thatch roofs; half are octagonal cabanas placed at the edge of the coral cliffs for privacy and views, and half are in a two-story wing in the garden dotted with cacti, almond trees, and traveler's palms. You want the former, unless you're on a really tight budget. They all have old-fashioned ceiling fans to augment the new-fashioned air-conditioning, but they come with modern non-1960s amenities like minibars and personal safes. You freshen up in topless shower stalls, lounge on chunky wooden chairs, sleep in custom-designed four-poster beds topped with netting, and enjoy unspoiled, unhurried nature. The owners have finally gotten around to putting enough lights and enough wattage to let you study each other after dark — or even do a crossword puzzle together. Stepladders and steps carved into the cliffside take you into or, if you dive in, out of the crystal-clear waters of

Pristine Cove. The Rockhouse will rent you snorkeling gear or kayaks. The restaurant, open from 7am to 11pm, delights guests with the Rockhouse Special: three courses with a rum punch for $22. 28 rooms. Doubles: $100–$225, winter 2002–03. *Rockhouse, P.O. Box 3024, West End Road, Negril, Jamaica. Telephone/fax: 876/957-4373; e-mail: info@rockhousehotel.com; Web: www. rockhousehotel.com.*

Idle Awhile

NEGRIL

The downside of Negril's West End is that you don't get to feel the sand beneath your feet; the downside with Negril Beach is that its 7 miles of sand are lined with uninspired all-inclusives. Now there's an alternative: The family that owns the 134-room Swept Away all-inclusive just down the road recently unveiled a small, boutique-y getaway on the beach. It's close to the action without pinning you down with all-inclusive rates. Idle Awhile fills a sliver of a plot between two other small hotels and some of the rooms may pick up traffic noise (avoid #102), but it sports a lot more pizzazz than you normally find around these parts. Swept Away's signature features like lots of ceiling fans, entire walls of hardwood louvers, lush tropical greenery, and spacious well-furnished verandas are dressed up with imaginative use of colors and wood — bold reds match on sofas, chairs and bedspreads. The 40-channel TV sets are neatly tucked out of sight in wooden cabinets. The one-bedroom suites (extra large for the money) have full kitchens, daybeds, and hammocks. There's a small bar-restaurant, The Bamboo Beach Bar, practically on the sand (the volume on the CD player seems to be under control) where you can have a jerk chicken for $8 at lunch or Jamaican steamed fish for $13 at dinner, unless you enjoy the freedom of non-inclusive rates and make a reservation at nearby Mariposa Italian Restaurant, one of the best on the island (people drive down from swank resorts like Tryall and Round Hill to dine here).

Guests of Idle Awhile have access to the 10-acre Fitness and Sports Center at Swept Away, with a shuttle bus to get them there and back. It may not be as endearing as its name, but here's a pleasant alternative to the standard Negril Beach lodgings. 13 rooms and suites. Doubles $170–$275 EP, winter 2002–03. *Idle Awhile, Negril, Jamaica West Indies. Telephone: 877/243-5352 or 876/957-3302; fax: 876/957-9567; e-mail: info@idleawhile.com; Web: www. idleawhile.com.*

The Dominican Republic

*I*t's the other part of Hispaniola, Columbus's favorite La Isla Española, which it shares with Haiti. The first permanent European settlement in the Americas was here, in a place called Montecito, founded the year after Columbus arrived in 1492. A few years later, Columbus's brother, Bartolome, founded a city on the banks of the Ozama River and named it New Isabella; we now know it as Santo Domingo. At one time, Santo Domingo was the most important city in the Caribbean, and it was from here that renowned conquistadors set forth on their expeditions to colonize the surrounding lands — Diego Velázquez to Cuba, Hernán Cortés to Mexico, and Juan Ponce de León to Puerto Rico, which is less than 60 miles to the east. In recent years, the Dominican government has been forging ahead with an impressive program to preserve and restore the old colonial city. It's well worth a visit (although it would be nice if they picked up the garbage more often).

The main resort areas — Puerto Plata and Punta Cana — are lined with all-inclusives, so the main choice boils down to one of the most remarkable resorts in the Caribbean: Casa de Campo, near La Romana.

HOW TO GET THERE   For vacationers bound for Casa de Campo, the least stressful way to get there is via American Airlines's flights from Miami directly into La Romana, the resort's spanking-new air terminal.

> For information on the Dominican Republic, call 212/588-1012 or visit www.dominicana.com

Casa de Campo

LA ROMANA

☆ ☆ ☆	☾ ☾ ☾	❻ ❻ ❻ ❻	$ $ $
ATMOSPHERE	DINING	SPORTS	RATES

The original "ambience" here was designed by Oscar de la Renta and many celebrities have indeed built private homes on the property, but La Romana's "house in the country" is a pleasant, informal resort with few airs — designed not so much for beautiful people as for active people. And how!

Two golf courses (one seaside, one inland) designed by Pete Dye are the pride of the project, and with reason. Both are highly rated by pros, but for average duffers they promise more frustration than relaxation. A third Pete Dye course for resort guests (as opposed to villa owners, who have their own 18) opened in 2002 and is equally challenging. Tennis facilities are so extensive they get a "village" all to themselves across the main road, where you'll find 13 Har-Tru courts (10 with lights), ball machines — even ball boys. There are, on a casual count, 14 swimming pools, as well as 150 quarter horses and 150 polo ponies in the equestrian center. Even the polo fields come in multiples — two practice fields, two playing fields.

William Cox was the architect who pulled the whole thing together and created a sprawling complex that nevertheless manages to be compatible, more or less, with its Dominican surroundings. Buildings (never higher than two stories) are finished in stucco, with native stone, rough-hewn local hardwoods, and roofs of red tile or, on the public buildings, typical island thatch.

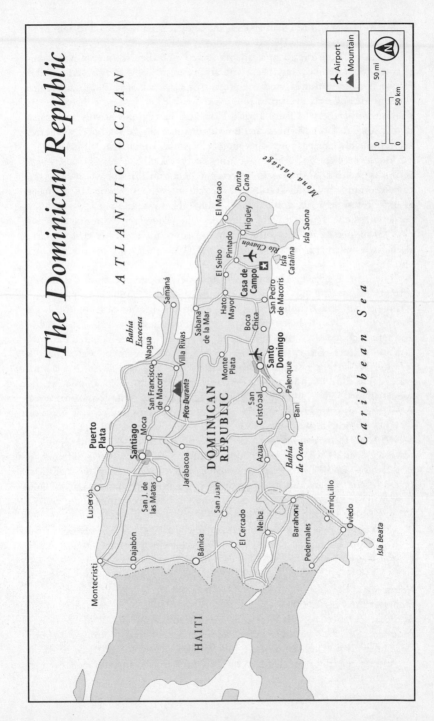

Guest rooms are finished in mahogany, with louvered doors and windows, minibars, and (get this!) Bose wave radio systems.

All in all, Casa de Campo doesn't sound like the creation of a big corporate conglomerate, but that's exactly what it is — or was. The Gulf+ Western Corporation started the project in a corner of its 7,000-acre sugar plantation, but sold everything — sugar, land, hotel, horses, golf balls — to the Fanjul brothers of Palm Beach, Florida, a family also heavily into sugar plantations. As homeowners themselves on the Casa de Campo estate, they were probably eager to buy up a project 11 times larger than Monaco.

However, Casa de Campo is getting to be more *casa* (house) than *campo* (country), with new villas going up everywhere. You almost have to plan your travels around this hotel as diligently as you might plan a tour of Caribbean islands: Tennis is here, golf is there, stables thataway, and the closest beach somewhere else. The first thing guests do when they arrive is rent a "touring cart" or moped to avoid waiting for shuttle buses. In fact, smart guests reserve their carts when they reserve their rooms. (Villa guests are provided with a cart.)

The hotel is organized around a handsomely designed core of restaurants, lounges, terraces, patios, courtyards, and a spectacular split-level pool with swim-up bar and thatched-roof lounge. Grouped around it are the hotel rooms. Golf villas are half a mile or so east; the equestrian center, polo fields, and tennis courts are across the main island road; Altos de Chavon, the resort's arts and culture village, with a range of restaurants, boutiques, and ateliers, is a few miles farther east. There are private homes on the hill (some for rent; others, like the Pucci place, strictly private) and private homes down by the spectacular shoreline and the fairways (which have to put up with some noise form the airport). In all, there are almost 300 rooms for rent at Casa de Campo — some regular guest rooms, others villa suites.

With all those rooms, all those acres, and a staff of 2,000, management obviously can't keep an eye on every detail. Even so, the staff is pleasant (if not always polished), rates are reasonable, and you can eat well at modest prices (there you are, out in the boonies, miles from the nearest cantina, and they don't try to gouge you — you can have a huge custom-made breakfast for just $14).

Even if you never catch so much as a glimpse of the polo-playing, party-giving, trend-setting socialites who fill the usual glossy articles about Casa de Campo, here's a place where you can never say you're bored. Ever.

Name: Casa de Campo
Manager: Ana Lisa Brache
Address: P.O. Box 140, La Romana, Dominican Republic
Location: On the southeast coast, 60 min. from Santo Domingo airport, 2 hours from the capital itself, but the easiest way to get there is via an American Airlines jet direct to the new La Romana International Airport (code: LRM)

Telephone: 800/877-3643
Fax: 305/858-4677
E-mail: res@pwmonline.com
Web: www.casadecampo.cc
Reservations: 800/877-3643 toll-free direct, or 305/856-5405 Premier World Marketing
Credit Cards: American Express, MasterCard, Visa
Rates: $287–$710 (Dec 21–Apr 20); service charge 10%; off-season 30% less
Rooms: 300 hotel rooms and 150 villas and homes of various sizes; all rooms have air-conditioning, ceiling fans, wet bar and stocked minibar, coffee-maker, hair dryer, balcony or patio, direct-dial telephones with voice mail and dataport, cable TV; homes and villas have full kitchens
Meals: Breakfast, lunch, and dinner somewhere on the resort or at Altos de Chavon; 7am–midnight in one or another of the 10 restaurants (some with recorded or live music, sometimes louder than you'd like); the beach-side El Pescador and Lago Grill are particularly attractive (dinner $25–$80); informal dress, but long trousers for men everywhere after 6pm and jackets or collared shirts in the hotel's Tropicana and Casa del Rio restaurants; limited room service, limited menu, $5 extra per tray
Entertainment: Bars, lounges, recorded and live music, dancing, disco, folklore shows, occasional concerts and recitals at Altos de Chavon
Sports: Beach at the resort plus another offshore on Catalina Island, and 14 pools, some semiprivate; you pay for just about everything else (rates are average) unless you're on a special inclusive package — options include boat trips to Catalina Island, snorkeling, windsurfing, Hobie Cats, Sunfish sailing, scuba, deep-sea fishing, water-skiing, tennis (13 Har-Tru courts, 10 with lights, full pro shop), an enlarged fitness center (racquetball, mas-sage, sauna, exercise equipment), 250-acre trap and skeet-shooting club, 110-station shooting center, horseback riding (western and English, with vaquero guides only), polo instruction and rentals (winter only), golf (3 superb Pete Dye courses, plus a fourth course reserved for homeowners), massage in your room or in the fitness center
PS: Some kids (but first-rate "camp" activities usually keep them tucked away on their own), some groups — all of which can be avoided most of the time, except on the beach; open year-round

The U.S. Virgin Islands & Puerto Rico

Call this "Suburbia South."

With a few delightful exceptions, these islands are just about everything you're trying to escape — shopping centers, real-estate billboards, telephone poles, traffic jams, crowded restaurants. However, since they are politically part of the United States, Puerto Rico, St. Thomas, St. Croix, and St. John have their attractions, sometimes bountiful. Not least of these is the fact that you don't have to worry about passports, don't have to fidget in long lines on arrival while some official thumbs his way through immigration formalities, don't have to wait at Customs behind returning islanders laden with suitcases and cartons that have to be painstakingly inspected and evaluated. These islands need no introduction, but a few comments might be helpful.

When most people think of Puerto Rico they think of San Juan, which, impressive though it may be from a commercial and political point of view, is no longer a true tropical hideaway. But how about Old San Juan? The old city, with its narrow streets and fortresses, is still one of the unique places of the Caribbean. Even UNESCO thinks so: It designated six monuments in Old San Juan as World Heritage Sites. Moreover, when you get beyond the city, Puerto Rico can be a stunningly beautiful island. Head for the rain forest. Try a drive along the roadway that runs east to west along the Cordillera Central. And the modern *autopista* from San Juan to Ponce is a spectacular and effortless route across the mountains.

St. Thomas and St. Croix have had more than their share of problems in recent years, not the least of them hurricanes. The islanders also blame a hostile mainland press for bad publicity, but you should read the lurid headlines in their own local papers. Both islands are low on the list of priorities for this guidebook, not because of any latent unrest, but because they are just a bit overdeveloped for comfort. Charlotte Amalie is a near-constant traffic jam. Poor Christiansted should be one of the gems of the Caribbean, but its lovely old Danish buildings are almost swamped by masses of power cables and carbuncled telephone poles. Your best bet on either island is to get to your hotel and stay put. Otherwise, you'll have to deal with their taxi drivers, not the Caribbean's most obliging fellows.

St. John is the delightful, enchanting standout — just 28 square miles, almost half of them national park. Cruz Bay, the main town, looks nothing like a suburb of Florida (or anywhere else, for that matter), and there are more than enough beaches, coves, and mountain trails for everyone.

HOW TO GET THERE   San Juan's Luis Muñoz Marín International Airport is the largest in the Caribbean (they've spent millions in the past few years expanding and improving it — and they're still at it, as of this writing); it's served by nonstop flights from 20 or so cities in North America and one-stop direct service from as far away as Los Angeles. From New York alone, there are almost 20 scheduled flights every day — including five flights daily on newcomer JetBlue. American Airlines has expanded its activities at the airport, which is now the hub of inter-island services to almost everywhere via American Eagle, which utilizes small, efficient aircraft. *Note:* When using these services, remember that what you consider carry-on luggage may have to be checked for the smaller flight, so pack accordingly.

For St. Thomas, your airlines are American, Continental, Delta, and US Airways. The only nonstop flight to St. Croix is on American from Miami. Otherwise, there are plenty of commuter flights from St. Thomas and San Juan, including a new service by Cape Air and by Seabourne Seaplanes, the latter downtown-to-downtown rather than airport-to-airport. You might also want to check into the schedules of Cape Air, which has a busy service between the islands.

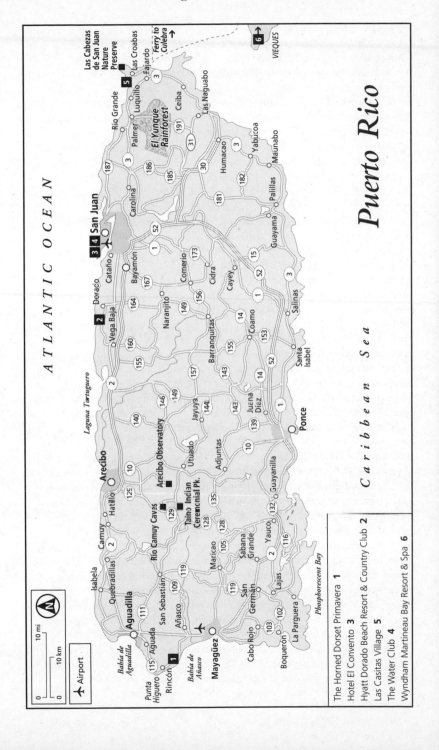

Puerto Rico

The Horned Dorset Primavera **1**
Hotel El Convento **3**
Hyatt Dorado Beach Resort & Country Club **2**
Las Casitas Village **5**
The Water Club **4**
Wyndham Martineau Bay Resort & Spa **6**

There's no airport on St. John, of course, so you get there on ferryboats from Charlotte Amalie or Red Hook on St. Thomas. If you're staying at Caneel Bay, you will be transported in style on one of the resort's private launches after catching your breath at the resort's private, air-conditioned lounge at St. Thomas's airport.

Note: One of the fun things to do on the U.S. Virgins is to take a day trip by ferryboat or sailing catamaran to the British Virgins, but since no passports are required for the American islands, lots of visitors can't make the trip because the British Islands insist on passports. Remember to pack your passport, just in case.

> For information on St. Thomas, St. John, and St. Croix,
> call 212/332-2222 or visit www.usvitourism.vi;
> for Puerto Rico, 800/866-7827 or www.prtourism.com.

Hyatt Dorado Beach Resort & Country Club

DORADO, PUERTO RICO

☆ ☆ ☆	Y Y Y	❻ ❻ ❻ ❻	$ $ $ $
ATMOSPHERE	DINING	SPORTS	RATES

The setting is one of the most majestic of any resort in the Americas: an estate of 1,000 acres and thousands of coconut palms, winding fairways and manicured lawns, and a pair of crescent beaches. A botanical bonanza of African tulip and almond trees, sweet immortelle, and fiddle-leaf fig line the pathways and patios.

When I first came here in 1963, a few years after it was opened by Laurance Rockefeller's Rockresorts crew, those crescent beaches were ringed with just 150 guest rooms, in decorous two-story wings hidden among the leafy palms. Today, the room count has doubled; the sports facilities, then the first-rate playground of a mere 300 guests, are still excellent, but now they're used by 600 guests and a local country club numbering 500-plus members.

Moreover, the 1,000 acres are shared with a sister hotel of more than 500 rooms, a mile down the coast. Nothing very new in that, of course: The seven-story Cerromar has been there for some time now, and it too is under the Hyatt banner (it's now the grandly named Hyatt Regency Cerromar Beach Resort & Casino). Cerromar is largely given over to groups and conventions whose members have charging privileges at both hotels, so the custom-built trolleys that shuttle between the two resorts seem to carry more bodies bound for Dorado than vice versa. On a recent visit, I found that the clientele at Dorado Beach was not at all what Rockefeller had in mind 37 years ago — they did nothing to add to the elegance of the original.

But there certainly are pluses, especially for sports buffs: When you include the sports facilities at Cerromar, you now have four championship golf courses (designed by Robert Trent Jones; all in tip-top condition, and they've just added a swank new clubhouse). There are 15 tennis courts, a few lighted for night play, and a Lisa Penfield Windsurfing School — and for anyone who overdoes it, the Spa del Sol stands ready with yoga, massage, and salt glows.

What the Hyatt people have also done is lavish millions just on updating and renovating the rooms. New colonial-style furniture enhances the Caribbean mood. Each room has a minibar and a safe, and the centerpiece of guest rooms on the upper floors is a sturdy carved pencil-post bed; beach-level guests have to settle for a pair of double beds.

The original deluxe beachfront rooms are the favorite of longtime guests, but the top-of-the-line accommodations are actually the Regency Casita Rooms, located between the pool and the beach with split-level layouts and skylights above bathtub-size shower stalls. However, the patios ought to have dividing walls or latticework to maintain a sense of privacy.

Which room should you choose? The dozen or so "standard" rooms facing the fairways are the least expensive (and perfectly acceptable in terms of facilities); the "superior" rooms are closest to the swimming pool and dining rooms; "deluxe" designates rooms fronting the beach, with those in the East Wing (the originals) closer to the golf and tennis pro shops.

The Surf Room, where dinner is served from 6:30 to 9:30pm, is hardly the most romantic room in the Caribbean, even with its 3,600 square feet of windows facing the sea (it's scheduled for remodeling to improve visibility). But Su Casa, the original estate house, most certainly is romantic, with candlelit tables, cool courtyards, and foliage-draped stairways — a welcome holdover from the original Dorado.

Moreover, Su Casa has a relatively new chef, Alfredo Ayala of San Juan's renowned Chayote, and the much-improved cuisine includes such nouvelle Caribbean dishes as Caribbean lobster tail with ginger and rosemary butter, served with fried green plantains and a chayote salad. But when spending $60 for dinner, I expect my waiter to greet me with a more professional salutation than "Yes, my friend, what can I get you?"

Name: Hyatt Dorado Beach Resort & Country Club
Manager: Fred Findlen
Address: Road 693, Dorado, Puerto Rico, 00646
Location: On the island's north shore, 22 miles west of San Juan, about 45 mostly untropical min. by shuttle van from the airport ($17 per person each way)
Telephone: 787/796-1234
Fax: 787/796-2022
Web: www.hyatt.com
Reservations: 800/233-1234, Hyatt Worldwide

Credit Cards: All major cards

Rates: $395–$705 EP (Jan 3–Mar 31); tax 12%, service charge 15%; off-season 40% less

Rooms: 262 rooms and suites in two- and three-story wings, most of them strung along the beach; each with marble bathroom (some shower only), bathrobes, lanai or balcony, air-conditioning, ceiling fans, stocked refrigerator, iron, coffeemaker, safe, TV, clock/radio, direct-dial telephone, hair dryer

Meals: Breakfast 7:30–11am (a super buffet for $18 — eat late and skip lunch), lunch noon–4pm, dinner in any of 5 restaurants (although they may not all be open, depending on the season) plus another 5 at Cerromar Beach, prices $60–$100; jackets requested in the Surf Room (and may be necessary, given the refrigeration level of the air-conditioning); room service to 11pm at extra charge; live music by Su Casa (mostly Spanish-style ballads by strolling musicians)

Entertainment: Music for dancing, movies; plus the large casino, dance club, and assorted lounges at Cerromar Beach

Sports: 2 reef-protected crescent beaches, 2 pools (one 82-footer with tournament lanes), walking/jogging trails; golf (36 holes, plus another 36 at Cerromar), 7 tennis courts (2 with lights, pro shop, plus additional courts at Cerromar), Lisa Penfield Windsurfing School and watersports, catamarans, nasty little jet skis, bikes, Spa del Sol (at Cerromar) at extra charge

PS: The hotel hosts groups up to 300, which may or may not strain the golf and tennis facilities; during holidays there are lots of children, but they have their own day camp; open year-round; no rules regarding cellphones

The Horned Dorset Primavera

RINCON, PUERTO RICO

☆☆☆☆	♈ ♈ ♈	❻	$ $ $ $
ATMOSPHERE	DINING	SPORTS	RATES

Here you are on the unspoiled western coast of Puerto Rico, where jungle-choked mountains give way to fields of sugarcane, surrounded by acres of tropical lushness dipping gently toward the sea, yet you're staying in a place named after a breed of English sheep. What gives here?

Let's get the name out of the way: Partners Harold Davies and Kingsley Wratten own a highly acclaimed restaurant in upstate New York called the Horned Dorset because, as I understand it, they also did some farming. When they went scouting around the Caribbean looking for a likely site for a second inn, they settled on this island of perpetual spring, so they tacked on the Spanish word for spring, primavera. I immediately dubbed it The Primavera, but everyone else has settled on Horned Dorset, so Horned Dorset it is.

This Horned Dorset is identified by discreet gateposts and the Relais & Châteaux symbol, located along the kind of side road where you don't expect to find a Relais & Châteaux property. Down a steep driveway you go to a tree-shaded parking lot, from which you get your first view of the estate and its enchanted garden with winding pathways and stairways with white balusters. In the foreground, there's a large swimming pool ringed by a broad sunning terrace with white umbrellas, loungers, a bar, and a barbecue (not many inns this size lay on the pampering so lavishly). Then you glimpse the grand two-story white manor in Spanish-Mediterranean style, topped by a red clay–tile roof, with white columns and a double stairway sweeping up to the dining room on the upper floor, and an open lobby leading to the Caribbean. To the right, Mediterranean-style villas housing the guest rooms dot the flowery hillside and skim the wall beside the beach.

Each room is a gem, decorated with native red-tile floors and fitted with four-poster beds and mahogany furniture that was custom-designed and handcrafted in nearby Ponce. Louvered French doors open to balconies and patios facing the sea; the bathrooms are opulent (almost too opulent for the setting), with Italian marble and footed bathtubs finished off with brass fixtures from France. A couple of years ago, the owners added a new two-story wing, Casa Escondido, with even grander lodgings — suites with private plunge pools and lawns and patios, and two with private rooftop decks. These suites share an imposing library/lounge. For lovers, the prime nest is a freestanding hillside cottage with dramatic views from a private swimming pool, fitted with a hand-painted "tent" on the ceiling and a custom-designed four-poster bed facing French doors that let bleary eyes wake up to views of bougainvillea, palms, and sun-glinting sea. Not for nothing is it named Casa Mirador (loosely, "house with a stunning view").

Last year, the inn unveiled 22 luxury, two-floor Villas at Horned Dorset, on a bluff overlooking the gardens and the sea, in a design reminiscent of the colonial townhouses in Old San Juan, each with an 8 × 10-foot private plunge pool and furnishings (four-posters, pedestal sinks, oval tubs). These villas are designed, alas, for air-conditioning rather than louvers and ceiling fans (a shame, given such a cool location), but they do add an extra degree of privacy for the Greta Garbos of this world. The choicest suites are probably the eight facing the sea directly, numbers 8 through 15, and of these you might opt for #15 because its celebrity owner modified the design to install louvered doors and windows rather than sliders.

Beyond luxurious comforts and peace and tranquility, the Horned Dorset offers nothing. This is, as the brochure promises, "a place without activities." By day, the popular agenda seems to be a morning dip in the ocean or a workout in the new fitness room; a leisurely breakfast of fresh mango and pineapple on the terrace, and coffee from the mountain plantations; an hour or two in one of the bamboo loungers with a good book; light lunch on the pretty terrace or around the pool; siesta; and an afternoon stroll along the ribbon of beach.

Well, it's not exactly without activities. Evenings begin with tapas at 6:30pm on the terrace facing the sea or in the lounge, with its splendid, hand-carved, antique mahogany bar, shelves of curl-up-on-a-lounger reading (Hortus Vilmorinianus anyone? Maybe *Discourses of Epictetus?*), the soft chatter occasionally interspersed with raucous commentary from Pompidou, a colorful macaw in a magnificent cage.

In its way, a Horned Dorset dinner is, if not an activity, at least an event. The main restaurant is upstairs in what looks like the salon of a Spanish grandee, surrounded by 14 mahogany doors and decorated with jacquard tapestries and softly glowing chandeliers. Until recently, dinner at the Horned Dorset was a formal, six-course *menu gastronomique,* but when the kitchen was taken over in 1996 by Aaron Wratten, Kingsley's son, the emphasis switched to a more relaxed prix fixe of just three courses, enhanced with *amuse-gueules* (cocktail snacks) and sorbets, fresh snapper and kingfish supplied by the eccentric fisherman who lives just along the beach, lobster from pots "you can swim out to" — or something extravagant like grilled foie gras served over sweated spinach on a pineapple slice. Notes the youthful Wratten, "With a small inn, we can get to know our guests' preferences and tailor our menus accordingly." Now there's a second restaurant adjoining the lounge on the main floor of the lodge, Le Bistro, with additional tables set up beneath sunshades on the lawns beside the beach.

It's a beguiling getaway, in other words, whether for a few days of unabashed idling or as the ideal stopover on a round-the-island tour (an idea I recommend highly). Just make sure you stay more than one night, though — The Horned Dorset Primavera is the sort of place you want to savor.

Name: The Horned Dorset Primavera
Owner/Manager: Wilhelm Sack
Address: Apartado 1132, Rincón, Puerto Rico 00743
Location: On Puerto Rico's west coast, just 15 min. north of Mayaguez (which you can reach via a 20-min. American Eagle flight from San Juan), or 2 hr. by car from San Juan via the northern highway and autopista; the hotel is located on Route 429, just outside Rincón at Marker Km. 3.0
Telephone: 787/823-4030 or 787/823-4050
Fax: 787/823-5580
E-mail: hdp@cqui.net
Web: www.horneddorset.com
Reservations: 800/633-1857, toll-free direct or 800/735-2478, Relais & Châteaux
Credit Cards: American Express, MasterCard, Visa
Rates: $700–$1,000 MAP (Dec 16–Apr 4); tax 12%, service charge 15%; off-season 35% less
Rooms: 31, all suites, in 8 two-story Mediterranean-style villas, all with marble bathroom, four-poster bed, air-conditioning and ceiling fans, sitting area, unstocked refrigerator; plus the Casa Mirador suite with private plunge pool — no phones, no TVs

Meals: Breakfast 7–10am; lunch noon–2:30pm on the terrace, in the new indoor/outdoor Le Bistro; or beside the pool; dinner 7–10pm in the formal, usually air-conditioned dining room (about $130) or the Le Bistro (approx. $100); informal dress — "no shorts or bathing suits in the public rooms after 6:00pm," but jackets are worn more often than not; room service for breakfast only; classical guitar during dinner (unamplified)

Entertainment: Cocktail hour, parlor games; salsa bars nearby, casino in Mayaguez

Sports: 2 freshwater pools, 27 private plunge pools, narrow beach; fitness center; surfing, watersports, tennis, and golf nearby

PS: No children under 12; "no cellphones in public areas"; open year-round

The Water Club

SAN JUAN, PUERTO RICO

☆☆☆   ♈♈♈   ❻ $ $ $
ATMOSPHERE   **DINING**   **SPORTS**   **RATES**

Don't arrive here in a hepped-up passionate mood because it may take you longer than usual to get from the front desk to your room — like so many other guests you might find yourselves spending so much time studying all the quirks and whimsy of the design.

San Juan's first boutique designer hotel (or at least the first one smack on the beach), The Water Club has a name and a backdrop of sea that designers can't resist turning into a theme. First, you step through glass doors with wavy motifs to find a waterfall behind glass at the front desk. You walk across blue-tiled floors surrounded by flowing white cotton (water, waves, get it?). When you step into an elevator, you're confronted with another waterfall behind glass. Walk down the sand-colored corridors and you find lots of votive candles casting a soft glow at one end, with a mermaid's legs clad in snorkeling fins jutting from the wall at the other end. Concealed speakers echo the sound of gently lapping surf. After dark, the windows of your room are bathed in a sea-blue glow from recessed lights. Even the bars don't let you forget that this is The Water Club — they're named Liquid, Wet, and Moist. I normally approach these designer boutique hotels with caution because some of them are gratingly pretentious, showcases for show-off decorators, but this one doesn't seem to take itself too seriously. It's a refreshing splash of humor on a strip of uninspired hotels, partly because its major mover-and-shaker, David Kurland, is a man with a neat-o sense of humor who also happens to have solid hotel credentials (he helped revitalize the El San Juan Hotel just along the beach).

The basic structure is hardly impressive, a run-of-the-mill 11-story hotel dating from the '90s but virtually unrecognizable today, except perhaps for the size and proportions of the rooms. The five suites are spacious enough but the guest rooms barely accommodate all the accoutrement of a modern hotel — the TV, CD player, minibar, and all those extras. Here things are arranged ingeniously and, in some cases, custom-designed to fit and enhance the setting. The beds are angled to take in the view, which also gives the designers space to attach an aluminum desk/dresser on the rear of the headboard. The closet is designed to accommodate clothes and the minibar *and* glasses — so don't bring lots of slinky evening gowns, as there's barely space for slacks and skirts. But you do get TV, a CD player, a rack full of design and fashion magazines, a board marked "Desires" for writing down instructions to the maids and staff, and a "do not disturb" sign that says DON'T EVEN THINK ABOUT IT.

But there's so much going on in the hotel itself (surprisingly, for an 84-roomer) that most of the time you will spend in your room will probably be spent in bed anyway. There's a lively bar/lounge, Liquid, off the lobby, where you can also have breakfast or light meals most of the day (if you don't mind the nonstop jazz and pop); up on the roof, you can enjoy a dip in the pool by day or, in the evening, sprawl on a futon by the faux fire and admire the city lights spread out around you.

The intention, as you've already guessed, is to make The Water Club a hip part of the swank San Juan scene (the place may get a tad noisy at times if you plan on turning in early), but, for many *Sanjuaneros,* the star of this Club is not the drinking spots. Its the Tangerine, the second floor restaurant that takes its cue from a fruit rather than the sea — with one tangerine-colored chair at each table, and a large painting of a tangerine on the wall. Of the 84 seats, the most romantic are outdoors on a terrace above the traffic, looking through the palm fronds to the beach and sea. Chef Cesar Fernandez conjures up cuisine that blends Asia and the Caribbean and a few other cultures; between his double-cut rack of lamb with a taro-root crust or herb-crisped, pan-seared halibut and the breezy, candlelit setting, Tangerine is one of the most inviting restaurants in the city. If you go touring beyond the city, don't forget to order a boxed lunch from the "You, too, can fly first class" menu — it's supposed to be for the flight home, but the food is so delicious lots of guests simply have it for picnics.

The Water Club couldn't have picked a worse time to open its wavy glass doors — October 2001 — but it quickly caught on and has since managed to attract lots of celebrities (Donatella Versace, Marc Anthony, Billy Dee Williams, Derek Jeter) and lots of singers and bands. Not surprisingly, for where else in San Juan can you get this kind of attentive, friendly service; this kind of style; *and* a beach across the street for just over $200 in winter (there are 25 rooms at the $209 per night rate).

Name: The Water Club
Owner/Manager: David Kurland
Address: 2 Tartak Street, Isla Verde, Puerto Rico 00979
Location: On a private street, across the street from the beach, near the "biggy" hotels, just 10 min. and $10 from the airport

Telephone: 787/728-3666
Fax: 787/728-3610
E-mail: info@waterclubsanjuan.com
Web: www.waterclubsanjuan.com
Reservations: 800/337-4685
Credit Cards: All major cards
Rates: $289–$349 EP, suites $695 year-round EP; taxes 12% extra, tipping optional; off-season 20% less
Rooms: 84 rooms and suites, all with air-conditioning, cable TV, CD players and discs, 2-line telephones, minibars, safes, telescopes for bikini watching in suites
Meals: Breakfast 7–11am, lunch noon–3pm, dinner 6–11pm in the Tangerine (approx. $80–$90), finger foods and sushi under the stars on the roof; background recorded music; casual but stylish dress; 24-hr. room service at extra charge
Entertainment: The bars — Liquid, Moist and, especially, Wet on the roof
Sports: Pool, fitness center; the beach across the street, watersports, golf or tennis at extra charge
PS: Not many children; open year-round,

Hotel El Convento

OLD SAN JUAN, PUERTO RICO

☆☆☆	Y Y	✪	$ $ $
ATMOSPHERE	DINING	SPORTS	RATES

The love-nooks here were the cells of Carmelite nuns back in those lusty days when the Spanish conquistadors were all over town, and this sanctuary was probably the only place where a maiden could remain a maiden.

The great mahogany doors of the convent still open to the same tiny *plazuela*, Plaza de las Monjas, where old men play dominoes, and priests and penitents cross on their way into the tall blackness of the 14th-century cathedral. The 300-year-old convent actually went through its own martyrdom, serving as a garage for sanitation trucks before it was rescued 30 years ago by a group of bold and farsighted people, including a Woolworth heir. They restored the fabric; imported authentic antiques from Spain; decked the halls and gallerias with paintings, tapestries, swords, and Andalusian tiles; and filled the guest rooms with hand-carved chests and high-backed chairs upholstered in brocades and velvets, turning the convent into one of the Caribbean's loveliest luxury hotels.

A new band of dedicated owners has come to the rescue once more. They've cleaned out the clutter of recent years and reduced the number of rooms from almost 100 to 58 (on the three upper floors, reached by private elevator from the lobby). They restored the guest rooms to their former charm, some with four-poster beds and ceiling beams, and added new window treatments that incorporate both glass panels and hardwood shutters.

The lower floors, grouped in graciously arched gallerias around a central patio dominated by a spreading 150-year-old tree, are now given over to half a dozen boutiques and three restaurants and cafes with indoor and outdoor dining. The ill-conceived swimming pool that ruined the courtyard a few years ago has been removed and replaced by the Cafe del Nispero, named for the centuries-old, four-story nispero tree that dominates the patio. Two other restaurants, El Picetao in the galleria and the street-level Cafe Bohemio, have turned the new Convento into the socializing spot in Old San Juan, where young *Sanjuaneros* gather to drink, gossip, and flirt over tapas, empanadas, and ceviches.

The downside: All this joie de vivre (the music in particular) can filter up to the guest rooms in a most un-Carmelite way (although, to be fair, most of the diners leave before 11pm). The upside: The old patio pool has been replaced by a much more private plunge pool and Jacuzzi on a red-tiled terrace on the fourth floor, with striking views across the harbor. The lobby terrace on the third floor below has become a popular rendezvous where guests can help themselves to the buffet continental breakfast or sip wine and nibble cheese at sundown — both buffets are on the house.

I stayed at El Convento many times during its heyday in the 1960s, and like so many other admirers of Old San Juan, I was saddened to watch the hotel's slow decay. Now it's back, hurrah! — one of the most unusual, most delightful inns anywhere in the Caribbean.

Name: Hotel El Convento
Manager: Consuelo MacMurray
Address: 100 Cristo St., San Juan, Puerto Rico 00902
Location: In the heart of Old San Juan, about 25 to 35 min. by taxi from the airport ($20), 5 min. from the cruise-ship piers
Telephone: 787/723-9020
Fax: 787/721-2877
E-mail: elconvento@aol.com
Web: www.elconvento.com
Reservations: 800/468-2779, Small Luxury Hotels of the World
Credit Cards: All major cards
Rates: $275–$1,200 CP (Dec 1–Apr 30); service charge 11%; off-season 40% less
Rooms: 58 rooms, including 4 suites, all with air-conditioning and ceiling fans, 2-line telephones, dataports, TV/VCR, CD/stereo, in-room safe, refrigerator with chilled water, and marble bathrooms with bathrobes, slippers, and hair dryer
Meals: Complimentary breakfast on the roof terrace or in your room, 7:30–10:30am, room service from the Cafe del Nispero (11am–9:30pm); 2 other private restaurants in the building — El Picetao and Café Bohemio

Entertainment: Wine and cheese every afternoon 5:30–7:30pm; honor bar on the deck; plenty of boîtes nearby

Sports: Small pool, Jacuzzi, and 8-station fitness center (available around the clock) — all free; watersports, tennis, and golf can be arranged at nearby hotels

PS: Few children; open year-round

Las Casitas Village

LAS CROABAS, PUERTO RICO

☆☆☆   ♈♈♈   ❻❻❻❻ $ $ $ $ $
ATMOSPHERE   **DINING**   **SPORTS**   **RATES**

You walk to your suite along flower-decked alleyways, past fountains, arches, and a *plazuela* with a bell tower. Where the village square and marketplace should be you'll find a swimming pool, hot tub, and terrace restaurant, Le Bistro.

Your 900-square-foot suite (best locations are suites with numbers 5010–5070 or 5250–5300), outfitted in a sort of Spanish-grandee style, comes with a "butler" who will run your bath and place scented candles around the tub. Or, unpack and press your resort togs. Or, fetch your meal from the restaurant and set it on your private dining table, complete with fresh flowers and unscented candles.

This Mediterranean village is set on a high bluff above another sea, the Caribbean, at the northeastern tip of Puerto Rico. Look east and the panorama of sea and islets is awesome; look west and the vista is awesome in its own man-made way — a sprawl of balconied concrete around pools and waterfalls, palm trees, and gardens. This is the Wyndham El Conquistador, big brother to this hotel-within-a-hotel. Thank your lucky stars that you and your fellow Casitas guests (178 of them) belong to a privileged elite, with your own entranceway, your own reception, your own bistro French chef, and first dibs on the luxurious 26,000-square-foot Golden Door Spa; whereas the hordes in yonder El Conquistador may not intrude on your privacy, you, on the other hand, can enjoy all the activities over there — restaurants, bars, pools, casino, golf, tennis. Anytime you feel like going to the beach, you can hop on their funicular, ride it down to the marina, board the resort's launch, and cruise over to El Conquistador's private island; but the only one of your facilities available to El Conquistador guests (by appointment only, of course) is the Golden Door Spa, with its 25 treatment rooms, a wraparound fitness room almost as spacious as most spas, and, for fanatics going for the burn, 12 Schwinn spinners.

After a day of spinning, running, swimming, jumping, golfing, and snorkeling, how nice to retreat to the peace and quiet of your village-within-a-city and call your butler. Ask him to run your bath — with extra bubbles and candles.

Name: Las Casitas Village, A Grand Bay Hotel & Resort
Manager: Jose Negron
Address: 1000 El Conquistador Avenue, Las Croabas, Puerto Rico 00738
Location: About 1 hr. by coach or limo from the airport, transfer by coach included in rate (if you want a private town car, it's $150 per person round-trip)
Telephone: 787/863-6484
Fax: 787/863-6758
E-mail: None
Web: www.wyndham.com
Reservations: 800/996-3426, Wyndham Resorts
Credit Cards: All major cards
Rates: $1,350–$2,500 1-bedroom suites, sunset-view or oceanview (Dec 20– Apr 15), tax 12%, service charge 10% extra; off-season 40% less
Rooms: 90, including 38 one-bedroom suites, all with separate living room, balcony, air-conditioning, ceiling fans, 2 TVs, VCR, CD/stereo, with 3 multi-line telephones with voice mail and dataport, full kitchen, coffeemaker, in-room foot massagers, fully stocked honor bar, personal safe, Jacuzzi, bathrobes, hair dryer, 24-hr. butler service (Las Casitas has been so popu-lar with CEOs and Mariah Carey and others who seek privacy that Wyndham is building an additional 67 suites, which should be ready in June 2004. Until then, be careful that you don't find yourself in an oceanview suite overlooking a construction site.)
Meals: Breakfast 7–11am, lunch 1–3pm, dinner 6:30–9:45pm (about $76), all in the 90-seat Le Bistro, indoors or alfresco; "collared shirt and slacks for men"; light recorded music; 24-hr. room service at extra charge; plus 13 restaurants at El Conquistador
Sports: Pool and hot tub exclusively for Las Casitas guests; everything else (golf, tennis, watersports) at El Conquistador, most of it at a price, except the funicular and the launch to the beach; horseback riding, Golden Door treatments, and Golden Door fitness center are extra
PS: Some children on weekends and holidays (they have their own activities camp); open year-round

Wyndham Martineau Bay Resort & Spa

VIEQUES, PUERTO RICO

☆☆☆☆   ☿☿☿   ❻❻❻ $ $ $ $
ATMOSPHERE   DINING   SPORTS   RATES

Vieques? Isn't that the place the U.S. Navy bombs? Did — but no more. The navy pulled out in May 2003, a few months after the resort opened its doors — and a few years after the resort was actually completed. If you keep tabs on these things, Martineau Bay is the resort that was supposed to join the Rosewood group (think Caneel Bay, Little Dix Bay) but then put up the shutters in 1999 before it even opened. Now the Puerto Rican owners have called in the Wyndham people to run the place with a cadre of management staff recruited from El Conquistador and Las Casitas (see above), Wyndham's other luxury resorts just across the channel on the mainland.

Now vacationers have the best of two worlds: timeless, unspoiled island, brand-new luxury lodgings. Vieques first. Because the navy had commandeered so much of this 22 × 4 mile island, developers have stayed away, despite a wealth of beautiful coves and beaches (if you want a beach all to yourselves, this is the place). There isn't a single traffic light on the island, the airport can't handle anything larger than a 70-seater, and if you see wire fences around properties, it's to keep out wild horses rather than nefarious people. Apart from the beaches, Vieques is not the prettiest of islands but it has that elusive, somnolent quality of an island time has passed by — which is fine by the 10,000 or so residents, many of them retirees, artists, and writers from northern climes.

So what you have now is that rarity these days, an unspoiled Caribbean island (the navy property has been turned out to the U.S. Department of the Interior) with luxury lodgings, outstanding cuisine, and more than a dash of sophistication. The architecture of Martineau Bay is vaguely plantation style (sloping metal rooflines, wraparound verandahs, decorative woodwork), a collection of 16 coral-colored villas, some two stories, some three stories, strung out on either side of the Great House, along the beach or around the pool. Most of the 42 acres are impeccably groomed lawns and flower beds. For some guests, the most appealing feature of the rooms may be the size — around 600 square feet, enough space for a sitting area, a large oval bathtub acting as divider between the bedroom and the bathroom (with a roll-down bamboo shade for anyone who wants more privacy), and a separate shower and separate john. The furnishings are top-quality, custom-designed for high-end Rosewood rather than medium-high-end Wyndham, and made in Bali, the Philippines, and Mexico — mahogany credenzas for the TV, woven quilt-style headboards, black oxidized faucets and sinuous iron door handles. Blue-and-white tiles for decoration and terra-cotta tiles for the floor. Louvered shutters replace curtains and drapes, sliders lead to balconies fitted out with armchairs, ottomans, and side tables, all in teak. Very attractive, very comfortable, even quite romantic. Since all rooms are identical (suites are two rooms, with extra sofas, credenzas, dining tables, and wet bars), you might want to choose your digs based on location: ocean front or garden view (the latter saves you a few dollars), lower floor for convenience or upper floor for privacy; rooms with numbers beginning 1 to 4 are quieter because they're on the opposite side of the Great House from the pool but close to the spa.

The resort's self-contained, 5,000-square-foot spa is set beside the beach with four treatment patios and rooms overlooking the sea and four more around a fountained courtyard. Right now it's called just The Spa, but ultimately it will carry the Golden Door banner. The small casino, which had yet to open in spring 2003, will feature tables and 70 slot machines.

The resort restaurant, Paso Fino (named for Puerto Rico's unique fine-gaited horses), was conceived on a grand scale with soaring ceilings, gargantuan wrought-iron chandeliers, bamboo screen dividers, and 24 multi-paned windows separating the interior from the spacious terrace. Elegant place settings include Italian china and Mexican hand-painted underplates and accessories. On the terrace you have sea breezes and the chirring of tree frogs; indoors you have air-conditioning and taped music that sometimes gets mangled by the cathedral ceiling and rafters. The biggest surprise of this newcomer may be the cuisine.

The veteran Wyndham chef/consultant, Ramesh Pillai, hails from India and has a passion for Indo-Latino fusion dishes — it's amazing what a little guava jelly or cardamom can do, respectively, to an Indian or Caribbean recipe. One of the first things he did at Martineau Bay was install an authentic tandoori oven so that executive chef, Victor Cruz, can produce tasty dishes like tandoori chicken with guayaba and mancheco cheese and tandoori frito Isla Nena filete chillo. Even the inevitable surf-and-turf offering comes out here refreshed and enhanced with subtle spicing as lobster and filet tango. I must have sampled half the dishes on the Pillai/Cruz menu so let me suggest a few standouts — empanada de vegetales and South Indian fried shrimp with mango relish among the appetizers. Herb sautéed dorado with mango chutney and yuca mofongo, masala-crusted double lamb chops, and Caribbean spiced pork with calabaza risotto among the entrees.

Despite the caliber of the cooking at Paso Fino, you ought to sample some of the eating spots elsewhere on the island. The most obvious stop is Esperanza, a dreamy, backwater village on the south shore, with a string of eating spots (Bananas, Chef Michael's, Posada Vista Mar) lining the blue and white malecon, or waterside promenade. Since you're going to pay about $30 round-trip by taxi, you might as well rent yourself a car and make Esperanza a stop on your island sightseeing tour, with maybe an hour or two of beach time. Sandy Beach is a good bet because it's near Esperanza and has brand-new facilities.

Wyndham Martineau Bay may not be the next Little Dix or Sandy Lane, but it has a lot going for it — stylish lodgings, exceptional dining, plenty of diversions. The youthful staff, 250 strong and mostly from Vieques, may still be unseasoned (most of them had never seen an underplate until a few months ago), but they're eager to show their paces and they greet you warmly — every time you step into the lobby, every time you sit down in the restaurant. You can't say that about every resort in Puerto Rico.

Name: Wyndham Martineau Bay Resort & Spa
Manager: William Ben Tutt
Address: State Road 200, Vieques, Puerto Rico 00765
Location: On the north shore of the island, about 5 min. and $7 by taxi from the airport (which in turn has frequent 25-min. flights on four airlines from San Juan International)
Telephone: 787/741-4100

Fax: 787/741-4105
E-mail: None
Web: www.wyndham.com
Reservations: 800/996-3426, Wyndham Resorts
Rates: $369–$850 EP, Dec 20–Apr 15; 9% and 11% per paid resort fee extra; off-season, 40% less
Rooms: 156, including 20 suites, in 16 two-story and three-story villas, all with patio or balcony, air-conditioning and ceiling fans, multi-line telephones, hair dryers, bathrobes, Golden Door toiletries, minibars, coffeemakers, satellite TV and Denon CD players, Jacuzzi tubs in suites
Meals: Breakfast 7–10am, lunch 11am–4pm at the pool bar, dinner 6–10pm in Paso Fino Restaurant (approx. $70–$80); 24-hr. room service at extra charge; resort casual dress (but no shorts in the dining room after 6pm); taped music in the dining room and occasional musical evenings at the pool
Entertainment: Small casino, some live music
Sports: 3 small beaches, pool, fitness center, all free; kayaks, sailing, windsurfing, snorkeling gear, tennis (2 courts, no lights); spa treatments at extra charge
PS: Expect some kids on weekends; open year-round

Caneel Bay

ST. JOHN

☆☆☆☆   ♈♈♈   ❻❻❻❻ $ $ $ $
ATMOSPHERE   **DINING**   **SPORTS**   **RATES**

Where else in the Caribbean — where else in the world — will $300 a day or thereabouts get you a resort with seven beaches (each lovelier than the next); a private peninsula of 170 acres surrounded by 6,500 acres of national park on land and 5,600 acres of national park underwater; where you can hike along paths lined with flamboyant, tamarind, and shower of gold; snorkel among peacock flounders and trumpet fish; spot a yellow-bellied sapsucker or pectoral sandpiper, maybe even a bobolink; build up your strength on a five-course breakfast, buffet lunch, and five-course dinner in some of the best restaurants in the Caribbean; and then bunk down in a double-size love nest open to the breezes and bird songs?

True, $300-plus a day is the basic summer rate (at least for 2003), but you still get all the attractions that presidents, vice presidents, bank moguls, gospel biggies, French counts, and senators pay almost twice as much for in winter.

Caneel is Caneel 12 months of the year, in season or out of season — just about the ultimate in seclusion, tranquility, and a sort of eco-euphoria. You almost have the feeling you're camping out here, but with a roof over your head rather than a tent, a bed under you rather than a sleeping bag, and real china rather than plastic plates.

There are 166 rooms at Caneel Bay (for every room an acre of landscaped parkland!); most of them are right on beaches, a few are on headlands, and 34 hillside rooms are in the Tennis Gardens, on the rise behind the courts, with a few bungalows off by themselves on the edge of the national park. A pair of shuttle buses circle the grounds every 15 minutes, but it's still worthwhile to give some thought to where you'd like to be. My preference is leeward Scott (single-story wing), but others prefer the windward Hawksnest (two-story, balconies for morning sun and afternoon shade, but these rooms have glass windows) for its views of offshore islands. Rooms at Turtle Bay, perhaps the prettiest beach, are close to the old estate house restaurant, and a few are actually in the estate house and may pick up the sounds of what passes as conviviality in these sedate parts, but room number 93 has a particularly bosky balcony.

The most secluded quarters are in the famous Cottage 7, once a home of the Rockefeller family, now the haunt of assorted VIPs who can conveniently park their bodyguards in the attached servants' quarters. Adjoining Cottage 7, rooms 61 through 66 are on a headland, secluded from the rest of the hotel, with their own patch of sand; on Caneel Bay itself, rooms 26 through 29 are especially popular because they're farthest from the public areas yet close to the main dining room. Up in the Tennis Gardens, rooms 132 through 141 are particularly spacious.

Since Caneel Bay, like its sister resort down the channel, Little Dix Bay, found itself taken over by Rosewood Hotels of Dallas a few years ago, many island lovers have been agog to see what would ultimately transpire. Not much — at least on the surface.

Traditionally, the exteriors have been painted in colors (variously described as "Madonna gray" or "Rockefeller putty") that blend unobtrusively into the surrounding nature, and the interiors have been only marginally more colorful. Don't knock it — it's always been very soothing even if slightly fuddy-duddy. The Rosewood people have installed new fabrics and whatnots to add discreet splashes of color, green decorative tiles in the bathrooms, and two-tone wicker-and-rattan or cane-and-bamboo furniture, including a few pieces from the Orient that look good but don't sit well with the old-timers. And for good reason — these people tend to settle in for weeks at a time, traveling with an average of five suitcases per couple; now they find that they have no place to store their fancy togs.

These rooms used to surprise some vacationers who thought that $300 a night rates included air-conditioning, room phones, and television. The rooms didn't even have glass in the windows facing the bay, just screens and jalousie louvers, and the wall opposite had only rough-hewn stone and jalousies screened by dense foliage. Four ceiling fans and the trade winds kept the rooms cool, and that's the way the longtime guests want it; they're the sort of people who could afford to stay anywhere, but choose to come back here year after year, in many cases more than 20 years. These are people who can survive happily without TV or radio or room phones — "After all," as one of them remarked, "calm is what we come for in the first place." Until 2000–01, that was the case; now Caneel has air-conditioning, with screens and louvers

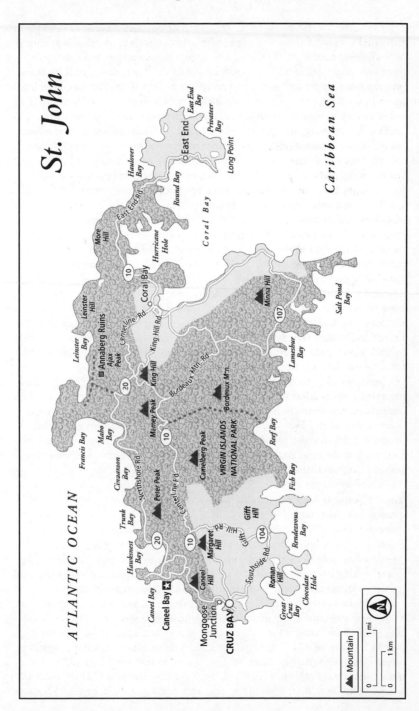

St. John

ATLANTIC OCEAN

Caribbean Sea

▲ Mountain

0 ___ 1 mi
0 ___ 1 km

to be sure, so that guests still have the option of opening their doors and getting cross ventilation. But the effect of living in the "outdoors" is gone, to a large degree; moreover, since the air-conditioning machinery is outside to eliminate indoor hum, the tranquility of a walk through the grounds has been compromised by whirring (and sometimes rattling). This may not be a big deal if you're heading to Caneel for the first time, but for anyone accustomed to the former park-like peace, it's an aggravation.

The Rosewood people, faced with the task of filling the resort year-round, have also opted to make it livelier, presumably to appeal to a younger clientele. Inevitably, this means amplified music, so it's more important than ever to ask for (1) a room away from the main lounge pavilion to avoid the boom-ta-boom of today's throbbing pop, and (2) a room away from those assigned to families (another recent innovation).

Caneel guests have a choice of three dining pavilions: the main one by the beach, one in a former plantation house, and another in a former sugar mill. Menus combine traditional American and traditional Caribbean with dashes of Pacific Rim to keep everyone happy. But a highlight of Caneel is still the grand lunch buffet beside the beach.

For active vacationers, there are no fewer than 11 tennis courts (no lights, though, because they'd spoil the magical after-dark atmosphere), a freshwater pool (but no diving, too noisy), Sunfish sailing, and snorkeling gear — all included, like the seven beaches and the 170 serene acres, in the room rate.

Caneel also has its own fleet of launches plying between the resort and St. Thomas, plus its own air-conditioned lounge at the airport, so guests enjoy VIP treatment and refreshments even before they set foot on the resort's private dock. Apart from a few nitpicks (sometimes the music is too loud), Caneel is one of those holdouts that really goes all out to pamper guests with personal attention (staff members outnumber guests by a good margin) and cloak them in an atmosphere of calm and serenity. As one lady remarked on the launch, "We've been going there for 20 years, and I always think of my 2 weeks there as therapy."

Name: Caneel Bay
Manager: Brian Young
Address: P.O. Box 720, Cruz Bay, St. John, U.S. Virgin Islands 00831-0720
Location: 4 miles across the channel from the tip of St. Thomas; the resort has its own air-conditioned lounge at St. Thomas's airport, and the hosts there will take charge of transferring you and your luggage to the resort — by taxi to Charlotte Amalie, where you board a private 58-ft. launch, *Caneel Bay Mary II,* for the 45-min. trip direct to the Caneel dock (included in the rates) or after dark by water taxi from Red Hook
Telephone: 340/776-6111
Fax: 340/693-8280
E-mail: caneelbay@worldnet.att.net
Web: www.caneelbay.com
Reservations: 888/767-3966, the resort's U.S. office

Credit Cards: All major cards

Rates: $450–$1,100 EP (Dec 20–Mar 31); service charge 10%; off-season 30% less

Rooms: 166 in a variety of one- and two-story wings strategically located around the property, with a few suites in cottage no. 7; all with air-conditioning, ceiling fans, louvers, balconies or patios, wall safes, minibars — but no TVs, radios, or phones (although there are phone pavilions outside the rooms)

Meals: Continental breakfast 6–8am, full breakfast 7:30–10am, lunch 11:30am–2pm, afternoon tea 4pm, dinner 7–9pm (about $110), in the breeze-cooled dining pavilion, the hillside Equator Restaurant, and the air-conditioned Turtle Bay Estate House; collared shirts, slacks, and "closed-in shoes" for gentlemen after 6pm in Turtle Bay (where jackets are not unusual, although not required), more casual in the main dining pavilion; "dry bathing suits and beach wraps and sandals at all times, no shorts or blue jeans after 6pm"; piano player in the Turtle Bay Estate House, some recorded music in the Equator; room service for breakfast only, $2 extra per tray

Entertainment: Live music every evening (guitar, combo, "slightly amplified"), dancing most evenings, movies every evening, nature lectures, backgammon, Scrabble, chess

Sports: 7 beautiful beaches, good swimming and snorkeling, freshwater pool behind the tennis courts, Sunfish sailing, windsurfing, kayaks, nature trails, tennis (11 courts, Peter Burwash pro shop, no lights), new 14-station fitness center (open 24 hr.), shuttle launch to St. Thomas (unlimited trips) — all free; massage, Self Centre, scuba (from the dock), sailboat cruises, boat trips to St. Thomas (popular for shopping) and Little Dix Bay, 90 scenic minutes away on Virgin Gorda at extra charge

PS: Caneel "welcomes children of all ages" year-round, entertains them in their own activity rooms, and installs families in their own clusters of rooms to avoid too much disruption of the tranquil setting; the resort is also, for the first time, accepting small meeting groups Apr–Nov; cell-phones for rent; open year-round

Point Pleasant Resort

ST. THOMAS

☆☆	⅄ ⅄	❽ ❽	$ $ $
ATMOSPHERE	DINING	SPORTS	RATES

Now a quarter of a century old, the 15-acre Point Pleasant has a settled look, blending into its surroundings as easily as any gnarled old seagrape or mampoo tree. Colors, materials, and designs are all natural, although a post-hurricane revamping has brightened up the interiors. Most of Point Pleasant's accommodations are in airy hillside dwellings, some in one-story cottages, others in three-story, condo-style structures. It's a bit too "condo" for some (in fact, all of the units are individually owned), but they are very comfortable and efficient, and all have kitchens. Walls are mostly windows and glass doors and can stay open to the trade winds because there's nothing on this breezy hillside to screen out.

The terrain (there's a shuttle bus to help you get around) may determine which unit you check into — high for breezes, swimming pools, and hiking trails, or just above the beach for swimming and watersports. The beach is small, so many guests traipse around the foot of the bluff to the larger swatch of sand at the Renaissance Grand Beach Resort. Some of my favorite rooms were up top because of the views of surrounding bays and islets, but many of them have been ruined by the penitentiary-like Wyndham's Sugar Bay Beach Resort across the bay.

A beachside cafe, Fungi's, makes life easy for water sprites; in the evening the attraction is the much-acclaimed Agavé Terrace Restaurant, in an alfresco hillside setting overlooking the bay and beach.

Name: Point Pleasant Resort
Manager: Joanna Patterson-Rizkallah
Address: 6600 Estate Smith Bay #4, St. Thomas, U.S. Virgin Islands 00802
Location: In the northeast of the island, half an hour and about $18 by taxi from the airport
Telephone: 340/775-7200
Fax: 340/776-5694
E-mail: PointPleasantResort@worldnet.att.net
Web: www.pointpleasantresort.com
Reservations: 800/777-1700, Colony Reservations
Credit Cards: American Express, Diners Club, MasterCard, Visa
Rates: $255–$575 EP (Dec 20–Apr 3); 8% tax and 12% service charge extra; off-season 25% less
Rooms: 128 suites from Juniors to two-bedroom suites, on the hill or beside the shore; all with balconies, fully equipped kitchens with microwaves and coffeemakers (small grocery store on premises), direct-dial telephones, ceiling fans and air-conditioning, satellite TV, clock/radio, in-room safes
Meals: Breakfast 7–10am, lunch 11am–8pm in Fungi's on the Beach, dinner 7–10pm in the Agavé Terrace Restaurant (about $60–$70), informal dress; no room service; live music 2 nights a week
Entertainment: Weekly managers' cocktail parties; shuttle bus to Charlotte Amalie and Magens Bay
Sports: Tiny beach (others nearby), 3 freshwater pools, snorkeling gear, tennis (1 court, with lights), nature trails — all free; dive shop, boat trips, golf nearby at extra charge
PS: Open year-round; some executive groups; some children

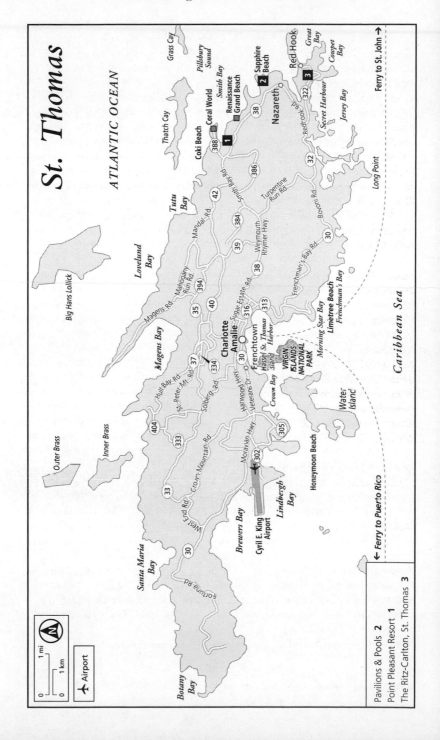

St. Thomas

ATLANTIC OCEAN

Caribbean Sea

Pavilions & Pools **2**
Point Pleasant Resort **1**
The Ritz-Carlton, St. Thomas **3**

Pavilions & Pools

ST. THOMAS

☆ ☆ ☆   ❻ $ $ $
ATMOSPHERE   **SPORTS**   **RATES**

The genies who designed this place proceeded on the premise that if we all had three wishes, they would be for (1) a tropical house on a tropical island, (2) a private swimming pool, and (3) no down payment, no mortgage. Sure enough, they've made all three wishes come true. Well, more or less.

The pavilion part of their wish fulfillment consists of a cabana-style suite (there are two basic designs, one slightly roomier than the other) of big, open, bright rooms with one long wall of sliding glass doors and full-scale kitchens. On the other side of the door lies the pool part: a completely private patio with a completely private swimming pool that's yours to do whatever you've always wanted to do in a swimming pool. A stout wall and plenty of tall spiky tropical plantings guarantee that peeping Toms can't peep.

Unlike most hotels with individual pools, Pavilions & Pools gives you one big enough (16×18 ft. or 20×14 ft.) for something more athletic than just dipping your toes. With most Caribbean hotels still frowning on topless tanning, you may be grateful for the chance to color in your white spaces without causing a riot. The rigorous privacy of the place, however, extends beyond your doorstep. To some, that's a plus. To others, a minus.

Because there's no central pool and no beach, and with only limited meal service, you're scarcely aware of anybody but the two of you and the friendly people who run the hotel and happily help you arrange side trips, rent cars, call airlines, reserve tables at restaurants, and so on. All activities outside your own room are at the hotel next door on Sapphire Beach. That includes tennis, any watersport you can think of, meals other than those you prepare in your own kitchen (the maids do the washing up), or snacks from the Fish Pond Café off the lobby.

P & P keeps right on being one of the Caribbean's most popular ways of getting away from it all — and it's now virtually a brand-new refurbished retreat without losing any of its unique ambience. If you both agree that a king-size bed, a pool, and thou are enough, come and join the crowd. Even though you'll never know they're here.

Name: Pavilions & Pools
Manager: Mackenzie "Mack" Farquhar
Address: 6400 Estate Smith Bay, St. Thomas, U.S. Virgin Islands 00802
Location: In the east, near Sapphire Bay, 30 min. and $14 by taxi from the airport
Telephone: 340/775-6110
Fax: 340/775-6110
E-mail: relax@vipools.com
Web: www.pavilionsandpools.com

Reservations: 800/524-2001, toll-free direct
Credit Cards: American Express, Discover, MasterCard, Visa
Rates: $250–$285 CP (Dec 20–Mar 31); tax 8%; service charge 10%; off-season 30% less
Rooms: 25 villas with private pools, king-size beds, kitchens, air-conditioning and ceiling fans, hair dryers, in-room safes, direct-dial telephones, cable TV, some with "garden" showers; Fish Pond Café open 8am–9pm for continental breakfast and simple dinners (about $50), honor bar
Entertainment: You; TV with 50 U.S. channels; cocktail party Tues nights
Sports: Private pools; snorkeling, tennis, golf, and watersports nearby
PS: Some, but not many, children; open year-round

The Ritz-Carlton, St. Thomas

ST. THOMAS

☆ ☆ ☆ ☆   ♈ ♈ ♈   ❻ ❻ ❻ ❻ $ $ $ $ $
ATMOSPHERE   DINING   SPORTS   RATES

At first sight you might think that the Caribbean sun has gone to your head: Is that really a Renaissance palace in the U.S. Virgin Islands?

It's not the heat, it's not a mirage, it's just the upshot of one Englishman's fantasy — Michael Pemberton, the original owner (it's now owned by Marriott and managed by Ritz-Carlton). He did things with his customary taste and scoured the world to find the best: hence, antique chandeliers and tapestries imported from Italy, and lovely coral-pink marble from Portugal.

This imposing salmon-pink palazzo is the centerpiece, with front desk, concierge, boutiques, and fitness room. The rest of the hotel, strung out along a more or less private beach, is more down-to-earth. Directly below the lobby is a pink-stucco complex of lounges and bars; pathways of fossil stone lead to a lip-level pool, acres of beautiful gardens, and a natural salt pond that's a sort of spa for geese and iguanas. And somewhere behind all those Renaissance-style facades and pink pavilions lurks the state-of-the-art paraphernalia that makes the hotel self-dependent — reverse osmosis water plant, sewage treatment plant, and an "ecologically sound heating system that eliminates boilers burning fossil fuels."

The guest rooms are housed in three-story wings of Mediterranean-style architecture with yellow-ocher stucco, lots of arches, lots of wrought-iron balconies — all facing the beach and sea and each with a balcony framed by a stucco arch or overhung with a tiled ramada. The marble-clad bathrooms come with separate toilets, twin vanities, hair dryers, and lounging robes. The guest rooms have just been restyled with mahogany furniture in traditional Caribbean style, new carpeting, new bedspreads and drapes, and new 29-inch televisions tucked into the armoires. The four one-bedroom and two-bedroom suites offer more of the same, measuring more than 1,000 square feet, not counting the double balcony, which has space for a pair of loungers as well as table and chairs (the ocean-view rooms have table and chairs only). A newly completed $75-million expansion added 24 rooms and 24 suites on a key-activated club floor with a private lounge, and an 8,700-square-foot spa to upgrade the pampering.

All in all, it's more sumptuous than anything else on the island. But for my money, I would have preferred ceramic tile or wood floors rather than wall-to-wall carpet, and I would have welcomed louvers in addition to the sliding-glass doors so that I could feel the gentle wisp of the trade winds.

Some guests might also grump about too little closet and drawer space. There would be reason to do so if this were a resort where you had to haul along trunks full of your fanciest togs because you were expected to dress up every evening, but it isn't — casual elegance is the order of the day. The dress code requires neither jackets nor ties, although I suspect that during the winter season many guests will, in fact, gussy themselves up, since the setting for dinner, The Dining Room, is rather posh — a pink-stucco pavilion of exquisite proportions facing the moonlit water of the bay, now enhanced with mahogany doors and Frette linens. Tables are widely spaced, the atmosphere is conducive to leisurely dining, and the service is attentive and not too pushy. The Dining Room, despite its beachside setting, is now air-conditioned, but guests can still dine under the stars at The Café, where Monday evenings are given over to a Caribbean Night, Friday to a seafood buffet. After dinner, guests can enjoy a new feature: live classical or jazz guitar music by the fountain in the courtyard of the palazzo, from 9pm to midnight. Another new feature of life in the palazzo is afternoon island tea in the Florentine Room, featuring local therapeutic blends served with pastries — all prepared in the home of the island-lady in charge of the entire presentation.

The 15 acres of gardens are one of the most impressive features of the resort, with more than 125 species of flowering plants and dozens of types of greenery. Plants climb the walls, rim the balconies, and encircle the pond. Shower of gold vies for attention with tree of life, and an expert green thumb could spot close to 20 species of palms, and rarities such as the four-sided lucky nut tree.

Maybe it was the gardens, the beguiling staff, or the spit and polish of the place, but on the ride back to the airport I finally reconciled myself with a Renaissance palace on a Caribbean beach. St. Thomas, with all its shopping malls and condos and traffic, is not really "Caribbean" — and, even if it's a tad pricey (after all, someone has to pay for all those pampering people), Ritz-Carlton swank is just what this island needed. And just what's needed for people in search of luxury without leaving U.S. territory.

Name: The Ritz-Carlton, St. Thomas
Manager: Jamie Holmes
Address: 6900 Great Bay, St. Thomas, U.S. Virgin Islands 00802
Location: On the eastern end of the island, 30–40 min. and $20 by taxi from the airport, 20–30 min. from all the shops in Charlotte Amalie

Telephone: 340/775-3333

Fax: 340/775-4444

E-mail: reservations@ritzcarlton.com

Web: www.ritzcarlton.com

Reservations: 800/241-3333, toll-free direct

Credit Cards: All major cards

Rates: $450–$605 EP (Jan 1–Apr 30); tax 8%, service charge 10% extra; off-season 30% less

Rooms: 200 rooms and one-bedroom suites, all with air-conditioning and ceiling fans, veranda or balcony, direct-dial telephones (3 per room), stocked minibar, 29-in. cable TV, bathrobes, in-room safe, tea/coffeemaker, clock radio, lighted makeup mirror, and hair dryer

Meals: Breakfast 7–10:30am, lunch noon–3pm, and light snacks throughout the day at the poolside Café Iguana or beachside Coconut Cove, dinner 6–10pm (about $90–$100), in one of two restaurants — one breeze-cooled, one air-conditioned; "casual elegance" — which means shoes and shirts in the lobby (no swimsuits), footwear at all times, dress shirt and dress slacks in the evening; recorded classical music in The Dining Room; room service 24 hr. a day, limited menu at extra charge

Entertainment: Bar, some live entertainment on the Café Iguana terrace, including a folklore show on Monday

Sports: 125-foot lipless freshwater pool, tennis (2 Omniturf courts, with lights, new Peter Burwash pro shop), fitness center, snorkeling gear, windsurfing, kayaking — all free; scuba and spa services at extra charge; day sails and evening cruises on the 53-ft. *Lady Lynsey* catamaran (the one President Clinton chartered); golf nearby

PS: Some children; open year-round

The Buccaneer

ST. CROIX

☆☆☆☆   ♆♆   ❻❻❻❻ $ $ $
ATMOSPHERE   **DINING**   **SPORTS**   **RATES**

If setting alone were the deciding factor, the Buccaneer would win hands down as the most attractive resort on St. Croix. Its 300 rolling acres incorporate a challenging but not overwhelming golf course, tidy lawns, the circular stone base of an old sugar mill on the hill, and three coves of white sand lined by stands of coconut palms. Tropical flowers vie with the pink-and-white buildings to splash the hillsides with color. Every way you turn you have another glorious view of sea or bay and Christiansted (from this location, a pretty picture of pastel stucco without the unsightly spaghetti of utility poles and cables).

Guest rooms are deployed around the grounds in a variety of one-, two-, and three-story buildings, some on the crest of the hill, some halfway down the hill, others beside the beach. Which one you choose will probably be determined by whether or not you want a steady breeze, whether you want to be closer to the beach than the golf course, and so on — but let me suggest that you consider the beach rooms (known as deluxe oceanfront) that curve around the point between Cutlass and Beauregard beaches; on the ridge, the choice lodgings, apart from room 212 in the main building, are the Ridge Rooms, a parade of little row houses looking across the fairways and sea to St. Thomas, 43 miles away, renovated in 2000 with whirlpool tubs, granite-topped vanities, and queen-size, four-poster beds.

The Armstrong family, owners since the hotel opened in 1947, have been turning their attention to the restaurants, bringing in chef Dennis Giacontiere, whose Mediterranean/Italian cuisine has transformed The Terrace into one of the choice dining spots on St. Croix.

The public areas are now much jollier environments. Even so, the Buccaneer doesn't set out to attract luminaries and glitterati; despite the fact that its most secluded beach is named Whistle (as in whistle before you get there to let people know you're coming — just in case), the Buccaneer tends to have a fairly conservative clientele. But the real attraction here, besides those beautiful grounds and the complimentary full American breakfast in the restaurant, is the range of sports activities — golf, eight tennis courts with lights, and a full range of watersports right at your doorstep. And then, of course, there's the able, responsive staff, many of whom have been with the Armstrongs forever.

Name: The Buccaneer
Owner/Manager: Elizabeth Armstrong
Address: P.O. Box 25200, Gallows Bay, St. Croix, U.S. Virgin Islands 00824-5200
Location: On the beach at Gallows Bay, about 10 min. from Christiansted, 25 min. and $14 for two by shared taxi from the airport
Telephone: 340/773-2100
Fax: 340/778-8215
E-mail: mango@thebuccaneer.com
Web: www.thebuccaneer.com
Reservations: 800/255-3881, toll-free direct or 800/223-1108, Ralph Locke Islands
Credit Cards: All major cards
Rates: $295–$525 with full American breakfast (Dec 20–Apr 1); no service charge, tipping optional; off-season 20% less
Rooms: 138, including 13 suites, in 8 categories, each with air-conditioning and fans, bathrobes on request, refrigerator, direct-dial telephone, TV, safe, balcony or patio
Meals: Breakfast 7:30–10:30am, lunch 11:30am–5:30pm in a couple of beachside pavilions, dinner 6–9:30pm in 3 indoor and outdoor restaurants (about $75), dress casual but "no shorts on the Terrace after 6pm"; limited room service, all meals; some live music

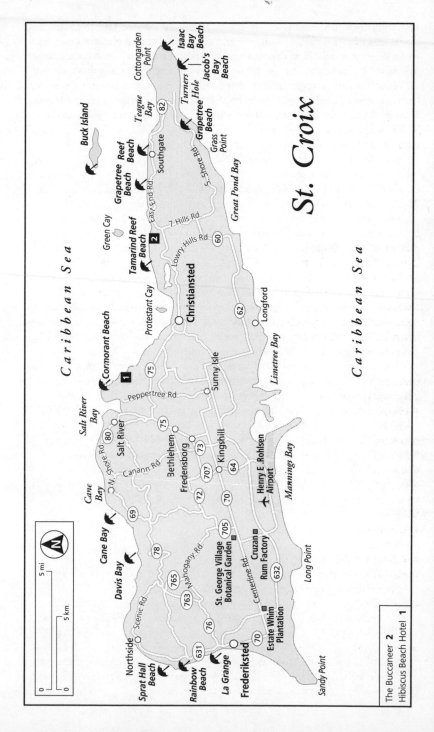

St. Croix

The Buccaneer **2**
Hibiscus Beach Hotel **1**

Entertainment: Nightly movie in the Cottonhouse Movie Theatre, live music
5 evenings a week, including steel bands, calypso, and guitarists
Sports: 3 beaches, 2 freshwater pools, health spa, new fitness club, floats,
kayaks, snorkeling gear — all free; tennis (8 championship-caliber courts,
2 with lights, $16 per hr., pro shop), golf (18 holes, pro, $60 per round, cart
extra), windsurfing, rowboats, Sunfish sailing, boat trips, horseback riding
on the west end of the island, treatments in the renovated Hideaway Spa at
extra charge
PS: Some families, some business groups in the off-season; open year-round

OTHER CHOICES

Hibiscus Beach Hotel

ST. CROIX

The 20-year-old Hibiscus offers beachside lodgings for less than $200 in
winter — that's as good a reason as any for putting it on your list of getaways.
At these rates you can't expect class, but the rooms are really quite pleasant —
they're decorated in island pastels with ceramic-tile floors and pale coral furniture, equipped with balconies, TVs, minibars, direct-dial telephones, air-
conditioning and ceiling fans, safes, clock radios, and showers rather than
bathtubs. A beachy but breezy bar/restaurant terrace among the palms is perfect for socializing (except when there's live music and the volume is too
loud). Thirty-seven rooms and one efficiency apartment. Doubles: $190–$290,
winter 2002–03. *Hibiscus Beach Hotel, 4131 La Grande Princesse, St. Croix, U.S.
Virgin Islands 00820-4441. Telephone: 800/442-0121 or 340/773-4042; fax:
340/773-7668; e-mail: hibiscus@viaccess.net; Web: www.1hibiscus.com.*

The British
Virgin Islands

here are they? When Winston Churchill was asked this question in the House of Commons, he is said to have replied: "Presumably as far as possible from the Isle of Man." In fact, the British Virgins are more than 3,000 miles from the Isle of Man, but only 60 miles from Puerto Rico and a 20-minute boat ride from St. Thomas. There are 60 of them strung along Sir Francis Drake Channel, where the wily Elizabethan mustered his ships before attacking the Spanish garrison at El Morro in San Juan. The main islands are Tortola (Spanish for turtle dove), Beef, Peter, and Virgin Gorda ("the Fat Virgin" — named by Christopher Columbus, who had obviously been too long at sea by this point); none of them is as big as Manhattan, and if you squeezed them all together, they would still be smaller than, say, Nantucket. These Virgins have no hang-ups. They're quite content to lie there drowsing in the sun, loyal outposts of Queen Elizabeth II. Britain sends over a governor who nominally attends to matters like defense and the law courts (which operate on the British system). Otherwise, the islanders elect their own executive council and run their own affairs, such as they are. But they're no dummies, these islanders, as they know which side of the bread their butter is on: Legal tender is the U.S. dollar rather than the British pound sterling.

These are quiet islands for quiet people. There's no swinging nightlife here and no casinos. What little sightseeing exists is usually done by boat rather than car. But what the Virgins dish out in return is glorious sea, glorious scenery, and glorious serenity.

HOW TO GET THERE   Service has greatly improved in recent years with the introduction of dependable flights by American Eagle, LIAT, Cape Air, and the brand-new Caribbean Sun from San Juan and St. Thomas, 10 or more times a day each way, getting you to the remotest B.V.I. hideaway in time for a stroll on the beach before dinner. A few inter-Caribbean airlines also fly to Tortola from islands other than Puerto Rico and St. Thomas, but you'd better check with your travel agent rather than the Internet for details.

Two points to remember: First, always collect your luggage at San Juan or St. Thomas, rather than checking it through. The American Eagle services have cut down on the delays in transferring baggage, but it's still wise to handle the chore yourself, rather than waiting for delayed luggage to arrive on the next flight (which may be the next morning). This is still true despite the fact that B.V.I.'s airport on Beef Island has been expanded with a brand-new two-story, air-conditioned terminal (nice, but it takes away some of the backwater quality of arriving here). Second, there's an alternative transfer to the B.V.I. from St. Thomas, longer (1 hr.) but less expensive (about $20 per person each way): by twin-hulled, air-conditioned ferryboats, each carrying 60 to 80 passengers, leaving from the ferryboat dock in Charlotte Amalie (about 10 min. by taxi from St. Thomas airport) to West End or Road Town on Tortola, continuing, in some cases, to Virgin Gorda.

> For information on the British Virgin Islands, call 800/835-8530 or 212/696-0400, or visit www.bviwelcome.com.

Long Bay Beach Resort

TORTOLA

☆☆☆	♈♈♈	❻❻	$ $ $
ATMOSPHERE	DINING	SPORTS	RATES

"Long" in this case means 1 mile, give or take a yard or two — 1 mile of white sand and glistening sea with sheltering headlands at either end, tucked

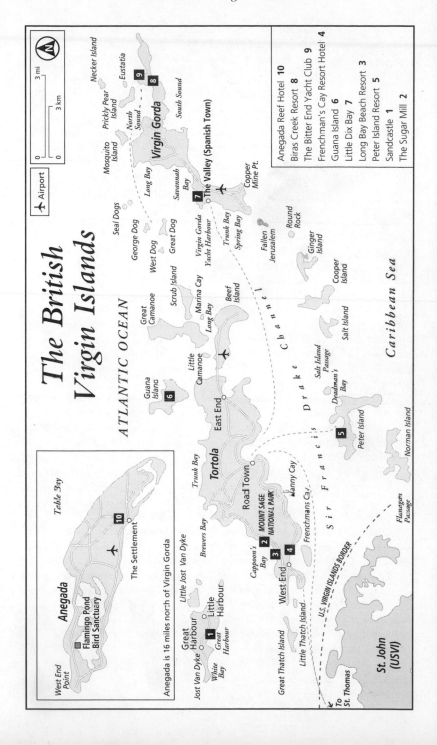

The British Virgin Islands

ATLANTIC OCEAN

Caribbean Sea

Anegada Reef Hotel **10**
Biras Creek Resort **8**
The Bitter End Yacht Club **9**
Frenchman's Cay Resort Hotel **4**
Guana Island **6**
Little Dix Bay **7**
Long Bay Beach Resort **3**
Peter Island Resort **5**
Sandcastle **1**
The Sugar Mill **2**

Airport

Anegada is 16 miles north of Virgin Gorda

away on the northwestern corner of the island, far from the crowds (not that there are ever real crowds on this friendly little island).

Long Bay, the resort, is really a 52-acre estate, with the ruins of a centuries-old sugar mill beside the beach, rooms and suites strung out along the sea and notched into the leafy hillside, and a nine-hole pitch-and-putt golf course weaving through the gardens and lawns between the beach and the hill. The resort has undergone a major transformation in recent years, almost doubling in size to 114 rooms and suites and introducing soothing coral-hued decor with jaunty island fabrics and cane furniture. Some of the rooms have bamboo four-posters and 120-square-foot decks cooled by paddle fans; the priciest units have full kitchens, microwaves, and Jacuzzis. All the lodgings come with air-conditioning and ceiling fans, refrigerators, coffeemakers, clock radios, cable TV, and direct-dial telephones.

The hillside studios and rooms are 50 to 100 yards uphill from the beach, but the advantage of these lodgings is that guests wake up to a more stunning view — the beach and the breakers, the headlands and offshore islets, and scores of scudding sails in the channel between Tortola and the island of Jost Van Dyke. The newest rooms ring the new pool, ideal for pool lovers, but maybe a tad noisy for folks who prefer the lulling sound of gentle surf.

Much of what makes Long Bay an exceptional value is the sense of space and privacy that comes with all those acres of gardens and lawns and a mile-long stretch of sand. But there's also the fact that all guests, no matter how much the room rate, have a choice of sporting activities that come free of charge: pitch-and-putt, two freshwater swimming pools, a well-equipped fitness/massage center, and two all-new tennis courts. The beach is one of the best walking and jogging strands in the British Virgins; in winter, it's true, the sea may be more appropriate for board surfing than swimming (there's a more sheltered beach around the bend), but in spring, summer, and fall the water is usually perfect for dipping and dunking. Other watersports (scuba diving, sport-fishing, sailing) are available just over the hill in Soper's Hole, and the resort's new branch of Virgin Adventure Tours offers sea kayaking and ecology tours.

There are also several fine eating spots, from beachside shacks to luxury inns, within a 10- to 15-minute drive, but Long Bay itself offers a couple of fine restaurants. The hillside Garden Restaurant (so popular it has been enlarged) is set amid rocks and greenery that make a romantic backdrop for candlelight dining. Despite the classy setting, dress is informal and there's live music two or three evenings a week. The poolside/beachside Beach Café at the old sugar mill, with tables and sunshades set up on the terrace beneath the seagrape and almond trees, is open from daylong breakfast through lunch to dinner beneath the stars. Prices here are reasonable — about $60 for a three-course dinner for two, without drinks. But the best place for a sundown drink or nightcap may well be the terrace of your own hillside room or studio with that great panoramic view.

Name: Long Bay Beach Resort
Manager: Bern Gabel

Address: Tortola, British Virgin Islands
Location: On the north shore, 20 min. and $20 by taxi from Road Town, 40 min. and $40 from the airport
Telephone: 284/495-4252
Fax: 284/495-4677
E-mail: info@longbay.com
Web: www.longbay.com
Reservations: 800/729-9599, toll-free direct
Credit Cards: American Express, MasterCard, Visa
Rates: $255–625 EP (Jan 2–Apr 5); taxes and service charge 17% extra; off-season 45% less
Rooms: 157 in 6 categories, all with ceiling fans and air-conditioning, balcony or deck, unstocked refrigerator, coffeemaker, clock radio, direct-dial telephones, remote-controlled cable TV; some with microwave, some with full kitchen (but for the use of owners only, not guests), some with barbecue grill; the resort also has several private villas for rent
Dining: Breakfast 7:30am–4pm, lunch 11am–4pm (at the beach terrace), dinner 6:30–9:30pm at the Beach Café (about $60) or in the Garden Restaurant (about $80); informal dress; no room service
Entertainment: Recorded classical music in the bar, live music 2 or 3 evenings a week on the bar deck or the Beach Cafe
Sports: Mile-long beach (good for bodysurfing in winter, good for snorkeling in summer, not always great for swimming), 2 freshwater pools, tennis (2 courts, with lights), fitness center, 9-hole pitch-and-putt course — all free; spa, sea kayaks, snorkeling gear, surfboards at extra charge
PS: Some children; open year-round

The Sugar Mill

TORTOLA

☆☆☆	YYYY	⚽	$ $ $
ATMOSPHERE	DINING	SPORTS	RATES

You might think that travel writers and food critics, who hear endless accounts of the agonies and travails of innkeepers, would steer firmly clear of such a profession. Not in this case. Critics Jeff and Jinx Morgan came over from San Francisco in the mid-1980s, plunged into the deep end by acquiring this delightful 20-roomer, and forged ahead, upgrading cuisine, service, and ambience. And still, come hurricanes, come hassles, they manage to find time to write.

The Sugar Mill is the weathered stone ruins of a 300-year-old mill and distillery set in a hilly garden above the sea, surrounded by flamboyant and wild orchid trees. To this basic setting, the Morgans have added three trellised gazebos beside the bar, where most of the evening mixing and chatting takes place, and a beach bar/restaurant called Islands, featuring moderately priced Antillean fare such as rotisserie and jerk chicken.

No matter where you eat, you don't have far to walk afterward: past the pool and up the hill to cantilevered cottages with traditional island furnishings, or, if you like to be a little on your own, just across the driveway to room 109.

Guest rooms here are not luxurious by any means, but they're spacious (although some bathrooms are a tad cramped); they've all been significantly livened up with cheerful fabrics and white wicker rockers, and each comes with a pantry or kitchen for folks who are checking in for more than a couple of nights. The views from the balconies are almost worth the price of admission. Room 109 is a dinky blue-and-pink gingerbread cottage with a few extra square feet of flooring, a couple of wicker armchairs, a small circular dining table, and a big tiled shower stall (although the view is somewhat hemmed in by the bougainvillea and hibiscus and you may pick up some noise from the roadway beyond the hedgerow).

It's the reputation of the kitchen that lures vacationers and islanders over to this corner of Tortola. The setting is picture-perfect: candlelight flickering on gray stone accented by the colors of Haitian primitive paintings, ceiling fans turning slowly beneath the hip-roof ceiling, tree frogs singing, glasses clinking, and friends exchanging greetings. There must be many diners who wish dinner would last another course or two, just to sample some of the other dishes from the Morgans' own recipe book. Why settle for West Indian Regimental beef curry and forgo snapper with red-pepper relish? Or almond-crusted lamb loin instead of tropical game hen with orange-curry butter? The range of desserts makes you wish the Morgans would toss in the towel and start a neighborhood pastry shop: coconut cloud tart, cappuccino mousse with crème de Kahlúa, piña colada cake, and meringue seashells with banana cream.

There may be other fine restaurants on the islands, but few have such a congenial atmosphere. Sugar Mill is sort of the tropical equivalent of one of those tiny *auberges* in Burgundy, with fine food and a few rooms for staying over. But here you wake up to perfect days and sparkling sea and no abbeys, châteaux, or musty museums that must be visited. Here you just slip into days of lazing — rum French toast on the breakfast terrace, a dip in the garden pool. Read a book and shuffle to the beach-bar for a long, boozy lunch that slowly fades into a siesta. Another dip, a walk to the village, a piña colada, and before you know where you are it's time for sundowners in the gazebo bar and thoughts of tomato-ginger-wine soup and grouper in banana leaves with herb butter.

Name: The Sugar Mill Hotel
Manager: Patrick Conway
Address: P.O. Box 425, Tortola, British Virgin Islands
Location: On the northwest shore, near Long Bay, about 45 min. and $36 by taxi from the airport, but only 10 min. and $6 from the ferry dock at West End
Telephone: 284/495-4355
Fax: 284/495-4696

E-mail: sugmill@surfbvi.com
Web: www.sugarmillhotel.com
Reservations: 800/462-8834, toll-free direct
Credit Cards: American Express, MasterCard, Visa
Rates: $215–$620 EP (Dec 21–Apr 14); service charge 10%; off-season 30% less
Rooms: 24 in various cottages in the garden, all with remote-controlled ceiling fans and air-conditioning, hair dryers, balcony; apartments with cable TV/VCR, refrigerator and/or pantry
Meals: Breakfast 8–10am on the terrace below the bar, lunch noon–2pm in Islands beach bar, dinner 7–9pm in the main dining room (about $100), 6:30–9pm in Islands beach bar, Jan–May (about $30); casual dress, "though a touch of glamour is never out of place"; no room service
Entertainment: Bar, board games, library
Sports: Circular freshwater pool, small beach for sunning, snorkeling gear, other watersports nearby
PS: No children under 11 Dec 21–Apr 14 (but they are welcome free of charge the rest of the year); closed Aug and Sept

Peter Island Resort

PETER ISLAND, TORTOLA

☆☆☆☆☆	♈♈♈	❻❻❻	$ $ $ $
ATMOSPHERE	DINING	SPORTS	RATES

Sun! Breezes! Sailboats! Seclusion! This private 1,800-acre Virgin Island, just across from Road Town in Tortola, would seem to have everything going for it, but it has never quite reached the heights it should have.

It came on the scene more than 20 years ago, the plaything of an ultra-rich Norwegian ship-owner who built an efficient but dull little Bergen-in-the-sun with two-story A-frame chalets like those found along the fjords of Norway — perched on the breakwater to preserve the purity of the beach. Later owners added 20 stunning rooms of bluestone and cedar beside the beach, with lots of louvers and tiny patio gardens, but subsequently "modernized" them with air-conditioning and sliding-glass doors. Farewell, romance; hail refrigeration! But now it's back to romance.

What Peter Island Resort has going for it is its beaches, five of them, but especially Deadman's Bay, one of the most ravishing half moons of sand in the Caribbean. Here guests can lounge in the trade winds beneath the palms; sail, windsurf, and wobble around on floats; or, at the far end, in a grove of trees, play tennis or dine in a lovely beachside pavilion. The focal point of the resort, though, is what was originally intended as a yacht club, beside a marina that sometimes is, sometimes isn't, functioning as a marina.

In 1997, then-owners Amway Hotel Corporation of Michigan brought in a new manager, Wayne Kafcsak (well-known to habitués of Bitter End Yacht Club) and undertook a major overhaul. Everyone had high hopes that maybe the resort would finally reach its potential. It certainly looked that way until a hurricane zeroed in on the resort, washed away the marina dining room and swimming pool, and uprooted trees and plantings. I saw it a few weeks later, scarred and bleak, but by the time they were up and running again, another freak storm came in and trashed the place again. A few months later, Kafcsak and his crew had everything shipshape and looking better than ever. It helps, of course, when the owners (now just one, the Van Andels, of the two families that own Amway) have bundles of cash and love spending it on the resort because they love vacationing there themselves.

The A-frames on the breakwater have been transformed from their Bergen stodge to Caribbean calypso pastels, enlarged with the addition of balconies and patios, and generally brought up to the standard expected in the type of high-end resort this was always intended to be. The spacious beach-front suites have been, well, transformed — louvered French doors opening to the balconies replace the motel-like sliding-glass panels; although the air-conditioning is still there, guests can once more enjoy the gentle breezes flowing through from the balconies to the bathrooms, which are now separated from the sleeping area with a wall of glass next to two-body tubs. The main dining room on the breakwater, once an architectural folly, is now much more inviting with large windows knocked into the fortress-like walls so that diners have a view of the sea with their rum-basted tropical lamb satay with grilled pineapple. And it now has an alfresco terrace beyond the louvered walls. The wine cellar now boasts a selection of 250 vintages from around the world, and once a week a dozen guests get together with the manager for a wine-pairing dinner in the private wine room. Although the musicians have been told to turn down the amps, dining here can still be marred by intrusive musicians; so you may find yourselves spending most of your evenings at the revamped Beach Grill, enjoying the Mediterranean/Italian cuisine and the whispers of palm fronds. The coconut palms on Deadman have been replaced (and then some); the redesigned reception pavilion now actually guides your eyes seaward instead of blocking the view, and the concrete around the marina has been softened with decorative tiles and mountainous plantings of hibiscus and bougainvillea and tropical greenery — you know, just the usual little improvements one makes when one has $40 or $50 million to play with.

The other thing Peter Island Resort has going for it is Peter Island itself. All that space for just 100 guests! Visiting yachts are steered to moorings in an adjoining bay, but guests who feel like a change of pace from Deadman can have the staff drive them around this headland or that headland to one of nine (nine!) other unspoiled, untrampled strands. The staff will even lay out a picnic if you give them plenty of warning. *Tip:* Get an early start and you can have tiny first-come-first-tanned Honeymoon Beach all to yourselves.

Name: Peter Island Resort
Manager: Jeffry Humes
Address: P.O. Box 211, Road Town, Tortola, British Virgin Islands
Location: Across the channel from Road Town on Tortola, a trip of 20 min. aboard a 46- or 65-ft. luxury power yacht (regular ferry service 9 times a day between the 2 islands, twice a week to St. Thomas and Virgin Gorda; the airport shuttle launch makes several runs a day, depending on arrivals, with fresh supplies of rum punch for each run; you can also charter helicopters form St. Thomas or San Juan direct to the island)
Telephone: 284/495-2000
Fax: 284/495-2500
E-mail: reservations@peterisland.com
Web: www.peterisland.com
Reservations: 800/346-4451 or 770/476-9988, the resort's stateside office or 800/323-7500 Preferred Hotels
Credit Cards: All major cards
Rates: $840–$1,200 FAP (Dec 20–Apr 4); taxes and service charge 17% extra; off-season 30% less
Rooms: 52, including 30 oceanview rooms overlooking Sprat Bay and Sir Francis Drake Channel and 20 beachfront rooms on Deadman's Bay, plus 2 hilltop villas (from $990); all with balconies or patios, air-conditioning and ceiling fans, kingsize beds, hair dryer, bathrobes, minibar, tea/coffeemaker, direct-dial telephones, personal safes; beachfront Junior Suites have Jacuzzi tubs; for 2003–2004, the resort will have two more superluxurious, four-bedroom villas perched on a couple of ridges above the beach
Meals: Breakfast 8–10am, lunch 12:30–3pm, afternoon tea 4pm, dinner 7–9pm in Tradewinds main pavilion, cooled by fans and breezes, or alfresco Deadman's Bay Beach Bar and Grill (about $100, for visitors); proper attire ("cover-ups at lunch, shirt with collar, no open shoes or sandals, shorts are not appropriate after 6pm") required in the dining room after 6pm; complimentary room service breakfast only, 8–10am
Entertainment: Bar/lounge, specialty dinners in the Wine Room, library with large-screen TV and parlor games, live entertainment (amplified, but not too loud — hopefully) during and after dinner for listening and/or dancing
Sports: Freshwater pool, 5 beaches (including isolated coves with transportation and picnic baskets supplied), windsurfing, floats, sailing (catamarans, Lasers, Sunfishes, Hobie Cats), kayaks, snorkeling, tennis (4 Tru-Flex courts, 2 with lights, Peter Burwash pro shop), mountain bikes, fitness center, miles of hiking trails — all free; scuba diving, water-skiing, treatments at new $35-million Solé spa due to open in late 2003, charter boats for fishing and sailing at extra charge; ashore/afloat vacations on the lovely double-ender Silmaril
PS: Some children; cellphones don't work here; closed Sept; open year-round

Guana Island

GUANA ISLAND

☆☆☆☆　　　Y Y　　　　❻❻　　　　$ $ $ $
ATMOSPHERE　　**DINING**　　　**SPORTS**　　　　**RATES**

The hotel boatman meets you at the airport, drives you half a mile or so to the jetty, stows your luggage aboard a 28-foot Bertram, and then casts off for a 10-minute ride to the island — past the eastern tip of Tortola, past Great Camanoe, around the rock formation that gave the island its name, and into White Bay.

There you're greeted by a dazzling sight — glistening water, glistening sand. Instead of the inn being buried among the palm trees, it perches on the hill, in the midday haze, looking for all the world like a hilltop village in the Aegean. As you approach the private dock, a Land Rover winds down the hill to meet you. Step ashore and you're in another world: Even the run-of-the-mill Caribbean seems a long way from here.

Guana Island was built in the 1930s as a private club on the foundations of a Quaker sugar and cotton plantation. The native stone walls are 2 feet thick, with graying whitewash and green shutters. The rustic library and lounge suggest the country home of a well-bred but overdrawn gentleman farmer; the main dining terrace is a trio of tables beneath a ramada and framed by pomegranate and ginger thomas trees, cape honeysuckle, and white frangipani. From the Sunset Terrace, fragrant with jasmine and carpeted with blossoms from the pink trumpet tree, stone paths and steps wind through archways of trees and off into the hillsides. The loudest sound is a kingbird, perched on the highest bough of the highest tree. The views are stunning — hills and coves, slivers of white sand and blue bays, sailboats beating to windward, and vistas of distant islands.

Guana Island is not the sort of place you come to for stylish accommodations and luxurious conveniences (for that, head for Little Dix Bay on Virgin Gorda or The Ritz-Carlton, St. Thomas). Some people, indeed, may find the lodgings here almost monastic, with their classic simplicity — whitewashed stucco walls, rattan-and-wicker furniture, rush rugs, hand-woven bedspreads in pretty patterns, bathrooms with unusual free-form showers. But in their restrained way, these rooms have great refinement — they're little gems of comfort, charm, and romance.

The most romantic of these rooms may be the Barbados Cottage — self-contained, spacious, with a very private balcony overlooking the Atlantic. But I'd happily settle into Fallen Jerusalem, with its mesmerizing views all the way to St. Thomas. Lovers who really want to be alone opt for the North Beach Cottage, a beach house facing the sea on the other side of the island, with its own living room and kitchen, open shaded terraces, and a private sea pool; indoor perks here include a phone, VCR, and CD player. A golf cart gets you to and from the main lodge.

This is a place that either grabs you instantly or leaves you wondering what the fuss is about. It has something of the charm and coziness of the best small inns of New England or Burgundy. Guests mingle on the Sunset Terrace or in the rattan-furnished lounge for cocktails at 7pm; dinner is served by candlelight, everyone gathered around the three tables on the main dining terrace or, by request, at tables for two on nearby tête-à-tête terraces. Dinners have always been something to look forward to on Guana and not just for the jolly, dinner-party ambience. Unspoiled getaway it may be, but the chefs always manage to brighten the evening with sophisticated fare — freshly caught lobster thermidor or seafood curry with mango chutney, beef Wellington or rack of lamb — with convivial wine to match. After dinner the party atmosphere continues in the lounge, where guests reassemble and exchange travel tales over coffee and cognacs. Or, you may prefer to slip into the corner library and browse through the 1933 Encyclopaedia Britannica.

By day, Guana Island is 850 acres of ineffable peace. Since the only way to get here is by boat, the island's seven beaches are virtually private, and two of them are so secluded they are accessible only to waterborne castaways. Indeed, so serene is the entire setting that when you finally hoist yourselves from your loungers on White Bay's 600 feet of white sand and peer across the dappled water, all you see is the lightly settled (but soon to be condo-covered) side of Tortola. The meadow beside the beach is given over to a croquet court and two tennis courts, one Hydrocourt (similar to clay), the other Omni; the Salt Pond in the center of the island is heaven for bird spotters, a preserve for black-necked stilts and red-billed tropics, plovers, blue herons, and a small flock of flamingos.

The island is, in fact, a designated nature preserve and wildlife sanctuary, with its own ongoing program that brings together scientists of various disciplines for learned networking every October. The director of the project, biologist Dr. James Lazell, says, "This island has more species of flora and fauna than any island yet studied in the West Indies and probably in the world." That may be overstating things a little, but it's no exaggeration that people who enjoy a relaxed, soft-spoken, almost genteel atmosphere will love it here.

As we were saying, this is not an everyday Caribbean island.

Name: Guana Island
Manager: Bridgette Roger
Address: Box 32, Road Town, Tortola, British Virgin Islands
Location: A private island northeast of Tortola, 10 min. by taxi and boat ($70 for two, round-trip) from Beef Island Airport
Telephone: 284/494-2354
Fax: 284/495-2900
E-mail: guana@guana.com
Web: www.guana.com

Reservations: 914/967-6050, the resort's stateside office or 800/223-1108, Ralph Locke Islands
Credit Cards: MasterCard, Visa
Rates: $850 FAP (Dec 16–Apr 15); taxes and service charge 17% extra; off-season 25% less; North Beach Cottage $1,500 in winter
Rooms: 15, cooled by breezes and ceiling fans, all with private bathroom and terrace; for total seclusion there's North Beach Cottage, with a bedroom, living room, and kitchen on its own ⅓-mile-long coral beach
Meals: Breakfast 8–10am, lunch 1pm, afternoon tea and cookies 4pm, cocktails 7pm, dinner 8pm (6:45pm for children, if there are any on the island) with a fixed menu (alternatives are available); informal (jackets optional, but sometimes worn in Jan and Feb); no room service; no intrusive music
Entertainment: Library, Scrabble, backgammon, conversation, music only when guests request it
Sports: 7 beaches (2 accessible by boat only), snorkeling cove (gear available free), tennis (2 courts, 1 Hydrocourt, 1 Omni, no lights), croquet, walking trails, 14-ft. Sunfish and Laser sailboats, kayaks, windsurfing — all free; water-skiing, powerboats for rent (fishing gear available), Bertram cruiser for charter; scuba available at extra charge
PS: Check with the inn about rules regarding children as they vary. Posted rule is that "cellphones can only be used out of sight and hearing of other guests"; closed Sept–Oct

Little Dix Bay

VIRGIN GORDA

☆☆☆☆☆	⦿⦿	❻❻❻	$ $ $ $ $
ATMOSPHERE	DINING	SPORTS	RATES

From the beach, all you can see of Little Dix are a few thatched sunshades and the conical cedar-shingled rooftops of the soaring dining pavilion peeking above the palms and casuarina trees. The native stone and hardwood guest cottages, cloaked by seagrape and tamarind trees, are strung out along the beach.

And what a beach! A curvaceous half mile of white powdery sand, sheltered by low headland at both ends and a picturesque reef just offshore. It's the classic beach scene, and Little Dix is among the classiest of resorts.

Like its sister resort, Caneel Bay, Little Dix is now managed by Rosewood Hotels of Dallas (owners of the highly acclaimed Mansion on Turtle Creek in Dallas) and went through a change of lifestyle a few years ago. Now all the rooms have air-conditioning (a no-no during the years when Little Dix was owned by its founder, Laurance Rockefeller), and the trademark walls of louvers have been replaced by a combination of panels of hardwood louvers and glass windows. Interiors have been spruced up with tropical fabrics in sea-echoing shades and floral patterns, wicker and rattan chairs with ottomans, and colorful tiled bathrooms. But the rooms still retain their basic Caribbean flavor, with native stone walls and slowly turning paddle fans.

Most distinctive among the resort's 97 rooms and suites are the 30 beachside hexagonal cottages, 13 of them perched on stilts, with patios, hammocks, tables, and chairs at garden level. Of the others, rooms 121 and 122 at the Cow Hill end of the garden are quietest and have the best views; I also used to recommend rooms 77 to 80 at the Savannah Pond end, but this corner of the property has now been delegated as the likeliest spot for families with children. The resort finally bit the bullet, acknowledged that more of its guests are traveling with kids, and erected a whole new Children's Grove with playrooms and playgrounds, and ringed by walls so that the toddlers are not spilling all over the pathways and tripping up the grown-ups.

Another innovation of the Rosewood regime is a new emphasis on dining. The grand buffets are still there at lunchtime, but in the evening guests have more options — Caribbean/international beneath the four Polynesian pyramids of the Pavilion or Italian/seafood in the old Sugar Mill restaurant. Another innovation, which may or may not please the regulars, is that two of the tennis courts now have lights — another no-no in the Rockefeller days because the glare ruined the magical atmosphere of the softly lighted gardens. But there's still no TV in the rooms: Anyone who must have a daily dose of CNN has to mosey over to the pavilion just off the bar and dining room. The most recent innovation is a full-service spa located on the bluff, a collection of small cottages with patios overlooking the sea, where the treatments are inspired by indigenous botanical sources. You can also opt for massages in the private Spa Suite, in a pavilion by the edge of the sea, or in the intimacy of your room.

Little Dix is still a place for taking life in nice easy doses (with a staff of 325 catering to the whims of just 200 guests, the taking doesn't get much easier). Twenty of those employees are gardeners who fuss over every blossom as if it were a paying guest, and one of the joys of Little Dix is strolling hand in hand along pathways lined with frangipani, oleander, and fragrant Jerusalem thorn.

Name: Little Dix Bay
Manager: Peter Shaindlin
Address: P.O. Box 70, Virgin Gorda, British Virgin Islands
Location: If you are traveling via Tortola/Beef Island, you'll be picked up at the airport, driven to the dock, and put aboard the private launch direct to the resort — a cool, refreshing trip of 15 to 20 min., with tropical drinks on the house to speed you on your way; you can now also board a private launch in St. Thomas, after being greeted at the airport, for a 1-hour trip direct to the resort marina, with the crew offering drinks and processing Customs/immigration and check-in forms en route (the trip is very scenic, since you pass several other Virgins along the way)
Telephone: 284/495-5555
Fax: 284/495-5661

E-mail: littledixbay@rosewoodhotels.com
Web: www.rosewood-hotels.com
Reservations: 800/767-3966, Rosewood reservations
Credit Cards: American Express, Diners Club, MasterCard, Visa
Rates: $450–$1,100 EP (Dec 20–Mar 31); service charge 12%; off-season 45% less
Rooms: 97 double rooms, various combinations of one- and two-story villas, plus two-bedroom cottages, all showers (no bathtubs), all with air-conditioning, stocked refrigerator, wall safe, telephone, balcony or patio, ceiling fans (no radios, no TV); new last year are a two-bedroom and a three-bedroom freestanding villa on the west end of the beach, each with a private pool, garden shower, and lots of privacy behind custom-designed wrought iron gates
Meals: Breakfast 8–10:30am, continental breakfast 7–10am, lunch 12:30–3pm at the Beach House Grill or Pavilion, afternoon tea 4:30pm, dinner 7–9pm (about $90, in the Pavilion, the Sugar Mill, or the Beach House Grill — all breeze-cooled); jackets no longer required after 6pm in the pavilion but men are still expected to wear long trousers, shirts with collars, and closed-toed shoes, and "swimwear, shorts, jeans, and tennis shoes are not permitted after sunset"; room service during dining-room hours, no extra charge
Entertainment: Guitarist, steel band, combo, or dancing 7 nights a week, library, games parlor with big screen TV and VCR; local bars and bands a short taxi ride away
Sports: ½-mile beach, snorkeling gear, small sailboats (and instruction), water-skiing, snorkeling trips, water taxis to adjacent beaches, new fitness center, tennis (7 courts, 2 with lights, pro shop) — all free; spa treatments and day sails on 46-ft. *Spirit of Anegada* ($105 per person, including lunch and open bar) at extra charge; scuba, Jeep safaris can be arranged
PS: Small groups (10–15) for lunch once or twice a week, usually from Little Dix's sister resort, Caneel Bay (a ferry runs between the resorts Mon, Wed, and Fri); children are now welcome and have their own kids' cottage, so well equipped that even their parents may not see much of them; no cell-phones allowed in the dining room or on the beach; open year-round

Biras Creek Resort

VIRGIN GORDA

☆☆☆☆   ⅊⅊⅊   ❻❻❻ $ $ $ $ $
ATMOSPHERE   DINING   SPORTS   RATES

When you first glimpse it, as you barrel across the North Sound, it looks for all the world like a Crusader castle: a circular stone fortress with a peaked roof sitting atop a low hill. But climb the hill and there's no mistaking it for what it is, a one-of-a-kind hideaway for people who want seclusion without giving up too many creature comforts.

The turret-like structure turns out to be the clubhouse, bar, and dining room — three shingled roofs over a framework of heavy hewn beams, opulently furnished with custom-designed rattan chairs and tables, boldly patterned Caribbean fabrics, island ceramics, and a huge tile mural. The guest rooms are over the hill on the bay, tucked among seagrape and almond trees, their backs turned to the Western world. These spacious beachside suites, two to a cottage, were recently redecorated with pricey-looking furniture indoors and out; prettified with bright swirling fabrics and charming appliquéd doodads; and enhanced with coffeemakers, refrigerators stocked with Argentine white wine and Heineken, and private safes (there are no door keys here). The bathrooms abut neat little outdoor shower patios with potted plants and tall walls to hide your hides. Each room comes with a quiet private patio, a great spot for putting your feet up and reading a tome from the clubhouse library. What you really want here is one of the two Grand Suites. They'll set you back $200 or $300 a night so you may want to save this for an anniversary, but they're among the loveliest in the islands — spacious, high-ceilinged, tile-floored living room with springy sofas and armchairs, a bedroom you could waltz around in, both with large shutters opening to Bercher's Bay. But it's the bathrooms that will wow you. They have the signature Biras outdoor shower plus a freestanding claw-footed tub in the middle of the room, a full-length mirror propped against one wall, and louvered French doors that open to bring in the sounds of the rolling surf so that you can whoop and holler your head off in the tub without anyone knowing what you're up to. Not that there are likely to be any other guests in that far-flung corner of the beach.

That's the signature of Biras Creek, a place of solitude and sophisticated simplicity; but since the inn was taken over in 1995 by a new owner, a Dutch businessman (and longtime guest) by the name of Bert Houwer, several minor innovations have appeared. Just down the hill from the clubhouse, a new shingle-roof, open-air pavilion known as the Arawak Room hosts the weekly staff-guest cocktail party and hides inveterate sports buffs who must watch major events on a big-screen TV/DVD. Television still hasn't penetrated the guest rooms, but air-conditioning units have been installed in the bedrooms to complement the ceiling fans and sliding-glass doors in place of the more romantic louvers (apparently lots of guests couldn't sleep with the sound of the surf through the open louvers and needed the soothing sounds of an air conditioner's hum).

In the beginning, the Biras Creek kitchen and wine cellar ranked among the finest in the Caribbean, but in recent years the caliber of the cuisine lost its luster. Now Houwer has a new chef from various Relais & Châteaux inns in England, Neil Hitchen, whose tasty lobster medallions with fresh truffle vinaigrette and grilled veal loin with eggplant caviar are followed by complimentary Port and Stilton from a large wheel (a nice touch!). The lunchtime beach barbecues, 3 days a week over at Deep Bay, are still a great chance for guests to get to know one another over a few glasses of Chardonnay.

The barbecues set you up nicely for a siesta on the beach or your private patio. But on non-barbecue days, what is there to do when you're up this particular creek? Well, there's shell gathering on the long, breeze-swept beach outside your cottage, and there's floating, wallowing, or swimming in the big freshwater pool overlooking Bercher's Bay. Play snooker or billiards in the game room. Take a Boston Whaler out into North Sound and find your own deserted beach (the resort will give you a chart and even a quick lesson on running a Boston Whaler).

Or you might start by wandering off together over miles of nature trails, by foot or by bike. The surrounding acreage — 140 acres all told — is more than just scenery. It's a living, breathing nature preserve created with equal regard for the animals that live there and the people who come to look at them. Trails wind through a desert-like pasture and mangrove swamps so natural you can step right over a 3-foot iguana and it'll never blink. Guests armed with trail maps can keep themselves walking for 12 minutes or an hour and a half, visiting cactus forests and stands of turpentine trees (locally dubbed "tourist trees" because they're tall, bright red, and peeling).

And then there's just winding down and savoring the cherished solitude of a Relais & Châteaux hideaway in the Caribbean.

Name: Biras Creek Resort
Managers: Michael and Luciana Nijdam
Address: P.O. Box 54, Virgin Gorda, British Virgin Islands
Location: On North Sound, accessible only by boat — 30 min. aboard the private 39-ft. Bradley, *Princess II*, which is included in the rate
Telephone: 284/494-3555
Fax: 284/494-3557
E-mail: biras@biras.com
Web: www.biras.com
Reservations: 800/223-1108, Ralph Locke Islands
Credit Cards: American Express, MasterCard, Visa
Rates: $750–$1,050 FAP (Dec 17–Apr 1); tax and service charge 17%; off-season 30% less
Rooms: 33, all suites, all but 9 directly on the bay, all with air-conditioning and ceiling fans, stocked refrigerator, coffeemaker, "garden" shower, telephone, CD players in suites, hair dryer, bathrobes
Meals: Breakfast 8–10am, lunch 12:30–2pm, dinner 7:30–9pm (about $120 for nonguests), all in the hilltop pavilion except for beachside barbecue lunches 3 days a week; slacks and "shirts with collars" (but not jackets) required after 6pm; no room service; live music 3 times a week, "quiet during dinner, louder later"
Entertainment: Mostly yourselves, except for the live music and board games, unless you want a boatman to take you around the headland to the bars at Bitter End or Saba Rock

Sports: 2 virtually private sandy beaches, freshwater pool, tennis (2 courts, with lights), windsurfing, snorkeling gear, 26-ft. sailboats, Hobie Cats, motorized dinghies, hiking trails, garden walks, bicycles, watersports instruction — all free; scuba diving, water-skiing, deep-sea fishing, and sailing trips can be arranged at extra charge

PS: No children under school age, but otherwise families are welcome; a popular option here is the Sailaway Package combining a few days ashore, a few days aboard the resort's 44-ft. sloop; open year-round

The Bitter End Yacht Club

VIRGIN GORDA

☆ ☆ ☆   Υ Υ   ❻ ❻ ❻ $ $ $
ATMOSPHERE   DINING   SPORTS   RATES

The first thing you discover about this wonderfully windblown little place is how apt its name is. To get there involves two, maybe three flights, followed by a powerboat ride almost straight to your doorstep.

Well, getting to heaven isn't easy, either.

As for Bitter End, it's worth the trip. How often, after all, do you have a chance to spend your days and nights on land or sea — or both?

Choose sea and you get your own seagoing sailboat — a floating suite, fully equipped and provisioned even if you never leave your mooring. It's a Freedom 30 sloop, easy to handle on voyages to Peter Island and Norman, Treasure, and other nearby cays. Yet whenever you come back, all the landlubber conveniences of the hotel are waiting for you, from hot showers to waiters to live music, movies, and camaraderie.

Choose land and you get plenty of options: beachside or hillside room or a North Sound suite in a "chalet" fashioned from fir and topped with an Antillean-style red roof. Some cottages stand on stilts a few paces from the shore, and others are cantilevered from the boulders and have undisturbed views of sails and islets; the chalet suites (known as Commodore Club Suites) are two to a cottage on a hillside dotted with prickly pear and mother-in-law cactus. Ceiling fans cool the interiors (the North Sound suites also have air-conditioning); acres of sliding-glass doors open, in some cases, to semiprivate sun decks with hammocks; and the furnishings are comfortable rattan and wicker, decorated with colorful serapes and batiks.

Now, what happens if you can't decide between a sea or land vacation? You still get your days afloat because you have at your disposal an entire fleet of sailing craft — all day, every day, and at no extra charge. To Bitter End's credit, when they list sea kayaks as an attraction, they don't mean just a couple of them — they mean four singles and four doubles. When they say they offer sports boats and catamarans, they mean top-of-the-liners like Bradley 22 self-drive powerboats and 30-ft. Freedom 30s. You actually have more than 100 craft to choose from.

Although there are lodgings here for only 170 land-billeted guests, Bitter End is on nearly every seasoned sailor's Caribbean itinerary, which means that it's hardly ever a deserted little backwater (actually, at times it can be almost raucous), even in summer. The sea-breezy Clubhouse dining pavilion flutters with hundreds of burgees left behind by the constant tide of salty visitors. Actually, the decor in this pavilion gives you a major clue to Bitter End's success. In its present form, the resort was created by a Chicago steel tycoon, the late Myron Hokin, who sailed in here with his kids and grandkids many moons ago aboard a chartered ketch; because his family liked the place so much, he bought it. It was much more primitive then, powered by an erratic generator, so Hokin moved in some of the bric-a-brac he'd collected in years of sailing. Hence, the dining pavilion is draped with Grandma's decorative glass-and-bamboo lamps from Bali, Dad's stuffed tarpon and sailfish, and weathered bottles salvaged from wrecks by Grandpa. A few years back, the patriarch toyed with the idea of selling the place, but the family stepped in and said no way. Now Bitter End is cherished and coddled by three generations of the family, and chances are that during your stay you'll be served a drink by Rolita, who's been a waitress here for 24 years.

If you don't consider yourselves to be a waterborne family like the Hokins, don't let that keep you away from Bitter End. Come down and take lessons at the Nick Trotter Sailing School, whose instructors are there for anyone who has never so much as hoisted a jib, as well as for old salts who want to learn new tricks at the starting line. Once you've worked your way up from Sunfish to Freedom 30, come back for one of the frequent sailing weeks, especially the Pro-Am Regatta in early November, when you might find yourself crewing for an Olympic helmsman.

Even the scuba diving ranges from the simple to the serious. There's great coral-hopping just about anywhere you stick your mask in the water. Deeper down, Horseshoe Reef is littered with the skeletons of doomed galleons. The resort will set up instruction, trips, and dives (one of the few things you have to pay for, so you might want to consider one of the resort's Dive Adventure Packages).

And don't worry about missing anything when you're underwater. When you go back to The Clubhouse or The English Pub, sea dogs from around the world will still be sitting around nursing their grog, swapping salty tales, and tucking into the hearty meals prepared by a crackerjack team of chefs.

Name: The Bitter End Yacht Club
Manager: Mary Jo Ryan
Address: P.O. Box 46, Virgin Gorda, British Virgin Islands
Location: At John O'Point, at the east end of North Sound; fly to Tortola (Beef Island Airport), where a taxi will take you to the jetty to board the North Sound Express — powerboats with two 225-horsepower engines that carry up to 36 passengers and get you to the resort in about 30 min. ($20 one-way, although the fee is included in some of the resort's packages)

Telephone: 284/494-2745
Fax: 284/494-4756
E-mail: None
Web: www.beyc.com
Reservations: 800/872-2392, toll-free direct
Credit Cards: All major cards
Rates: $585–$1,850 MAP (Dec 20–Apr 30); taxes and service charge 18% extra; off-season 20% less
Rooms: 85, in a variety of villas and bungalows dotting the hillside on both sides of the dock; each with private bathroom, tiled shower, telephone, refrigerator (unstocked, but there's a commissary at the dock), balcony/deck, ceiling fans (air-conditioning in the North Sound suites); also, a two-bedroom Estate House with kitchen and spectacular views
Meals: Breakfast 8–10am, lunch 12:30–2pm, dinner 6:30–9pm in the Clubhouse Steak & Seafood Grille, the English Carvery, the English Pub, indoors and outdoors, ($60–$80); casual dress; no room service; some live music or tapes
Entertainment: Sunday Regatta Party, manager's welcome party Mon, live music 3 nights a week, movies or TV every evening in the alfresco Sand Palace
Sports: 3 beaches (none of them terrific, but adequate), freshwater pool, hiking trails, fitness course, snorkeling gear, windsurfing, windsurfing clinics, sailboats (Sunfishes, Lasers, Rhodes 19s, J24s, Vanguard 15s, Optimus, etc.), boat trips on 56-ft. power catamaran *Corinthian* or the 48-ft. catamaran *Paranda* (lunch included), skiffs with outboard motors, rowing sculls, sea kayaks, introductory sailing lessons — all free; windsurfing instruction, Freedom 30 sloops, Bradley 22 powerboats, private sailing lessons, and scuba diving with the famed Kilbride team at extra charge
PS: Although there are several special events for kids throughout the year, the resort is never overrun with children; no guidelines regarding cellphones — "they haven't been a problem"; open year-round

OTHER CHOICES

Anegada Reef Hotel

ANEGADA

Anegada is the last little speck of the British Virgin Islands before you hit open ocean and, days later, Africa. A small Clair Aero plane flies in several times a week, but the thrill-a-minute way to get there is by boat — if you can find a skipper foolhardy or skilled enough to get you there. The island is really the top of a reef surrounded by more reef, and since its highest point is the tallest palm tree, boats are practically on top of the reef before they know the island is there. Hence all the bits of mast and hull popping up from the water — it's said that 200 galleons, caravels, and luxury yachts have gone down on these reefs in the past 300 years. Obviously, then, it's not an over-crowded island, which means that Lowell Wheatley's Anegada Reef Hotel is a far cry from San Juan.

The hotel's 20 rooms are simply furnished with wicker and rattan, newly refurbished with sand-drift-colored walls and bright tropical fabrics. There are no phones, no TV, and you'll have to read your thrillers by the light of 60-watt lamps; but the rooms do have coffeemakers, tiled tubs/showers, and air-conditioning to augment the ceiling fans. Half the rooms face a garden at the rear; the others face the marina up front. There's a small beach beyond the thatched sunshades, but if you walk or drive a short distance, you come to glorious sand. The attractions of such an authentically Caribbean location are beguiling: There are dining tables by the water's edge and beneath the stars with music for dancing. The lobster is brought in fresh from the boats tied up outside your window, and everyone who comes ashore in the pleasure craft sidles up to the bar and sits around sipping tall drinks and swapping tall tales while they wait for their lobsters to be cooked — right there on the beach, on a steel drum over charcoal with a secret barbecue sauce. There's a small surcharge for the lobster, but otherwise all meals come with the low room rates — enough of a bargain to justify venturing through the coral heads and wrecks to get there. 20 rooms. Doubles: $250–$275 with all meals, winter 2002–03. *Anegada Reef Hotel, Setting Point, Anegada, British Virgin Islands. Telephone: 284/495-8002; fax: 284/495-9362; e-mail: info@anegadareef.com; Web: www.anegadareef.com.*

Sandcastle Hotel

JOST VAN DYKE

Jost Van Dyke is the island off the northwest corner of Tortola — a Robinson Crusoe place with no airstrip, few inhabitants, and a few restaurants that cater mostly to people stepping ashore from charter yachts. Dinner at Sandcastle is by candlelight, and water is heated, if at all, by the noonday sun. Which is, for many escapists, what the Caribbean is all about. Sandcastle is right on the beach (a beauty, shared with a couple of private homes that lie empty much of the time, a campground, and some low-key beach bars). There's no dock. You just roll up your trousers or skirt and wade through the surf to get here, after a choppy ride by water taxi or ferry from West End in Tortola. Activities revolve around the breezy beach bar and the watersports — windsurfing, Sunfish sailing, kayaking, snorkeling, rafting. But most of the time guests just seem to lounge around in hammocks, wearing to dinner what they wore to breakfast. Menus feature sandwiches at lunch, Continental fare at dinner. Six rooms in four *rondavel* (thatched) cottages. Doubles: $140–$250, winter 2002–03. *Sandcastle, White Bay, Jost Van Dyke, British Virgin Islands. Mailing address: 6501 Red Hook Plaza, Suite 201, St. Thomas, U.S. Virgin Islands 00802-1306. Telephone: 284/495-9888; fax: 284/495-9999; e-mail: relax@sandcastle-bvi.com; Web: http://sandcastle-bvi.com.*

Frenchman's Cay Resort Hotel

TORTOLA

The cay in question is located at the west end of Tortola, linked to its south shore by a narrow bridge and jutting into the sea so that guests may enjoy ravishing views of sea and islets and the Sir Francis Drake Channel. The villas rest on the rise above the coral-fringed sea, each with a kitchen, dining room, sitting room, attractive, if undistinguished, island furniture, ceiling fan, and balcony for sea gazing. The 12 acres of relaxing garden incorporate an Omniturf tennis court, six hammocks beneath a cluster of seagrape trees, a sea pool, a headland for snorkeling, a swimming pool, and an octagonal pavilion that houses the reception area, the bar, the Clubhouse Restaurant, and something like 700 paperbacks. What more could you want for a relaxing vacation? How about kayaks, Sunfish sailboats, and windsurfers, available for rent? 9 one- and two-bedroom villas. Doubles: $247–$470, winter 2002–03. *Frenchman's Cay Resort Hotel, P.O. Box 1054, West End, Tortola, British Virgin Islands. Telephone: 284/495-4844 or 800/235-4077 (for reservations only); fax: 284/ 495-4056; e-mail: fmchotel@surfbvi.com; Web: www.frenchmans.com.*

The Dutch Windwards

The Dutch West India Company

that sent Henry Hudson scouting around the northeast coast of America also sent its ships and captains to the Caribbean; and Peter "Pegleg" Stuyvesant, the hobbling Hollander who became governor of New York City, tried to dislodge the Spanish from St. Maarten only to have the Spanish dislodge his leg. What 21st-century lovers will find in this corner of the Dutch Caribbean is a trio of islands — two of them totally unspoiled and serene (Saba and St. Eustatius), and one (St. Maarten/St. Martin) that offers only pockets of serenity since it tries to be a valid alternative to

San Juan and the U.S. Virgins for vacationers who want hamburgers, casinos, and lively, varied nightlife.

Saba is the phantom silhouette you see on the horizon when you're sitting on the waterfront in St. Maarten. It's really the tip of a volcanic cone, a straight-up-and-down island with one roadway and a thousand inhabitants, completely unlike any other island in the Caribbean (for a start, it doesn't have a beach). What it does have is a haunting, tranquil, otherworldly charm; it's strictly for lovers who are content to be on their own (or, in recent years, for scuba divers who crave a change of aqueous scenery).

Likewise for St. Eustatius (or Statia, as it is sometimes called), except that you'll find beaches (sort of) here. Statia should be popular with Americans for historic reasons: The Dutch garrison of Fort Oranje fired the first salute to the brand-new American flag during the War of Independence. For its pains, the island was zapped by England's Admiral Rodney, and Oranjestad, once the busiest harbor in the Indies, is now a half-submerged ghost town — but a treasure trove for snorkelers and scuba divers.

Because the Dutch ended up splitting the island with the French, St. Maarten is also St. Martin. When you go from one side to the other (there's no frontier, no Customs), you're going from France to Holland — literally, because the French side is part of the Republic of France and the Dutch side is part of the Kingdom of the Netherlands. Between them, they offer you something like three dozen white, soft, powdery beaches; duty-free shopping; nightlife; scores of interesting restaurants; and more construction and concrete trucks than you probably want to encounter on your vacation.

HOW TO GET THERE   Try American, Continental, Delta, and US Airways from various points in the U.S. — but this is a fluid situation because some of the carriers have just "discovered" the island or may be flying only on weekends or during peak season.

Many of these flights arrive and depart within a short time of one another, and the nondescript airport can't always cope efficiently — although you're expected to fork over a departure tax of a whopping $20. On your return flight, pay a $20 per person fee and you can use the airport's new VIP retreat, Soualiga Lounge.

Windward Airways (sometimes known as Winair) flies several times a day to Saba and St. Eustatius, each about 20 minutes away, unless you stop off at one or the other on the way. Landing in Saba is an experience in itself that's probably worth the $120 round-trip ticket ($66 for midweek day trips): The only way the Sabans could find a flat surface for the runway was to chop off the top of a hillock beside the sea, so touchdown here is like landing on an aircraft carrier (World War II vintage at that). But it's no problem for such advanced STOL planes as Windward's Twin Otters (which also, by the way, have picture windows to let you see where you're going — and how you're getting there). You can also get to Saba two or three times a week by boat from St. Maarten — for times, check with your travel agent.

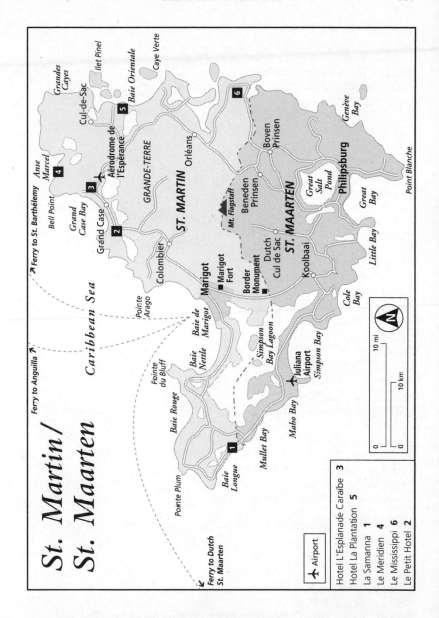

St. Martin/
St. Maarten

Caribbean Sea

Grandes
Cayes

Cul-de-Sac

Ilet Pinel

Baie Orientale

Caye Verte

Anse
Marcel

Ferry to St. Barthélemy

Bell Point

Aérodrome de
l'Espérance

GRANDE-TERRE

Grand
Case Bay

Grand Case

Colombier

Pointe
Arago

Baie de
Marigot

Ferry to Anguilla

Pointe
du Bluff

Baie
Nettle

Baie Rouge

Pointe Plum

Baie
Longue

Muller Bay

Maho Bay

Simpson
Bay Lagoon

Juliana
Airport

Simpson Bay

ST. MARTIN

Orléans

Mt. Flagstaff

Beneden
Prinsen

Boven
Prinsen

Marigot

Marigot
Fort

Border
Monument

Dutch
Cul de Sac

ST. MAARTEN

Koolbaai

Cole
Bay

Great
Salt
Pond

Phillipsburg

Great
Bay

Little Bay

Genève
Bay

Point Blanche

Ferry to Dutch
St. Maarten

✈ Airport

10 mi

10 km

N

Hotel L'Esplanade Caraïbe **3**
Hotel La Plantation **5**
La Samanna **1**
Le Meridien **4**
Le Mississippi **6**
Le Petit Hotel **2**

For information on St. Maarten, call 800/786-2278 or visit
www.st-maarten.com; St. Martin, 877/956-1234 or www.st-martin.org;
Saba, 011/599-416-2231 or www.sabatourism.com;
St. Eustatius, 011/599-318-2433 or www.statiatourism.com.

La Samanna

ST. MARTIN

☆☆☆☆☆	♈♈♈♈	➏➏➏	$ $ $ $ $
ATMOSPHERE	DINING	SPORTS	RATES

Step from the patio of your suite and you're right on the beach, surrounded by seagrape trees, just 20 paces from the sea. You couldn't find a more pristine beach-filled location.

Or skip the beach altogether, climb the stucco steps beside your thatched veranda, and head for your own little rooftop sun deck. It's totally secluded up there. Only the frigate birds could be shocked at the goings-on, and they're too busy diving for dinner.

Yet your lodgings are among the swankiest in the Caribbean, and just a few paces away, along paths that wind through hibiscus, bougainvillea, and allamanda, you can sit down in style at one of the most sophisticated restaurants in the Caribbean.

I can remember, in fact, the days when there was nothing on this beach. A couple of sun worshippers could have the entire place to themselves, and I was miffed when I learned that a guy, some New York industrialist called James Frankel, was about to build a resort on "my" beach. As it turned out, this James Frankel was a man of refined taste and substantial resources with, we came to learn later, a romantic streak. So he and his architect came up with a Mediterranean-Casablancan mélange of whitewashed stucco with graceful domes and inviting arches, a series of villas with bright-blue doors and window trim strung out along the beach among the casuarinas and seagrapes, with a two-story main lodge crowning the bluff at one end. Terraces lead down to a large blue-tiled pool, surrounded by colorful blossoms and greenery — the bar is topped by a multicolored Indian wedding tent — and St. Martin disappears, shut off from the resort by 55 acres of grounds.

A few years ago, I had a coffee with Frankel and asked him, as a much-traveled cosmopolitan, to describe his favorite hotel. He waved his arm around to embrace his beloved La Samanna and said, "This place, but without the guests." There were times, for sure, when the service could be offhand and irritating for people who weren't insiders like Richard Nixon, Jackie Kennedy, and Billy Graham, but I always admired Frankel and loved the resort.

So, like many other La Samanna fans, I've been on tenterhooks over the past few years since ownership passed to Orient Express Hotels, the people who own the Cipriani in Venice and the Windsor Court in New Orleans, among others. Well, here's what happened: Orient Express has tacked an extra floor onto the main building and filled it with a king-of-the-hill presidential suite (three rooms, which can be rented in toto or separately, furnished with vaguely Oriental-French-Colonial artifacts), reconfigured some suites to make them more spacious and more luxurious, modernized the bathrooms and restyled the windows in the beachside suites, redesigned the swimming pool (gone are the ravishingly blue tiles to make way for an infinity rim), added a beach/bar bistro (a welcome addition and very pleasant), installed TV sets that pop up at the press of a button from custom-made bamboo cabinets placed at the foot of the beds, and added a small but plush Phytomer spa with a Thalatherm Dome for hotel guests only. They've also spent a king's ransom on the gardens, from the royal palms and red ixora that line the driveway, to the jasmine and ylang-ylang that scent the evening air, to the bromeliads and orchids that lend their colorful accents to the lobby and lounge. Orient Express has also acquired 45 extra acres and plans to add a wing of "executive suites" out on the bluff, and a 50-seat boardroom-style meeting complex.

Old-timers might have qualms about all this activity, but anyone lucky enough to visit La Samanna for the first time will think, Wow! This is it! This is what life is all about! It's still an exceptional getaway and in some ways an improved one: The beach bar saves drowsy sun worshipers the long trek back to the terrace for a bite to eat; the staff is sharper and more cordial. Making life easy for guests is what it's all about in a place like this: They keep rental cars on the property — small Mercedes sedans at that — but for security reasons they can no longer have you checked in in advance at the airport (instead, they recommend that you buy a $20 pass to the airport's air-conditioned VIP lounge). And then there's La Samanna's much-lauded restaurant. It's still the epitome of stylish alfresco dining, with a romantic terrace shaded by a thatched ramada, on the bluff overlooking the full sweep of Baie Longue. The new executive chef, Erwan Louaisil (from the Tour d'Argent in Paris and the Louis XV in Monaco), matches his Parisian peers sauce for sauce and seems to have a generous budget for flying in the finest fresh fish and produce from Paris for masterpieces like *filet de canard roti et sa cuisse confit au jus, accompagnes d'un petit bouquet amer au croustillant de pain d'epice, jus au poivre doux de Jamaique* (duck breast and confit leg braised in its own juice and served with crispy spice bread and Jamaican sweet pepper sauce). Although some intangible thing may have been lost in the transfer from owner-visionary to corporate committees (as one Frankel admirer puts it, "The sexiness is gone"), La Samanna is still a place of magic.

Name: La Samanna
Manager: John P. Volponi
Address: P.O. Box 4077, 97064 St. Martin Cedex, French West Indies
Location: On Baie Longue, 10 min. from Juliana Airport, $20 by taxi (you can also ask the hotel to send a car, which you'll pay for, of course)
Telephone: 590 590/87-64-00
Fax: 590 590/87-87-86
E-mail: reservations@lasamanna.com
Web: www.orient-expresshotels.com
Reservations: 800/854-2252 or 212/575-7030, the resort's New York office
Credit Cards: All major cards
Rates: $765–$1,690 CP (Jan 3–Apr 27); tax 5% extra, service charge included; off-season up to 40% less

Rooms: 81 rooms and suites, all oceanfront, all with veranda or patio, air-conditioning and ceiling fans, direct-dial telephones, TV/VCR, stocked refrigerator, hair dryer, bathrobes; some with rooftop sun deck

Meals: Buffet breakfast 7–11am, lunch 12:30–2:30pm, dinner 7–10:30pm (about $100–$120), in the main restaurant; casual but stylish dress ("long pants and collared shirts for men, and dress, skirts, or pants for the ladies"); 24-hr. room service at extra charge

Entertainment: Bar, local bands poolside on weekends, piano in lobby-lounge, game room, small library, video library with 100 Academy Award winners; the resort also keeps its own fleet of Mercedes rental cars on the property (guests elsewhere usually have to trot back to the airport or into town to pick up their cars)

Sports: Mile-long beach, infinity lap pool, tennis (3 courts, with lights, tennis pro), 7-station fitness pavilion with AAFA-certified trainer, snorkeling gear, windsurfing, water-skiing, kayaks — all free; scuba diving (on property) and sunset cruise on powerboat at extra charge; horseback riding, sailing, fishing, scuba diving, golf nearby (the course is currently in a scruffy state)

PS: Some children during holidays; "cellphones don't work in this secluded location"; closed Sept–Oct

Le Meridien

ST. MARTIN

☆☆☆	ΥΥ	❻❻❻❻	$ $ $ $
ATMOSPHERE	DINING	SPORTS	RATES

The full name is Le Meridien L'Habitation and Le Meridien Le Domaine. Too many words for a title — especially for a pair of hotels that are not really that exceptional.

What they do have going for them is a relatively secluded setting on an island that's getting to be uncomfortably congested: an impressive sweep of sand about half a mile long surrounded by sheltering hills. This is a perfect spot for a 300-room, two-story hotel like L'Habitation, even with a marina attached; but it's getting to be a bit crowded now that it has a neighbor right next door, another 120 rooms in Le Domaine. Each hotel has a different owner, although they're both managed by the French chain Meridien; the front desk for both is the lobby of L'Habitation, a sunny two-story space with white marble floors, white walls, and tasteful displays of colorful island doodads.

Still, if you want to be on St. Martin, if you want comfortable lodgings, and if you want good food and lots of activities, the Meridien hotels have much to commend them. The plantings at both locations are flourishing, so you no longer feel as if you're looking directly into the rooms across the garden (ask for a room facing the central garden — the "rear" rooms are dreary), and L'Habitation has been rejuvenated by the Meridien people with bold colors and sunny fabrics (although the rooms still lack individuality).

On the other hand, no one can say that the rooms at the new Le Domaine lack individuality, just a touch of common sense. The designer has managed to avoid the tyranny of four square walls, and the bathtubs are tucked into a corner of the room with a surrounding curtain for the modest bather; but the closets are back at the entrance, so you'd better plan ahead or you may be tracking bathwater all over the white ceramic-tile floor. Utilities like TVs and minibars are neatly tucked into a corner cupboard, the sheets are by Porthault, and the decor is pleasant enough with antiqued furniture and papier-mâché bananas and fish. The suites on the upper levels have the same eccentric arrangement of tubs, large balconies, and sitting areas with a sofa your back will probably resent after a very short time. Again, all ingeniously designed, but not very practical.

Some positive notes: The owners of Le Domaine spent $1 million on landscaping, with pretty paths and globe lamps to lead you back to the lobby, and the gardens were beautiful even before the hotel opened. Meridien's signature restaurant, La Belle France, is physically attractive, the service is attentive and pleasant, and the food is above par for an island hotel. La Domaine's La Veranda restaurant, also in plantation style, is also physically attractive, but the service is variable and the food so-so. The music in the pool bar is far too loud, even if it does end at 11pm, and I don't appreciate a maid arriving on my doorstep at 8:30am on departure day insisting on checking a minibar that was never stocked in the first place.

Name: Le Meridien
Manager: Didier Martin
Address: BP 581, Anse Marcel, 97056 St. Martin Cedex, French West Indies
Location: At Marcel Bay, on the northern shore, about 30 min. and $35 by taxi from Juliana Airport, 15 min. and $28 by taxi from Marigot (with shuttle bus to Marigot several times daily)
Telephone: 590 590/87-67-00
Fax: 590 590/87-30-38
E-mail: resasxm@powerantilles.com
Web: www.lemeridien.com
Reservations: 800/543-4300, Meridien Hotels
Credit Cards: All major cards
Rates: $350–$1,400 EP (Dec 21–Mar 27); service charge included; off-season 30% less
Rooms: 396 in all, including 50 one-bedroom Marina Suites, all with balconies or lanais, marble bathrooms, satellite TV, stocked minibars or refrigerators, direct-dial telephones, bathrobes; Marina Suites have complete kitchens
Meals: Breakfast 7–10:30am, lunch noon–4pm, dinner 7–10:30pm ($64–$120) in 1 of 3 indoor/outdoor restaurants, plus a cafe at the marina and another restaurant in the hilltop sports complex; informal dress; live music

(guitar, piano) in the main restaurant; full room service during dining-room hours at extra charge

Entertainment: Live music every evening somewhere on the property, complimentary shuttle bus to casinos on Dutch side (at 9:30pm)

Sports: Lovely sheltered beach, 2 freshwater pools, Jacuzzi, paddleboats, kayaks, floats, snorkeling gear, archery, minigolf, jogging trail, gymnasium, tennis (6 courts, with lights, pro shop, shuttle bus to courts) — all free, except for use of lights on tennis courts; water-skiing, parasailing, WaveRunners, motorboats, horseback riding, squash, and racquetball at extra charge

PS: Some business groups, lots of children at holidays (but they have their own club); cellphones don't function in this location; closed Sept

Le Mississippi

ST. MARTIN

☆☆	Y	❻	$ $ $ $
ATMOSPHERE	DINING	SPORTS	RATES

To get there, you have to drive all the way over to the other end of the island on a road engineered on the same basic principles as a roller coaster. The final lurch brings you to the crest of a hill and your first heart-stopping glimpse of the eponymous bay — a circular lagoon and a narrow, rocky inlet (now surrounded by small hotels) and St. Barthélemy off in the distance.

By day, you lounge; in the evening, you feast.

The beach is just down the road, but the 8-year-old Mississippi is one of those non-beachside places where you rarely roam far from your private deck, reading or snoozing or smooching, occasionally immersing yourselves in your private whirlpool for two. When the sun goes down, slip into slacks and walk the hundred or so paces to one of the most refined little restaurants on the island.

Your cottage here is fashioned from Guayana redwood, a romantically designed hexagon with walls and doors of louvers, subdivided into a living room, a bedroom dominated by a romping-size bed topped by Cleopatra-style netting, and a bathroom that's almost entirely a shower stall prettily decked out with colorful tiles from Provence.

There are just six of these hexagons. The remaining 13 suites are in two-story villas in a vaguely Colonial Plantation style (remember, Louisiana and those Mississippi delta parts were once a French colony). They're attractive in their more traditional way, with marble bathroom (some with two bathrooms), kitchenettes, rattan furniture, Designer Guild fabrics, lots of louvers, and large hardwood decks. Double entry-doors, one solid, one with louvers, let you decide whether you want air-conditioning or flow-through breezes. Suites on the second floor have high ceilings and extra "loft" bedrooms, with vistas of Oyster Pond marina and resorts in one direction and the Caribbean in another (beyond an abandoned and unkempt resort that slightly mars the view).

Now, the feasting part. The hotel's Restaurant Mahogany is basically another of those hexagons, with louvered walls opening to the lap pool, communal Jacuzzi, and tropical shrubbery. It's quite modest, but it serves ambitious dishes — grilled mahimahi with warm olive-oil vinaigrette or rosette of Peking duck with lavender honey — in a very relaxed, low-key setting.

Then, feeling well fed and content with the world after a bottle of Saint-Veran, you retrace those 100 paces back to your deck, shed your resort togs, and dawdle with a moonlight dip in your whirlpool.

Name: Le Mississippi
Manager: Claudie Vial
Address: Oyster Pond, 97150 St. Martin, French West Indies
Location: On the eastern coast, almost right on the border between the French and Dutch sides, 30–45 min. and a $35 cab ride from the airport
Telephone: 590 590/87-33-81
Fax: 590 590/87-31-52
E-mail: contact@lemississippi.com
Web: www.lemississippi.com
Reservations: Direct
Credit Cards: American Express, MasterCard, Visa
Rates: $198–$308 including breakfast and service charge (Dec 16–Mar 30); local tax $3 per person a day extra; off-season 45% less
Rooms: 13 in 3 two-story villas, 6 in individual cottages, all with air-conditioning and ceiling fans, TV/VCR, JVC CD players, minibars or refrigerators, hair dryers, personal safes, bathrobes, Hermès toiletries, terraces; cottages have whirlpools, suites have microwaves and Jacuzzi bathtubs
Meals: Breakfast 7:30–10am, lunch noon–2pm, dinner 7–9:30pm in the Restaurant Mahogany ($120); room service for breakfast only at no extra charge; no shorts in the evening; quiet recorded music, mostly jazz
Entertainment: Piano player (occasionally); plenty of bars and clubs nearby in Oyster Pond
Sports: Lap pool with whirlpool; complimentary shuttle to nearby beaches and watersports
PS: Few children; open year-round

Hotel La Plantation

ST. MARTIN

☆ ☆	⅄	✪	$
ATMOSPHERE	DINING	SPORTS	RATES

The setting used to be beguiling (the famed Orient Bay, with its variety of beachside eateries serving everything from tapas to hamburgers to grilled lobster, is just down the hill and across the street), but the government has allowed way too much building between Le Plantation and the beach, with the result that the beach can be a zoo, except on late afternoons, midweek. The inn itself, though, has many attractions worth noting — such as attractive Colonial-style architecture with verandas, spacious rooms with raftered ceilings, chunky but comfy rattan furniture, hand-stenciled decorations in jaunty pastel colors on furniture and walls. Each room comes with air-conditioning, direct-dial phones, satellite TV, kitchenette, and a personal safe — and other features you might not expect in a hotel with rates beginning at under $200 in winter.

The 7-plus acres of tropical gardens are well tended, the staff is cordial and helpful, and language is no problem, since manager Julia Peacock hails from Scotland. A small fitness center lurks in the basement, and a swimming pool edges up to a pleasant dining terrace and pavilion. What more could you want? Well, the beach and the recreational scene.

Walk the 100 or so yards to Orient Bay and you'll find more watersports than you can squeeze into a week, including trips to offshore islands. Orient Bay is, it should be noted, a naturists' beach, and if you find it unsettling to nibble lobster with all those fleshy distractions, take a short taxi ride to Grand Case and another collection of charming (but pricier) dining spots. Remember, though, there's also that moderately priced (and quieter) restaurant beside the pool in a relaxing garden back at La Plantation.

Name: Hotel La Plantation

Manager: Julia Peacock

Address: Orient Bay, 97150 St. Martin, French West Indies

Location: About 30 min. and $45 by taxi from Queen Juliana Airport (let the hotel know when you're arriving and they'll arrange for a trusty driver to meet you)

Telephone: 590 590/29-58-00

Fax: 590 590/29-58-08

E-mail: hotel@la-plantation.com

Web: www.la-plantation.com

Reservations: Direct

Credit Cards: American Express, MasterCard, Visa

Rates: $180–$305 CP (Jan 4–Apr 11); tax 5% extra, service charge included; off-season 10% less

Rooms: 52 studios and suites in villas consisting of 2 studios and 1 suite, air-conditioning and fans, mosquito netting, direct-dial phones (with free AT&T access), safe, and TV; studios have kitchenettes, suites have full American-style kitchens

Meals: Breakfast 8–10am, lunch noon–2:30pm, dinner 7–10pm in the garden terrace, Café Plantation ($30–$40); informal dress; room service breakfast only; guests also have charge privileges at 5 restaurants right on the beach — Coco, Bikini, Waikiki, Kintiki, and Kakao

Entertainment: Going out to dinner on the beach or in Grand Case

Sports: Freshwater pool, gym at the hotel; miles of sand and oodles of watersports at Orient Bay (the hotel will drop you off in a minibus and collect at the appointed hour); horseback riding nearby

PS: Not many children

Saba

ATLANTIC OCEAN

0 — 1 mi
0 — 1 km

✈ Airport
▲ Mountain

SABA MARINE PARK

Torrens Bay

Diamond Rock Island

Well's Bay

○ Hell's Gate

Cove Bay

Sandy Cruz Walk

▲ Mt. Scenery

The Gap

1

▲ Big Rendezvous

2

Windwardside

3

The Bottom

St. John's

Tent Point

Booby Hill

○ Fort Hill

Fort Bay

SABA MARINE PARK

Caribbean Sea

The Cottage Club **2**
Queen's Garden Resort **1**
Willard's of Saba **3**

Willard's of Saba

SABA

☆☆☆ **ATMOSPHERE**　　Y Y **DINING**　　🌐 **SPORTS**　　$ $ $ **RATES**

To find the highest hotel in the Kingdom of the Netherlands, take a Winair Twin Otter on the 20-minute flight from St. Maarten to Saba. The tiny Dutch island of Saba (all of 5 sq. miles) is that green volcanic peak leaping abruptly from the sea, straight up to 2,855 feet, its precipitous slopes dotted with tiny white cottages with red corrugated roofs. There's one main road — up one side, down the other — plus 1,064 concrete steps up through the ferns and mango trees to the peak of Mount Scenery. Scuba divers come here for dramatic, uncrowded underwater trips, but regular visitors have been vacationing here for years for total seclusion, tranquility, and a chance to catch up on their reading and thinking.

Willard's of Saba doesn't just happen to have the same name as the Washington, D.C., landmark — it was built by a great-grandson of Henry

August Willard, who put his name on what was then the capital's top lodgings (and, in the process, gave us the word "lobbying"). This property comes
on a much smaller scale, of course — no more than 14 guests at a time — but
it has a more dramatic setting, 2,000 feet up (hence "the highest in the
Kingdom of the Netherlands," as owner Brad Willard Jr. puts it, since no part
of Holland is higher than the Empire State Building).

From the hot tub or 20 × 40-foot pool, guests can look directly down the
cliff side to the thrashing waters below or across the sea to seven neighboring islands. Three of the rooms (the most spacious is about 400 sq. ft.) are in
the main lodge; the remaining four are in cottages notched into the hillside.
Surprisingly, given the location, they're among the most stylish lodgings of
any small inn in the Caribbean — white-on-white color schemes, Tennessee
ceramic tiles underfoot, furniture of Pacific Northwest cedar and heavy-duty
rattan, original island paintings on the walls, ceiling fans overhead (at this
altitude, who needs air-conditioning?), all done with contemporary colors
and flair.

Likewise the dining. Manager Corazón de Johnson doubles as chef and
brings the fine touches of her native Philippines to her eclectic cuisine (she
happens to have a degree in nutrition, is a champion swimmer, and looks
uncannily like opera diva Kiri Te Kanawa). Lucky guests of Willard's can
spend their days lounging on the grand ocean liner-like deck around the
pool, playing tennis on the inn's private court, or toasting the sunset from the
hot tub; then they'll sit down to an evening of Shanghai rolls with zosette
sauce, breaded chicken coujons with red hot sauce, broiled red snapper with
rainbow dressing, or chicken breast baked with a peach sauce and mozzarella.
Or, for something really exotic, a special lava-stone grill of shrimp, chicken,
or beef cooked right at the table. All of this deliciousness can be followed by
maruya, a special dessert of banana and local jackfruit wrapped in a crepe,
which is fried and served with homemade vanilla ice cream.

How did all this sophistication happen to come to Saba? Willard, a retired
lieutenant general in the Army Corps of Engineers, came to Saba 5 years ago,
as so many others do, to dive the virgin waters. He loved the place so much
that he bought a vertical acre of land (how they calculate an acre up here is
something you can puzzle out in the hot tub) and applied his engineering
savvy to constructing his mountain goat of an inn.

It may not be appropriate for acrophobes and children, but Willard's of Saba
certainly adds a new dimension to this most unusual up-and-down island.

There's nothing to do here but relax and take great chugalugging gulps of
fresh air. Maybe you'll hike up Mount Scenery, drive down to The Bottom
(Saba's capital), or stroll through the winding streets of Windwardside. Divers
have now discovered Saba in a big way, but most of the time you'll eat, have
a rum punch in the sun, eat, snooze, take a dip in the pool, eat, and make love.

In fact, you'll probably want to spend most of your time at the hotel, given
the price you now have to pay. I was a big fan of Willard's when it opened
because the setting was so dramatic, the welcome was warm, and the prices

were manageable. Now, alas, my enthusiasm is tempered by Four Seasons' rates without the Four Seasons' perks.

Name: Willard's of Saba
Manager: Corazon de Johnson
Address: P.O. Box 515, Windwardside, Saba, Netherlands Antilles
Location: Away up there, about 20 min. by taxi from the airport, $15
Telephone: 599/416-2498
Fax: 599/416-2482
E-mail: willards@unspoiledqueen.com
Web: www.willardsofsaba.com
Reservations: 800/504-9861
Credit Cards: American Express, Discover, MasterCard, Visa
Rates: $400–$700 EP (Dec 15–Apr 14); service charge included; off-season 15% less
Rooms: 6 rooms and 1 suite, all with ceiling fans, ceramic-tile floors, tiled bathroom (shower only, some with bidet), cable TV in some rooms — no phones, no air-conditioning (at this altitude you sometimes sleep under blankets)
Meals: Breakfast whenever, lunch noon–3pm, dinner 6–10pm (about $60–$70), all on the terrace or in the dining room; casual dress but "long trousers after dark — in any case you'd want long trousers and long sleeves at this altitude"; quiet New Age tapes in the background; no room service; honor bar
Entertainment: Counting the offshore islands
Sports: Solar-heated lap pool, hot tub, tennis (1 court, no lights) — all free; hiking and diving nearby
PS: "We discourage children under 14 because of the location"; open year-round

Queen's Gardens Resort

SABA

☆☆☆	Y Y	⚽	$ $ $
ATMOSPHERE	DINING	SPORTS	RATES

It sits thousands of feet above the sea, among breadfruit trees and Norfolk pines, wild orchids, and papayas, the terraced stone garden shaded by towering mango trees. The view beyond the pool takes in the island capital — the hamlet known as The Bottom — a panorama of headlands and a broad expanse of sun-sparkled sea.

It's not the sort of place where you expect much in the way of style and refinement, so it comes as a pleasant jolt to find that the guest rooms are fitted out with Dutch and Oriental antiques, the massive wooden buffet table in the dining room was once a Chinese hand-carved bed, and the loungers around the pool are made of teak and solid brass.

Queen's Gardens consists of three four-story structures notched into Tryon Hill, their white facades trimmed with green shutters popping up out of the mountain greenery. Opened in 1996, the resort suffered a few missteps along the way, but it finally seems to be getting its act together. The rooms are spacious and airy with white walls, white ceramic tile floors, sparkling white bathrooms, and white netting draped over pencil-post beds. Oriental parasols peek above antique Dutch armoires; dining nooks may be decked out with antique bench-tables.

There are hiking trails up here, but the only exercise at the hotel is the pool and a tiny gym. The dining terrace, dominated by an oversize wrought-iron gazebo, is a charmed setting of alfresco dining, but you'll probably want to have at least one lunch indoors because the Mango Royale Restaurant is so inviting. Dinner will cost about $80 for two, but that brings you double cloths on the tables, hefty cotton napkins, and sparkling glassware surrounded by wrought-iron chandeliers and a large wall tapestry.

At times, it's hard to believe you're thousands of feet up among the tropical greenery of a beach-less, backwater island.

Name: Queen's Gardens Resort
Manager: Paul Boetekees
Address: Troy Hill Dr., Saba, Netherlands Antilles
Location: High up and tucked away, 15 min. and $18 from the airstrip
Telephone: 599/416-3494 or 599/416-3496
Fax: 599/416-3495
E-mail: queens@gobeach.com
Web: www2.gobeach.com/saba/queens.htm
Reservations: 800/613-1511, toll-free direct
Credit Cards: American Express, MasterCard, Visa
Rates: $230 and up CP (Dec 15–Apr 15); add 15% for service charge and taxes; in summer 30% less
Rooms: 12 including suites, all with ceiling fans (no air-conditioning — you don't need it at this elevation), 24-channel cable TV, telephone, showers only, coffeemakers, minibar, refrigerator; some suites with kitchens
Meals: Breakfast 7:30–11am, lunch noon–3pm; dinner 6:30–10pm (about $80); soft recorded classical music; casual dress; room service during dining-room hours at extra charge
Entertainment: Local steel band for the Wed Caribbean Night
Sports: Pool, 3-station gym; diving and hiking nearby
PS: Not really suitable for children, given the layout; open year-round

OTHER CHOICES

Hotel L'Esplanade Caraïbe

ST. MARTIN

Most of the overbuilding on this island has been churning out undistinguished structures that mar the landscape rather than fit in unobtrusively, but here's an exception. Decked around with hibiscus and bougainvillea, L'Esplanade sits on a rise just outside the village of Grand Case, that culinary mecca, within walking distance of half a dozen of the island's best beaneries — and one of its prettiest beaches. The white-walled, red-roofed Mediterranean-style structure is elegantly enhanced with decorative tiles, balustrades and pergolas, and hardwood trim. It houses just 24 rooms and suites, some duplex, all with spotless kitchenettes (full-size fridge, four-burner stove, microwave), satellite TV, direct-dial telephones, air-conditioning and ceiling fans, and hair dryers. Very comfortable, very spacious — some of them are up to 370 square feet. Balconies have stunning views of the sunset — and of the new swimming pool with balustrade and a swim-up gazebo/bar. A stepping-stone pathway leads to a beach 5 minutes away. 24 rooms and suites. Doubles: $270–$370, winter 2002–03. *Hotel L'Esplanade Caraïbe, P.O. Box 5007, Grand Case, 97150 St. Martin, French West Indies. Telephone: 590 590/ 87-06-55; fax: 590 590/87-29-15; e-mail: esplanade@pobox.com; Web: http:// www.lesplanade.com.*

Le Petit Hotel

ST. MARTIN

This find is a sister of the Esplanade (above), in the same tile-and-arches style, but set right on the beach at the opposite end of Grand Case. Just nine rooms and one suite, each measuring a spacious 240 square feet, similar to the Esplanade rooms with ceramic tile floors, television, air-conditioning to augment the ceiling fans, and kitchenettes with microwave, toaster, and coffeemaker (if you call ahead, they'll stock your fridge with your favorite goodies — the cost, of course, goes on your bill). Le Petit Hotel has an extra perk: Each suite has its own direct phone line, in case you're planning to call all your friends back home and let them know how much you're enjoying the good life in Grand Case. From suite 1 you can step directly onto the beach; studios 7, 8, 9, and 10, on the second floor, have high ceilings, open sun decks, and semi-reclining chaises overlooking the bay and beach. You can have breakfast served in your room, but there's no restaurant. When it's time to dine, all you have to do is walk along the beach to a score of charming eating spots. 10 rooms. Doubles: $270–$370, winter 2002–03. *Le Petit Hotel, 248 Boulevard de Grand Case, Grand Case, 97150 St. Martin, French West Indies. Telephone: 590 509/29-09-65; fax: 590 590/87-09-19; e-mail: info@lepetithotel. com; Web: www.lepetithotel.com.*

The Cottage Club

SABA

Brick pathways wind through bushes of bougainvillea and frangipani, the lap pool is ringed by a broad sunning deck with stunning views, the stone Colonial-style clubhouse incorporates a small lounge with stereo, CDs, and shelves of paperbacks. Each of the 10 rooms is a dinky Saban-style gingerbread cottage, set on a hillside about 900 feet above the sea, with steady breezes to take care of all the cooling. Each is functionally but tastefully decorated with ceramic tile floors, double bed at one end, kitchenette at the other, dining tables and cable TV between. The rooms also have balconies for sunset watching — a great spot for relaxing with a cool beer after a day spent climbing up the 1,064 steps to the peak of Mount Scenery, between tree ferns and banana trees, past wild orchids and heliconia. 10 rooms. Doubles: $145, winter 2002–03, including tax and service charge. *The Cottage Club, Windwardside, Saba, Netherlands Antilles. Telephone: 599/416-2386; fax: 599/416-2476; Web: http://cottage-club.com.*

The Queen's Leewards

he six islands that make up this group are, with one exception, former British islands that now owe allegiance to Queen Elizabeth II as head of the Commonwealth. The exception is Anguilla, whose citizens decided to secede from the St. Kitts/Nevis partnership and remain a Crown Colony, governed more or less directly by London.

Antigua claims that lovers can spend a year on the island and visit a different beach each day. Maybe so, but once you see the beaches at, say, Jumby Bay or Curtain Bluff, you'll wave good-bye to the others. Most of the tourist resorts are in the northwest, vaguely between the airport and St.

John's, the capital; with the exception of the offshore Jumby Bay, most of the hideaways in this guide are toward the south of the island, where the country is more lush, the hills are higher (all the way to 1,319 feet at the curiously named Boggy Peak), and picturesque English Harbour fairly oozes with memories of those dashing young 18th-century officers about town, Commander Horatio Nelson and Prince William Henry, Duke of Clarence. Enjoy the beaches, even if you don't make it to all 365 of them, but be sure to make time for English Harbour, Nelson's Dockyard, and Shirley Heights.

St. Kitts, alias St. Christopher, may not be the most gorgeous island in the Caribbean, and you have probably seen more romantic beaches; the central part has been developed (hotel, condos, golf, casino) for a mass tourism that has yet to descend, but the mountainous western half is authentic Caribbean, with foothills of sugarcane, narrow coast-hugging roads, and huddled villages. Two attractions worth the bumpy drives: the spectacular fort perched on Brimstone Hill (take a picnic) and Romney Manor, a batik workshop in a lovely old plantation house.

Nevis — now there's a fabulous little island. Slightly mystical, slightly spooky, with centuries-old plantations, tumbledown hamlets, rain forests, and a mountain with its head in the clouds (hence Columbus's designation *nieves,* or snow). Alexander Hamilton was born here, the illegitimate son of a Scottish planter (his restored home is now a museum); Fanny Nisbet lived here with her husband until he died, and she was later wooed, won, and wed by Nelson in the parish of Fig Tree. If they returned for a reunion, they'd find that their island hadn't changed all that much — people still seek solace in the mineral baths, where England's aristocracy came to frolic.

Anguilla is set apart from the others by geography as well as politics. It's just to the north of St. Martin, a 20-minute ferryboat ride from Marigot. It's long, flat, and physically as undistinguished as the eel for which it's named, but if you want beautiful beaches, here are beautiful beaches and mellow, friendly people. In the past several years, a few new hotels have made people sit up and take notice. But Anguilla is a long, long way from being over-developed, crowded, or spoiled — although there are now six traffic lights on the island and its first golf course is in the works.

Montserrat, 15 minutes by air southwest of Antigua, was one of the most lush and prettiest islands, with its steep hills and dales, glens and glades, until Soufrière Hills volcano began erupting. As of spring 2001, Montserrat is still in a state of recovery, with few tourist facilities. A ferryboat runs daily between the island and St. John on Antigua, and if you want to stay over for a night or two, there are two or three small guest houses and B&Bs. We can only wish the islanders an eventual recovery.

HOW TO GET THERE   For Antigua, American, US Airways, BWIA, Air Jamaica and Continental from New York; American from Miami and San Juan; Air Canada and BWIA from Toronto. For St. Kitts, there are now direct flights from Philadelphia on US Airways and connecting flights from San Juan (American Eagle and LIAT), St. Maarten (LIAT or Windward), or Antigua

(LIAT). For Nevis, the usual flight path is via St.Kitts, but it's worthwhile to look at other possibilities from St. Maarten and St. Kitts. Now that the Nevis runway has been extended and a new two-story — wow! — terminal completed (much to the delight of guests of Four Seasons, many of whom fly in on their own aircraft), American Eagle now flies direct to Nevis from San Juan, eliminating the change in St.Kitts. Most inns on Nevis will recommend a seat on a shared charter; it costs a few dollars more, but it can save a lot of time and anguish, and the inn can probably make all the arrangements. The local Nevis airline tries to meet every jet arriving on St. Kitts. There is also ferryboat service between St. Kitts and Nevis, a 1-hour trip and a lot of fun, but the airline and ferry schedules rarely mesh. Guests of the Four Seasons, of course, have their own luxury launches between St. Kitts and the resort, or, as frequently happens, they have a small charter plane waiting for them on the runway.

For Anguilla, the most convenient way these days seems to be the twice-daily nonstop flights (40 min.) from San Juan on American Eagle; the alternative is St. Maarten, with connecting flights (10 min.) on Windward or a shared charter on Tyden Airways (your resort can arrange this). There is also ferryboat service 12 times a day between Anguilla and Marigot (on the French side) — again, a fun way to go, but inconvenient if you have more than light carry-on luggage.

> For information on Antigua and Barbuda, call 888/268-4227 or visit www.antigua-barbuda.org; Anguilla, 800/553-4939, 516/425-0900, or www.anguilla-vacation.com; St. Kitts and Nevis, 800/582-6208 or www.stkittsnevis.com; Montserrat, 664/491-2230 or www.visitmontserrat.com.

Malliouhana Hotel

ANGUILLA

☆ ☆ ☆ ☆ ☆   ⵛ ⵛ ⵛ ⵛ   ❻ ❻ ❻ $ $ $ $ $
ATMOSPHERE   DINING   SPORTS   RATES

When I first saw Anguilla's Mead Point in the early 1980s, it was a craggy coral headland flanked by two dream beaches — one a cove, one a ribbon of white sand — where "someone was planning to build a luxury hotel more beautiful than La Samanna." Ho-hum. How many times have we heard that over the years?

The next time I went there, someone was building a hotel. The stark headland was now a stark construction site. During my tour of the cinder blocks and piled pipes, I met a young couple who had come over for the day from La Samanna just to see this new place they'd heard about. They were so impressed they left behind a $1,000 deposit for the following February, for a room that didn't exist in a hotel yet to be built. I knew then that I was present at the birth of a legend.

From the day it finally, formally opened in November 1984, people have clamored to get a room at Malliouhana. And most of the people who go there book on the spot for the following year. And who wouldn't want to return as often as possible to Malliouhana's delights? Thirty flowery acres with royal palms for shade, sea bean for greenery, purple and yellow allamanda for splashes of color, night-blooming jasmine for fragrance. Two beaches, one almost a mile long, the other a secluded cove, both with beach bars and loungers (the hotel assigns eight members of the staff just to look after two beaches!). A 20,000-bottle wine cellar, a kitchen headed by a Michelin two-star chef from Paris. Villas whose bathrooms rival other hotels' bedrooms for size and appointments. A staff that outnumbers guests two to one.

Step into the grand, open-sided atrium lobby with its arched galleries and imposing paintings by Haiti's Jasmin Joseph and you feel like you're in a sort of Caribbean château. Settle into the plethora of pillows in the lounge's plump banquettes and admire the intricate raw-silk tapestries and hand-carved wooden figurines (mostly lions in honor of owner/manager Leon Roydon). The playground just beyond is a stunning landscape rather than a multilevel swimming pool.

The Roydons, père et fils, on the spot day and night keeping an eye on things, have pulled out all the stops for their guests. They deploy a staff of 34 for just over 100 pampered vacationers — 17 of that a team of gardeners to keep the crotons and hibiscus picture-perfect. Guest rooms are a carefree, non-bed-bumping 20 × 18 feet (a couple of feet larger in the villas), with decks only a few feet smaller. Interiors were designed by the esteemed Larry Peabody, with the same sensuous ambience he contrived for the much-lamented Habitation LeClerc in Haiti. Filtered sunbeams dapple hardwood louvers and quarry tile floors. Blossomy vines spill in profusion over balcony balustrades. Soft, indirect lighting transforms lush planters and leafy ficus into mini-Edens. It's an atmosphere calculated to induce instant indolence. In addition, each villa comes with its own service pantry, a godsend for those of us who enjoy dawdling bathrobe breakfasts on the balcony, attended by not one but two maids — the first to set up the table and flowers, the other to serve piping-hot croissants and pour freshly brewed tea. Granted, such a breakfast will set you back a tidy sum, but think what it does to set you up for another day of dallying.

Interiors are basically the same throughout the hotel, but location might make a minor difference. Assuming you have a choice (which might mean going in, say, June or July), rooms 109, 209, 110, and 210 would be my picks, although Leon Roydon's favorite is 101, above the bar and with a particularly large balcony. The most popular villas are those on the cliff beyond the pool, for the view; room 300 has its own Jacuzzi; the two directly on Mead's Bay are for people who are water sprites. I spent time in a Garden Villa (that is, looking at the hotel rather than the sea, but surrounded by flowers) and didn't feel deprived in the slightest. Six enormous two-terrace Junior Suites perch on the bluff above the cove — quiet and secluded — but that much farther from the dining room and tennis courts ("farther" meaning all of

Anguilla

ATLANTIC OCEAN

Seal Island

Prickly Pear Cays

Scrub Island

Island Harbour

Savannah Bay

Sandy Island

Crocus Bay

The Valley

Road Bay
Sandy Ground

The Quarter

Forest Bay

3 **4**
South Hill

Little Harbour

West End

5
Blowing Point

1 **2**
Rendezvous Bay

Shoal Bay West

Caribbean Sea

✈ Airport

0 ___ 5 mi
0 ___ 5 km

N

Cap Juluca **2**
CoveCastles Villa Resort **1**
CuisinArt Resort & Spa **5**
Malliouhana Hotel **4**
La Sirena Hotel **3**

3 minutes' stroll). The newest (1996) quarters are a pair of super suites within one villa that can be rented (and often are) as 8,500 square feet of private luxury with a private pool and its own artifacts and Jasmin Joseph mural. Each suite comes with private outdoor Jacuzzi, terraces for sunning and sitting in the shade, 12-suitcase closet, and a bathroom so sumptuous there's room for an exercise machine — and the twin washbasins are so far apart you almost have to signal to each other by semaphore.

Many people travel much more than 3 minutes, of course, to dine here (if they can get a reservation), for the terrace restaurant is one of the undoubted lures of Malliouhana. Again, Leon Roydon wanted the best, and since one of his longtime friends was none other than the late Jo Rostang of the Michelin two-star La Bonne Auberge in Antibes, he invited him to direct the Malliouhana kitchen. Now, Rostang's son Michel from Paris supervises the kitchen and cuisine. Anguilla is no Riviera with an infinite supply of fresh produce, but given the shortcomings of a Caribbean island, the Rostang corps does a commendable job of creating an Antillean Antibes. The setting helps immensely: an open fan-shaped pavilion above a sparkling sea, a hardwood canopy rising over giant ginger and stephanotis trees, with that final touch of civilized well-being — the pleasures of a well-endowed wine list (1,240 selections, 30,000 bottles in stock, up to $2,000, but most are in the $35–$45 range), the product of Leon Roydon's long-standing oenophilia.

All of this may make dining at Malliouhana sound like a stuffy activity. Far from it. The cuisine may be French, the china Limoges, the crystal French, and the cutlery Christofle, but the guests are as casually but stylishly dressed as they would be in St. Tropez. And the resort as a whole is as sports-oriented as it is luxurious — and now almost all the sporting activities are available at no extra charge, including the smart gymnasium/exercise pavilion above the beach, its walls open to the sea and sky.

You'd expect to find a place like this on the French Riviera, but on an unspoiled Caribbean backwater such as Anguilla, it's a marvel.

Now, to make a marvel more marvelous and to keep regular guests happy, the Roydons have added a new pool and restaurant beside the beach, and a dazzling 15,000-square-foot oceanfront spa with three private spa suites, fitness center, Ultra Bath therapy, and a large outdoor whirlpool overlooking the bay. Who could have imagined all this luxury and pampering all those years ago?

Name: Malliouhana Hotel
Owners/Managers: Leon and Nigel Roydon
Address: P.O. Box 173, Meads Bay, Anguilla, British West Indies
Location: On Mead's Bay, on the northeast shore of the island, about 10 min. and $16 by taxi from the airstrip, 6 or 7 min. and $14 from the ferryboat pier at Blowing Point
Telephone: 264/497-6111
Fax: 264/497-6011
E-mail: malliouhana@anguillanet.com
Web: www.malliouhana.com
Reservations: 800/835-0796, toll-free direct
Credit Cards: American Express, MasterCard, Visa
Rates: $575–$2,900 EP (Dec 18–Mar 31); service charge 10%, "added in lieu of gratuities"; off-season up to 50% less
Rooms: 55 rooms, one- or two-bedroom suites, in the main building or villas, overlooking beach or garden, all with air-conditioning and ceiling fans, balcony and/or lanai, stocked minibar with ice maker, telephones, television in suites, 2 with Jacuzzi, 1 with private pool
Meals: Breakfast anytime in your room, lunch noon–4pm in the moderately priced beachside Bistro or dining terrace, dinner 7:30–10:30pm (about $140), served in the breeze-cooled dining terrace; informal but stylish dress; no recorded music; room service 7:30am–11pm (special menu)
Entertainment: Elegant bar/lounge, 2 TV rooms (cable and video), library, backgammon, chess, cribbage
Sports: 2 beautiful beaches (1 long and public, 1 virtually private cove, both with beach bars, good swimming, and snorkeling), 5 freshwater pools (1 for laps), heated Jacuzzi, tennis (4 courts, with lights), Sunfish, Laser, and catamaran sailing, windsurfing, water-skiing, air-conditioned exercise

room (Nautilus devices, Aerobicycles, weights), trips to adjoining islets — all free; massage, scuba diving, 35-ft. powerboat for fishing available on the premises at extra charge

PS: Some kids (who now have their own half-a-million-dollar beachside playground, complete with nannies); "We request that guests do not use cellphones in the restaurant"; closed Sept–Oct

Cap Juluca

ANGUILLA

☆☆☆☆☆	⛄⛄⛄	❽❽❽	$ $ $ $ $
ATMOSPHERE	DINING	SPORTS	RATES

Let's start with the bathrooms: tubs for two, with Italian-porcelain headrests and faucets, separated by a wall of glass from a sunbathing patio; floors and walls are marble, doors are louvered Brazilian hardwood, the walk-in closets could accommodate Elizabeth Taylor's wardrobe with hangers to spare (well, her swimsuits, anyway); and dimmer lights and ceiling fans add just the right romantic touch.

Granted, not all the rooms and suites have the double tubs and patios, but even the few with only showers stand out from the crowd — just as the resort itself is unique. Cap Juluca is located on the leeward side of the island, on a heart-stoppingly beautiful mile of white sandy beach called Maundays Bay, with Cove Bay (another mile or so of sand) on the other side of a low headland; 179 acres of land and lagoon surround the guests and hold the world at bay. The distinctive architecture is a sort of Moorish/Patmos/Xanadu, a series of whitewashed one- and two-story villas with domes and cupolas, arches and pseudo-parapets peeping through the palms and wispy casuarinas. If you think it's all very beautiful by day, wait until you see how ravishing it can be after dark, when soft lights add their flicks of magic. And if you think that's ravishing, time your trip to coincide with a full moon and you'll think you've finally escaped this humdrum world.

If you read somewhere recently that the beach had washed away, forget it: Part of the beach disappeared in a storm, as beaches are wont to do in these parts, but the resort spent a cool $1 million replacing the sand, and the beach is back to its usual eye-catching self.

The resort has been a-building since 1988, but Cap Juluca is almost finally finished, with the recent addition of six pool villas (each with three or five bedrooms grouped around a walled garden and secluded pool) and a beachside playground with swimming pool, bar/cafe, and shrub-screened tanning areas. After spending $11 million on a complete rehab of every suite and every shrub, redoing the restaurants and kitchens, adding a third restaurant, topping the main lodge terrace with an extraordinary big white sunshade-cupola, the owner is now in the process of building a 12,000-square-foot spa and eight new villas out on the bluff beyond Pimm's Restaurant. Until it's finished, you can have your Volcanic Earth Ritual or Rice and Spice Scrub in your secluded bathroom patio or on your terrace. I'm not sure the spa is such a great idea — there's something deliciously relaxing about lying on your private terrace being oiled, rubbed, lava-scrubbed, pummeled, and pampered to the sound of surf, surrounded by a garden full of thryallis and oleander, dwarf gardenias and buttonwood.

Last time around, I stayed in pool villa number 5, or rather one suite thereof, a 1,540-square-foot expanse with a sky-lit circular dining nook, a spacious living room with a wall of folding hardwood louvers, and an equally spacious bedroom with shuttered doors leading to a large, shaded terrace. I lost track of the light switches. But even if I never stay in anything grander than one of the original rooms (a mere 790 sq. ft.), I'll never feel deprived because they are so exquisitely decorated: banquettes piled high with pillows, walls of louvered shutters leading to enormous patios with arches framing a dazzle of flowers and hammocks slung between the seagrape trees. Each group of rooms and suites comes with its own maids' pantry, where your breakfast is prepared to order every morning, then brought to your room by two maids: one to set the table with linen and silverware, the other to set out the fruits, juices, and freshly baked croissants.

Service with a capital S is, of course, a major enticement of a swank resort like Cap Juluca, and with two staffers per room, this one can offer service well above the Caribbean norm. Sure, there are minor shortcomings — those huge bathtubs sometimes take an eternity to fill, and sometimes the maids talk too loudly outside your louvers when you're still half asleep.

But just when you think there's nothing else the good people at Cap Juluca can do to fill a vacation with romance, you walk back along the beach-side path after dinner at Pimm's, past gardens fragrant with jasmine and frangipani, open the door to your suite, and find that the maid has not only turned down the bed but also turned down the lights and lit the candles in the storm lanterns. The world here is suffused with magic. Candlelight flickers on red tiles and antiques. Beyond the louvered hardwood shutters, the surf sighs and the moon silvers the sea.

Name: Cap Juluca
Manager: Eustace ("Guish") Guishard
Address: P.O. Box 240, Maundays Bay, Anguilla, British West Indies
Location: On the leeward coast, about 15 min. and $20 by taxi from the airport, $18 from the ferryboat dock (the resort has someone at the airport to meet you; on the way out, for a fee, you can have the resort check your bags and get your boarding pass in advance)
Telephone: 264/497-6666
Fax: 264/497-6617
E-mail: capjuluca@anguillanet.com
Web: www.capjuluca.com
Reservations: 888/858-5822
Credit Cards: American Express, MasterCard, Visa

Rates: $620–$2,115 CP (Dec 18–Mar 31); service charge 10%; off-season 40% less

Rooms: 98 rooms and suites in various configurations in 18 one- and two-story villas strung out along the edge of the beach, all with marble bathroom (some with shower only), hair dryer, bathrobes, covered terrace or patio, hammock and lounger, stocked refrigerator/ice maker, air-conditioning and ceiling fans, direct-dial telephone with dataport; some suites with kitchenettes, some with private or semiprivate plunge pool, some with rooftop sun decks

Meals: Breakfast served in villa at any time after 7:30am, lunch noon–2:30pm, snacks 11am–7pm, afternoon tea 4:30pm, dinner 7:30–10pm in one of 3 restaurants (about $80–$100); informal dress but generally stylish; recorded music in the dining rooms (occasionally too loud), some live music for dancing; room service all meals at extra charge

Entertainment: 2 bars, live music several evenings a week, movies nightly in the media room, library/game room

Sports: 2 miles of beach, snorkeling gear, windsurfing, water-skiing, sailing, croquet, tennis (3 courts, with lights, with pro), state-of-the-art fitness center — all free; boat trips and sunset cruises at extra charge; exotic spa treatments available in suites until new 12,000-square-foot spa is built on the headland

PS: Children 6 and over during high season, kids' activities for all ages at Easter and during summer; open year-round

La Sirena Hotel

ANGUILLA

☆ ☆	Y	❻ ❻	$ $
ATMOSPHERE	DINING	SPORTS	RATES

It may not have the cachet of Malliouhana or Cap Juluca — neighbors that are two of the classiest, most expensive resorts in the Caribbean — but this small, friendly hotel has other charms. First of all, with a room rate of around $260 a night in winter, it's much easier on the pocketbook. Second, many couples seeking to get away from it all may actually prefer the casual, more relaxed beach ambience of La Sirena. You don't have to worry about staining the chair cushions with suntan lotion, and the rooms, each with a balcony or patio, are spacious enough to function as comfortable retreats. Best of all, the beach — a mile-long, half-deserted, glistening white strand — is only a 4-minute stroll away. It's the same beach used by high-paying guests at Malliouhana, and to get to it, all you have to do is stroll a hundred yards down the hill, past a scattering of private homes.

The three-story hotel rises above a spread of lawns, gardens, and a large swimming pool; stone pathways lead through the gardens to the six villas, a

Jacuzzi, and a second, more secluded pool. The Spanish-Mediterranean architecture — white walls and arches, wooden balconies, ochre-tiled roofs — is complemented by a decorating scheme of wicker furniture and terra-cotta tile floors.

Each of the 24 guest rooms and suites has a minibar concealed in a light wicker chest, a bed with an arched wicker headboard, and contemporary accoutrements, such as halogen bedside lamps and a clock radio. The balcony or patio is furnished with a canvas deck chair and a table, and the bathrooms have large, tiled showers and fine toiletries. Only the closets are a bit skimpy; the Swiss owners must assume that their guests travel light.

For the best views and highest ceilings, reserve a room on the upper floors; two of the rooms on the third floor have wraparound views and lead to a roof terrace. Those guests seeking absolute privacy and extra space should check out one of the six villas, three with two bedrooms and three with three bedrooms. Each costs about the same as a single room at many of the more exclusive resorts.

The dining room I found to be "uninspired" has been converted into a couple of suites, and the restaurant downstairs, overlooking the pool and garden, is now known as the IN Cafe. It's fairly casual; if you want to dine in style, I suggest you head for the more elegant dining rooms along the same stretch of beach. The lower room rate you're paying at La Sirena will put enough change in your pocket to let you splurge at the dining table without guilt.

Name: La Sirena Hotel
Manager: Rolf Masshardt
Address: P.O. Box 200, Mead's Bay, Anguilla, British West Indies
Location: On mile-long Mead's Bay, 10 min. and $17 by taxi from the airport
Telephone: 264/497-6827
Fax: 264/497-6829
E-mail: lasirena@anguillanet.com
Web: www.la-sirena.com
Reservations: 800/331-9358, toll-free direct or 800/223-9815, International Travel & Resorts
Credit Cards: American Express, Discover, MasterCard, Visa
Rates: $265–$410 EP (Dec 15–Apr 15); service charge 10%; off-season 40% less
Rooms: 24 rooms and suites, all with balcony with deck chair, tile floors, telephone, clock/radio, ceiling fans in all rooms, air-conditioning in most, hair dryer, minibar; 4 new suites (2 upstairs in the main building in what used to be the second restaurant, 2 in the garden), all with kitchenettes; plus 6 fully equipped villas in the garden
Meals: Breakfast, lunch, dinner (in dining room, about $80–$90); casual dress; villas have full kitchens and barbecue equipment; room service for breakfast only
Entertainment: Barbecue dinner with live music on Mon and Thurs, recorded music in bar-lounge; cable TV and VCRs for rent

Sports: 2 freshwater pools, snorkeling gear — all free; massage (that's something new here), water-skiing, windsurfing, tennis, day-trips to adjoining islands can be arranged at extra charge; and there's now a PADI dive shop on the property
PS: Some children, especially on weekends; "U.S. cellphones need a conversion, European models can pick up the St. Martin signal from the second floor"; open year-round

CoveCastles Villa Resort

ANGUILLA

☆ ☆ ☆ ☆	⛉ ⛉ ⛉	❻	$ $ $ $
ATMOSPHERE	**DINING**	**SPORTS**	**RATES**

So distinctive is its postmodern architecture that CoveCastles is one of the first sights that catches your eye as you fly into or sail toward Anguilla. The stark white sculpture is two stories high with rolled-over rooflines on the bay side, presumably rising directly from the seagrape-covered dunes. They make an artistic statement of some sort; *Architectural Digest* and other knowledgeable magazines laud the design, but for others it's gratingly un-Caribbean.

Originally, CoveCastles consisted of only three-bedroom villas, which were hardly ideal for lovers other than movie celebs who could afford to rent the entire place just for a twosome. But new "Beachhouses," two-bedroom villas that can be rented as one-bedroom suites for a double rate, make CoveCastles much more appealing for readers of this guide. For my money, the earlier villas were more appealing because they had walls of louvered Brazilian hardwood doors rather than glary wall-to-wall, floor-to-cciling sliding-glass doors.

Yet even ardent traditionalists are likely to be seduced by the secluded setting, half-mile beach, refined luxury, and attention to detail — the champagne on ice awaiting your arrival, the exquisite hand-embroidered linens that caress you at night, Buccellati table settings, raw silk upholstery on the rattan loungers, and the inviting Pawley Island hammocks on the oversize terra-cotta verandas.

The kitchens give new meaning to the words "fully equipped," with their Braun juicers, Krups coffeemakers, 12 cruets for oils and dressings, and in mine (admittedly, a four-bedroom villa) no fewer than six types of drinking glasses, 72 in all. Oddly enough, my bathroom had no hook for a bathrobe — and if they're going to place the bed facing the wall-to-wall window, why block the view of the sea and the hills of St. Martin with a white TV set perched on a wicker trunk at the foot of the bed?

Despite kitchens that look like a sound stage for Martha Stewart, one of the villas shelters a hideaway 20-seat restaurant with a two-story ceiling and oversize wicker armchairs and traditional island pottery overflowing with anthuriums and ixora. You know you're in for serious dining when the waiter arrives with an amuse gueule of succulent scallop mousse wrapped in sole with red caviar followed by *carre d'agneau rote en croûte de pain d'épice au jus Creole* or *choucroute garnie de langoustines locale, sauce Noilly Prat.*

The restaurant is open for breakfast, lunch, and dinner, but the Lyonnaise chef, Dominique Thevenet, keeps his brigade on duty throughout the day to prepare tasty tidbits — say, *tarte tiede aux legumes de Provence et fromage de chevre* or *tranche de boeuf Black Angus grillée avec oignons sur baguette* — to be served with your Buccellati place setting on the shady, red-tiled veranda a few yards from the gently lapping surf.

Name: CoveCastles Villa Resort
Manager: Sylvene Petty
Address: P.O. Box 248, Anguilla, British West Indies
Location: On Shoal Bay West, 20 min. and $22 by taxi from the airfield, 15 min. and $18 from the ferryboat pier
Telephone: 264/497-6801
Fax: 264/497-6051
E-mail: covecastles@anguillanet.com
Web: www.covecastles.com
Reservations: 800/223-6051, Ralph Locke Islands
Credit Cards: American Express, MasterCard, Visa
Rates: $805–$1,190 EP (Jan 5–Apr 15); service charge 10% extra; off-season 25% off
Rooms: 8 two-bedroom beachhouses and 6 villas, all with ceiling fans, cable TV/VCR, CD player, direct-dial telephone with voice mail, fully equipped kitchen; one of the new Grand Villas ("5,000 square feet of dramatic living space") has a small private pool because it's at the end of the beach with a few rocks
Meals: Breakfast 8–10am, lunch noon–2pm, dinner 7–9pm (about $100); casual but stylish dress ("no shorts in the evening"); room service all day at no extra charge
Entertainment: Yourselves (you're on the quiet end of the island so any nightlife is a 20-min. drive away) or the videocassette library
Sports: ½-mile beach, tennis (1 court, with lights), kayaks, Sunfish sailing, snorkeling gear, bicycles — all free; scuba, water-skiing, sailing trips can be arranged at extra charge
PS: Few children; closed Sept to mid-Oct

CuisinArt Resort & Spa

ANGUILLA

☆☆☆☆   ♉ ♉   ❻❻❻ $ $ $ $
ATMOSPHERE   **DINING**   **SPORTS**   **RATES**

The first thing you notice about CuisinArt (after the spelling, which we'll get to later) is the garden — masses of red and purple bougainvillea, trim well-water lawns, trim driveways leading to the three-story, stacked white villas in vaguely Mediterranean style. A cool passageway leads the eye past the reception desk and boutiques to a broad terrace, a swimming pool, a cascade, and a blue-tiled channel that leads to the beach. Off to the right, looking like the white bridge of a classic ocean liner, is the Venus Spa.

This place, this CuisinArt, got a lot of buzz when it opened in 1999, but it's hard to see what all the fuss was about. Sure, the setting is pretty, the gardens are graceful, the food is good, but there are lots of other resorts (on Anguilla for starters) that have impressive settings, gardens, and cuisine. The architectural hints of the Mediterranean and the Greek Isles, coming after La Samanna on St. Martin, Cap Juluca, Malliouhana, and the Sonesta on this island, are becoming something of a cliché. It has a lot of the expected features — sumptuous bathrooms, big balconies, top-quality furnishings — but somehow it doesn't add up to personality. The Venus Spa helped a lot. It was the first deluxe spa on the island, and it quickly gained a following for its beautifully designed treatment rooms, fitness center, and rooftop cafe.

Which leaves the rooms. If you're looking for space, you'll find plenty of it here — maybe to the point where you wish they'd install another planter or objet d'art to fill up some of the bare corners. The bathrooms are something else — oodles of space, oodles of marble, separate tubs and showers (with the marble floors thoughtfully coarsened to keep feet from slipping), and top-of-the-line toiletries and gizmos. And there's the clue to the place.

The hair dryer is by Conair, part of the mini-empire that also produces the Cuisinart blenders. When he decided he also needed a resort, the owner added the extra capital since the words "Cuisine" and "Art" sum up his philosophy. Since his background is Italian, that means Mediterranean cuisine and Mediterranean art. The cuisine is provided by European chefs performing in an exhibition kitchen in an air-conditioned restaurant named Santorini (you can also dine alfresco in the garden); the art comes from a collection of original European paintings, some of which are for sale (and there are those among the guests who are probably thinking, the sooner they sell the better).

What sets CuisinArt apart is its hydroponic garden. Other resorts have tackled this technique in the past but none seems to have succeeded like CuisinArt. A large greenhouse just inside the entrance coaxes along flowers and fruit, vegetables, and herbs for the kitchen. The result: the freshest salads and the most colorful gardens on the island.

Name: CuisinArt Resort & Spa
Manager: Rabin Ortiz
Address: P.O. Box 2000, Rendezvous Bay, Anguilla, British West Indies
Location: About 15 min. and $22 by taxi from the airport, 15 min. and $16 from the ferryboat dock
Telephone: 264/498-2000
Fax: 264/498-2010
E-mail: None
Web: www.cuisinartresort.com
Reservations: 800/973-9356, toll-free direct or 800/223-6800, Leading Hotels of the World

Credit Cards: American Express, MasterCard, Visa
Rates: $501–$1,300 CP (Dec 15–Mar 31); service charge 10% extra; off-season 40% less; penthouse suites extra
Rooms: 93 rooms and suites, all with air-conditioning and ceiling fans, direct-dial phones with dataports, clock/radios, cable TV/VCR, hair dryers, bathrobes, balconies, some with CD players, some with pantries
Meals: Breakfast 8–10am, lunch noon–3pm in the garden or the spa, dinner 7–10pm in the Santorini Restaurant (about $100–$120); casual but elegant dress code (no shorts); room service during dining-room hours at extra charge
Entertainment: Occasional live music
Sports: Beach, pool, tennis (3 Astroturf courts, with lights), snorkeling gear, windsurfing, water-skiing, fitness center, billiard room, croquet, sauna — all free; spa treatments at extra charge; scuba diving and sailboat cruises can be arranged
PS: Few children (but they have their own playground); no guidelines regarding cellphones ("not yet, at least"); closed Sept

The Golden Lemon

ST. KITTS

☆☆☆☆	♈ ♈ ♈	☻	$ $ $
ATMOSPHERE	DINING	SPORTS	RATES

Take a 17th-century French manor house (in a walled garden beside a grove of coconut palms) and fill it with antiques and bric-a-brac. Paint the exterior a bright lemon yellow, tuck a pool into a corner of the leafy garden, and you'll have a handsome country inn in the tropics.

But you still wouldn't have the legendary Golden Lemon.

The Golden Lemon is indeed all of these things — a 17th-century manor of volcanic stone with a wood-framed upper floor, an 18th-century addition, and a gallery with a wide-plank floor surrounding it. From the gallery, you look out to unspoiled Caribbean — a reef, a lagoon, a beach of black sand, and the palm trees, tall and spindly and well into their second century. In the walled garden, loungers invite guests to relax among the trees, and white tables and chairs set on the arcade beneath the gallery beckon for lunch or a drink. All very romantic for escapists who want to savor authentic Antillean surroundings (the inn is located at the end of a narrow street in a simple fishing village). But there's more to the Golden Lemon than that.

It was the old manor's good fortune to be spotted by a connoisseur with a sharp eye who recognized the house's thoroughbred qualities in its then-dilapidated state. At the time, Arthur Leaman was an editor with *House & Garden* magazine who also happened to be an avid collector with an eclectic array of antiques — four-poster beds, mahogany tables, blue delft tulipieres from Holland, clocks from Italy.

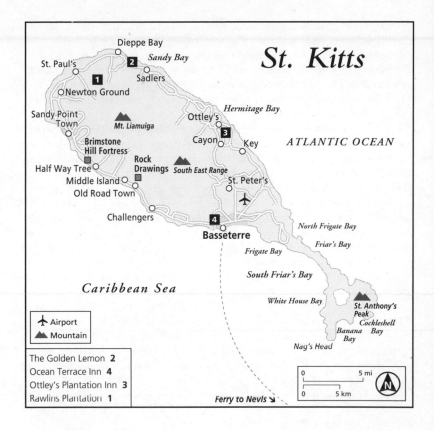

Dieppe Bay

St. Paul's   2 Sandy Bay

Sadlers

1

Newton Ground

St. Kitts

Sandy Point Town

Mt. Liamuiga

Hermitage Bay

Ottley's

3

Cayon   Key

ATLANTIC OCEAN

Brimstone Hill Fortress

Rock Drawings   *South East Range*

Half Way Tree

Middle Island

Old Road Town

St. Peter's

Challengers

4

Basseterre

North Frigate Bay

Friar's Bay

Frigate Bay

South Friar's Bay

Caribbean Sea

White House Bay   St. Anthony's Peak

Cockleshell

Banana Bay   Bay

Nag's Head

✈ Airport
▲▲ Mountain

The Golden Lemon **2**
Ocean Terrace Inn **4**
Ottley's Plantation Inn **3**
Rawlins Plantation **1**

0   5 mi
0   5 km

N

Ferry to Nevis ↘

Leaman has an extraordinary and enviable ability of taking a castoff and, by deft juxtaposition or downright alchemy, turning it into an heirloom. Each room at the Great House is different, each a masterpiece of composition and color (I have a hunch that if you stood on your head in one of the rooms here, you'd still have a picture-perfect interior). I can never decide which is my favorite — the Hibiscus Room, say, with its two white canopy beds, or the Batik Room with steps up to the big antique double beds — but every detail reflects Leaman's refined sense of style, so much so that you're so busy admiring the grace notes in the bathrooms that you don't even notice you're stepping into a prefab plastic shower stall. Rooms on the upper floor, it should be noted, are wood framed and not infallibly soundproof, but your compensation for keeping your voices down or overhearing extraneous sounds is breakfast on the gallery. First, the maid announces the meal's arrival by the sounds of a table being set with a tray full of playful lemon-motif mugs and plates; then she returns with pewter dishes of homemade preserves, perfectly browned toast, perfectly timed scrambled eggs, a thermos of coffee — all served course by course. It gets your day off to a very slow, very stylish start — just the way life should be at the Golden Lemon.

For guests who want more substantial accommodations, there are newer wings of duplex one- and two-bedroom villas across the garden beside the volcanic shore — some with decks overhanging the sea, most with small private pools. The interiors, needless to say, are exquisite: some with canopy beds, some with bull's-eye orrery windows that dapple sunlight on the ceramic tile floors. The prices are extravagant at first glance but considering the setting and surroundings, not outlandish.

Evenings have always been special at the Golden Lemon. For one thing, the walled garden setting out front and the jungle-like garden at the rear become quite magical with soft lighting and soft breezes. The antiques-filled dining room sparkles in the soft light of candelabra and chandeliers. Traditionally, Arthur Leaman hosts a sort of captain's table, but tables are also set for twos and fours, with guests rotated so that everyone has a chance to mix, if that's what they want. Leaman's patrician presence and wit still turn evenings into house parties, especially since the guests next to you in the bar may be paying their 20th visit in 20 years. Dinner is a fixed menu, and the inn's cooks always come up with something to look forward to; but repeat guests know to rev up the taste buds for Sunday brunch and the inn's West Indies rum beef stew, liberally laced with Mount Gay.

The Golden Lemon, let me quickly add, is not for everyone. Its devotees are mostly designers and writers, young Californians, young Washingtonians, and people in the theater. As gracious as Arthur Leaman may be, he doesn't want his inn (and the solitude of his guests) disturbed by cruise-ship passengers. There was a time when Leaman claimed that since "you can take only so much of paradise" no one was allowed to stay longer than 2 weeks — but fortunately he has mellowed. Stay as long as you like.

Name: The Golden Lemon
Owner/Manager: Arthur Leaman
Address: Dieppe Bay Town, St. Kitts, St. Kitts and Nevis, West Indies
Location: In the village of Dieppe Bay Town, on the northeast coast, about 30 min. and $30 by taxi from the airport (let the hotel know when you're arriving and they'll arrange for a dependable driver to meet you)
Telephone: 869/465-7260
Fax: 869/465-4019
E-mail: info@goldenlemon.com
Web: www.goldenlemon.com
Reservations: 800/633-7411, Caribbean Inns Ltd.
Credit Cards: American Express, MasterCard, Visa
Rates: $325–$495 CP (Dec 16–Apr 15); service charge 10%; off-season 25% less
Rooms: 32, 8 inn rooms in 2 buildings, all with private bathroom, ceiling fans, balcony or patio; kitchens in the 16 new condo units, 2 sharing 1 pool, the others with private pools
Meals: Breakfast 7:30–10am, lunch noon–3pm on the patio, afternoon tea 4pm ("real tea, not bags"), dinner 7–9pm (about $70–$80, in the fan-cooled main

dining room); informal dress ("no wet bathing suits at lunch"); room service $5 extra charge

Entertainment: The bar (occasionally with live piano music), quiet recorded music, backgammon and parlor games in beautifully designed library

Sports: Beach, 20 × 40-foot freshwater pool (plus private pools in the villas), snorkeling gear, "tremendous reef" — all free

PS: No children under 18; no cellphones in bar, restaurant, or tennis court; closed Sept 1–Oct 15

Rawlins Plantation

ST. KITTS

☆ ☆ ☆ ☆	ΥΥΥ	❻	$ $ $
ATMOSPHERE	DINING	SPORTS	RATES

Don't be put off by the bumpy, hilly dirt road that meanders through the fields of sugarcane. Granted, 260 acres of the sweet stuff are hardly a romantic introduction to a hideaway, but press on up the hill and around one last bend and you arrive at a 12-acre oasis of clipped lawns and clumps of croton, breadfruit, and African tulip trees. Up ahead, the cane fields rise to the foothills of forest-clad Mount Misery; behind you, the fields fall off to the sea and distant views of St. Eustatius.

At 350 feet above the sea, Rawlins is exactly the sort of cool, calm place you relish returning to after a sticky day at the beach or a hike through the rain-forest foothills beneath canopies of trailing vines and wild orchids. Some guests actually make it all the way up to the peak, 4,000 feet above the sea, where misery must seem like cloud nine. Owners Paul and Claire Rawson will arrange picnic outings up the mountain, part of the way by Jeep, the rest on foot, fortified by their special rum punch. They've also flattened a corner of their lawn into that rarity — a grass tennis court.

But essentially, this is an inn for relaxing. You'd never get me near the beach or up a hill. Sit on a picket-fenced porch and read a book. Dunk in the spring-fed pool that was once the mill's cistern. Sit on the veranda of the great house at sundown, gin-and-tonic in hand, and chat with fellow guests, or simply dream sundown dreams. Check out the library. Watch the sunset's glow on Statia. Listen to the birds and tree frogs. This is what people have in mind when they dream about a place to unwind — really unwind.

The inn still looks like a gentleman's plantation — white great house at the center, cottages for managers and overseers in the gardens, and a white lattice gazebo beside the pool. The circular stone base of the 17th-century windmill is now a duplex suite, much favored by honeymooners — pretty red-and-white sitting room downstairs, white cast-iron double bed upstairs; another pink and pretty suite has a king-size bed and a semi-sunken bathroom with semi-sunken tiled bathtub, and there's a new gazebo patio for relaxing in the shade. The remaining guest rooms, each named for the tree outside its windows, reflect the ambience of colonial times, with mahogany floors and rush rugs rather than fitted carpets, ceiling fans rather than air-conditioning, wicker and rattan rather than leather, and mosquito nets for decoration rather than protection. The fabrics may be more colorful than they were in the old days, but it's all very tasteful and low-key. No television, no telephones. Plumbing and electricity are just about the sole concessions to the 20th century.

The former boiling room, where the cane was converted to molasses, is now a flower-draped, stone-floored patio where guests gather for drinks before moving to the indoor/outdoor dining salon. Dining has always been especially pleasurable here. Rawlins has never promised "the finest Continental cuisine" or made any of the fatuous claims of some island inns. What Claire Rawson and her local cook serve are perfectly prepared local dishes with their own embellishments and Claire's "lightly French accent." Thus, guests gathered on the veranda can while away sun-dappled noondays while nibbling on flying-fish fritters, rice with akee and dill, soups (breadfruit, eggplant, or cucumber with fresh mint), curries garnished with garden-fresh avocados and papaws. In the evening, candles sparkle on gold-and-white Royal Doulton and servings of, say, crab and callaloo soup, St. Kitts shrimp with orange butter, roast lamb with mango sauce, and, for dessert, bananas in puff pastry with local mountain oranges.

Between them, Rawlins Plantation and The Golden Lemon have created a haven for the lovers of fine food who wend their way to this unspoiled corner of the Caribbean year after year — Rockefellers, Cabots, Rothschilds, peers of the realm, doctors and lawyers and writers — anyone who recognizes an exceptional value.

Name: Rawlins Plantation
Owners/Managers: Paul and Claire Rawson
Address: P.O. Box 340, St. Kitts, West Indies
Location: At Mt. Pleasant Estate, near Dieppe Bay Town; directly across the island from the airport, about 30 min. and $28 by taxi (let the Rawsons know when you'll arrive and they'll send a driver to meet you, "probably Kenmore, who'll wait forever in case your flight is late")
Telephone: 869/465-6221
Fax: 869/465-4954
E-mail: rawplant@caribsurf.com
Web: www.rawlinsplantation.com
Reservations: Direct
Credit Cards: American Express, MasterCard, Visa
Rates: $460 MAP (Dec 15–Apr 15); service charge 10%; off-season 30% less
Rooms: 10, in various cottages, including the Sugar Mill Suite and 1 two-bedroom cottage with 2 sitting rooms, all with breezes and ceiling fans, private bathroom, hair dryer, balcony or patio

Meals: Breakfast 8–9:30am, buffet lunch 12:30–2pm on the veranda, afternoon tea 4pm, dinner 8pm (about $100 for nonguests), fixed menu, in the dining room; informal dress but no shorts; no music

Entertainment: "Good conversation," parlor games, library with more reading material than you can handle on a single vacation

Sports: Small spring-fed pool, croquet, tennis (1 grass court, cramped, no lights) — all free; full-day cruises on catamaran to Nevis and crater trips by Jeep and foot can be arranged

PS: Cellphones and children under 13 "not encouraged"; closed mid-Aug to mid-Oct

Ottley's Plantation Inn

ST. KITTS

☆ ☆ ☆ ☆   ♈ ♈ ♈   ❻ $ $ $
ATMOSPHERE   **DINING**   **SPORTS**   **RATES**

The Ottley sugar plantation was founded in the early 1600s and the Great House was built in 1832, but its career as an inn didn't begin until 12 years ago. It was bought by the Keusch family, former bookstore owners in New Jersey, who saw the tumbledown estate as the perfect means for fulfilling their dream of becoming Caribbean innkeepers. After a year of scraping paint, hammering, and chipping (to say nothing of a month or two of renovation after Hurricane Hugo paid a brief call), their fantasy finally came true.

The Great House, a two-story manor of brimstone walls, looks the part with its wraparound veranda, yellow storm shutters with white trim, and Brazilian hardwood doors — features that give the structure the appropriate tropical flavor. It sits on 35 acres of splendid grounds, with a row of coconut palms in the front and the peak of Mount Liamuiga in the distant rear. Stone paths lead past crumbling statuary, allamanda-draped terraces, silk-cotton and cinnamon trees, and massive strangler figs to a mango orchard.

In the inn itself, overstuffed rattan chairs and paisley Sheraton sofas on the veranda and in the great room are an invitation for afternoon tea taking or just plain lounging around. Stunning Portuguese rugs accent the hardwood floors, and an antique Chippendale-style bar in the Great Room sets just the right tone for sundown socializing. A small anteroom with DVD and VCR functions as an entertainment center and library.

Ottley's 24 guest rooms are all variations of tropical villa style with touches of English country and Caribbean colonial, enhanced by wicker and rattan furniture, floral chintz bedspreads and upholstery, antiques, and bric-a-brac. Island prints decorate the white walls, while woven mats from Dominica cover the white plank floors. Thoughtful touches include new reading lights beside the comfy armchairs (the touch of a former bookseller) and plentiful supplies of beach towels. Some of the rooms are quite large for a plantation-style inn, with high-peaked ceilings and floor dimensions of 24 × 24 feet. Several of the bathrooms are also unusually generous, with separate dressing areas and tiled bathtubs and showers. A favorite with privacy seekers is the English Cottage, the former cotton house, which has mullion windows, a separate sitting room, and a small patio looking out to sea. In its former incarnation, Princess Margaret reportedly stayed here, but she wouldn't recognize its newly enlarged bathrooms, lattice-fenced sunning decks, and tiled plunge pool. All the rooms are cooled by breezes and ceiling fans (air-conditioning is available as well). The Royal Suites, in new cottages lining the driveway, are especially appealing with their lush individual gardens, spacious verandas, and sumptuous bathrooms.

The founders' daughter, Nancy Lowell, and her husband, Martin, run a tight ship with a staff of 40 (a guest-to-staff ratio of almost 1 to 1). The inn's restaurant, the Royal Palm, is highly regarded for its innovative menu and is popular with local gourmands, but overnight guests have first dibs on the 22 tables, set up beneath ceiling fans and opening onto the swimming pool. And it's just a short walk, up or down, to some of the loveliest love nests in the Caribbean.

Name: Ottley's Plantation Inn
Owners: The Lowell and Keusch Families
Address: P.O. Box 345, Basseterre, St. Kitts, West Indies
Location: About 15 min. from Basseterre, 12 min. and $15 from the airport (let the hotel know your flight number and they'll send a reliable driver to meet you)
Telephone: 869/465-7234
Fax: 869/465-4760
E-mail: ottleys@caribsurf.com
Web: www.ottleys.com
Reservations: 800/772-3039, toll-free direct
Credit Cards: American Express, Discover, MasterCard, Visa
Rates: $280–$730 MAP (Dec 15–Apr 15); service charge 10%; off-season 25% less
Rooms: 24 in 5 categories, 9 in the Great House, 15 in cottages, all with private bathroom, air-conditioning and ceiling fans, balconies or patios, direct-dial telephone, minibars, in-room safes
Meals: Breakfast 7–10am, lunch 12–3pm, dinner 7–10pm, in the pavilion known as the Royal Palm (dinner about $130 for nonguests); "smart casual" at dinner, no shorts or T-shirts; Sun champagne brunch; recorded music; room service for all meals at no extra charge
Entertainment: Bar/lounge and poolside bar, TV room with VCR and extensive DVD library (TV sets on request, some rooms only), parlor games, live music Fri evenings
Sports: 60-foot-long spring-fed pool, tennis court (with lights), croquet lawns, hiking trails from the back door — all free; beaches nearby (transportation daily); golf, horseback riding, and sailing can be arranged
PS: Small children not encouraged; closed Sept–Oct

Nisbet Plantation Beach Club

NEVIS

☆ ☆ ☆ ☆   Ⓨ Ⓨ Ⓨ   ⊛ $ $ $ $ $
ATMOSPHERE   **DINING**   **SPORTS**   **RATES**

It's now 10 years since David Dodwell of The Reefs resort in Bermuda bought this legendary inn and slowly and tastefully transformed it into his own vision. The tiny pink cottage with gingerbread trim, called Gingerland, that once housed the reception desk has been turned into a boutique and a new pavilion added next door for a more spacious, more efficient lobby.

But that's just the beginning. By adding a timbered complex on the beach incorporating a freshwater pool and an open-air restaurant called Coconuts, Dodwell has given guests the opportunity to dine beneath the stars with the rumbling of the surf just a few feet away. Then there are the new lodgings. The two-story, pale-yellow villas that house the 12 air-conditioned Premier rooms are somewhat obtrusive, given that all the other plantation buildings have one story and are half-concealed by the shrubbery. Inside, however, the rooms are large and pleasant, with wet bars and refrigerators, king-size beds on elevated platforms, and sitting areas with comfortable sofas. Each bathroom has a wall of closets and an elevated bathtub. The walls, ceramic floors, rafters, and wicker furniture are white; wooden window louvers and ceiling fans help keep the rooms pleasantly cool.

The Great House, connected to the beach by a 200-foot-long *grande allée* lined with coconut palms, has been rejuvenated with new shutters around the screened veranda and a bright floral fabric on the sofas and chairs. Thankfully, the atmosphere of a gracious, peaceful, generations-old country house, complete with antiques-filled salons that function as dining rooms, has been retained (although I wish they'd revert to the old practice of house wines with dinner — it added a nice house-party touch). The square two-story dwelling is a sterling example of a traditional Nevisian plantation: It's built of native stone with a screened porch reached by an imposing flight of steps. In bygone days, when Nevis was wall-to-wall plantations, this was the estate of a Mr. William Nisbet, who lived here with his lovely young bride, Fanny (a few years later, she was widowed and went on to more universal fame as the wife of Admiral Horatio Nelson). The house is not the one in which the Nisbets lived, but rather an authentic-looking reconstruction.

All of the hotel's original gingerbread cottages, scattered under the coconut palms, have been spruced up with lighter furniture, stocked refrigerators, bathrobes, and Gilchrist & Soames toiletries. The layout in most of these is two rooms per bungalow, arranged so that bathrooms rather than bedrooms abut one another and porches face away from their neighbors. Furnishings are island-simple but comfortable and relaxing, and the newer bungalows have screened porches.

Despite the changes, Nisbet, which I first saw 20-odd years ago, will always have a place in my heart. True, its original 12 rooms have mushroomed to 38, and the inn is no longer quite so unique; true too that the extensions to the nearby airport are likely to make aircraft noise a factor somewhere down the road; but first-timers seeking a romantic escape will not be disappointed.

Name: Nisbet Plantation Beach Club
Manager: Don and Kathie Johnson
Address: St. James Parish, Nevis, West Indies
Location: On the northeast coast, just 1 mile from the airstrip, $8 by taxi, and 8 miles and $16 by taxi from Charlestown
Telephone: 869/469-9325
Fax: 869/469-9864
E-mail: nisbetbc@caribsurf.com
Web: www.NisbetPlantation.com
Reservations: Direct or 800/742-6008, Island Resorts Reservations
Credit Cards: American Express, MasterCard, Visa
Rates: $475–$710 MAP (Dec 21–Apr 16); service charge 10%; off-season 30% less
Rooms: 38, 12 in two-story villas, 26 in cottages and bungalows, all with private bathroom (16 with shower only), some with air-conditioning, all with ceiling fans, in-room safe, private porch; Junior Suites with minibars, wet bars, and towel hampers
Meals: Breakfast 8–10am and lunch 12:30–2:30pm (at the beach restaurant, Coconuts; box lunches available with advance notice for those going on an excursion), afternoon tea 4–5pm (in the lounge), dinner 7:30–8:30pm (in the fan-cooled dining room, about $110 for nonguests); informal but stylish dress; some live music; room service for continental breakfast at no extra charge
Entertainment: Beach bar (open 10am–6pm), Great House bar (open 6pm to late evening), library, backgammon, Scrabble, piano, occasional local bands, TV in lounge (but rarely used)
Sports: Beach, beachside freshwater pool, snorkeling, croquet, tennis (1 court, no lights) — all free; other watersports about 3 miles down the road at Oualie Beach and Newcastle Marina; golf nearby; boat trips, horseback riding, taxi tours, air charters to other islands can be arranged
PS: Some children, but not really suitable for the very young; closed Sept to mid-Oct

Four Seasons Nevis Resort

NEVIS

☆☆☆☆   Y Y Y   ❻❻❻❻ $ $ $ $ $
ATMOSPHERE   DINING   SPORTS   RATES

I've been carping about this place ever since I first heard that one of my favorite coconut groves was going to be carved up for a luxury resort (and, of course, it was no fault of Four Seasons that Hurricane Hugo came along

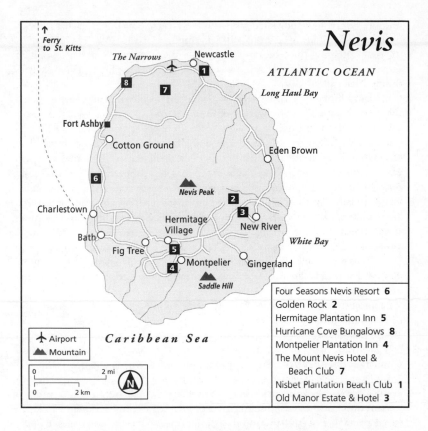

Ferry to St. Kitts

Nevis

The Narrows   Newcastle   ATLANTIC OCEAN

Long Haul Bay

8   7

Fort Ashby ■

Cotton Ground

Eden Brown

6

Nevis Peak

Charlestown

2

3

Hermitage Village   New River

Bath   White Bay

Fig Tree   5

4   Montpelier   Gingerland

Saddle Hill

✈ Airport
▲▲ Mountain

Caribbean Sea

0   2 mi
0   2 km

N

Four Seasons Nevis Resort **6**
Golden Rock **2**
Hermitage Plantation Inn **5**
Hurricane Cove Bungalows **8**
Montpelier Plantation Inn **4**
The Mount Nevis Hotel &
    Beach Club **7**
Nisbet Plantation Beach Club **1**
Old Manor Estate & Hotel **3**

in the midst of the construction and did its own thorough job of scything still more trees). Farewell, densely planted grove! What are we left with?

For starters, a breathtaking golf course. Since the surrounding landscape is virtually unspoiled nature, these fairways benefit from the happy confluence of forest, sea, and gullies set off by the mystical backdrop of a perfect volcanic cone wreathed in clouds.

Then, too, we have Luxury with a capital L. Four Seasons didn't earn its present preeminence with no-frills lodgings, so here we have the lot — 130 square foot bathrooms with acres of marble, separate showers, and soaking tubs and toilets; closet safes; stocked refrigerators; direct-dial telephones; credenzas with concealed 15-channel television and VCR; ceiling fans and air-conditioning; and spacious screened porches — all refurbished in 1998 and 1999 after a couple of check-ins by hurricanes. (There are several suites, but given the size and amenities of the regular rooms, I can't see any reason for upgrading.)

The public rooms are just as grand: a soaring lobby/lounge accented with antiques and with floor-to-ceiling glass doors that open to the terrace; a wood-paneled, library-style lounge/bar; and two high-ceilinged, chandelier and crystal dining rooms, each air-conditioned and seating about 140 diners indoors with a few additional tables on the terrace, serving food that's sumptuous but safe. The most noticeable revamping for the 2000 reopening was the eye-catching pool/beach complex — an extra pool, a new poolside restaurant, more deck space, more sand (imported) on the beach. So what's my problem, then?

For my money, it's all more Four Seasons than Nevis. It just seems such a shame that with all the resources of Four Seasons (the budget for this resort was said to be $75 million, and the recent rehabbing cost another $45 million), with all their proven good taste and all that talent at their disposal, they could not have come up with the perfect small resort for a perfect small island. Instead, we have 10 cottages that could be plopped down in Colorado or Maui with only minor adjustments, despite lavish trimming with gingerbread and giving each one an island plantation name. Granted, uninspired architecture is less of a drawback now that the lavish plantings are blooming and sprouting and someone has affixed trellises to the walls to encourage vines. The interiors seem to have been inspired less by a sense of place than by the corporate manual, so no Four Seasons fan will find anything out of place; but island lovers may wake up discombobulated, wondering where the hell they are.

The Four Seasons people, to their credit, have been very concerned from the start about fitting into their new surroundings, aware that they were making an unusual impact on the delicate social, professional, and environmental balance of Nevis. After all, they were opening a world-class resort with a guest count that doubled the island's capacity overnight, with a championship golf course on an island that can count its regular players on one hand, and with potential wages beyond the average Nevisian's dreams, on an island hitherto known only for modest inns. So they went to extraordinary expense and care to adapt to Nevis and mounted an impressive program we needn't detail here, other than noting that they shipped their rookie staff off to learn about luxury service in various Four Seasons hotels in the United States. Even when they added a spa in 2002, they designed it as a garden, filled with local gingerbread houses, pools, waterfalls, and flowerbeds.

And service is what Four Seasons is all about, after all, and here it has many refinements: a staff of 680 for 392 guests, golf carts patrolling the fairways with light refreshments, chilled towels and Evian spritzers for sunbathers and tennis players, and thicker padding on the loungers than at other resorts. When you rent golf clubs, they're late-model Callaways; when you open your confirmation reservation, you'll find one of those immigration cards required to enter the islands (you don't have to worry about the stewardess on the flight not handing them out); and when you want to go jogging, the resort has jogging gear for rent. There's a qualified nurse on the property, and if you want a partner for a game of tennis or a round of golf when there are no guests available, Four Seasons will trot out one of their management people, all of whom are encouraged to polish up their games and keep their gear on hand just in case. Service beyond the call of duty, you say? Not quite: They do this so that the staff can get feedback on service and facilities direct from the guests (like, at these prices, why is there no towel hamper in the bathroom?).

Accessibility is a drawback, I suspect, for people spending that kind of money on a vacation. For many people, Nevis is a favorite hideaway because you have to put in extra effort to get there, but Four Seasons tackles the problem with its usual thoroughness: Because most guests are likely to be arriving via St. Kitts, Four Seasons's people meet their flight there, serve drinks in a private air-conditioned lounge, and then transfer them to a commuter plane for Nevis (a lot of Four Seasons guests, of course, fly directly to Nevis in their private jets — that's why Nevis has been so busy extending its runway). But let me end on a positive note: The summer rate — $325 compared with $675 in winter — is an exceptional value. Sign on for, say, the 7-day tennis package and it's almost a steal.

Name: Four Seasons Nevis Resort
Manager: Robert Whitfield
Address: P.O. Box 565, Charlestown, Nevis, West Indies
Location: On Pinney's Beach, just outside Charlestown, 15 min. and $12 by taxi from the airfield, 40 min. by private launch from St. Kitts — a few min. by air on Nevis Express, which meets every American Eagle flight arriving at St. Kitts ($35 per person each way)
Telephone: 869/469-1111
Fax: 869/469-1040
E-mail: None
Web: www.fourseasons.com
Reservations: 800/332-3442, Four Seasons in the U.S.; 800/268-6282 in Canada
Credit Cards: All major cards
Rates: $675–$750, one-bedroom suites to $2,625 EP (Jan 3–Apr 14); service charge 10%; off-season 60% less
Rooms: 196, including 10 Four Seasons and 2 Presidential Suites, all with screened porch, air-conditioning, ceiling fans, stocked refrigerator, remote cable TV/VCR, direct-dial telephones, closet safe; also some villas for rent along the fairways
Meals: Breakfast 7am–noon, lunch noon–5pm in the Dining Room, Cabana, or Clubhouse, dinner 6–10pm in the Dining Room or Grill Room (about $90–$100); local band at poolside restaurant; "gracious informality ... after sunset, we would recommend collared, buttoned shirts, full-length trousers, and closed-in footwear for gentlemen"; 24-hr. room service
Entertainment: Lounge-bar, billiards, Nintendo, Sony PlayStations, movie library; trips to St. Kitts on the resort's private twin-hulled launch
Sports: 2,000 feet of beach, 2 freshwater pools with whirlpool and lap lanes, croquet, small-boat sailing, pedalos, windsurfing, snorkeling gear, aqua-cycles, exercise room (Lifecycles, Stairmasters, sauna, whirlpool) — all free; golf (18 holes), tennis (10 courts, clay and all-weather, with lights, Peter Burwash pro shop), water-skiing, treatments at new state-of-the-art health spa at extra charge; scuba diving by arrangement

PS: Some children (they're tucked away in their own game room and have separate dining hours), some executive seminar groups; open year-round; also available for rental are privately owned two-, three-, and four-bedroom villas at Four Seasons Resorts Estates — from $2,650 a night

PPS: American Airlines, which serves St. Kitts out of San Juan, now has an office on the grounds of the Four Seasons with complete check-in facilities — a godsend, like that private lounge at the St. Kitts airport

Montpelier Plantation Inn

NEVIS

☆ ☆ ☆ ☆	♈ ♈	☻	$ $ $ $
ATMOSPHERE	DINING	SPORTS	RATES

In the beginning was the plantation, where, one day in 1776, beneath a shady silk cotton tree, a local widow named Fanny Nisbet wed a naval officer who later became a naval legend, Admiral Lord Nelson. You can still see the couple's signatures in the wedding register at the nearby Fig Tree Church. Then in the Sixties, Montepelier was acquired by an aristocratic young English couple, James and Celia Milnes Gaskell, who took the tumbledown plantation and set about rebuilding the great house, propping up the old stone windmill, planting eight bungalows around the garden, and adding a unique swimming pool surrounded by decorative canvas murals of bucolic local life. It became one of the Caribbean's most appealing small inns, a choice getaway for lovers who wanted solitude and serenity and, above all, privacy (Princess Diana and her two lads spent an unhounded week there). After 30 years of tending, coddling and feeding guests, the Gaskells decided to move to a villa just down the hill and sell their cherished inn to an American international banker, Lincoln Hoffman and his wife Muffin, who have left the day-to-day running to his son, Tim, and daughter-in-law, Meredith.

The guest rooms, happy to say, have changed only marginally, their white ceramic tile floors and white walls serving as backdrops to four-poster or bamboo beds with white netting, cool Swiss cotton and Porthault cotton bed covers, bamboo headboards, and wicker and glass end tables. What's been added are friendly frills — fresh fruit and bottled water daily, bamboo racks for the Gilchrist & Soames toiletries, lots of fresh flowers, and nightlights. (The Hoffmans may add air-conditioning in some of the rooms — hardly necessary at this elevation.) Now Montpelier has reappeared rejuvenated and restyled — but without losing much of its character, except, perhaps, for its plummy Englishness, and retaining most of its staff and its chef, Mark Roberts.

The changes begin at the front office, which now has a desk rather than a counter and interesting local bric-a-brac decorations. The breakfast terrace has been brightened with stylish knickknacks but otherwise remains the same understated, low-key place to begin another day of tranquility. The main changes are in what has always been for me (and probably for most guests) the most charming part of Montpelier—the lounge bar, the so-called Great Room, in the old longhouse, a comfy English parlor with gray stone rather than chintz. The Hoffmans have dressed it with some imaginative details: the mirror, which is a gargantuan wooden template of a sugar mill gear wheel (a holdover from sugar mill days), oversize stone lamps, and the plump chairs and sofas upholstered in Brunschwig Fils Ananas Exotique fabrics.

What the Gaskells referred to as their Ballroom (but which probably never heard the sound of a quadrille) is now a private dining alcove dominated by a large circular mahogany table with whimsical bamboo and pineapple decorations. Outside on the covered dinner terrace, the Western Veranda, two more of those Bunyanesque templates serve as a room divider, which most guests won't notice as they tuck into Mark Roberts' chilled cucumber, mint, and yogurt soup; roasted loin of pork and cassis; and raspberry terrine with a guava coulis.

Name: Montpelier Plantation Inn

Owners/Managers: The Hoffman Family

Address: P.O. Box 474 Nevis, St.Kitts & Nevis, West Indies

Location: In the hills, 750 feet above sea level, 30 min. and $22 from the airport

Telephone: 869/469-3462

Fax: 869/469-2932

E-mail: info@montinn.com

Web: www.montpeliernevis.com

Reservations: Direct

Credit Cards: MasterCard, Visa, American Express

Rates: $430–$505 CP (Dec 16–Apr 27); service charge 10%; off-season 30% less

Rooms: 17 in 8 bungalows, including 1 suite, all with patio, ceiling fans, king or twin beds, four-poster or bamboo beds with white netting, full tub and shower, tea/coffeemakers, safe, direct-dial telephone, bathrobes, hair dryer; the solitary suite has a separate living room with double sofabed

Meals: Breakfast 8:15–10am, lunch noon–2:30pm in the patio, complimentary afternoon tea 3:30–5:30pm beside the pool, dinner 8pm on the western veranda ($100); casual dress (but long trousers for men — and at 750 feet up you might want to take along a cardigan or wrap); room service for breakfast and light dinners at no extra charge; quiet recorded music in the Great Room lounge

Entertainment: During the winter season, evenings of dancing to the Honey Bees native band; occasional beach barbecues with beach cricket; library and card room, but mostly mingling with the other guests

Sports: 60 × 30 ft. swimming pool, tennis (1 court, no lights, rackets and balls available); free shuttle to private beach and beach bar, 20 min. away, where snorkeling gear is complimentary; other watersports can be arranged at extra charge

PS: Children welcome, if 8 years or older, throughout the year; "cellphones don't work in this location"; closed Sept

Golden Rock

NEVIS

☆ ☆ ☆	☉ ☉	❻	$ $
ATMOSPHERE	DINING	SPORTS	RATES

Orchids grow by the stone patio; hummingbirds flit from blossom to blossom and from saman tree to saman tree. You're 1,000 feet above sea level, in a flowering 25-acre garden surrounded by 100 private acres of tropical greenery, with a misty rain forest an hour's hike from the pool.

Golden Rock is a 200-year-old sugar estate, its counting house converted into a reception room and office, its original windmill an unusual duplex suite with stone walls, two antique four-posters, and a private sun deck at the rear. The remaining rooms, in pastel-colored bungalows widely spaced among the allamanda and bougainvillea, have one-of-a-kind mahogany four-poster beds and verandas with views of unspoiled countryside and unending sea. Three newer rooms are located one level down the hill, between the rose garden and the herb garden, but still with that stunning view. All the rooms have been refurbished with white ceramic-tile floors and enlarged tiled bathrooms, but best of all they have roomy verandas with huge panoramic views.

The dining room is a garden porch in the old vaulted "longhouse," where candlelit dinners — say, pumpkin soup, lobster on the half shell, or curried lamb with hot Nevis sauce, and mango mousse or banana cream with meringue — are served in the old-time plantation style with Pam Barry dining every evening with her guests at a communal table.

It's an unhurried life up here, at the end of a long bumpy driveway lined by poinsettia and flamboyant. Unhurried breakfast on your veranda, unhurried lunch on the patio, unhurried drinks in Mervin's bar, unhurried dinner in the garden porch. This is a place for reading (in the "secret garden" orchid courtyard, for example), for backgammon or Scrabble, maybe a game of tennis, surely a dip in the big spring-fed pool. Twice a day, Pam Barry offers her guests a trip to one of two private beaches or to town, and twice a day, many of them decide not to leave the garden or gazebo. Saturday evenings the gardener picks up his bamboo flute and leads his group, the Honey Bees, through their repertoire of local airs.

But most of the time the loudest noise is the sighing of the breeze in the saman trees.

Name: Golden Rock
Owner/Manager: Pam Barry
Address: Box 493, Nevis, West Indies
Location: In the parish of Gingerland, 1,000 feet in the hills, give or take an inch, about 25 min. and $22 by taxi from the airfield

Telephone: 869/469-3346
Fax: 869/469-2113
E-mail: gdhobson@golden-rock.com
Web: www.golden-rock.com
Reservations: Direct or 800/223-9815, International Travel & Resorts
Credit Cards: American Express, MasterCard, Visa
Rates: $210–$275 EP (Dec 24–Apr 14); service charge 10%; off-season 30% less
Rooms: 16, including the Sugar Mill Suite, all with veranda, shower only, four-poster bed; the Sugar Mill Suite has an additional sleeping gallery, stone-walled shower, and huge antique four-posters (king-size upstairs, 1 queen and 1 twin downstairs)
Meals: Breakfast 8–10am, lunch noon–2:30pm (both alfresco on the terrace), afternoon tea 4–5pm, dinner 7:30–9pm (in the indoor garden pavilion, fixed menu, $90); informal but jackets not inappropriate (partly because of the elevation); lunch is also served at the private beach bar on Pinney's Beach
Entertainment: Bar/lounge, parlor games, billiards, darts, some recorded music in bar ("never in the dining room"), live music Tues (calypso) and Fri (steel band with fish barbecue), telescope for stargazing
Sports: Spring-fed pool, tennis (1 court, recently resurfaced but with constricted alleys, no lights) in the garden, transportation to the inn's private beach properties (20 min. away) twice daily, snorkeling gear — all free; guided hikes through the rain forest; other watersports can be arranged nearby
PS: Some children, not many; "cellphones don't work well at our location"; closed Sept

Hermitage Plantation Inn

NEVIS

☆ ☆ ☆ ☆　　　Y Y Y　　　❻　　　$ $ $
ATMOSPHERE　　　DINING　　　SPORTS　　　RATES

Alexander Hamilton found it to his liking, we're told. So did Horatio Nelson. And so today do bevies of contemporary knights and lawyers, actors, and low-key rock singers. Certainly this place has been around long enough to have welcomed Nelson and Hamilton: The Great House is something like 300 years old, all shingles and rafters and in remarkably fine (if somewhat fragile) fettle for its age. Its book-laden foyer leads to a roomy, raftered lounge furnished with Victoriana and assorted period pieces, the setting for house-party-style gatherings before the pumpkin fritters and shrimp in vodka sauce or after the last crumb of Key lime pie has been plucked from the plate; the trellised dining veranda, just off the lounge, blends nicely with its venerable surroundings.

The Carriage House, in traditional Nevisian style, houses three of the guest rooms. The remaining lodgings are in 11 new but traditionally styled cottages in the garden, up the hill a few paces behind the stone-decked, fresh-water swimming pool. The decor features four-poster canopy beds (on wood and foam bases), Schumacher bedspreads with pastoral patterns, frilly pillow-cases, sturdy wardrobes, and showers, tubs, and Victorian fixtures in all the bathrooms. The luxury quarters also have small kitchenettes.

Like so many Nevis plantations, Hermitage sits high in the hills, in a garden terraced by hand-cut stone, flowering shrubs, and tangerine, lime, tamarind, and soursop trees. Owners/managers Maureen and Richard Lupinacci built a reputation for fine cooking and cordial hospitality when they ran nearby Zetlands Plantation. Their infectious charm and cuisine (fea-turing fresh local produce, including pork and lamb) bring their guests back year after year, and they now have a loyal following, turning the Hermitage into the tropical cousin of a quiet little country inn in Vermont — or, I should say, Pennsylvania's Bucks County, the Lupinaccis' original home. It's so peace-ful here that movie producers have been known to settle in for a week or two to work on scripts and shooting schedules. It's good value, too, a fact that wouldn't be lost on Scots-descended Alexander Hamilton if he were around today.

Name: Hermitage Plantation Inn
Owners/Managers: The Lupinacci Family
Address: Nevis, West Indies
Location: In the parish of St. John's Figtree, in the hills about 30 min. and $20 by taxi from the airfield
Telephone: 869/469-3477
Fax: 869/469-2481
E-mail: nevherm@caribsurf.com
Web: www.hermitagenevis.com
Reservations: 800/682-4025, toll-free direct
Credit Cards: American Express, MasterCard, Visa
Rates: $325–$790 CP (Dec 15–Apr 15); 8% tax and service charge 10% extra; off-season 30% less
Rooms: 15, all different, in 12 separate garden cottages, in 3 categories; all with showers/tubs, ceiling fans, balcony or patio, heirloom four-poster canopy beds, direct-dial telephones, antiques, tea/coffeemaker, safes, refrigerators; 7 Luxury Cottages have kitchenettes and TV/VCR; plus 1 fully equipped villa, the three-bedroom Manor House, with its own tiled pool and garden
Meals: Planters Breakfast 8–10am, lunch noon–2:30pm, afternoon tea 4pm, dinner 8pm in the covered veranda draped with flowering vines (about $110 for 4 courses); "evening wear is smart casual and shorts are not worn in the evening"; room service during meal hours; West Indian buffet with music on Wed evenings
Entertainment: Conversation around the bar, parlor games, TV room, scores of paperbacks, opera recordings

Sports: Pool, walking, trips to the beach by shuttle van, tennis court (no lights), snorkeling gear — all free; horseback riding and rides along the back roads in an antique carriage at extra charge

PS: Some but not many children; "cellphones don't work here"; open year-round

Old Manor Estate & Hotel

NEVIS

☆☆	ҮҮ	☻	$ $
ATMOSPHERE	DINING	SPORTS	RATES

Here you while away your hours among monkey-no-climb and gooseberry trees, surrounded by gardens that are almost an outdoor museum of colonial industry — dotted with antique pistons, gearwheels, and other metal sculptures from another era. Mount Nevis itself looms above the garden swimming pool, and the island of Nevis slopes off to the distant sea.

The ground floors of the 200-year-old original cut-stone buildings — sugar mill, hospital, smokehouse, and sugar factory — are topped with wooden-sided plantation-style structures with steep roofs and wooden verandas, painted in pleasing tones of off-white and coral. The guest rooms are spacious, uncluttered, comfortable, and not at all pricey.

One thing hasn't changed: the reputation of the Cooperage Dining Room. They take cuisine seriously here, growing their own spinach and lettuce in what used to be the settling tanks, serving such tasty dishes as Jamaican jerk pork, local wahoo steak seasoned with lime and butter, breaded escalopes of veal sautéed in butter and served with a champagne morel sauce. Friday night is given over to a lobster-and-steak buffet — with steel-band accompaniment. It's about the only time you'll hear anything louder than the trade winds rustling in the monkey-no-climb.

Name: Old Manor Estate & Hotel
Manager: John Maycock
Address: P.O. Box 70, Charlestown, Nevis, West Indies
Location: 800 ft. up the flank of Mt. Nevis, 20 min. and $22 from the airport
Telephone: 869/469-3445
Fax: 869/469-3388
E-mail: oldmanor@caribsurf.com
Web: www.oldmanornevis.com
Reservations: 800/892-7093, toll-free direct
Credit Cards: All major cards
Rates: $260–$320 EP (Dec 15–Apr 14); service charge 10%; off-season 30% less
Rooms: 15 rooms and suites in 4 buildings, with balcony or patio, ceiling fans and louvers

Meals: Breakfast 7:30–10:30am, lunch noon–2:30pm at the Cooperage or private beach bar, dinner 6:30–9pm (about $80); informal dress; room service 7am–8pm; Fri buffet with steel band
Entertainment: Bar adjoining the restaurant, billiards, game room, library, TV lounge
Sports: Swimming pool, Jacuzzi, miles of hiking trails, shuttle to beach — all free
PS: Few children; open year-round

Jumby Bay Resort

ANTIGUA

☆ ☆ ☆ ☆   ♉ ♉ ♉   ❸ ❸ ❸ $ $ $ $ $
ATMOSPHERE   DINING   SPORTS   RATES

So, you're looking for something secluded but still accessible? Jumby Bay, a private islet just off the northern coast of Antigua, may be the answer.

"Secluded" because its 300 acres are shared by not much more than 100 guests (in other words, 3 acres per guest), a flock of wild sheep, and a few whistling swans; "accessible" because all it takes to get there is a 3-minute taxi ride to the resort's dock, then, assuming schedules jibe, a boat ride of 10 minutes to the island, with the crew dispensing rum punches on the way. When you set foot on land once more, an electric buggy takes you across shaded, manicured lawns directly to your room.

Lovers have their pick of four styles of lodgings: the original octagonal huts, regular rectangular cottages, the two-story mission-style Pond Bay House at the far end of Jumby Beach, or, if they need lots of space, two- and three-bedroom suites in the town house–style Harbor Beach Villas, the latter slightly detached from what passes in these parts as the action. The huts and cottages are draped in tropical foliage that screens the private porches from passersby while wafting the scents of tropical blossoms through the rooms; in the cottages, huge bathrooms come with double washbasins and showers with additional alfresco showers in leafy courtyards that create a sense of elbow room with a touch of Blue Lagoon romance. The Pond Bay House lodgings are virtually mini-suites, designed on a sumptuous scale and with acres of panels and doors louvered with Brazilian walnut. Everything is freshly redecorated and refurbished by the Rosewood people, who have now taken over the running of the resort.

Let me pass along what every lover of the island wants to hear: Jumby Bay looks just great. Again. In return for the lofty rates, you'll enjoy a high level of mollycoddling — scads of big fluffy towels, waffle-weave cotton bathrobes, a bottle of champagne to welcome you to your suite, 150 new Caloi bicycles (a bike for everyone with 50 to spare, deployed on a use-'em-and-leave-'em

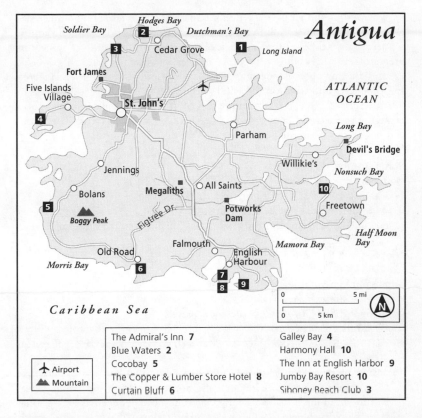

Antigua

Soldier Bay

Hodges Bay **2**

Dutchman's Bay

3

Cedar Grove

1 Long Island

Fort James

Five Islands
Village

St. John's

4

ATLANTIC
OCEAN

Parham

Long Bay

Devil's Bridge

Willikie's

Nonsuch Bay

Jennings

Megaliths

All Saints

10

Freetown

Bolans

5

Boggy Peak

Figtree Dr.

**Potworks
Dam**

Half Moon
Bay

Falmouth

Mamora Bay

Old Road

English
Harbour

Morris Bay

6

7

8

9

Caribbean Sea

0   5 mi

0   5 km

N

The Admiral's Inn **7**	Galley Bay **4**
Blue Waters **2**	Harmony Hall **10**
Cocobay **5**	The Inn at English Harbor **9**
The Copper & Lumber Store Hotel **8**	Jumby Bay Resort **10**
Curtain Bluff **6**	Siboney Beach Club **3**

✈ Airport
▲ Mountain

basis), and one other amenity you still *won't* find on this secluded and care-free spot, although some travelers often think of them as essential: room keys. You don't need them here.

Since eating and drinking are the island's main evening activities, the resort devotes a lot of attention to the dining experience; you can expect sophisticated cuisine in the very romantic candlelit restaurant, set in the courtyard at the refurbished 230-year-old Estate House. It is sophisticated and inventive. New chef Alex Chen Hui hails from Hong Kong but his career has also taken him to Europe, the U.K., and the Middle East, so his menus are eclectic, but some guests find his Oriental dishes such as hibachi filet of grouper on a bed of wok-fried buckwheat soba noodles more successful than western fare like roasted Long Island duck breast with goat cheese ratatouille. The price you pay for Jumby Bay's easy accessibility is the sudden racket of the occasional (very occasional) jet leaving the airport across the channel and lumbering heavenward quite close to the island.

The odd jumbo jet is only a minor blip on the bewitching tranquility and ravishing attractions of Jumby Bay — it is still one of the Caribbean's most refined resorts, no question, and few places give you this sense of space, this precious sense of seclusion. To prove it, hop on your bike and ride over to Pasture Bay, a protected nesting site for hawksbill turtles, the endangered Eretmochelys imbricata, on the windward side of the island. A real Robinson Crusoe sort of place, it has hammocks strung between the seagrape trees, a changing room, and a conveniently placed cooler with soft drinks, beer, rum, and ice, all on the house. Jets? What jets? World? What world?

Name: Jumby Bay Resort
Manager: Peter Bowling
Address: P.O. Box 243, St. Johns, Antigua, West Indies
Location: Just off the northeastern shore of Antigua, a 15- to 20-min. ride by taxi and private launch from the airport (included in the rate), and someone will be at the airport to greet you
Telephone: 268/462-6000
Fax: 268/462-6020
E-mail: jumbybay@rosewoodhotels.com
Web: www.jumbybayresort.com
Reservations: 888/767-3966, Rosewood Hotels
Credit Cards: All major cards
Rates: $950–$1,500 FAP+ (Dec 16–Mar 31); service charge 10%; off-season 40% less
Rooms: 39 rooms and suites plus 11 two-bedroom town house villas with private plunge pools, all with air-conditioning, louvers and ceiling fans, bathrobes, umbrellas and walking canes, minibars, coffeemakers, personal safes, hair dryers, radio/CD/cassette players, direct-dial telephones (with voice mail); luxury two-bedroom town house villas have kitchens, dishwashers, and cable TV; several private luxury villas also available for rent
Meals: Breakfast 7–10:30am and lunch 12:30–3pm at the veranda overlooking the beach, afternoon tea 3:30–5pm and dinner 7–10pm in the Estate House ($130); after sunset, men are requested to wear collared shirts and casual slacks but no jackets or ties are required; room service for continental breakfast only (7–10:30am) at no extra charge
Entertainment: Combo in the Estate House every evening, informal beach tours July through Nov, when you may catch a glimpse of the endangered turtles
Sports: 3 beaches, swimming pool, bicycles, tennis (3 courts, 2 with lights, pro shop), fitness room, snorkeling gear, windsurfing, sunfloats, Sunfish sailing, sea-cycling, water-skiing, 3 miles of hiking trails, beautifully upgraded croquet lawn and putting green — all free; spa treatments, day sailing trips, scuba, golf, and deep-sea fishing nearby
PS: Children are now welcome all year (they have their own playground by the town houses); cellphones "not allowed in dining room"; open year-round

Curtain Bluff

ANTIGUA

☆☆☆☆☆	♈♈♈	❻❻❻❻	$ $ $ $
ATMOSPHERE	DINING	SPORTS	RATES

Behold one of the loveliest settings in the Caribbean. A 12-acre headland with lagoon-smooth beach on the leeward side, breezy surfy beach to windward, rocky bluff at the tip. The flowers are brilliant, the trees tall and stately, the lawns primped to the nearest millimeter. And with rooms for just 140 vacationers, there's more garden than guests.

Curtain Bluff also happens to be one of the most consistently dependable, top-drawer resorts in the islands, thanks largely to the personality of its owner, the inimitable Howard Hulford. Just over 40 years ago, when he was piloting planes around the Caribbean for oil company executives, he used to fly over and lust after this south-coast headland, vowing that one day he would build a dream home there. In 1985, he and his wife, Chelle, moved into a spectacular dream home on the very tip of the bluff, but in the intervening years, he opened, modified, and perfected his stylish resort and welcomed people to Howard's Headland year after year, decade after decade.

For some people, though, Curtain Bluff seems to be too cultivated, too country-clubby. In the high season, you're expected to wear a jacket for dinner (ties are now optional), except Wednesday and Sunday, and judging by the sartorial propriety, guests must send their togs ahead on container ships. Dinner is a serious affair, in an elegant garden pavilion surrounded by lawns, a gazebo, the Sugar Mill Bar, and a dance floor beneath a tamarind tree. Add to that a well-rounded wine cellar that wouldn't look out of place in Beaune, and you may decide that dining here is the sort of event that makes all the dressing up worthwhile. Of course, you may also decide to forgo the dining room and have your dinner sent to your private balcony or patio, while you remain dressed in your bathrobe.

The suites are located in villas built step-fashion up the leeward side of the bluff. Living rooms measure a generous 17 × 20 feet, bedrooms a few feet more; each room (not suite, room) comes with a comfy balcony overlooking the sea, and the suites with duplex configurations also have open dining terraces and secluded patios strung with hammocks. Everything in the suites seems to come in multiples. Two ceiling fans per room (again, not suite, but room), plus another in the bathroom. There are his-and-hers lighted closets and twin vanities, plus three, sometimes four, telephones to a suite. The one-bedroom suites are fitted with 18 light switches — for fans, vanities, dimmers, terraces, and the track lighting that pinpoints gallery-caliber artwork, most of it commissioned for the Bluff. Fabrics and rugs are in delicate pastels, glass doors and screens positively glide, oversize rattan sofas and chairs billow with 18 cushions; Italian marble covers the walls and floors and separate shower stalls of the sumptuous bathrooms. Chelle Hulford designed and decorated these suites with great taste and has conjured up some of the grandest accommodations in the Caribbean. The grandest of these is probably the Terrace Room, at the top of the bluff, with a king-size four-poster bed and huge terrace.

Of the remaining deluxe rooms, one wing acquired a second floor in 2000 and has been converted into suites similar to those on the bluff — and it looks like the remaining wing will follow suit in the near future (all very nice for guests bedding down in them, but, for my money, the new portico to this wing tends to overwhelm the garden — used to be the first thing you saw when you drove in was garden, but now it's concrete).

It's all very relaxed and genteel here (there are no room keys and no one ever asks for them), but despite its country-club flavor, Curtain Bluff is far from being a pasture for geriatrics. It's actually one of the sportiest small hotels in the Caribbean. And, into the bargain, this is one of the best values, despite what, at first glance, might seem like stiff rates. All meals and all drinks are included, and most sports facilities are available at no extra charge. Even water-skiing. Even scuba diving! You pay extra only for day sails or half-day sails on the resort's yacht, *Tamarind*. From its decks, Curtain Bluff looks even more stunningly lovely than it did from the air all those 40 years ago. Which seems to be an appropriate spot to salute Howard Hulford's achievement — 40 years as one of the Caribbean's three or four top resorts, a record of consistency hard to beat. To celebrate those 40 years, Curtain Bluff has added a pair of stunning suites — Grace and Morris — with Jacuzzis on the balconies, exquisite appointments, and living rooms with an entire non-wall opening to the beautiful gardens.

Name: Curtain Bluff
Owner/Managers: Howard Hulford (owner), Robert Sherman (managing director), Calvert Roberts (general manager)
Address: P.O. Box 288, St. John, Antigua, West Indies
Location: On the south coast, next to the village of Old Road, 35 min. and $24 from the airport by taxi
Telephone: 268/462-8400
Fax: 268/462-8409
E-mail: curtainbluff@candw.ag
Web: www.curtainbluff.com
Reservations: 888/289-9898 or 212/289-8888
Credit Cards: American Express, Discover, MasterCard, Visa
Rates: $850–$2,995 FAP+ (Dec 19–Apr 14); service charge 10%; off-season 20% less
Rooms: 72 rooms, Junior Suites, and Executive Suites, in several wings, all with balcony or lanai, marble bathroom, bathrobes, ceiling fans (no air-conditioning), louvers and screened glass doors, direct-dial telephones, wall safes, minibars, some with Jacuzzis
Meals: Breakfast 7–9:30am, continental 9:30–10:30am, lunch 12:30–2pm (served in the open-sided garden pavilion or Beach Club), dinner 7–9:30pm (about $160, with wines, for nonguests) in garden pavilion; beach

barbecue buffet on Wed; "jackets required for gentlemen after 7pm, except Wed and Sun Dec 19–Apr 14; at other times we ask gentlemen to wear long trousers (no jeans, please), a collared shirt, and dress shoes in the evening"; limited room service at no extra charge

Entertainment: Bar, lounge, library, parlor games, TV/video room, live music for dancing every evening (combos, native bands, and so on, amplified but not loud), steel band with beachside buffet

Sports: 2 beaches (1 windward, 1 leeward), free-form swimming pool with two 75-foot lap lanes, hammocks, snorkeling gear, scuba (certified divers only), water-skiing, windsurfing, Sunfish sailing, sea kayaks, reef trips, deep-sea fishing, tennis (4 courts, with lights, pro shop), squash court, exercise room, croquet, putting green — all free; day and ½-day sails on the resort's own 47-foot sailboat at extra charge; golf 10 min. away

PS: "Please, no unaccompanied children in the bar after 7pm" and no children under 12 Jan 10–Mar 10; mid-May features a very popular pro-am tennis tournament; cellphones "discouraged in the bar and restaurant"; closed late July to mid-Oct

The Inn at English Harbour

ANTIGUA

☆ ☆ ☆	❦ ❦	◉ ◉	$ $ $
ATMOSPHERE	DINING	SPORTS	RATES

This was, until a few years ago, one of Antigua's most dependable and most popular small inns, especially with the British (especially since actor Richard Burton spent honeymoons here with two different wives). A few years ago, the Deeth family sold their cherished inn to an Italian family, who closed it down for a couple of years for renovations and expansions. Rumor had it the new owners would change everything, and old-time fans were having palpitations. Now the inn has reopened in 2002, and when you enter the hillside driveway and step into the breezy stone lobby and restaurant and pub-like bar, you'd never know (sigh) there had been a change of owner. It's only when you get down to the beach that you see changes — gone are some of the beach rooms, the grounds have been opened up, and two new wings of rooms have been added, well back from the beach behind an inviting pool. Designed in two two-story wings in Georgian style and named for British admirals, the new suites are more design coordinated than the back-to-basics rooms up on the hill. TVs and minibars are tucked into mahogany cabinets, king-size beds are draped in netting, the mahogany sofas are designed in plantation style, and the bathrooms have spacious tiled shower stalls and twin washbasins.

The focal point of the inn is still the sturdy, open-plan hilltop lodge, crafted from native stone, with quarry-tile floors and beamed ceilings. Chandeliers are fashioned from ships' wheels, and the bar has something of the air of an English pub, with high-backed booths, wooden tables, and, of course, a dartboard. In the adjoining lounge, the shelves are still stacked with copies of *Country Life* and the London newspapers. The dining room and its broad tree-shaded terrace has changed only in subtle ways but the menu is now a tad more continental than English.

What hasn't changed, of course, is the spectacular view of harbor and hills, yachts and powerboats.

Name: The Inn at English Harbour
Manager: Giannia Miani
Address: P.O. Box 187, St.Johns, Antigua, West Indies
Location: At English Harbour, on the south coast, 35 min. and $22 by taxi from the airport
Telephone: 268/460-1014
Fax: 268/460-1603
E-mail: theinn@candw.ag
Web: www.theinn.ag
Reservations: Direct
Credit Cards: All major cards
Rates: $224–$640 EP (Dec 20–May7); 10% gratuities and 8.5% tax extra; off-season, 25% less
Rooms: 34, including 24 suites, 6 hillside rooms, 4 standard beachside rooms, all with ceiling fans and air-conditioning, cable TV, bathrobes, hair dryers
Meals: Breakfast 7:30–9:30am, lunch 12:30–3pm at the beach bar, afternoon tea 5pm, dinner 7:30–9:30pm in the hillside restaurant (about $80); room service during dining room hours; after 6, long trousers for men ("no tees, no tank tops"); some background music
Entertainment: Beach barbecue and band every Thursday, library, board games
Sports: Beachside pool, kayaks, windsurfing, Sunfish sailing, snorkeling gear, rowboat, fitness center, tennis (2 courts, with lights) — all free; scuba diving nearby
PS: Children welcome, except in February; closed Sept 1–Oct 31

The Admiral's Inn

ANTIGUA

☆☆   Y Y $ $
ATMOSPHERE   **DINING**   **RATES**

In Nelson's pre-admiral days as commander in chief of the dockyard, this two-story, weathered-brick structure was an unglamorous corner of his domain — the storehouse for turpentine and pitch. You'd never suspect it today. It's now a lovely 30-year-old inn in a most unusual setting. A well-worn stone patio, set with tables and chairs and shaded by sun umbrellas and casuarina trees, leads to a lawn that ends at the water's edge. Just off to the right, a row of sturdy but stunted stone pillars are all that remain of the former boathouse, decapitated in a long-ago earthquake; just beyond that another section of the dockyard has become an annex of the inn with four more spotless guest rooms. Yachts lie at their moorings a few oar strokes offshore, and somewhere behind you the market women of English Harbour have festooned their stands with batiks, T-shirts, necklaces, and baubles.

The inn's lobby, a tiny desk beneath the stairs in a beamed bar/lounge, faces French doors that lead to the dining terrace. A dartboard adds the right Royal Navy touch; the burgees of 100 yachts and yacht clubs remind you that the Admiral's Inn is a favorite gathering place for sailing buffs. If the Flying Dutchman were to come ashore again one of these days, this would be a sensible place for him to search for a latter-day Senta.

Being a gathering place for yachtspeople, the inn may not be the most serene of hideaways, but it has a lot of charm and camaraderie. Guest rooms are small, simply but tastefully furnished, and cooled by ceiling fans or air-conditioning. Some of the rooms have patios. The prime nest (indeed, one of the prettiest in all of Antigua) is number 1, a large corner chamber with lacy curtains, straw matting, and canopied four-poster, king-size bed (two of the other rooms have queens, the others are twins). Because it's right at the head of the stairs, number 1 gets a certain amount of inn traffic outside its doors, and since it's directly above the bar, it picks up some of the chatter and jollity from rendezvousing voyagers. But the carousing generally ends around midnight, and then all you hear when you throw open the window shutters is the clank of the rigging on the sailboats.

The four rooms across the pillared lawn are a touch quieter — smallish in floor space but with high ceilings, whitewashed-stone walls, built-in dressers, modern plumbing, fans, and air-conditioning. Room A is the biggest, and, being at the harbor end of the row with louvered windows on three sides, it is also the brightest and breeziest.

Even if you don't have time to stay here, stop in for a drink or meal on the broad terrace — indoors beneath iron chandeliers, outdoors beneath the lacy casuarinas. The inn is a popular spot for lunch, which always features delicately seasoned pumpkin soup and fried snapper; the cost, excluding wine, will run about $65 for two people. The surroundings are delightful, the welcome friendly — it's another century, even if the yachts have aluminum rather than wooden masts.

Name: The Admiral's Inn
Manager: Ethelyn Philip
Address: English Harbour, P.O. Box 713, St. John's, Antigua, West Indies
Location: In Nelson's Dockyard National Park, on Antigua's south coast; 16 miles directly across the island from the airport (40 min. and $26 by taxi) and 14 miles from St. John's (30 min. and $23 by taxi)
Telephone: 268/460-1027
Fax: 268/460-1534
E-mail: admirals@dcandw.ag
Web: None

Reservations: 800/223-5695, American Wolfe International
Credit Cards: American Express, MasterCard, Visa
Rates: $130–$160 EP (Dec 15–May 5); service charge 10%; off-season 30% less
Rooms: 14, all with private bathroom (shower only); 8 with air-conditioning, all others with ceiling fans, some with small patios
Meals: Breakfast 7:30–10am, lunch noon–2:30pm, dinner 7:30–9pm (about $74), served indoors or on the terrace; casual dress (but not scruffy, despite the proximity of all those yachts); room service available
Entertainment: Steel band on Sat, dancing, some recorded music, darts
Sports: Snorkeling gear, Sunfish sailing — free; windsurfing, paddleboats, beach, watersports, boat trips, tennis, squash, scuba diving, and horseback riding, all nearby, golf ½ hour away
PS: Some (sometimes lots of) cruise-ship passengers, since you're right in the middle of what tourists come all the way across the island to see; especially busy during Sailing Week (late Apr, early May) and charter-yacht review week (early Dec); closed Sept 1 to mid-Oct

Siboney Beach Club

ANTIGUA

☆☆☆	⅄ ⅄	𝟞	$ $ $
ATMOSPHERE	DINING	SPORTS	RATES

Siboney is one of those small, quiet, laid-back spots where you can hang out in the bar/restaurant for hours, chewing the fat and enjoying sea breezes and island tales. This all-suite hotel was built by and is now owned and run by an easygoing, outgoing Australian, Tony Johnson, who arrived on the island by yacht more than 30 years ago and never left because he has "great windsurfing right on my doorstep."

Johnson has transformed a relatively undistinguished three-story complex into a lush retreat by planting a veritable jungle on the grounds — casuarinas, palms, bougainvillea, and hibiscus that have survived occasional tempests. An oval pool is tucked away in the greenery, loungers are set up among the palms, and seagrapes line the beach. Another palm tree grows right through the roof of the islandy restaurant, the Coconut Grove, where the bar is on land and the terrace is on the beach, and the decor reminds you of Polynesia.

The suites are furnished in contemporary style. Throw back the shutters and your living room becomes a terraced salon overlooking the garden. There's a small pantry/kitchenette tucked out of sight behind louvered doors, complete with refrigerator (unstocked), pots, cutlery, dishes, and a two-ring burner. In the bedrooms, air-conditioning augments the ceiling fans and louvers. The rooms on the upper floors have more privacy — if you don't mind the walk up to them — and you almost feel you're living in a tree house decked with flamboyant and bougainvillea.

There's nothing fancy or swank about Siboney, but it's the sort of place that appeals to English lords and incognito celebrities who yearn for seclusion and comfort, with a special old-time Caribbean charm and a friendly and competent staff. The turquoise sea is only paces away, and the mile-long beach offers the best of both worlds: It's quiet and uncrowded at Siboney, but with plenty of watersports shacks, restaurants, and bars a short walk away along the sand.

Name: Siboney Beach Club
Owner/Manager: Tony Johnson
Address: P.O. Box 222, St. John's, Antigua, West Indies
Location: On Dickenson Bay, about 15 min. and $13 by taxi from the airport, 10 min. and $7 from town
Telephone: 268/462-0806
Fax: 268/462-3356
E-mail: siboney@candw.ag
Web: www.siboney-antigua.com/
Reservations: 800/533-0234, toll-free direct
Credit Cards: American Express, MasterCard, Visa
Rates: $280–$330 EP (Dec 20–Apr 14); service charge 10%; off-season 40% less
Rooms: 12 one-bedroom suites, all with terrace, living room (fans and louvers), and bedroom (air-conditioning), refrigerator, direct-dial telephone, Pullman kitchen, shower, clock radio; TV on request
Meals: Breakfast 8–10am, lunch noon–3pm, dinner 6 10:30pm (about $70–$80) all in the Coconut Grove Bar/Restaurant; casual dress; recorded and occasional live music
Entertainment: Yourselves, but there are bars and casinos nearby
Sports: Mile-long beach, freshwater pool in garden; watersports, sailing, golf nearby
PS: Open year-round

Galley Bay

ANTIGUA

☆☆☆   ♈ ♈   ❽❽ $ $ $ $
ATMOSPHERE   DINING   SPORTS   RATES

This used to be an escapists' favorite, a no-frills but sophisticated retreat for Old Island Hands. A few years ago it was acquired by Antigua Resorts, enlarged, and turned into an all-inclusive like their other properties. In the previous edition of this guide, Galley Bay was relegated to the "All-Inclusives" chapter way at the end.

But I recently had a chance to spend a couple of days there and was so impressed that Galley Bay is now back as a featured resort despite its all-inclusive pedigree. Because truth to tell, there's none of the gung-ho, nonstop frenzy we associate with all-inclusives. If anything, Galley Bay is as laid-back as ever, with a clientele (youngish to elderly) that looks as though it would rather lie in one of the hammocks and read than stand on a pair of skis and chase a powerboat. There are no billboards of activities, and no cheerleaders to make sure everyone is participating.

The focal point of the resort is still the beachside thatched tepee above the bar by night, but by day some of the attention has drifted a few feet to the new swimming pool with its rocky cascade. Guests who like to step from their room straight onto the sand (or nod off to the sound of surf practically in their room) check into the beachfront bungalows; romantics bed down beside the lagoon in thatch-roofed, Polynesian-style quarters called Gauguin Cottages; and folks who like a few more frills and extra steps opt for the new deluxe rooms and suites in the newer two-story wings beyond the restaurant. The beachfront rooms are attractive but not so much different from well-designed (that is, with plenty of cross-ventilation) beachfront rooms elsewhere; the newer rooms and suites have bathrooms larger than you really need, with wet bars in the suites.

It's the Gauguin Villas that put Galley Bay in a class by itself in these parts. "Villas" is a slight misnomer: They really are pairs of *rondavels* (round huts), neither of them very large but each sensibly arranged, one for making love and sleeping, one for showering and dressing. Between the two is a breezeway with shoulder-high bamboo screens. They're kooky and romantic but also very practical: You come in from the sea and sand, head for the shower without tracking sand all over your bedroom, and then, all fresh and glowing, skip across your private breezeway and into bed — or lounge around dishabille, since the screens let the breezes through but keep peeping eyes out. The Gauguins have been brightened up by Antigua Resorts — lighter colors, brighter fabrics, more lights. They're really popular, these would-be Polynesians, but I'm always happy to check into one of the more orthodox beachfront rooms or suites.

Galley Bay now has two dining spots — the original beachside restaurant with its earthenware coal-pot theme (for indoor/outdoor dining) and the new Gauguin Restaurant, an open pavilion with a thatched roof and a series of attached "gazebos" jutting out towards the sea. The gazebos seat six, but the sympathetic maître d' can probably arrange for the two of you to have one all to yourselves. It's a charming way to dine and the food is much better than you might expect.

Name: Galley Bay
Manager: Britton Foreman
Address: Five Islands, P.O. Box 305, Antigua, West Indies
Location: On the island's west coast, 15 min. and $17 from the airport, 10 min. and $12 from St. John's
Telephone: 268/462-0302
Fax: 268/462-4551
E-mail: res@eliteislandresorts.com
Web: www.eliteislandresorts.com

Reservations: 800/345-0356, Antigua Resorts
Credit Cards: American Express, MasterCard, Visa
Rates: $690–$1,020 all-inclusive (Dec 21–Apr 18); off-season, 20% less
Rooms: 70 in 4 categories, all with air-conditioning and ceiling fans, minibars, hair dryers, coffeemakers, bathrobes — but no phones, no TV
Meals: Breakfast 7:30–10am, lunch noon–5pm, afternoon tea 4–5pm, dinner 7–10pm (the latter in one of two dining rooms); "collared shirts and long trousers, no jeans, no T-shirts, no shorts" in the evening; Thurs evening beach barbecue; room service for continental breakfast only; live music in the main dining rooms
Entertainment: Socializing in the bar, live music every evening ("lightly amplified"), games room, library
Sports: ½-mile beach (but beware of the red-flag warnings), swimming pool, tennis (1 court, no lights), 12-station fitness center; windsurfing, snorkeling gear, Sunfish sailing, bicycles, kayaks — all included; water-skiing, scuba, and golf can be arranged
PS: No children under 16 except the week of Christmas/New Year; open year-round

Blue Waters

ANTIGUA

☆☆	Y Y	🌀🌀	$ $ $
ATMOSPHERE	DINING	SPORTS	RATES

Long before you catch your first sight of the eponymous blue waters, you'll be charmed by the botanical flavor of the setting — down the steep hill, into the circular tree-shaded driveway, through the open lobby to the flower-decked terrace, pool, and beach. There are so many plants in these 14 acres it takes 10 full-time gardeners to keep the grounds spruce and dandy.

Two-story wings of rooms lead off on either side of the high-ceilinged, open-to-the-breezes lobby and Pelican Bar. Guest rooms (all of them face the beach) have recently been enhanced with stocked refrigerators, quieter split-unit air-conditioners, and, in some cases, more square footage by extending the original balconies. The newest cluster of one- and three-bedroom condo suites at the far end of the garden give guests even more room to lounge around (although some of the Hillside Suites have views of other condos rather than the sea or lawns).

There has always been a friendly, congenial atmosphere at Blue Waters, nurtured by senior staffers who have been around for years (it's been around for 35 years but a new owner has given it a major revamping). Nice people is still one of the resort's lures, but that lovely confluence of sea and beach and garden — especially the garden, the sheer profusion of hibiscus and pink ixora, white lantana, and red ginger — may be what makes it so popular with the British.

Even for guests with no horticultural bent, there are plenty of opportunities to enjoy the setting in romantic ways. Stroll past the plumbago and tamarind trees to the breakwater known as North Point. There you'll find a tiny gazebo, just big enough for two (except when taken over by a wedding party), where you can get away from the chatter and laughter, listen to the waves, marvel at the blue waters, maybe even discover another shade of blue.

Name: Blue Waters
Manager: Keith Martel
Address: P.O. Box 356, Soldiers Bay, St.Johns, Antigua, West Indies
Location: On the north coast, $15 min. and $12 by taxi from the airport
Telephone: 268/462-0290
Fax: 268/462-0293
E-mail: bluewaters@candw.ag
Web: www.bluewaters.net
Reservations: Direct
Credit Cards: American Express, MasterCard, Visa
Rates: $320–$1,125 CP (Dec 21–Apr 10); 10% service charge and 8.5% government tax extra; off-season 30% less
Rooms: 77 in two-story wings, all with balconies or loggias, air-conditioning and ceiling fans, minibars, safes, hair dryers, cable TV, direct-dial telephones, tea/coffeemakers, bathrobes; the promontory on the west end of the property, a 3-min. walk from the lobby, is now crowned by Rock Cottage, a gorgeous two-bedroom villa with private jetty
Meals: Breakfast 7:30–10:30am, lunch 12:30–2:30pm in the alfresco Palm pavilion, afternoon tea 4–5pm, dinner 7–10pm in the pavilion or the air-conditioned Vyvien's ($80); casual dress ("but feet covered, body covered, no shorts, no tank tops, no jeans after 6"); room service $5 charge
Entertainment: Buffets and live music for dancing 2 or 3 times a week
Sports: 2 beaches, freshwater pool, snorkeling gear, Laser and Hobie Cat sailing, kayaks, windsurfing, pedalos, tennis (1 court, with lights), 11-station fitness center, games room — all free; beauty salon and spa at extra charge; golf and scuba diving nearby
PS: Some children; "even local cellphones don't work in this location"; open year-round

K Club

BARBUDA

☆☆☆☆	♟♟♟	❻❻	$ $ $ $ $
ATMOSPHERE	DINING	SPORTS	RATES

When the Milanese fashion mogul Mariuccia Mandelli, a.k.a. Krizia, got around to choosing her "personal Eden," she opted for Barbuda.

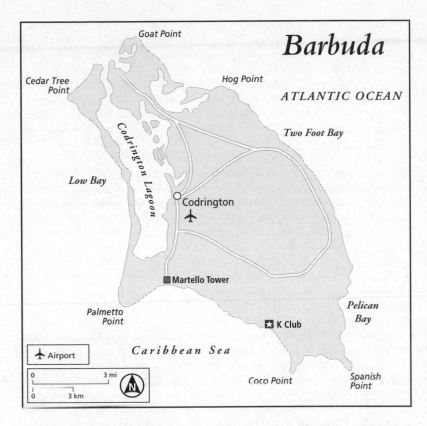

Barbuda? That flat pancake of an island with a nondescript village and a bird preserve where ornithologists from far and wide come to study the frigate bird? That speck of island about 20 minutes by air north of Antigua?

The very same. Because what Barbuda has (apart from no hassles) is a never-ending beach — one of those strands of the softest sand that seems to go on and on, running along most of the island's southwest coast. At the south end of the beach, there's a small, clubby resort called Coco Point Lodge, but otherwise there was virtually nothing here until Krizia came along. She and her husband, Aldo Pinto, used to vacation at Coco Point, then decided to build their own resort. Which, after several stops and starts and false alarms, they did.

Usually when an owner or the spouse of an owner decides to design a hotel, the results can be a bit of a hodgepodge (there are, of course, some eminent exceptions); but when that owner happens to be a world-class modiste of impeccable taste and, moreover, someone answerable, apparently, only to herself and her husband/manager for the bottom line, then the ingredients are in place for something special. And something special this is.

Her $30 million, 241-acre country club comes with a wondrous sense of space and beachiness, with everything open to the trade winds and the sea. Her architect, Gianni Gamondi, has given the spread a contemporary flavor, but (bless him) has kept within the Antillean vernacular — 36 white square cottages with lots of louvers and high-pitched roofs widely strung out along the beach, no rooftop higher than the palm trees. Even the staff housing has more class than the guest rooms in many other hotels.

Everything here is a reflection of Krizia's tastes, down to the Krizia-designed doorknobs. Decor is awash in the house color, a delicate green some-where between turquoise and aquamarine (turquamarine, perhaps?). In fact, the place is so color-coordinated that I suspect if an errant yellow-breasted bananaquit appeared on the breakfast table, it would be shooed off pronto.

As well as being uncommonly stylish, the K Club's suites and villas are unusually spacious. The 20×20-foot bedrooms incorporate reading corners with armchairs and ottomans and still don't feel cluttered. Wooden cathedral ceilings 14 feet high and white ceramic-tile floors add to the sense of spa-ciousness. The walk-in closets could hold enough Krizia dresses to give her Milanese seamstresses carpal tunnel syndrome. The shower stalls are big enough to party in; I love them, but I suspect some folks will say, "With all this space, why no tub?" — the answer probably being, "We want to conserve water."

All this refined decor notwithstanding, I'd probably wrap myself in my yukata (Krizia's custom-designed cotton lounging robe) and spend most of the time outdoors on my spacious private deck. Each suite has a swank white-on-white alfresco kitchenette — an inexplicable luxury since all meals are included in the rate, but it's useful to have the refrigerator close at hand. For siestas, there are bamboo shades to block out the glare and big bamboo loungers that look vaguely like litters once used to carry missionaries around Africa.

I could happily dine at K Club for a week without feeling deprived of having no other place to go on the island. Even if there were, chances are it wouldn't be half as attractive as this one. The dining pavilion is part of the main lodge, beside the beach and open to the breezes with demerara shutters, its lofty ceiling supported by 146 turquoise columns and cooled by a battery of paddle fans. As you might expect, the linens and place settings (Granito Tognana Porcellana) are impeccable. The staff — mostly villagers without any hotel experience — are well trained, helpful, and, on the whole, adept.

Nor would I feel deprived by a lack of daytime bustle. There's that deck for starters. Oh, the reading I could do there (many of the books in the club library are in Italian — anyone for *Ultima Fermata a Brooklyn* or *Le Avventuri di Huckleberry Finn*?). The pool is a dazzler, with the Krizia logo fashioned in tiles on the bottom. One day I'd grab a picnic basket and have the boatman zoom me along in his Boston Whaler to Spanish Point — a lagoon, a reef, and a beach, deserted except for the crews of the odd charter yacht.

Name: K Club
Manager: Antonio Delpin
Address: Barbuda, Antigua & Barbuda, West Indies
Location: On the island's leeward coast, about 20 rutted min. from the airfield (the hotel sends a Nissan Patrol to meet you); the resort will also arrange the last leg of your trip from Antigua on a 7-passenger Islander for about $290 per passenger round-trip (but beware — the brochure promises a

trip from New York of "only 3½ hrs. [plus 15 min.]," but if I were you I'd count on an extra hour rather than 15 min. because of immigration and Customs on Antigua)

Telephone: 268/460-0300

Fax: 268/460-0305

E-mail: kclub@candw.ag

Web: www.lhw.com/kclub

Reservations: Direct or 800/223-6800, Leading Hotels of the World

Credit Cards: American Express, Diner's Club, MasterCard, Visa

Rates: $1,300–$3,000 FAP (Nov 16–Apr 30); service charge 10%; off-season 15%

Rooms: 36 cottages in various configurations, all with air-conditioning and ceiling fans, huge bathroom (showers only, yukatas, hair dryers, generous supplies of Krizia amenities), direct-dial telephones, refrigerator and wet bar on the terrace

Meals: Breakfast 7–11am, lunch 12:30–3pm, dinner 7–10pm (lunch $100, dinner $160 for nonguests); casual but elegant dress ("no jackets required"); room service during meal hours; recorded Caribbean music in the background

Entertainment: Comfy bar/terrace, library, TV/VCR lounge, steel band Sun evening (but "no amplification ever" — hooray!)

Sports: 4 miles of beach, heated seawater pool, Jacuzzi, tennis (2 Astroturf courts, with lights, with pro), snorkeling gear, golf (9 holes, carts and clubs available) — all free; massage, water-skiing, windsurfing, and boat trips at extra charge

PS: No children under 12; cellphones don't work on the island; closed Sept–Oct

OTHER CHOICES

Hurricane Cove Bungalows

NEVIS

Great view (the humped outline of St. Kitts just a mile across the channel), quiet location (a steep rise above a cove — don't let the name deter you; it means it's sheltered from big blows), and come-hither rates (from $95 for two in summer) make this a valid alternative to the island's inns. The mini-resort consists of 12 timber bungalows cantilevered out from the hill, looking, with their glassless shuttered windows, raftered ceilings, and wraparound verandas, perfectly natural in their island setting; but, in fact, they're prefab structures from, of all places, Finland. Each bungalow has a shower rather than a bathtub, a well-equipped kitchen, and mosquito netting to jazz up the country-style, wood-framed bed. Five bungalows have private pools, and there's a small pool on the grounds, built into a 250-year-old fortification, plus watersports and a nearby beach. 12 bungalows. Doubles: $190–$295 for one-bedroom, winter 2002–03. *Hurricane Cove Bungalows, Nevis, West Indies. Telephone and fax: 869/469-9462; e-mail: hcove@caribsurf.com; Web: www. hurricanecove.com.*

The Mount Nevis Hotel & Beach Club

NEVIS

From the dining terrace, bougainvillea draping a white pergola frames a picture postcard: the hotel's 60-foot tiled swimming pool, the green flanks of Mount Nevis, the shoreline of Nevis, the strait that separates Nevis from its sister island, St. Kitts, and then the humpback silhouette of St. Kitts itself. With food like this (try the lobster wontons with ginger-soy dipping sauce, or grilled snapper with mango and tomatillo salsa) and a view like this, you may never get out to explore some of the other fine restaurants on the island.

The hotel consists of the main lodge and its restaurant, then, slightly detached across sloping lawns, three two-story condo-style blocks of rooms and suites, all done in Caribbean contemporary style with rattan and cane, and outfitted with ceiling fans and air-conditioning, TV, and VCR. Some even have full kitchens. Nothing grand, nothing stylish, just very comfortable lodgings run by a very gracious, hospitable couple, Sally and Adly Abdel-Meguid.

But, you say, you want a beach? Just drive down the hill to the hotel's beach club, where you'll find a swath of sand, watersport gear, and a beach-side restaurant serving light meals. The drive down and up is not very exciting, but jot down the Mount Nevis as a smart alternative for folks who find the island's traditional inns too traditional and the Four Seasons too pricey. 32 rooms. Doubles: $245–$310 EP, winter 2002–03. *The Mount Nevis Hotel and Beach Club, P.O. Box 494, Charlestown, Nevis, West Indies. Telephone: 800/756-3847 or 869/469-9374 ; fax: 869/469-9375; e-mail: mountnevis@aol.com; Web: www.mountnevishotel.com.*

Ocean Terrace Inn

ST. KITTS

OTI, as it's affectionately known, has always been a sort of clearinghouse for what used to be known as commercial travelers, the traders and dealers of inter-island business, but it has some appeal for pleasure-bent travelers, too. For a start, the garden. The terraces of the Ocean Terrace Inn, which tumble down a hillside on the outskirts of Basseterre, have been imaginatively reformatted in recent years to include three swimming pools, a grotto, a waterfall, a whirlpool tub, and two swim-up bars, surrounded by dense clumps of foliage and flowers. The original guest rooms have been upgraded and another batch of more upscale rooms added, most of them with views of the bay, the waterfront, or the hills of the Southwest Peninsula. Although you get lots of features (a balcony, air-conditioning and ceiling fans, cable TV, international direct-dial telephones, refrigerators, coffeemakers, hair dryers), the rates are reasonable, making OTI a sensible choice for lovers who want to be closer to the action than the famed trio of inns at the other end of the island. 78 rooms and suites. Doubles: $170–$300 EP, winter 2002–03. *Ocean Terrace Inn, P.O. Box 65, Fortlands, St. Kitts, West Indies. Telephone: 800/524-0512 or 869/465-2754; fax: 869/465-1057; e-mail: otistkitts@caribsurf.com; Web: www. oceanterraceinn.net.*

The Copper & Lumber Store Hotel

NELSON'S DOCKYARD, ANTIGUA

Don't let the name faze you — even if you find it in a dockyard. It's a national park kind of dockyard, and, indeed, the Antigua National Park has now taken over this lovely restoration, once a critical unit of the main Caribbean port of the British Navy back in the 18th century. For history buffs, the adjoining museum has relics of its most famous commander, Captain Horatio Nelson; for yachting buffs, Nelson's Dockyard is the Caribbean's most popular, best-equipped marina and re-victualing base. Throw open your shutters here and you'll look out on a unique setting of bollards and capstans, masts, and rigging.

The Copper & Lumber Store, now run by the Antigua National Park people, is a sturdy, two-story structure in Georgian/Admiralty style, built of native stone and hefty rough-hewn timbers that wouldn't have looked out of place on a ship of the line. The hotel is filled with antiques. The "office" is a 17th-century *escritorio* (writing desk) carted off as booty from a Spanish galleon; the weathered brick floors and walls of the lobby lead to a cloister-like patio and warehouse doors that open to lawns and the marina. All the guest rooms and suites have views of the harbor and yachts in one direction or another; all are furnished with period pieces accenting the basic decor of ceiling beams, hand-stenciling, and wallpapers and fabrics that are replicas of 200-year-old patterns. Although most people who stay here are overnighting before or after cruises, these are lodgings to settle into for a few days to explore the historic surroundings. The Copper & Lumber has its own pub restaurant, the Admiral's Inn is 2 minutes away, and there are several eating places just outside the Dockyard gates. But check the status of the hotel before you commit yourselves — ownership and management are shaky. 14 fan-cooled rooms. Doubles: $210–$360 EP, winter 2002–03. *The Copper & Lumber Store Hotel, P.O. Box 184, St. John's, Antigua, West Indies. Telephone: 268/460-1058; fax: 268/460-1516; Web: www.yachtcharterclub.com/copper-lumber.htm.*

Cocobay

ANTIGUA

You know those back-to-basics little wooden houses you see while you're driving around the islands? Here's your chance to stay in one, sort of. Veteran hotelier Andrew Michelin and his partners have built replicas of these pastel-colored "chattel houses" but given them some contemporary touches. The interiors are wood-framed and wood-floored in traditional style, but the hand-carved beds are topped with billowy white netting and covered with white bedspreads; the showers, tiled in blue and white, open directly to your private veranda, with a hammock at one end and a pergola at the other to coax thunbergia to grow and spread and turn your veranda into a flowery bower. Since the location is breezy (on a hillside above a beach), there's no need for air-conditioning, and you can rely on ceiling fans and lots of louvers for cooling. To make the place still more appealing, most of the stylish furniture is handcrafted locally. The rest of Cocobay centers on a hilltop pavilion restaurant (try the Caribbean seafood pie with snow peas), a hilltop pool, and an inviting bar/lounge, as well as beachy activities like windsurfing, Sunfish sailing, and kayaking. 41 rooms. Doubles: $460–$510 EP, winter 2002–03. *Cocobay Resort, Valley Church, P.O. Box 431, St. John's, Antigua, West Indies. Telephone: 800/816-7587; e-mail: info@cocobayresort; Web: www.cocobayresort.com.*

Harmony Hall

ANTIGUA

Unlike neighboring Nevis and St. Kitts, Antigua had no nifty little plantation inns — at least until now. This promising "newcomer" has actually been around for several years as an art gallery and restaurant built around a former sugar mill, with a few rooms tacked on as an afterthought; but new Neapolitan owners have now rejuvenated the place, enhancing the menu, fixing up the six existing rooms by adding Italian marble and tiles for the bathrooms and imaginative decor in the living area. Harmony Hall has always been an attractive spot for a day's outing — buying arts and crafts, having a dip in the pool, lingering over lunch — but now it's a place to consider for a moderately priced stay. There's a pool in the garden, a beach just down the hill. 12 rooms. Doubles: $155 CP, winter 2002–03. *Harmony Hall, Brown's Bay, P.O. Box 1558, St. Johns, Antigua, West Indies. Telephone: 268/460-4120; fax: 268/460-4406; e-mail: harmony@candw.ag; Web: www.harmonyhall.com.*

The French
West Indies

he *tricouleur* flutters above and
micro bikinis wiggle on Martinique, Guadeloupe, St.
Martin (the French half of the island otherwise known as
St. Maarten), St. Barthélemy, and a few out islands; French
savoir faire and joie de vivre have been transplanted
intact — in fact, they may even have gained from overlays
of tropical sensuousness. You'll find some of the best eating
in the Caribbean here, some of the sportiest highways, the
most stylish dressers, and, on the nudist beaches, the most
enthusiastic non-dressers. These are great islands, or integral
political units, of la belle France.

Martinique (50 miles long and 22 miles wide) is a lush, mountainous land with rain forests, plantations, fishing villages, and masses of wildflowers. It has enjoyed centuries of renown for its dusky maidens: Napoléon's Josephine is the most famous, but Martinique has also provided queens and consorts for a dozen other rulers — including Louis XIV and the Grand Turk of Stamboul. Fort-de-France, the capital, is an intriguing mishmash of West Indies seaport, the latest Peugeots, fishing boats, yachts, open-air markets, high fashion, and gourmet restaurants.

But the most interesting part of the island for my money is the spectacular north around Mont Pelée, especially the town of St. Pierre, known as the Paris of the Caribbean before it was destroyed when Pelée erupted one Sunday morning in 1902. The highway/road/path along the rugged northeast coast to remote Grand' Rivière is also worth an excursion and picnic.

Guadeloupe (from the Spanish Guadalupe and the Arabic Oued-el-Houb, meaning River of Love) is really two islands, Grande-Terre and Basse-Terre, linked by a pair of short bridges. The capital is also known as Basse-Terre, away in the south, shut off from the rest of the island by the magnificent National Park of Guadeloupe. But the action is up around Pointe-à-Pitre, which is rapidly beginning to look like a suburb of Paris. When *les citoyens* of Pointe-à-Pitre want to get away from it all, they board a ferryboat for the 60-minute ride to Terre-de-Haut, one of the islets that make up the tiny archipelago known as Les Saintes. It's about as quiet and unspoiled as they come, with an atmosphere that's French Antillean to the last Gauloise. This is one place where you may need an acquaintance with French beyond *bonjour* and *merci*.

Technically, St. Barthélemy, or St. Barths, is part of the *département* of Guadeloupe, although it's closer to St. Martin, which is (at least on the French side) in the same geopolitical boat. St. Barths is the tiniest (about 8 sq. miles) of the French islands and something of a curiosity: It and Les Saintes are the only islands in the Caribbean with a predominantly white population (mostly descendants of the original Breton settlers), and its picture-postcard port of Gustavia was formerly an outpost of Sweden. Despite its modest size, St. Barths manages to accommodate something like 60 restaurants.

HOW TO GET THERE   The simplest way to get to Guadeloupe and Martinique these days is via American Eagle flights from San Juan. In winter, North American Airlines flies direct to Martinique from New York every Sunday. You can also make relatively easy connections via Antigua or Barbados (on LIAT or Air Caraïbes) or St. Maarten and San Juan (on Air Caraïbes). There is also a twin-hull, high-speed ferryboat service between Guadeloupe and Martinique, with stops at Dominica along the way.

For St. Barthélemy, you first fly to St. Maarten for connecting flights on Windward, Air Caraïbes, or some other local airline (a total of about 16 departures a day, depending on the season). There are also a few scheduled

---

St. Martin Hideaways

Hotels on St. Martin, the French half of the dual St. Maarten/St. Martin, are listed with St. Maarten hideaways in the chapter on the Dutch Windward Islands. See page 107.

---

flights on inter-island airlines from San Juan and St. Thomas. For the faint-hearted, who may prefer not to endure the modified kamikaze approach to St. Barths's airstrip, there are also several sea crossings by launch or catamaran, although they may not connect with international flights and, therefore, may involve an overnight stay on St. Maarten/St. Martin. Ask your travel agent (or call 590 590/87-10-68) to check out the schedules for the efficient, comfy *Voyager I* and *Voyager II* or one of the ubiquitous sailing catamarans, if you're in no hurry to get there. Also, since St. Barths cannot handle aircraft after dark, savvy trip planners may want to have some kind of backup option in mind in case their U.S. flights are delayed and they find themselves stranded overnight on St. Maarten/St. Martin.

For information on St. Barths, call 410/286-8310; Guadeloupe, 011 590 590/82-09-30; Martinique, 800/391-4909 or visit www.martinique.org and www.touristmartinique.com.

François Plantation

ST. BARTHELEMY

☆☆☆☆   ♈♈♈   ✆ $ $ $ $
ATMOSPHERE   **DINING**   **SPORTS**   **RATES**

For more than 20 years, François Beret has been one of St. Barths's most esteemed restaurateurs, so his longtime fans have dutifully followed him to his new hillside inn. They applaud his restaurant, his cuisine, his wines, but his eyes really light up when you compliment him on his garden.

In this flowery minijungle, you'll find lantana and mango, palmier and amandier, filao and caoutchouc, "probably one of every type of tree that grows on the island," and 20 types of hibiscus in exquisite colorings, which Beret arranges in joyous bouquets to decorate his veranda. There are so many flowers and trees growing in this luxuriant garden that you barely see the inn and its dozen cottages until you're practically on the doorstep and walking beneath a cobalt blue pergola into the lounge.

François Plantation sits on a cool hillside near the hamlet of Colombier (not far from where the Rockefellers built their private hideaway), with sweeping views from the veranda and most of the cottages, the grandest panorama reserved for the small hilltop swimming pool with its sunbathing "island." The pastel-colored cottages are designed in traditional Antillean style — square wooden frames with steeply pitched roofs, raftered ceilings, terrazzo-tile floors, chunky pencil-post beds crafted of mahogany, with rattan stands to house refrigerators and television sets.

The veranda doubles as lounge and restaurant, the former furnished with cushioned rattan and plump sofas in shades that echo Beret's plantings, and the latter in Georgian-style mahogany tables and cane-seated chairs. Lavish greenery in pots and planters and the leafy garden just beyond the white balustrade give the place an authentic colonial look, while the fabrics and pastel prints add a dash of sophistication.

François Beret, although still the mastermind behind the menu and upholder of standards, now functions as the boniface in chief and has handed the kitchen brigade over to Chef Bruno Benedetti, an espouser of the gourmet olive oils of the Mediterranean and the spices of the Caribbean. The extensive a la carte menu includes turbot poached in bay leaf–flavored broth and tournedos of roasted ostrich with Cajun spices and other meticulously seasoned choices. The wine list has as many choices as there are blossoms in the garden.

Name: François Plantation
Owners/Managers: François and Françoise Beret
Address: Colombier, 97133 St. Barthélemy, French West Indies
Location: In the hills, about 7 min. and $12 from the airport or the main town of Gustavia
Telephone: 590 590/27-80-22
Fax: 590 590/27-61-26
E-mail: info@francois-plantation.com
Web: www.francois-plantation.com
Reservations: 800/932-3222, WIMCO
Credit Cards: American Express, MasterCard, Visa
Rates: $390–$440 CP (Dec 21–Mar 31); service charge included; off-season 35% less
Rooms: 12 colonial-style cottages, each with marble bathroom (twin vanities), air-conditioning and ceiling fans, direct-dial telephone, stocked minibar, coffeemaker, bathrobes, cable TV and stereo, wall safe
Meals: Breakfast 7:30–10am on the veranda; no lunch; dinner 7–10pm, also on the veranda (about $150–$180); dress informal; some quiet background recordings; room service for breakfast only.
Entertainment: Eating and thinking about eating
Sports: Hilltop freshwater pool, sun deck, 4-station fitness gazebo beside pool; beaches nearby (you really need a car)
PS: Not really suitable for children; closed Aug 1–Oct 15

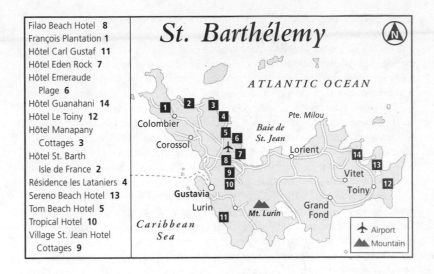

Filao Beach Hotel **8**
François Plantation **1**
Hôtel Carl Gustaf **11**
Hôtel Eden Rock **7**
Hôtel Emeraude
  Plage **6**
Hôtel Guanahani **14**
Hôtel Le Toiny **12**
Hôtel Manapany
  Cottages **3**
Hôtel St. Barth
  Isle de France **2**
Résidence les Lataniers **4**
Sereno Beach Hotel **13**
Tom Beach Hotel **5**
Tropical Hotel **10**
Village St. Jean Hotel
  Cottages **9**

Hôtel Carl Gustaf

ST. BARTHELEMY

☆☆☆☆	♈♈♈	✪	$ $ $ $
ATMOSPHERE	DINING	SPORTS	RATES

The 10-year-old Carl Gustaf is notched into a precipitous hillside on the edge of town, its suites cascading down from the lobby, just four suites on each level with a central stairway running down the middle.

Trouble is, there are 82 steps to the *escalier*, plus another score or so to reach the lobby and restaurant, so be sure to reserve a suite on the upper levels (rates are the same, regardless of location). Moreover, the lower the suite, the more the utility poles and power cables spoil the view. But what a view!

Gustavia, with its rectangular yacht-filled port and red-roofed wooden houses, has to be one of the prettiest sights in the Caribbean, and the panorama from the Carl Gustaf is quintessential Gustavia. So guests can enjoy the scene in uncrowded, scantily clad comfort, the architect has designed a living room with one wall removed, facing a broad wooden deck with wooden loungers — and a tiny plunge pool at the edge of each deck.

Carl Gustaf's cantaloupe-colored stucco cottages echo the style of the traditional St. Barths home — trim squares with steeply pitched red roofs. One-bedroom suites consist of the terrace, adorned with a pergola; the three-walled open-air living room, measuring around 300 square feet; a small pantry with minibar and two-ring burner; and a bedroom with two sets of French doors opening to the deck and the living room — it's just as well it has so much glass, as it's quite small. Ditto the bathroom (which has a shower only). Two-bedroom suites have an identical bedroom on the other side of the living room, plus what the brochure calls a "cabin" with two bunks for kids. It should be added, however, that the hefty rates bring many frills and refinements — Porthault bathrobes, Signoricci toiletries, two fax machines, three telephones, three TVs, a VCR, and pantries with full-size refrigerators and wet bars. A one-bedroom rates only one fax, two phones, and two tellies.

The best view in the house is from the lobby/bar/restaurant level, a white-on-white terrace enclosed in frameless glass screens, with a few tables on a tiny terrace beside a bikini-size pool that's more decorative than swimable. If you decide to eat here, let me point out that the view is best at lunchtime — in the evening the glass screens tend to reflect too much sparkle and glitter, dissipating the view.

There are, of course, lots of refined touches here. Blue-white-gold Haviland china for the filet of beef. Fretwork grills over the air-conditioning outlets (they look like they were done by one of the island's master carpenters, but, in fact, they were designed and worked by computers in Switzerland). The state-of-the-art halogen burners in the pantry. The fan-shaped headboards trimmed with Swiss fabrics. The paintings and lithographs of sailing ships in each suite. The flower-decked parking garage across the street. In fact, the Carl Gustaf would be a super-romantic hideaway if the rates were guillotined — say, by 30%. In that case, I could see myself very happily spending a couple of spellbinding nights here (the spellbinding part being the view, of course).

Name: Hôtel Carl Gustaf

Manager: Emanuelle Bourgueil

Address: Rue des Normands, Gustavia, 97133 St. Barthélemy, French West Indies

Location: In the foothills on the edge of town, about 5 min. from the airport, easy walking distance to the cafes and restaurants of Gustavia (the hotel van will meet you)

Telephone: 590 590/27-79-00

Fax: 590 590/27-82-37

E-mail: carlgustaf@compuserve.com

Web: www.carlgustaf.com

Reservations: 800/932-3222 or 401/847-6290, WIMCO

Credit Cards: American Express, MasterCard, Visa

Rates: $880–$1,250 CP (Dec 20–Apr 14); service charge included; off-season 25% less

Rooms: 15, 7 one-bedroom and 7 two-bedroom suites, all with indoor-outdoor living room, broad wooden deck, private plunge pool, air-conditioning, bathrobes, hair dryer, pantry, minibar, TV/VCR, CD/stereo, direct-dial telephones, fax machine; 1 Honeymoon Suite with whirlpool

Meals: Breakfast anytime, lunch noon–2:30pm, dinner 7–10pm (about $120); informal but stylish dress ("no shorts, no T-shirts, preferably no sandals"); piano in the evening; room service during dining-room hours

Entertainment: The bar, the view
Sports: Plunge pools, exercise room, sauna — all free; the nearest beach is a
    5 min. drive away, watersports 10 min. away
PS: Some children; open year-round

Hôtel St. Barth Isle de France

ST. BARTHELEMY

☆☆☆☆   ♈ ♈ ♈   ❻❻ $ $ $ $
ATMOSPHERE   **DINING**   **SPORTS**   **RATES**

What this somewhat awkwardly named hotel has going for it is setting with
a capital S. It's on Anse des Flamands, one of the loveliest crescents of sand on
an island of lovely beaches, enclosed by two headlands, protected by a reef,
with a pair of islets just offshore to make it postcard-perfect. The world is
miles away, but comforts are no more than arm's length.

The hotel itself lies along both sides of a driveway. On the beach side, the
main clubhouse echoes a colonial plantation house (a handsome but con-
crete-heavy echo of a Great House), with flower-decked stairs curving up to
a broad veranda, 12 rooms, and an antiques-lined breezeway that leads to the
pool deck and beach. On the garden side, there are 16 cottages, a second pool,
and a couple of tennis courts set among tall latanier trees and flowering shrubs
(the plantings look better than ever).

When I first came here shortly after it opened in the early 1990s, I found
plenty to carp about — the dining, the layout, the gloominess of the garden
rooms — but time, experience, and, alas, a hurricane have contrived to
change many of these shortcomings.

The beachside pool, for example, seemed to me to be too close to the
ground-floor suites, but now, the original having been washed into the bay,
the new pool is set lower, giving guests more privacy. The old restaurant,
which was in the garden next to the lighted tennis courts, has been relocated
to the beach and set up in a new pavilion, La Case des Iles, a variation on a
traditional island house, or case. A 30-seat terrace was added. The storm also
dispatched some of the lataniers, but as a result the garden cottages now get
more light. And the original sourpusses have been replaced by a smiling crew
who now welcome the guests and go out of their way to please.

All 12 beachfront lodgings have balconies or patios overlooking the pool
and bay (although the verandas on the upper floor have too much concrete,
which blocks much of the view). Suites and rooms alike blend light colors,
mosquito netting, and fabrics with a smattering of mahogany furniture —
some antique, some reproduction, some Victorian, some colonial — set off by
smart, contemporary rattan and wicker. It's all very minimalist, but a couple
of potted plants or scatter rugs on the marble floors might make the lodgings
feel more cozy.

The pièces de résistance of Isle de France's rooms and suites are the enormous marble bathrooms, larger than the bedrooms in most St. Barths hotels. In the garden suites, large oval tubs for two are positioned alongside picture windows with tinted glass; folks on the outside, I was assured, can't look in. Maybe yes, maybe no (even a travel writer doesn't have license to go snooping around after dark to see if anyone's in the tub), but I suspect that most guests will keep the Venetian blinds tightly shut, especially when the lights are on. These cottages are pleasantly furnished, but they're designed for air-conditioning rather than breezes (alas, no ceiling fans), since neither the French doors nor the windows have screens — not a bright idea in a tropical garden.

But the nitpicking fades when you cross the driveway, mount the steps, and feel your first caress of trade winds and get your first glimpse of Anse des Flamands. This is true even in the evening, when the candles flicker in La Case de L'Isle and you sit down to Chef Mikael LeClezio's *filet de dorade coryphene rôti en barigoule* or *filet de boeuf truffé en pot de feu*. It's some sort of magic.

And not many resorts give you this kind of intimacy and personal service, plus two swimming pools, lighted tennis, and a fitness center, all at no extra charge. And, as of 2003, the Spa at hotel St. Barth Isle de France, designed by Molton Brown, the U.K. cosmetics company, includes a signature Molton Brown Serail Rainforest Room and a range of treatments inspired by the Caribbean, Europe, Asia, and the Middle East.

Name: Hôtel St. Barth Isle de France
Manager: David Walker
Address: P.O. Box 812, 97133 St. Barthélemy, French West Indies
Location: On Baie des Flamands, about 5 min. from the airport, 7 min. from Gustavia (the hotel minivan will collect you)
Telephone: 590 590/27-61-81
Fax: 590 590/27-86-83
E-mail: res@crownintmark.com
Web: www.isle-de-france.com
Reservations: 800/628-8929, Crown International
Credit Cards: All major cards
Rates: $595–$1,090 CP (Dec 20–Apr 15); service charge included; off-season 30% less
Rooms: 33, including 8 rooms and 4 suites in the main lodge, the remainder in garden cottages, all with air-conditioning, deck or veranda, cable TV, DVD players and stereo, stocked minibar, hair dryer, bathrobes, coffeemaker (with real coffee, not the usual little sachets); there's also a couple of new luxury two-bedroom suites
Meals: Breakfast 7–10am, lunch noon–3pm (including service on the beach), dinner 7–9pm (about $80–$100); casual but stylish dress; room service during restaurant hours at extra charge; some recorded music, usually jazz
Entertainment: Yourselves, DVD library — but there's plenty going on a short drive away

Sports: About ½ mile of beach, 2 pools (1 beachside, 1 in the garden that you often have all to yourselves), tennis (2 courts, with lights), snorkeling gear, air-conditioned squash court, fitness room — all free; spa treatments at extra charge; sailing and windsurfing nearby

PS: Some children; closed Sept 1 to mid-Oct

Hôtel Le Toiny

ST. BARTHELEMY

☆☆☆☆☆	ΥΥΥΥ	❻	$ $ $ $ $
ATMOSPHERE	DINING	SPORTS	RATES

The birdsong tells you the sun is up. You scramble down from your oversize four-poster, pad across the floor, slide open the glass doors, blink in the light, and then plop into your private swimming pool.

A few minutes later the sound of a Minimoke pulling up at the gate tells you it's time to slip into your embroidered bathrobe before the waitress appears with breakfast: freshly baked croissants, freshly squeezed fruit juice, homemade yogurt, a platter of fresh fruit, a thermos of coffee, and Bernardaud china — all carefully set on the patio dining table while you admire the view across the flower borders to the beach and palms, with Caribbean all the way to the horizon. Try not to slurp your coffee — you'll disturb the peace.

Le Toiny is the third of a trio of small hotels that opened on St. Barths in 1992, but it is moons ahead in romance. It consists of 12 island-style cottages notched into a rise a few hundred yards from the shore, each cottage on a different level to ensure privacy, each with a 20 × 10 foot swimming pool — designed with admirable refinement.

Each 1,076-square-foot cottage easily accommodates a large deck and covered terrace (with dining table, coffee table, chairs for each, and a pair of loungers); a living room with pantry, desk, fax, exercise machine, and chunky armoire holding a VCR and 21-inch TV; a bedroom with a four-poster bed so high you almost have to hoist yourself aboard and a matching armoire with another TV; a bathroom with walk-in closets, separate toilet, separate tub, separate shower with a big window overlooking the bay. Granted, size is not everything. What is so impressive about these lodgings is the care that's gone into the decor and the spare-no-expense attention to detail — big decorative porcelain vases atop the armoires, the selection of hand-milled soaps in a small wooden box, the tissues wrapped in dainty white lace napkins handmade by women over in the village of Corossol, and patio furniture that matches the lavender, mint, and peach hues of the drapes and bedspreads.

Each cottage has a view, though guests at the top of the hill see more of the Caribbean, and the maison du directeur comes with three bedrooms and a few additional refinements, and rents for just over $2,000 per night.

The main lodge houses a tiny lobby, furnished with Oriental antiques and tastefully arrayed doodads; the bar/lounge has the air of a colonial plantation house; and the adjoining 70-seat restaurant, named La Gaiac for the distinctive native tree, spreads out behind sliding floor-to-ceiling windows. The terrace incorporates a swimming pool (outside lunch guests may use the pool and dressing rooms), but the breezes on this corner of the island often rule out alfresco dining. The cuisine is impressive, masterminded by a youthful Frenchman ("one of the greats of tomorrow," he has been called) who honed his skills at some of France's most honored hotels and restaurants. The wine list complements the French-Caribbean cuisine very nicely.

The few reservations you might have about Le Toiny are the price (even with a private pool, even with a self-contained cottage, the rates are steep compared with those of neighboring islands); the lack of sports facilities on the premises (tennis is 5 min. away, watersports 10 min. away); and the nearby windward beach, which is better for surfing than for swimming. And given the breeze-cooled location, I would have preferred louvers rather than sliding-glass doors.

But for all those lovers whose idea of play is something other than tennis or water-skiing, Le Toiny is some kind of Eden.

Name: Hôtel Le Toiny
Manager: David Henderson
Address: 97133 St. Barthélemy, French West Indies
Location: On the "far" side of the island, at Anse de Toiny, about 15 min. by taxi from the airport (complimentary shuttle) or Gustavia
Telephone: 590 590/27-88-88
Fax: 590 590/27-89-30
E-mail: letoiny@saint-barths.com
Web: www.letoiny.com
Reservations: 800/932-3222, WIMCO
Credit Cards: All major cards
Rates: $1,480–$1,530 CP (Dec 20–Apr 30); service charge included; off-season 35% less
Rooms: 12 cottages, each a self-contained suite with private pool, pantry, ice maker, air-conditioning and ceiling fans, 3 direct-dial telephones, 2 TVs with DVD/VCR, fax machine, gym equipment, veranda/deck, bathroom with tub and shower, bathrobes, and hair dryer; the owner's suite also has a whirlpool tub and dining patio
Meals: Breakfast 7–10am, lunch noon–2:30pm, dinner 7–10pm (about $200) in the La Gaiac, although lunch may be served on the terrace beside the pool, trade winds permitting; casual but stylish dress; room service with dining-room menus to 11pm, limited menu thereafter; some soft background music (mostly classic jazz)
Entertainment: Small bar adjoining the restaurant, in-room massage at extra charge

Sports: Large freshwater pool, 12 private pools, snorkeling gear; beach (10-min. walk), tennis, and watersports nearby
PS: Few children; closed Sept–Oct

Hôtel Manapany Cottages

ST. BARTHELEMY

☆ ☆ ☆	Ⴘ Ⴘ	❻ ❻	$ $ $
ATMOSPHERE	DINING	SPORTS	RATES

The Manapany is tucked away on Anse des Cayes — at the bottom of a winding hill beyond a hamlet of unkempt homes with cluttered yards — but beside an invigorating expanse of sand and sea. It's been around since the 1980s, one of the island's stalwarts by this time, but now emerging from a much-needed buffing up.

It's a series of cottages, designed in traditional island style with red-shingle roofs and gingerbread trim, rising up the hillside from the beach and an egg-shaped pool. Each cottage consists of a suite with a large terrace and a room with a small balcony; the rooms are small, but the suites are spacious with full kitchenettes and ideal for lounging, with 20-foot screened terraces fitted out with wicker sofas, armchairs, coffee table, dining table and chairs. Soothing pastel fabrics set off white-on-white walls, ceiling, and floors. Beachfront rooms cost more, of course, but since most cottages on the lower levels tend to look out on other cottages, you may want to opt for one of the upper cottages clinging to the steep, terraced hillside. This imposes a bit of a hike down a somewhat precipitous path to get to the beach, pool, or restaurant, but the upper levels afford more breezes and a stunning view. The choice quarters are the new Junior Suites with louvered windows and views of the bay from your pillows, smart new furniture, bathrooms clad in marble from the hills around Rome, and floors laid with terra-cotta tiles from Valencia.

What used to be the Ouanalou Restaurant, a semi-open-air pavilion curving around the pool, is now the Ristorante Fellini because the owner is a good friend of the owner of the highly successful restaurant of the same name in Paris. The pastas are fresh and savory, of course, but the menu also acknowledges its French heritage and American clientele.

But quite apart from all these improvements (and the newly savvy staff), Manapany may be coming into its own: This is one of the few resorts on the island where you can park your rental car at your door. In fact, it's one of the few hotels where you can even find a parking space — and on this tight little car-glutted island, that's getting to be a major consideration for a carefree vacation.

Name: Hôtel Manapany Cottages
Manager: Federico Roy
Address: Anse de Cayes, 97098 St. Barthélemy Cedex, French West Indies

Location: About 5 min. from the airstrip (the hotel provides free transfers)

Telephone: 590 590/27-66-55

Fax: 590 590/27-75-28

E-mail: manapan@saint-barths.com

Web: www.lemanapany.com

Reservations: 800/847-4249, Mondotels

Credit Cards: All major cards

Rates: $460–$1,120 CP (Jan 7–Apr 15); service charge and taxes included; off-season 40% less

Rooms: 46 rooms and suites, all with air-conditioning and ceiling fans, balcony or patio, private bathroom (some with bathtubs), bathrobes, wall-mounted hair dryers, clock radio, color TV (in-house movies, English and French), direct-dial telephones, some with pantries and refrigerators

Meals: Breakfast 7–10:30am, lunch noon–3pm, dinner 7:30–10:30pm (about $100), all in the Fellini; "casual but correct dress — long trousers and shirts"; some live music, otherwise recordings; brunch seafood buffet on Sun, lobster barbecue Fri; 24-hr. room service (including full menu during restaurant hours), at extra charge after 10:30pm

Entertainment: Bar/lounge/terrace with piano, recorded music, billiards, cigar room/library, chess, Scrabble, backgammon; to say nothing of oodles of bars 10–15 min. away by Minimoke

Sports: Beach (windswept, with coral, not especially good for swimming or windsurfing), large egg-shaped freshwater pool with island deck for sunbathing, whirlpool, tennis (1 court, with lights, pro), snorkeling masks, exercise room with Universal equipment — all free; boat trips (with hotel-prepared picnics), scuba diving, body surfboards, sailing at extra charge

PS: Some children; "no cellphones in the restaurant"; open year-round

Filao Beach Hotel

ST. BARTHELEMY

☆☆☆☆	ＹＹ	❻❻	$ $ $ $
ATMOSPHERE	DINING	SPORTS	RATES

Riviera would give an arm and a leg to have a beach like the Filao's (broader than ever after a post-hurricane replenishment involving several barges of white sand).

This plush little hideaway is on one of the prime locations on St. Barthélemy, right on fashionable (and usually topless) St. Jean Bay, on that talcum-fine strand between the island's toy-town airstrip and the rocky promontory known as Eden Rock.

Hugging its plot of precious beach, the hotel meanders back along well-marked paths through gardens of seagrape trees livened with white hibiscus, allamanda, and red cattail — its own little botanical garden, lovingly tended by the manager's wife, Sylvaine. Red-roofed bungalows house 30 guest rooms, each named for a château in France, with the name (Villandry, Montlouis, whatever) etched on a ceramic owl above the door. Each room is generously furnished with double bed, daybed/sofa, plenty of chairs and tables, television, refrigerator, and both air-conditioning and ceiling fans. The roomy bathrooms incorporate tub, shower, and bidet — and they get upgraded almost every fall.

All 30 rooms in this Relais & Châteaux resort have been restyled with Italian floor tiles, but it's in the niceties that Filao scores — fresh flowers in every room, a continually replenished supply of bottled water in the fridge, an electric hair dryer in the bathroom, and chaises covered with comfy cushions in green-and-white stripes on each private terrace. You'll probably do more snoozing than sunning on your terrace because of the copious shade from the foliage, but almost certainly you'll have breakfast there, seated at the glass-topped table decorated with an island chart, pouring over the topography of St. Barthélemy, deciding which beach to visit once you've scooped up the last flakes of croissant.

After a morning's swim, you can look forward to a pleasant lunch at the Filao's beachside bar/restaurant, a peak-ceiling pavilion with lazily turning fans. It opens directly onto a raised wooden deck and an angular swimming pool, with the flags of France, Sweden, the United States, and Filao Beach fluttering fraternally in the trade winds above the topless sun worshipers. The Filao's light lunches (no, not the topless bathers, the lunches) draw a crowd from all over the island to nibble on the freshest lobster (the brother-in-law of one of the friendly, longtime staffers is a lobsterman), sip Sancerre, and look out across the sand to the sea breaking on the reefs.

Afterward, if you're feeling too sated for much else, you have to walk only a few steps to the beach and settle into a molded plastic lounger for a siesta. For something more active, the waters off St. Jean Bay, protected by those scenic reefs, are ideal for windsurfing — and there's a windsurfing concession on the beach that rents boards and offers instruction.

The delightful dining room is now open for dinner, where you can enjoy *filet de saumon estragon* or *gigot d'agneau à la Provençal* against a backdrop of Eden Rock bathed in floodlights, making it all more Riviera-like than ever. Then you can stroll back to Villandry or Montlouis along gently lighted pathways through the fragrant garden.

Note: That's how it is now but Filao Beach has been acquired by the Matthews team at Eden Rock, its next-door neighbor, and within a couple of years, the two hotels will be combined into one and the rooms at Filao will become suites. In the meantime, the estimable Pierre Verdier is running both hotels.

Name: Filao Beach Hotel
Manager: Pierre A. Verdier
Address: P.O. Box 667, 97133 St. Barthélemy, French West Indies
Location: On St. Jean Bay, about 1 mile from airport, free shuttle for guests

Telephone: 590 590/27-64-84
Fax: 590 590/27-62-24
E-mail: filao.st.barth@wanadaoo.fr
Web: www.filaobeach.com
Reservations: Direct or 800/525-4800, Small Luxury Hotels of the World
Credit Cards: American Express, Diners Club, Visa
Rates: $370–$680 CP (Dec 20–Apr 15); service charge included; off-season 30% less
Rooms: 30 (8 Deluxe Beachside, 10 Deluxe, 12 Garden), all with ceiling fans and air-conditioning, refrigerator, hair dryer, TV/VCR, safe-deposit box
Meals: Breakfast 7–10am, lunch noon–2:30pm, dinner 7–9pm (about $80–$100); casually elegant attire; room service for breakfast only
Entertainment: Yourselves if you stay on the property, *le tout* St. Barths if you go dining and drinking
Sports: Freshwater pool; beach swimming, snorkeling equipment, and windsurfers at extra charge
PS: Few children; closed Sept to mid-Oct

Hôtel Eden Rock

ST. BARTHELEMY

☆☆☆☆☆   ♈ ♈ ♈ ♈   ❻❻ $ $ $ $ $
ATMOSPHERE   **DINING**   **SPORTS**   **RATES**

The first inn on St. Barths (opened all of 50 years ago!) snagged the choicest site — a steep hillock of basaltic rock jutting into the bay of St. Jean, beach to the left, beach to the right — and its red-roofed gray stone cottages have been the island's most photographed landmarks ever since. Howard Hughes flew in once or twice, and Greta Garbo sometimes came here when she really wanted to be alone (there's still a Garbo Suite, very gussied up and tony). But in recent years the place needed a drastic overhaul.

Now it's had one. New English owners, David and Jane Matthews, took over in 1995 and spent a year or more fixing the place up, adding five rooms, a pool, and two more restaurants on the beach. Up on the rock, the plumbing was overhauled and the wiring replaced, vintage wooden boats sit at the dock, ships' running lamps and a World War II searchlight decorate the steps, and antiques and artworks add a touch of class to the rooms. The 16 rooms and suites — from "cabin" to "ocean suite" — are all different, from 151 square feet (the two cabins, really a giggle and really only for younger people) to 712 square feet, some with four-poster beds draped in gossamer netting, some with roomy balconies, some lined with cedar paneling or with walk-in showers built around natural rock. Each is a gem, and rooms that were once staid and gloomy now reverberate with a variety of decorative grace notes. The six hillside rooms, rather than the beachside lodgings, get the best views and coolest breezes — but in either location, you pay a premium for this prime setting.

With three restaurants (three — in a 24-roomer!) supervised by one of the island's most acclaimed chefs, Jean-Claude Dufour from Bordeaux, Eden Rock is also one of the island's hot dining spots. But with hamburgers costing $30 or so ("the chef doesn't want to cook hamburgers all day") it somehow enhances the impression that this hotel would really rather deal with stars and celebrities. But have some tapas at the On the Rocks Bar and you can have a jolly evening above the beach for $30 a head. The latest addition is a whirlpool spa somehow carved into or dug out of the rock. You can have treatments here in plenty of privacy — as though you needed massaging and dunking in this kind of relaxed, feel-good setting.

Name: Hôtel Eden Rock
Manager: Pierre Verdier
Address: St. Jean, 97133 St. Barthélemy, French West Indies
Location: On St. Jean Beach, 5 min. from the airport (free pickup), 10 min. from town (about $10 by taxi)
Telephone: 590 590/27-72-94
Fax: 590 590/27-88-37
E-mail: info@edenrockhotel.com
Web: www.edenrockhotel.com
Reservations: 800/576-6677, toll-free direct or 888/576-6677, Karen Bull
Credit Cards: American Express, MasterCard, Visa
Rates: $385–$1,750 CP (Jan 5– Apr 31); service charge and tax included; "cabins" from $385; off-season 20% less
Rooms: 8 rooms, 8 suites, all with air-conditioning, direct-dial telephones, TV/VCR, CD player, complimentary minibars, hair dryers, in-room safes, bathrobes, some with balconies or verandas; the owners' suite, Harbour House, is also available for rent at certain times of the year
Meals: Breakfast 7:30–10:30am, lunch noon–4pm, dinner 7–10pm in 3 restaurants, indoors or out, but not air-conditioned (ranging $60–$200); room service during restaurant hours at extra charge; elegantly casual attire; music (mostly trendy and recorded) in most restaurants
Entertainment: Just being there, checking out the other guests, CD and video library
Sports: Beach, swimming pool, Jacuzzi, pedalos, kayaks, snorkeling gear — all free; other watersports nearby
PS: Children are welcome, but it's unlikely you'll be overrun by them; closed Sept 1–Oct 15
PPS: See note above under Filao Beach regarding the merging with Eden Rock

Tom Beach Hotel

ST. BARTHELEMY

☆ ☆   Y Y   ✪ $ $ $
ATMOSPHERE   **DINING**   **SPORTS**   **RATES**

It seems hard to believe that another hotel could be shoehorned into the strip beside St. Jean Beach, but here it is — just 12 rooms, most of them at right angles to the beach, facing a courtyard with a pool. A footbridge spans the pool and leads to an attractive but sometimes noisy bar/restaurant by the edge of the beach.

Until 2000, Tom Beach was a so-so alternative to other hotels farther along the beach, but now a new owner has taken over, waved her magic wand, and transformed the place. Well, not so much a magic wand as a few rolls of colorful fabric that she has twisted around columns, draped here and swathed there, giving Le Tom a lot more of le pizzaz. Even the porte-cochere is a swirl of colorful draperies. There's new contemporary art on the walls, a leafy garden of ferns and rubber plants. The guest rooms are small but pleasantly comfortable, with clay-tile floors, pencil-post beds (some with dreamy netting), small patios or verandas, and such up-to-date amenities as TVs, direct-dial phones, and private safes.

The pavilion restaurant is a gallimaufry collection of vintage sofas and couches and wooden tables painted in dazzling fire-engine reds, royal blues, mustards, and yellows and planted higgledy-piggledy on the deck, in the sand, under thatched gazebos. "The menu ranges effortlessly from tapas (*accras de morue, tempura de crevettes*) to Thai platters, Creole platters, and fisherman's platters by way of BBQ ribs, chicken wings, and lamb chops."

You pay a hefty premium for being right on the sands of St. Jean, of course, and if privacy is your goal, you'd be better off at Le Toiny St. Barth Isle de France but Le Tom is fun, frolicsome, and very French.

Into the bargain, it has the island's only underground parking garage (fear not, it's so small it's hardly noticed, although it holds 24 cars).

Name: Tom Beach Hotel
Owner/Manager: Carole Gruson/Stephanie Manelli
Address: St. Jean, 97133 St. Barthélemy, French West Indies
Location: 4 min. from the airport (they'll collect you free of charge)
Telephone: 590 590/27-53-13
Fax: 590 590/27-53-15
E-mail: tombeach@wanadoo.fr
Web: www.tombeach.com
Reservations: Direct
Credit Cards: American Express, MasterCard
Rates: $295–$645 CP (Dec 21–Apr 16); service charge and taxes included; off-season 30% less

Rooms: 12 rooms, all with air-conditioning, king-size canopy bed, direct-dial telephone, in-room safe, minibar, TV/VCR and mini hi-fi, hair dryer

Meals: Breakfast 8–10:30am, lunch noon–4pm, dinner 7–10pm, all in La Plage beachside pavilion; recorded music (jazz, ambient); very casual; room service for breakfast only

Entertainment: Sipping a tí punch and listening to the recorded music, walking on the beach, checking out the bars nearby

Sports: Pool; plenty of watersports right and left along the beach

PS: Few children; open year-round

Hôtel Guanahani

ST. BARTHELEMY

☆☆☆	♈♈♈	☻☻☻	$ $ $ $
ATMOSPHERE	DINING	SPORTS	RATES

Fourteen swimming pools. A couple of tennis courts. A couple of restaurants. St. Barths has never had a resort so lavish.

Bay and beach, reef and islet, headlands and breeze-whipped sea — few resorts have a setting so beautiful. Guanahani sprawls over acres of landscaped hillside tucked into one corner of Grand Cul-de-Sac Bay, a reef-protected beach, with a low-profile hotel on one side, a grove of coconut palms belonging to Edmond de Rothschild on the other.

The island's largest resort, the 13-year old Guanahani got a little larger a couple of years ago when it added a new row of plank-walled bungalows facing a quiet bay above the Rothschild family compound (artfully concealed behind a bamboo fence). But it still has well under 100 rooms, deployed two or three to a cottage up and down the hillsides. The new rooms are eye-catchers, designed with a quirky Gallic flair: dashing candy-shop colors setting off curvaceous rattan headboards and bedside lamps, custom-designed cabinets for TVs and minibars, custom-designed desks and chairs, and lava-laminated washbasins. The spacious patios have wooden dining tables and slat-backed chairs; the bathrooms have marble shower stalls (no tubs), double vanities, waffle-weave robes, and Hermès toiletries. There are even Citroëns instead of the average resort's Ford Taurus.

The original rooms have been re-groomed, mostly with softer colors but still with the colonial pencil-post beds, terra-cotta tiles, antique armoires for TV, and minibars — the same basic look, in fact, so your choice of lodging may boil down to location, whether or not you want to be next to the beach and a few paces from the sea, or whether or not you want to be on the hillside to catch the views and breezes. I checked out one of each. Room 54 beside the beach may be too close to the beach bar and restaurant for some tastes, especially if the stereo is cranked up as it was when I was there; also, the room is fairly small, and at $770 a night in winter, you could get better value elsewhere on the island. Likewise, one of the newer suites, number 60, has a private pool, attractive decor, and a quiet location, but carries an extravagant price tag. Granted, Guanahani now includes tennis and nonmotorized watersports in the rate, but if you plan to spend most of your time just kicking back, look carefully at these prices.

No one can hope to run a successful hotel on St. Barths without paying almost as much attention to the kitchen as the decor, maybe even more. The Indigo Beach Restaurant, beside the beach and pool, is a Riviera-style cafe for casual lunches of grills and Chablis; the main showpiece is the stylish 40-seat Bartoloméo Restaurant, located at the top of the hill, with its soft candlelight, elegant Limoges porcelain, refined decor, and polished service.

Name: Hôtel Guanahani

Manager: Marc Theze

Address: Anse de Grand Cul-de-Sac, P.O. Box 609, 97098 St. Barthélemy, French West Indies

Location: On the Atlantic coast on Grand Cul-de-Sac Bay, about 15 min. from the airport in a courtesy air-conditioned minibus

Telephone: 590 590/27-66-60

Fax: 590 590/27-70-70

E-mail: guanahani@wanadoo.fr

Web: www.leguanahani.com

Reservations: 800/223-6800, Leading Hotels of the World

Credit Cards: All major cards

Rates: $490–$1,900 CP (Dec 19–Apr 31); service charge included; off-season 40% less

Rooms: 76 rooms and suites in 40 cottages, each with terrace/patio, fans and air-conditioning, minibar, satellite TV/VCR, radio, direct-dial telephone, bathrobes, hair dryers; 14 suites with private pools

Meals: Breakfast 7–10am, lunch noon–5pm in the Indigo Beach Restaurant (sometimes noisy), dinner 7:30–10pm in the fan-cooled Bartoloméo Restaurant (about $120–$140); informal but stylish dress ("shorts, T-shirts, swimsuits, or other similarly casual clothing are inappropriate after dark in the dining room and bar"); 24-hr. room service at no extra charge

Entertainment: Live piano jazz (quiet, most of the time) in the Bartoloméo; video library; Guanahani hosts an annual Gourmet Festival (Nov 1 through mid-Dec) and guests are invited to join in the fun

Sports: Beach (with a second swatch of sand on the other side of the Rothschild coconut grove), 14 individual swimming pools, 2 large pools and Jacuzzi beside the beach, snorkeling, tennis (2 hard courts, with lights), windsurfing, Hobie Cats, canoes, paddleboats, exercise room — all free; windsurfing lessons at extra charge; deep-sea fishing, sailing by arrangement

PS: Some children

Village St. Jean Hotel Cottages

ST. BARTHELEMY

☆☆☆　　　　Ⓨ Ⓨ　　　　🅞　　　　$ $ $
ATMOSPHERE　　**DINING**　　**SPORTS**　　**RATES**

Picture a hillside of blossoms and greenery with a handful of cottages tucked in among the hibiscus and bougainvillea. Add a blue-tiled pool with a terracotta deck and white sunshades, paint a backdrop of red roofs and blue sea, and then anchor the garden with an indoor-outdoor restaurant serving acclaimed Italian food. Voilà — one of St. Barths's most inviting small hotels!

Village St. Jean has been charming guests for more than 30 years (food guru Craig Claiborne came so often, he kept his personal pots and pans in his favorite cottage), always under the watchful, caring eye of the French-American Charneau family. All 20 cottages (including 14 suites and 6 regular "hotel" rooms) have air-conditioning and paddle fans, terraces or gardens, refrigerators, telephones, and radios; the suites have kitchenettes with four-ring burners and family-size refrigerators. The deluxe cottages have been spiffed up with new tiled bathrooms, new fabrics, antique wood and cane furniture from India, and top-of-the-line patio furniture that's so inviting you may want to throw dinner parties every evening, even if you're not Craig Claiborne (fear not — daily maid service includes dishwashing). Which cottage? Some are more private than others, but for views, none is grander than those from cottages 12 and 10. Take one look at those spacious decks and terraces with their plumply padded loungers and you might easily forget that the beach is just 5 minutes down the hill, especially now that the hotel rooms (one of the best values on the island) have been retiled, repainted, and reroofed. Sample the Italian delicacies in the spiffed-up Le Patio and you might forget all about dashing around the island in your Suzuki looking for a great place to eat.

Besides the pool, there is a Jacuzzi, a commissary (basics only), and a library/TV room with parlor games. But maybe the most appealing feature of Chez Charneau is the cost: Even in winter, doubles begin at just $160 (hotel rooms, with continental breakfast), rising to $360 for a deluxe cottage with terrace and Jacuzzi.

Name: Village St. Jean Hotel Cottages
Owners/Managers: The Charneau Family
Address: BP 623, 97133 St. Barthélemy, French West Indies
Location: On Colline St. Jean, a rise above the island's most famous beach, 5 min. by taxi from the airport (let them know when you're arriving and they'll collect you at no extra charge), 10 min. from Gustavia
Telephone: 590 590/27-61-39
Fax: 590 590/27-77-96

E-mail: vsjhotel@wanadoo.fr
Web: www.villagestjeanhotel.com
Reservations: 800/651-8366, direct
Credit Cards: American Express, MasterCard, Visa
Rates: $170-$370 CP (Dec 15–Apr 15); service charge 10%; off-season 30% less
Rooms: 20 cottages (14 suites and 6 rooms), with air-conditioning and ceiling fans, terrace or patio, direct-dial telephone, radio, hair dryer; deluxe cottages with CD/stereo, hammock, open-air kitchenettes (four-ring burners and refrigerators)
Meals: Breakfast 8–10am, dinner in El Patio 7:30–10:30pm (closed Wed; about $60); casual dress; limited room service
Entertainment: Library/TV room, parlor games; otherwise, plenty of diversions just down the hill
Sports: Pool, Jacuzzi; watersports nearby
PS: Few children; open year-round

Le Jardin Malanga

GUADELOUPE

☆☆☆　　　　Y　　　　◎　　　　$ $
ATMOSPHERE　　DINING　　SPORTS　　RATES

The Jardin in question is less of a garden than a plantation — a hillside of banana and breadfruit trees. Here and there the gardeners have trimmed and primped flowering shrubs and palms along the pathways that lead from the guest rooms to the main lodge.

The lodge is the former plantation Great House, built in the 1920s in traditional French colonial style, a weathered mahogany structure with a wraparound veranda and a cedar-shingle hip roof accented with three dormer windows. This is the socializing hub, a pleasant plank-floored salon of colonial minimalism. Settle into the planters' chairs for pre-dinner *planteurs;* the view from the veranda is stunning. Swim to the southern end of the pool, where the water cascades over the lip and you don't even have to crane your neck to take in the panorama: lush tropical hillsides with hardly any signs of the 20th century, and the sea far below, ribboned with the wakes of ferryboats and pleasure craft plying to and from the Iles des Saintes, whose craggy peaks loom a few miles offshore.

The pool provides the only activity here, apart from wandering among the bananas. Malanga would be a retreat for only the most self-contained of lovers if it weren't for the fact that it's in the most ravishingly beautiful corner of an island of striking natural beauty. Most of Basse-Terre (the western "wing" of butterfly-shaped Guadeloupe) is forested national park, its jungle-covered peaks looming over roads that lead to plantations (several with guided tours), venerable rum distilleries (more tours), hiking trails to hidden cascades and

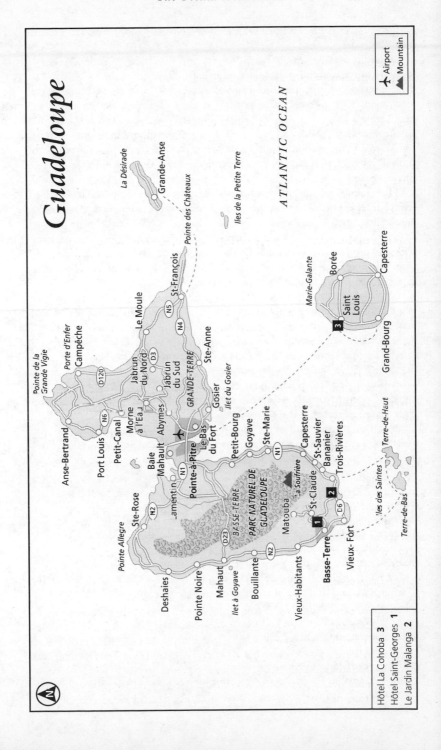

Guadeloupe

Hôtel La Cohoba **3**
Hôtel Saint-Georges **1**
Le Jardin Malanga **2**

✈ Airport
▲ Mountain

ATLANTIC OCEAN

La Désirade
Grande-Anse
Pointe des Châteaux
Îles de la Petite Terre

Pointe de la Grande Vigie
Porte d'Enfer
Campêche
Anse-Bertrand
Port Louis
Petit-Canal
Morne à l'Eau
Baie Mahault
Abymes
Pointe-à-Pitre
Le Bas du Fort
Le Moule
N5
N4
Jabrun du Nord
Jabrun du Sud
D3
D120
N6
GRANDE-TERRE
Ste-Anne
Gosier
Îlet du Gosier
St-François

Ste-Rose
N2
...amentin
N1
Petit-Bourg
Goyave
Ste-Marie
N1
Capesterre
St-Sauvier
Bananier
Trois-Rivières
Pointe Allègre
Deshaies
Pointe Noire
Mahaut
D23
Bouillante
Îlet à Goyave
BASSE-TERRE
PARC NATUREL DE GUADELOUPE
Matouba
St-Claude
la Soufrière ▲
2
1
D6
Vieux-Habitants
N2
Basse-Terre
Vieux-Fort
Îles des Saintes
Terre-de-Haut
Terre-de-Bas

Marie-Galante
Borée
Capesterre
Saint Louis
3
Grand-Bourg

N

gorges, and a coastline rimmed with cliffs and coves — all of it easy to explore from the hotel.

Le Jardin Malanga lies between the sea and the flanks of Soufrière, a volcano whose crater still puffs and steams high above the Caribbean. You can drive almost to the crater, a journey of roughly 40 minutes to 1 hour from your room. On the way back, stop off at Basse-Terre's latest attraction, the sparkling spa known as Manioukani, where you can order up a sea wrap or a jet shower. Then again, you can rise early one morning, slip on your sandals and shorts, grab your swimsuit, drive down the hill to the fishing village of Trois-Rivières, catch the ferry, and spend the day beaching and dreaming on Iles des Saintes.

The nicest thing about any of these side trips is coming home to Malanga for a late-afternoon swim in the pool, drinks on the veranda, and a candlelight dinner in the pavilion beside the main house. You sit down to the sort of homespun meal the planters themselves might have enjoyed, making do with the produce of the garden and the sea: lots of fresh fish, vegetables, and fruit, all presented and served with the touch of class that we've come to expect from even the humblest French restaurant.

All this despite the fact that Malanga is still a shoestring operation (opened in 1996, the inn has only nine rooms), and the staff seems to consist of no more than four people. But the ambience is warm and welcoming, the setting idyllic, and the rooms charmingly rustic but, in some ways, surprisingly sophisticated. The main house has three rooms, but the most desirable quarters are in the three hillside chalets, designed in the style, more or less, of the basic Creole case. Each has a balcony equipped with table, chairs, and hammock, and sliding doors lead to a snug bedroom with a queen-size bed, paddle fan, ceiling-high air conditioner with remote control, and snazzy contemporary light fixtures. But it's the bathrooms that shine, literally: gleaming white tiles on walls and floor, a sunken tub/shower beside a panoramic window, and a couple of cotton kimono robes that are great for lounging in hammocks and admiring the view.

Name: Le Jardin Malanga
Manager: Christel Mercier
Address: L'Hermitage, 21 Rue Jean Mermoz, 97116 Trois Rivières, Guadeloupe, French West Indies
Location: At the southern tip of Basse-Terre, just past the exit for Trois Rivières, about 50 min. from the airport ($60–$80 by taxi, if you arrive after dark and don't want to drive in strange terrain)
Telephone: 590 590/92-67-57
Fax: 590 590/92-67-58
Reservations: 800/322-2223 or 805/967-9850, French Caribbean International
Credit Cards: MasterCard, Visa
Rates: $202–$290 CP (Dec 15–Apr 15); service charge included; off-season 30% less

Rooms: 9 total, 3 in the main house, 6 in hillside cottages, all with remote-controlled air-conditioning and ceiling fans, tiled bathroom with bathrobes and hair dryer, veranda and hammocks (hillside rooms only)

Meals: Breakfast 7:30–10am, lunch noon–2:30pm, dinner (fixed menu) 7–9pm in the pavilion (about $70); casual dress; no room service; soft recorded music

Entertainment: The tree frogs and the birds

Sports: Beautiful pool, guided garden walks — all free; watersports, boat trips, and Manioukani Spa nearby at extra charge

PS: Closed Oct

Hôtel Saint-Georges

GUADELOUPE

☆ ☆	Y Y	🌐	$
ATMOSPHERE	**DINING**	**SPORTS**	**RATES**

Designed primarily for business travelers and assorted people doing business with the island government in its offices down the hill, this relative newcomer from 1997 may not be exactly romantic, but it does have a certain beguiling charm — and its location gives it more than usual interest.

The hotel's contemporary lines — three stories around a courtyard and pool — house rooms that are functional but hardly somber, with locally crafted rattan furniture and ceramic-tile floors, and as comfortable as any you'll find at this price. In fact, the rates are a prime attraction of the Saint-Georges — at $175 for a double, the attractive suites cost less than mere rooms in most other hotels on the island. And how often do you find a hotel at that price that throws in breakfast, free squash, and a fitness center?

The central courtyard, one floor up from the lobby, is the focal point of the hotel, with its pool and open-pavilion bar, the Mahogany. The bar counter is lined with a tempting array of aged and flavored rums, but its casual menu is even more appealing — *brochettes de viande* for $9, chef salad $6.50 — prepared and presented with style. The adjoining restaurant, Le Lamasure, is something of a status symbol for visiting and local gourmets, whose favorite specialty appears to be *fricassee de langouste au poivre rose* for $17.

But the reason you might find yourself checking into the Saint-Georges is the fact that when you drive a few yards to the main road and turn right up the hill, you arrive, less than 20 minutes later, at the peak of Soufrière. Here is a dramatic setting with extraordinary views, and just enough steam and odor to create that frisson you experience in the presence of a dormant but hardly extinct volcano.

Name: Hôtel Saint-Georges

Manager: Joachim Pourque

Address: Rue Gratien Parize, 97120 Saint-Claude, Guadeloupe, French West Indies

Location: In the village of Sainte-Claude, about 1 hr. from the airport ($60–$80 by taxi, if you arrive after dark and don't want to drive in strange terrain)

Telephone: 590 590/80-10-10

Fax: 590 590/80-30-50

Reservations: Direct

Credit Cards: MasterCard, Visa

Rates: $195 CP (Dec 15–Apr 15); service charge included; off-season 20% less

Rooms: 40, including 2 suites, all with TV, telephone, air-conditioning, smart tiled bathroom, tiny balcony

Meals: Breakfast 7:30–10am, lunch 12:30–2:30pm in Mahogany Bar or Le Lamasure, dinner 7:30–9:30pm (about $80) in Le Lamasure; casual dress in the bar, slightly dressier (but no jackets or ties) in the restaurant; room service breakfast only

Entertainment: Those aged and flavored rums, billiards (French rules), occasional barbecues, music on weekends

Sports: Free-form pool, air-conditioned squash court, 10-station fitness room — all free; watersports, hiking, and Manioukani Spa nearby

PS: Few children; open year-round

Hôtel La Cohoba

MARIE-GALANTE

☆   ☥   ◐◐ $
ATMOSPHERE   DINING   SPORTS   RATES

First off, où est Marie Galante? It's one of those specks of an island just off the southern coast of Guadeloupe, a 45-minute ride from Pointe-à-Pitre aboard a big twin-hulled launch. During the 17th and 18th centuries, lots of sugar, cotton, and tobacco were grown here, but the working plantations have more or less disappeared, except for a few rum distilleries, a few one-story villages, and several inviting beaches. Marie-Galante has long been a getaway mostly for Guadeloupeans when they get fed up with trying to find a parking spot in downtown Pointe-à-Pitre; now the island finally has a hotel to appeal to a wider flock, and although it's geared for a European rather than American clientele, it's still a worthwhile spot to keep in mind if you escape to the back of beyond.

Basically, Cohoba is a collection of bungalows and a pair of two-story motel-ish wings, housing all 100 rooms — big time for Marie-Galante — in soft pastel colors of aqua, coral, sky blue, and sand. But it's all so new that the bushes and blossoms haven't yet disguised the utilitarian architecture. Although it's promoted as a beach resort, the sand is a hundred or so paces away through a grove of cocotier and raisinier trees — a nice arrangement since this preserves the natural look of the beach, even if it means that none of the rooms has a beach view. It's a great walking beach, by the way, and in 20 minutes you can be in town, taking your pick of the local bistros and bars.

Not that you're likely to do so more than once or twice, because the surprise of La Cohoba is that the food in the pavilion-like dining room is of a much higher caliber than you'd expect in a budget-priced hotel. Try the *vivaneau gratinee* with tomatoes and ratatouille and the *tarte au coco sauce hibiscus,* and you'll forget that you'll be walking back to a love nest that's small and functional (though new and spotless). And since it isn't costing a bundle, you can splurge on another rum punch.

Name: Hôtel La Cohoba

Manager: TBA

Address: Cocoyer BP 59, 97112 Grand Bourg, Marie-Galante, Guadeloupe, French West Indies

Location: About 1 mile from the Grand-Bourg ferry dock or the airport but (despite the address) only ½ mile and $7 by taxi from the Saint-Louis ferry dock

Telephone: 590 590/92-50-50

Fax: 590 590/92-17-11

E-mail: cohoba@leaderhotels.gp

Credit Cards: American Express, MasterCard, Visa

Reservations: Direct

Rates: $135–$188 CP (Jan 8–Apr 15); taxes and service charge included; off-season 30% less

Rooms: 100 in 3 categories, all with air-conditioning, satellite TV, shower, separate toilet, hair dryer, direct-dial telephone, patio; premium rooms have kitchenettes and dining tables on large verandas

Meals: Breakfast 7 10am, lunch 12:30–2pm, dinner 7–9pm (about $60), all in an open pavilion off the lobby; no room service; dress casual; some recorded music

Entertainment: Some live music or folklore shows in the bar

Sports: Swimming pool, ½-mile beach, boules, tennis (2 courts, no lights) — all free; water-skiing, windsurfing, Hobie Cats, bicycles at extra charge

PS: Some children; closed Sept

Habitation Lagrange

MARTINIQUE

☆☆☆☆	⅂⅂	➑	$ $ $
ATMOSPHERE	DINING	SPORTS	RATES

The jungle greenery practically sneaks through the shutters into your room, and if you're lodged in the main house, you can reach out and pluck breakfast mangoes straight from the tree. Beyond the lawns and pool, a wooden bridge leads to a banana plantation that seems to go on forever up the narrow valley.

Habitation Lagrange is the brainchild of local hotelier Jean-Louis de Lucy, who used France's tax-shelter laws to restore a landmark rather than build yet another formula hotel from scratch. Although the plantation manor dates only from the turn of the century, it looks as if it should have been around when de Lucy's ancestors fled the French Revolution and settled on Martinique. The centerpiece of the estate is a two-story plantation Great House with a wraparound veranda and gracefully curving corners. Tall mahogany doors lead into a hallway with polished parquet and Oriental bric-a-brac, a library on one side, a wood-paneled bar on the other. The bar is the perfect spot for settling into one of the antique planter-style rockers, the kind with big footrests, and sipping a tí punch.

The 12 guest rooms are arranged around a garden — four in the Great House, two in a former stable wing, the remainder in a one-story wing that blends in nicely with the others. Furnishings are country Caribbean (cane and rattan, mahogany colonial-style pencil-post beds), but the designer telephones are dashingly modern. The big armoires were intended for TVs and VCRs, but the sets were late arriving for the opening of the inn, and the first guests persuaded de Lucy that TVs would be out of place. The rehabilitation of the estate was something of a family effort — de Lucy's wife sewed the drapes and bedspreads and framed the pictures; an uncle came down from Montréal to paint the murals in the main house; whoever happens to be on hand mixes the traditional tí punch in the bar.

Of special note is the cuisine. The food is decidedly French, but seasoned with island spices — nutmeg, cloves, and cinnamon. The service is gracious and unobtrusive, and the meals are delicious.

Life among the bananas is probably not for everyone. Beach lovers may be disappointed by the absence of talcum sand in these parts (the nearest decent beach is at Trinite, a 30-min. drive away), but Lagrange is not so remote that guests have to settle for an anchoritic existence. A drive of an hour or so takes you to some of the most opulent scenery in the Caribbean. My choices would be a morning trip to Grand' Rivière, or a day trip up the flanks of Mont Pelée, across to the Caribbean coast and the dolorous town of St. Pierre, snuffed out when Pelée erupted back in 1908. You can also take a trip down the center of the island, or over to the Trinite Peninsula for a swim and lunch at a waterside bistro.

On the other hand, the slow jouncing track back to the main road may persuade many travelers to stay put, and there's no reason to leave anyway. Lagrange rewards you with tranquility. Here there's time to sniff the jasmine and time to listen to birdsong by day and cicadas after sundown.

I like the garden best in the morning, with the rain pattering on the leaves as I am admiring breakfast. Not eating, just admiring: a bowl of freshly sliced bananas and mangoes from the garden, freshly baked croissants and toast wrapped in linen, a carafe of freshly squeezed fruit juice, all presented in a native basket artistically decorated with delicate ferns and red ixora.

For connoisseurs of real island ambience, Habitation Lagrange is hard to beat.

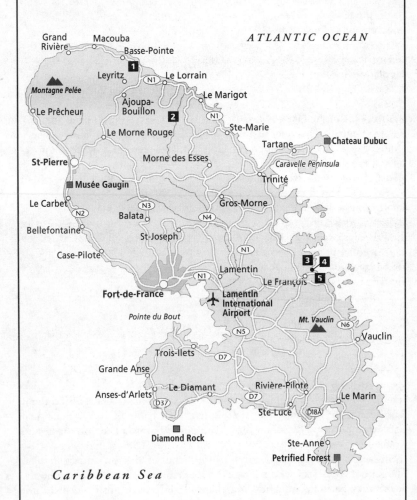

Martinique

ATLANTIC OCEAN

Grand Rivière
Macouba
Basse-Pointe
Leyritz **1**
N1
Le Lorrain
Montagne Pelée
Le Prêcheur
Ajoupa-Bouillon
Le Marigot
2
N1
Ste-Marie
Le Morne Rouge
Tartane
■ **Chateau Dubuc**
Morne des Esses
Caravelle Peninsula
St-Pierre
Trinité
■ **Musée Gaugin**
Le Carbet
N3
Gros-Morne
N2
Balata
N4
Bellefontaine
St-Joseph
Case-Pilote
N1
Lamentin
N1
Le François
3 **4**
5
Fort-de-France
✈ **Lamentin International Airport**
Pointe du Bout
Mt. Vauclin ▲
N6
N5
Vauclin
Trois-Îlets
D7
Grande Anse
Rivière-Pilote
Le Marin
Anses-d'Arlets
Le Diamant
D37
D7
Ste-Luce
D18A
■ **Diamond Rock**
Ste-Anne
Petrified Forest ■

Caribbean Sea

Frégate Bleue Inn **5**
Habitation Lagrange **2**
Hôtel Cap Est Lagoon Resort **4**
Hôtel Plantation Leyritz **1**
Le Plein Soleil **3**

✈ Airport
▲ Mountain

Name: Habitation Lagrange
Manager: Betty Mathieu
Address: 97225 Le Marigot, Martinique, French West Indies
Location: On the Atlantic coast, about 1 hr. and $70 by taxi from the airport; if you're driving yourself, it's just north of the village of Le Marigot, just past a sign announcing the Bassin Ecrevisse Seguinneau (a crayfish farm) on the left
Telephone: 596 596/53-60-60
Fax: 596 596/53-50-58
Reservations: 800/633-7411 or 843/785-7411, Caribbean Inns Ltd.
Credit Cards: All major cards
Rates: $305–$400 FAP (Dec 20–Apr 15); service charge included; off-season 25% less
Rooms: 12, 4 in the Great House (including a Junior Suite), 2 in a former stable wing, the remainder in a new wing, all with air-conditioning and ceiling fans, veranda or porch, direct-dial telephones, stocked minibar, bathrobes
Meals: Breakfast 7–10am, lunch noon–2pm, dinner 7:30–9:30pm (about $100), all served in the garden pavilion; casual dress; room service
Entertainment: Bar, billiards, parlor games, library of sorts
Sports: Curvaceous pool (not for laps), tennis (1 court, no lights), miles of walks; beaches down the coast, day trips to Les Ilets de l'Imperatrice (an intriguing property owned by the de Lucy family, a 45-min. drive away)
PS: Some children; open year-round

Le Plein Soleil

MARTINIQUE

☆	⅄⅄	❻	$ $
ATMOSPHERE	DINING	SPORTS	RATES

Set on a hilltop overlooking a palette-of-blues lagoon, The Full Sunlight (Le Plein Soleil) has the air of the distinguished home of a well-established gentleman planter, a large bungalow with peaked roofs, a deep overhang, and wraparound veranda.

In fact, it was built from scratch in 1999, the dream creation of a Parisian ad-agency art director who managed to shake off the shackles of long hours, big salaries, and uncomprehending clients. Running an inn is no picnic, of course, even one as beautiful as this, but how restful he has made life for his guests.

The three cottages that house the 12 guest rooms (2 up, 2 down) ring the rim of the hillside, a few yards down from the private hilltop villa of *le patron*. They're designed in simple island style, the interiors trimmed down to the basics (no TVs, no radios). The sort of people who will find happiness here are self-contained couples who want to lounge and read, nip off

to bed in the afternoon, and then wake up refreshed for an evening of socializing and dining — mostly island recipes like *tarte au epinard, loup sauce poires
et taglietelles,* and *bavarois a l'ananas.* The bar/lounge in the main lodge, fortunately, is a place where you could sit for hours just looking and admiring —
high raftered ceilings with a gallery at one end, eye-catching original art, and
a collection of wonderful decorative touches contrived from baskets, found
timber and driftwood, twigs, dried flowers, and calabash shells. Even Martha
Stewart would approve.

Name: Le Plein Soleil
Owner/Manager: Jean-Christophe Yoyo
Address: Pointe Thalemont, Mansarde Rance, 97240 Le Francois, Martinique,
   French West Indies
Location: On the eastern coast, about 25 min. and $30 from the airport
Telephone: 596 596/38-07-77
Fax: 596 596/65-58-13
E-mail: pleinsoleil@sasi.fr
Reservations: Direct
Credit Cards: MasterCard, Visa
Rates: $120–$142 EP (Dec 15–Apr 15); service charge included; off season
   30% less
Rooms: 12 rooms in 3 cottages (2 up, 2 down), 6 with air-conditioning, all
   with ceiling fans, direct-dial telephones, some with kitchenettes and ter-
   races (not very private)
Meals: Breakfast 7:30–9:30am, lunch 12:30–2:30pm, dinner 7:30pm ($70), all
   on the terrace of the main lodge; dress code "completely casual"; soft
   recorded jazz; room service for breakfast only
Entertainment: None
Sports: Small pool and snorkeling gear free; a small boat will take you from
   the hotel dock down the hill to the beach across the bay (about $50 for
   2–6 passengers)
PS: Few children; "cellphones are no problem with our kind of guest"; closed
   Sept

OTHER CHOICES

Tropical Hotel

ST. BARTHELEMY

Located up on the hill next to Village St. Jean, Tropical Hotel is a huddled
enclave of greenery and blossoms with just 20 rooms, some facing the sea,
some facing the gardens. There's a bar that serves light snacks around a small

pool. Guest rooms are small, but nevertheless manage to squeeze in modern amenities such as a TV, radio, direct-dial telephone, refrigerator, and, in the bathroom, a hair dryer. Jot this down as a possibility for the off-season — to my mind it's overpriced in winter, but almost half the price during the remaining 8 months of the year (except June and the first half of July, when it's closed). 21 air-conditioned rooms. Doubles: $180–$450, with continental breakfast, winter 2002–03. *Tropical Hotel, P.O. Box 147, 97095 St. Barthélemy, French West Indies. Telephone: 590 590/27-64-87; fax: 590 590/27-81-74; e-mail: tropicalhotel@wanadoo.fr; Web: www.st-barths.com/tropical-hotel.*

Hôtel Emeraude Plage

ST. BARTHELEMY

Another garden full of bungalows, this time by the edge of the beach in St. Jean. All 24 bungalows have kitchenettes, sun decks, and maid service; the atmosphere is totally beachcomber, and there are watersports facilities on the doorstep. 24 bungalows, 3 suites, 1 villa. Doubles: $350–$1,400, winter 2002–03. *Emeraude Plage, P.O. Box 41, 97133 St. Barthélemy, French West Indies. Telephone: 590 590/27-64-78; fax: 590 590/27-83-08; e-mail: emeraude-plage@wanadoo.fr; Web: www.emeraudeplage.com.*

Résidence les Lataniers

ST. BARTHELEMY

This is a sort of poor man's François Plantation without the restaurant — in a positive way, I hastily add. Like François, it's on a hillside, in this case over-looking Anse des Cayes and a grove of coconuts, and it, too, is a collection of tiny, island-style cottages around a small pool and terrace bar. Each cottage is outfitted with kitchenette, tiled showers, air-conditioning, and ceiling fans — and, despite its modest rates, refinements like hair dryers, TV/VCR, and remote control for the air-conditioning. Ask for one of four corner rooms — they have the largest terraces. No meals except breakfast. 12 rooms. Doubles: $305–$410, winter 2002–03. *Résidence les Lataniers, Anse des Cayes, 97133 St. Barthélemy, French West Indies. Telephone: 800/633-7411 or 590 590/27-80-84; fax: 803/686-7411; e-mail: yuana@wanadoo.fr; Web: www.yuana.com.*

Frégate Bleue Inn

MARTINIQUE

Six years ago Charles and Yveline de Lucy de Fossarieu, former owners of one of Martinique's most romantic inns, Hotel Plantation Leyritz, opened another small inn on the island's Atlantic shore, a simple modern house with gingerbread trim and much more modest than Leyritz. Their seven-room Frégate Bleue is nonetheless an enticing hideaway. Part of its appeal is the setting: It's located on a hilltop overlooking a large lagoon dotted with islets and reefs where islanders like to wade in the morning while sipping cool drinks. Each of the seven rooms is furnished in a tasteful assortment of antiques and period pieces, with carved pencil-post beds and Oriental rugs, ceiling fans (with air-conditioning as a backup), cable television, wet bar, and pantry. Five of them have balconies with that stunning lagoon view. Back in the garden, there is a swimming pool and a refreshment bar shaded by trees and perfumed by flowers. 7 rooms. Doubles: $210–$235, winter 2002–03. *Frégate Bleue Inn, 97240 Le François, Martinique, French West Indies. Telephone: 596 596/ 54-54-66; fax: 596 596/54-78-48; e-mail: fregatebleue@cgit.com.*

Hôtel Cap Est Lagoon Resort

MARTINIQUE

There was a time when Martinique had a topflight hotel in Bakoua Beach, but it has been through so many owners and changes of direction, it's no longer a player. Now Cap Est Lagoon Resort has come in to fill the gap, with 50 sexy deluxe suites, 35 of them with private swimming pools, all of them with air conditioner and ceiling fans, plasma screen TV, DVD, Internet access, cordless phones, espresso machine, and a maxibar rather than a minibar. Exotic wood shutters filter the sun, beds are draped with abaca cloth, and some suites have outdoor garden showers. The chef, maître d', and restaurant manager all come from places like Taillevent, Prunier, and Lucas Carton in Paris. Likewise, the spa is run by Sothys from the rue du Faubourg Saint-Honore in Paris. Outdoor diversions include tennis, windsurfing, kayaking, water-skiing. Cap Est is, as its name implies, located on the eastern side of the island, about 20 minutes from the airport. If only it was easier to get to the airport from the U.S. because Martinique has never known such luxury. 50 rooms. Suites: $300–$1,350, winter 2002–03. *Hôtel Cap Est Lagoon Resort, Le Francois, 97240 Martinique, French West Indies. Telephone: 596 596/54-80-80; fax: 596 596/54-96-00; e-mail: info@capest.com; Web: www.capest.com.*

Hôtel Plantation Leyritz

MARTINIQUE

Leyritz is a living, working banana plantation that's three centuries old, and the guardhouse, the slave quarters, and the Grand Manor House are all intact — but now instead of *planteurs* bedded down in them, you find vacationers. The former chapel and sugar factory have been transformed into beamed, stone-walled dining rooms with stenciled ceilings. At the bottom of a long emerald lawn, a swimming pool with marble dolphins sparkles like a big, cool sapphire. Accommodations here are comfortable, but far from luxurious. What wins Leyritz its following is that overworked catchall word, "charm." Everywhere you go, a miniature stone canal splashes fresh mountain water along your route — through the garden, past the guest rooms of the carriage house, cascading over the walls.

The 14 tiny cottages that once housed the plantation's slaves provide the most privacy — snug little tile-roofed warrens with foot-thick stone walls and windows discreetly screened by tropical flowers and mango trees. Rooms in the carriage house all have sun decks and the easiest route to the swimming pool — just 250 grassy feet down the hill; the smallest rooms are the newest — in a onetime dormitory. But probably the two most unusual places to hang your sun hat at Leyritz are what once served as the guardhouse and the master's kitchen — each gives you your own stone cottage surrounded by guava trees and manicured lawn. The guardhouse cottage gives you the best of both worlds: inside, a cool and shadowy stone-walled bedroom with slit windows just wide enough to poke a musket through, and outside, your own tiled patio with nothing in sight but a few million banana trees.

The problem here is that Hotel Plantation Leyritz is a tourist attraction by day — carloads and busloads of people from other hotels and cruise ships come to admire the corn-husk doll in the Musée de Poupées Végétales, drink at the bar, and nosh in the pavilion restaurant. After 4pm, of course, the day-trippers have gone and the hush returns, but it's not my idea of a secluded hideaway and nook. 67 rooms. Doubles: $130 with continental breakfast, winter 2002–03. *Hôtel Plantation Leyritz, 97218 Basse-Pointe, Martinique, French West Indies. Telephone: 596 596/78-53-92 or 800/823-2002; fax: 596 596/78-92-44.*

Auberge Les Petits Saints

TERRE-DE-HAUT

Here's another of those islands, one of Les Saintes off the coast of Guadeloupe, that turns the clock back decades. It's picture-postcard pretty: a circular anchorage surrounded by hills, a couple of forts, colorful fishing boats bobbing at their moorings, waterfront restaurants exuding joie de vivre, a narrow street lined with boutiques, souvenir shops, and art galleries. One of the best views of all this (against a dramatic backdrop of distant Soufrière on Guadeloupe) is from the flower-decked hill just above town, where Les Petits Saints hosts 20 guests in a quirky but quite charming series of rooms grouped around a small swimming pool and dining terrace.

The owners, Jean-Paul Colas and Didier Spindler, are also chefs (Jean-Paul entrees, Didier desserts), and their trellised terrace is probably the best dinner spot on the island. The cuisine is French-Creole smoked marlin, quail with pineapple and bourbon rice, scalloped wahoo with passion fruit sauce, banana tart or coconut charlotte with mango coulis — and dinner is served in a sprawling lobby/lounge/restaurant that's a mass of antiques. Les messieurs Colas and Spindler are also antiques dealers, spending one month each year touring the world in search of treasures. So, the terrace, lounge, and many of the guest rooms are fitted with objets from Nepal and Tibet, the Philippines, and Bali. Since they're all for sale, guests who fall in love with the couches they sit on or the tables they dine on frequently have them wrapped up and shipped home. What you see today may not be what you see when you return next year. Fun place. 10 rooms. Doubles: $80–$150 with continental breakfast, winter 2002–03. *Auberge Les Petit Saints aux Anacardiers, La Savanne, Terre-de-Haut, Guadeloupe 97137, French West Indies. Telephone: 590 590/99-50-99; fax: 590 590/99-54-51; e-mail: petitsaints@yahoo.fr; Web: www.petitssaints.com.*

The Queen's Windwards

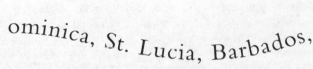

ominica, St. Lucia, Barbados,
Trinidad, and Tobago are not, strictly speaking, a geograph-
ical entity, and any sailors who think of them as "windwards" may find themselves way off course; but for lovers
and other romantics this is a convenient, if grab-bag, group-
ing. What these islands have in common is that they were
all, at one time or another, British dependencies.

Of the group, Dominica is the most fascinating — the
Caribbean as it must have been at the turn of the century,
or, once you get into the mountains and rain forests, as it
must have been when Columbus arrived here one *dominica*

(Sunday) in 1493. This is an island for travelers rather than vacationers, with real me-Tarzan-you-Jane countryside — untamed, forbidding landscapes, mountains a mile high, primeval forests, waterfalls, sulfur springs, lava beaches, and communities of the original Carib Indians.

St. Lucia has much the same topography as Dominica, but somehow it's a gentler island, its landscape softened by mile after mile of banana, spice, and coconut plantations, by bays and coves of white sand beaches. The road from the international airport in the south takes you along the windward Atlantic shore and across the mountains, but if you have time, take a drive on the regraded and repaved road down the Caribbean coast. It winds, snakes, twists, and writhes forever, but the scenery is impressive, and you pass Marigot Bay (a good lunch stop), Soufrière, and the famed Pitons, with possible side trips to volcanoes, sulfur springs, or rain forests.

Barbados is hardly a St. Lucia or Dominica in terms of scenery (it's relatively flat and pastoral except for a hilly region in the northeast), but it has a cosmopolitan air that few other Caribbean islands have, maybe because it has always been a favorite with the English gentry. Its main attraction, of course, is its scalloped western coastline, each cove with a lagoon-like beach. It may be rather crowded these days, but it still shelters most of the island's finest resorts. When it's time to take a break from sunning and swimming, however, Barbados rewards the leisurely tourist with a variety of sights, from caves and flower forests to plantation houses, forts, and venerable churches. There's even a house where George Washington slept when he visited his brother Lawrence.

Trinidad you can keep, at least in terms of lovers' hideaways. This island seems to get by on the strength of its carnival and, to some extent, the bustling, swinging, melting-pot qualities of its capital, Port of Spain. Its airport would be high on the list of places to avoid (even though it was recently upgraded) if it weren't for the fact that you often have to transit through there to get to a gem — Tobago.

Tobago is another story: 114 square miles of lush mountains, backwater fishing villages, beautiful beaches, and Buccoo Reef. It's certainly worth the trouble it takes to get there, if you want someplace offbeat and secluded. But go soon — four resorts have opened in recent months, including a Hilton, which is the lynchpin of an ambitious resort that will incorporate other international resorts, meeting facilities, and a couple of golf courses. Tobago is rapidly losing its innocence.

HOW TO GET THERE   To Barbados's Grantley Adams International Airport, there are American Airlines, Air Jamaica, US Airways, and BWIA from the States; American from San Juan; and Air Canada and BWIA from Toronto.

Getting to St. Lucia requires a little more attention because it has two airports: Hewanorra International in the south for jets, and the thoughtlessly named George F. L. Charles Airport (formerly Vigie) in the north for inter-Caribbean services. Choose carefully, otherwise you could waste half a day of your vacation (and until 2004, roadwork from Hewanorra to Soufrière adds at least half an hour to your drive — take a taxi to your hotel then rent a car from there). From New York, you can fly US Airways, Air Jamaica, and BWIA; from San Juan, American Eagle.

For Tobago, you usually first have to fly to Port of Spain on Trinidad — nonstop from New York on BWIA, from Miami on American and BWIA. The connecting flights are on jets. You might also want to consider getting there via Barbados or Grenada with easy connecting flights on LIAT or Caribbean Star, but, by the time you read this, your travel agent may be able to fill you in on direct flights from New York or Miami.

> For information on Dominica, call 212/949-1711 or visit www.ndcdominica.dm; St. Lucia, 800/456-3984 or www.stlucia.org; Barbados, 800/221-9831 or www.barbados.org; Trinidad and Tobago, 888/595-4868 or www.visitTNT.com.

Windjammer Landing Beach Resort

ST. LUCIA

☆ ☆	☕	🏀 🏀	$ $ $
ATMOSPHERE	**DINING**	**SPORTS**	**RATES**

Here are some of the most appealing lodgings on St. Lucia, even if they are in a town-house-style development and even if there have been several management changes since Windjammer opened in 1989.

The accommodations are all in dazzling white Mediterranean-style villas, spread over 55 acres of hillside, with lots of graceful touches and refinements that set them apart from run-of-the-mill resorts. Two- and three-bedroom villas come with their own private plunge pools, extra-spacious terra-cotta tiled patios, and glorious views of the ocean and surrounding hills. Couples on a splurge can rent a suite with a private pool in one of the two-bedroom villas for less than the usual foursome rate (villas 1, 2, 7, and 8 are particularly appealing).

Dotted around elsewhere on this hillside estate are one-bedroom villas with their own large swimming pool. Each of these 1,300-square-foot villa suites comes with a complete kitchen (including microwave), TV, terrace, air-conditioning (bedrooms only), and ceiling fans. Some of the bathrooms offer the same stunning views as the balconies.

The public areas, like the private quarters, are among the most attractive — at least architecturally — on the island. A split-level lobby/lounge flows into a poolside bar and a multilevel thatched dining pavilion overhanging the sea, all done in pickle pine with designer fabrics in soothing pastel shades. The cuisine is varied and appetizing; the staff is welcoming and eager to please. Windjammer's beach is not the greatest, but it's par for the course on St. Lucia, augmented with fine white sand imported from Barbuda and enough watersports and activities to fill your days. The new hilltop Serenity Spa is a big plus.

The drawback for visitors may be the terrain. The steep hills can be negotiated only by jitneys (no private cars throughout most of the property). Because there are only six electric carts to cover the entire estate, you may find yourself waiting around for transportation, even though the vehicles operate around the clock. Another possible drawback is the private pools: Some of them are private only in the sense that you have one all to yourself, but they are sited in such a way that people walking up and down the pathways may look directly down on your frolicking — although the resort is adding new lattice screens to alleviate the problem. Be warned!

Name: Windjammer Landing Beach Resort
Manager: Tony Bowen
Address: P.O. Box 1504, La Brelotte Bay, Castries, St. Lucia, West Indies
Location: On the northwest coast, about 15 min. and $20 by taxi from George F. L. Charles Airport, 20 min. from Castries; 90 min. and $80 from Hewanorra Airport
Telephone: 758/456-9000
Fax: 758/452-0907
E-mail: windjammer@candw.lc
Web: www.windjammer-landing.com
Reservations: 800/958-7376 or reservations@windjammer-landing.com
Credit Cards: All major cards
Rates: $280–$495 EP (Jan 5–Apr 4); tax 8%, service charge 10% extra; off-season 35% less
Rooms: 90 villas (35 one-bedroom, 25 two-bedroom, 26 three-bedroom, 4 four-bedroom), 21 superior one-bedroom units with garden view, 21 deluxe one-bedroom units with ocean view. All villas and units have air-conditioning (bedrooms only) and ceiling fans, refrigerator and tea/coffeemaker, private patios or terraces, cable TV, telephones, CD player, radio, safe, hair dryer, and bathrobes; some have separate living rooms and kitchens or pantries. All two- and three-bedroom villas, and a few one-bedroom villas, have private plunge pools
Meals: Breakfast 7:30–11am, lunch 11am–5pm, dinner 6–10pm (about $80–$100) at Jammer's Bar & Grill or Papa Don's; casual dress; limited room service at extra charge
Entertainment: 2 bars, some live music around the main pool 6 nights a week (which you'll hear in the restaurants), special shows 2 nights a week; shuttle service into Castries ($10 round-trip) twice weekly; cybercafe Café Labrolette
Sports: 2 large freshwater pools, 56 private villa pools, man-made sandy beach, tennis courts (2 Astroturf courts, with lights, rackets available), windsurfing, kneeboards, kayaks, volleyball, snorkeling gear, Sunfish sailing, fitness center, paddleboats — all free; water-skiing, boat trips, scuba, spa treatments at extra charge; horseback riding and golf nearby
PS: Some children of all ages, especially holidays, with a full children's program year-round; cellphones for rent; open year-round

Anse Chastanet Beach Hotel **5**
East Winds Inn **3**
Jalousie Hilton Resort & Spa **7**
Ladera Resort **6**
The Royal St. Lucian Hotel **1**
Ti Kaye Village **4**
Windjammer Landing Beach Resort **2**

St. Lucia

Cap Estate
Gros Islet
Anse Lavouette
Rodney Bay **1**
Choc Bay
Labrelotte Bay **2** **3**
Grande Anse Bay
Vigie Airport
La Toc **Castries**
Graand Cul de Sac Bay
La Sorcière
Marigot Bay
Roseau Bay
Fort Charlotte
Anse-La-Raye
4
Canaries
Dennery
5
Soufrière
La Soufrière
Petit Piton
7 **6** Fond St. Jacques
Micoud
Caribbean Sea
Gros Piton
Choiseul
Savannes Bay
Hewanorra Airport
Vieux Fort   *Maria Islands*

BARRE DE L'ISLE

ATLANTIC OCEAN

0   5 mi
0   5 km
N

✈ Airport
▲ Mountain

East Winds Inn

ST. LUCIA

★★☆
ATMOSPHERE

🍷🍷🍷
DINING

🌐
SPORTS

$ $ $ $
RATES

Inns don't come more beachcomber-ish than this — on a private bay with seagrapes and coco palms separating the white sand from a peaceful garden of mango and pomegranate trees and colored with hibiscus and bougainvillea. You come across this garden setting almost as a surprise, an oasis at the end of 800 yards or so of what feels like the most potholed road on an island of potholed roads, with a turquoise chattel house guarding the entrance to the resort. The birdsong tells you you're someplace special. Off to the left on a low rise is a cluster of lime-green cottages, below them a group of hexagonal cottages, a free-form pool with a swim-up bar, and then an open-sided clubhouse with a bamboo bar and piano lounge. Now the birdsong switches to squawks as Mac and Erik, the mascot parrots, hold forth in their giant cages beside the new thatched-roof Piton Bar, where folks gather at sunset to drink rum punches.

The 10 hexagonal cottages are the originals — traditional old-style Caribbean lodgings with jalousie windows, tiled floors, wicker furniture, and island decorations — no frills except for a refrigerator in the closet. They're still popular with regulars despite the arrival a few years ago of the 16 lime-green cottages, the deluxe lodgings, which come with king-size beds, sunken stone-lined showers that are halfway open to the breezes, and unbeachcomber-ish amenities like TV/VCRs and wet bars, the latter set up on private beaches well-screened by lush foliage.

Mealtimes have become something special here. For a start, cocktails and wines (60 choices!), like the meals, are included in the rate. Lunch is a grand buffet (take your plate out to one of the thatch-shaded gazebos set in the sand). The four-course dinners might include award-winning dishes like stingray terrine (more delicious than it sounds) and pan-fried pork loin with four-spice sauce, or St. Lucian roots stew and red snapper in ginger sauce (you know the fish is fresh here — you see it arriving every morning in the fisherman's pirogue).

There's nothing pretentious about East Winds. The owner, Giuseppe Olivares, walks around barefoot, setting a very laid-back and relaxing air. As one guest wrote in the visitors' book, "The most relaxing, friendly, good-value holiday we have ever enjoyed. We shall return." For a real back-to-basics, lolling-around vacation, be guided by the East Winds.

Name: East Winds Inn
Owner/Manager: Giuseppe Olivares/Gareth Leach
Address: P.O. Box 1477, La Brelotte Bay, Castries, St. Lucia, West Indies
Location: On the northwest coast, about 15 min. and $20 by taxi from George F. L. Charles Airport and Castries; 90 min. and $72 from Hewanorra Airport
Telephone: 758/452-8212
Fax: 758/452-9941
E-mail: eastwinds@candw.lc
Web: www.eastwinds.com
Reservations: 800/225-3186, Karen Bull Associates
Credit Cards: American Express, MasterCard, Visa
Rates: $730–$1,080 FAP, including drinks (Dec 17–Apr 3); tax and service charge included; off-season 30% less
Rooms: 30 single-story cottages — 10 superior hexagonal cottages, 16 deluxe traditional cottages, and 1 four-bedroom villa, with patio, ceiling fans (no air-conditioning), refrigerator, tea/coffeemaker, hair dryer, in-room safe; deluxe cottages with TV/VCR, king-size bed, and sunken shower; all rooms face the gardens, no direct water views
Meals: Breakfast 7:30–10am, lunch 12:30–2pm, afternoon tea 4–5pm, dinner 7:30–9:30pm in the informal open-air restaurant on the beach (about $135 including drinks for nonguests); limited room service; some music from the bar
Entertainment: Live music (jazz, calypso, "shak-shak," piano) every night in the bar/restaurant, steel band at Saturday lunch; videotapes available for loan (no charge)

Sports: 1 large free-form swimming pool with self-service swim-up bar, small but inviting white-sand beach, snorkeling gear, pedalos, straddle canoes — all free

PS: No children under 12 Feb 1 through Mar 6; mainly British clientele; open year-round

Ti Kaye Village

ST. LUCIA

☆☆☆	ΥΥ	⊖	$ $
ATMOSPHERE	**DINING**	**SPORTS**	**RATES**

Nestled on a steep cliff overlooking the Caribbean, secluded, tasteful, and casually elegant, Ti Kaye is a special place. The recent creation of 34-year-old St. Lucian–born Nick Pinnock, with designs by architect Wayne Brown, one of the founders of Anse Chastanet, this is a true Caribbean resort laid out on 16 acres of lush vegetation, with 19 St. Lucian gingerbread style individual cottages and 14 rooms in duplex cottages, all with stunning water views and the promise of a spectacular sunset.

All 19 cottages are identical: a spacious bedroom with St. Lucian–style furniture made of white cedar from the property, a king-size four-poster bed, large windows with louvers, and an outdoor garden shower. French doors open to an expansive veranda where you can flop into a double hammock and in four of the cottages you can plop into a plunge pool, complete with night lights. Banana trees, magenta bougainvillea, and a host of tropical plantings frame the spectacular vista (Ti Kaye Village is designed to be eco-friendly and is in line for a Green Globe award from CAST, the Caribbean Association for Sustainable Tourism).

A steep staircase (166 steps — count them) leads down to a cove with silver sand, crystal-clear water, and a well-equipped dive shop. This is Anse Cochon Bay, home to St. Lucia's most popular shipwreck dive site, "Lesleen M," and beautiful coral reefs — a haven for snorkelers and scuba divers. Unfortunately, of course, this makes the cove a popular destination for catamarans loaded with day-trippers, snorkelers, and divers from other resorts. Best plan: Go to the beach in the morning, leave before noon, then return after the catamarans leave, around 4 pm. Just before sunset, you can watch the fishermen from nearby Anse La Raye, pulling a giant net from their pirogue towards the beach. Guests who would rather lounge around the quiet pool can absorb the panorama from high above with Martinique's soaring Mont Pelé on the horizon.

Kai M'jame (House of Food in the local patois) is the perfect setting for a romantic dinner overlooking the seascape: No walls — just soft white curtains billowing with the breeze and candles flickering on the neatly set tables. Chef Paul Yellin (a Bajan-American raised in Brooklyn) combines classic and Caribbean cuisine in signature dishes like beef tenderloin with coffee glaze, mahimahi with banana-lemon butter, grilled shrimp with tamarind and rum glaze. The menu changes every day. Paul took over Ti Kaye's kitchen in January 2002, after stints with Hans Schweitzer at the Sandy Lane Hotel in Barbados, and in 2001 he won first prize at the Jamaica Spice Food Festival. It's not just the setting that makes this a special place.

Name: Ti Kaye Village

Manager: Jeannine Davis

Address: P.O. Box GM669, Castries, St. Lucia, West Indies

Location: On the west coast of St. Lucia, on Anse Cochon, about halfway between Soufrière and Castries, and a mile off the main road. 80 min. and $45 by taxi from Hewanorra International Airport, and 40 min. and $30 by taxi from George F. L. Charles Airport.

Telephone: 758/456-8101 or 758/456-8102

Fax: 758/456-8105

E-mail: info@tikaye.com

Web: www.tikaye.com

Reservations: Direct

Credit cards: All major cards

Rates: $180–$320 CP (Dec 16–Apr 15); tax 8%, service charges10%; off-season, 20% less

Rooms: 8 oceanfront cottages, 4 with a plunge pool; 11 oceanview cottages; 14 oceanview rooms in 7 duplex cottages. Amenities include air-conditioning and ceiling fans, small refrigerator, telephone with direct dial, safe-deposit box, hair dryer, coffeemaker

Meals: Breakfast 8–10am, lunch noon–3:00pm, dinner 7–9:30pm, at Kaj M'jamé (about $79); casual dress; recorded background music

Entertainment: Every full moon, bonfire on the beach, with music, drinks, and food. Fri shuttle takes guests to nearby fishing village Anse La Raye for "Seafood Friday." Live West Indian music once a week

Sports: Swimming pool, small fitness center with Cybex equipment — free; scuba diving at extra charge; whale-watching, rainforest and volcano hiking tours, excursions to Castries and Soufrière by water-taxi can be arranged

PS: Mostly European clientele, children 12 years and older welcome; open year-round

Anse Chastanet Beach Hotel

ST. LUCIA

☆☆☆☆ ATMOSPHERE | Y Y DINING | ❸❸❸ SPORTS | $ $ $ RATES

Don't come here for three-speed showerheads and Porthault sheets. The luxuries at Anse Chastanet run deeper and dearer. First, there's the Caribbean's most spectacular view, a Bali Ha'i of jagged mountains soaring out of the sea that would have sent Gauguin diving for his umbers and indigos. Then there's the hotel's simple good taste, from handmade mahogany bed tables to the twist of immaculate madras on every waitress's head.

But you find something else here that is all too rare in the Caribbean these days: a caring and a closeness, not just between owner and guests or staff and guests, but with the whole tiny community — taxi drivers, schoolgirls, fishermen, banana cutters.

Artfully tucked away in a 5,000-acre estate in one of St. Lucia's most remote back pockets, Anse Chastanet proves hard to get to even once you get there. Its private roadway rocks and rolls you up and up and up until at the end of it all you discover the beginning of the hotel, spiraling up higher still into the hills or down to the sea.

Octagonal whitewashed guest cottages cantilever from the hibiscus like vacationers who can't get enough of that view. The style is beach functional: wraparound windows and terraces, paddle fans, island-crafted furniture of local wood, crisp madras and muslin at the windows and on the beds, ingenious three-dimensional burlap wall hangings, original artworks, and wood-trimmed showers. All of it is born of the theory that beach houses are for sleeping. The prime lodgings are the 11 suites built in 1990, a notch or two up the hill, ranging from 900 to 1,600 square feet, some with ceilings soaring 20 feet high, and some with bathrooms larger than most hotel rooms. Each of these suites has a breathtaking view, whether it's facing north across the luxuriant dell and beach or south to the Pitons. Among the premium suites, 7B has a perfectly framed view of the peaks; 7S's bed has been set at an angle for a classic view of the Pitons; 7F has a 180° vista and a shower with a perfect Piton view; suite 14B, slightly futuristic in looks with a soaring ceiling, sports a free-form stucco shower open to the breezes with a 30-foot-high St. Lucian fir tree in the middle; 15B suggests a sort of tree house with its wraparound louvers opening onto dense foliage. The 12 spacious rooms tucked behind the beach are handsome and luxurious (room 11 is best in terms of privacy).

In recent years, the owners, Nick and Karolin Troubetzkoy, have been inviting distinguished European and American artists to vacation at Anse Chastanet in return for paintings. As a result, the little resort tucked away on a hillside in St. Lucia has one of the best collections of gallery-caliber art of any hotel anywhere. They've even published a catalog of Anse Chastanet paintings. For the rest, there is a series of multilevel open-air terraces, dining rooms, and bars, and, at the bottom of a long hillside stairway, a graceful ¼-mile beach of fine volcanic sand the color of pussy willows.

But who says you have to stay at home? Take a picnic lunch to the hotel's private waterfall. Get a native guide to paddle you around the neighboring mountain islands. Give your camera a workout in Soufrière, a tumbledown fishing village as picture-perfect as a movie set. Tour an authentic French colonial banana plantation. Soak your weary bones in the hot mineral baths of a tropical rain forest. Visit a volcano. Or sample the hottest diversion: Spend a morning or afternoon mountain biking on Cannondale 800s through the

Troubetskoys' adjoining estate, on miles of easy or single-track trails to a height of 900 feet or so.

Currently the owners are constructing 24 new suites, a sort of "executive club" complex with its own concierge desk, restaurant, and spa. Each suite will have a private plunge pool but, in the Anse Chastanet tradition, will have no fourth wall, no TV, no phone, no radio, and no room service, and maids will be summoned by tugging a cord. Some guests are hoping that the new complex might lead to a new, less bumpy access road — without endangering the resort's sense of tranquility and privacy.

Name: Anse Chastanet Beach Hotel
Owners/Managers: Nick and Karolin Troubetzkoy
Address: P.O. Box 7000, Soufrière, St. Lucia, West Indies
Location: On the southwest coast, 90 min. and $55 by taxi from Hewanorra Airport, 2 hr. and $80 from George F. L. Charles Airport or Castries (the fare is included in the weekly scuba package or escape package); the hotel will have someone meet you at the airport if you let them know when you're arriving
Telephone: 758/459-7000
Fax: 758/459-7700
E-mail: ansechastanet@candw.lc
Web: www.ansechastanet.com
Reservations: 800/223-1108, Ralph Locke Islands
Credit Cards: American Express, Diners Club, MasterCard, Visa
Rates: $445–$795 MAP (Dec 20–Apr 15); 8% tax and 10% service charge extra; off-season 20% less
Rooms: 49, 12 in spacious hillside villas, 25 in the hillside cottages (of which 5 are suites), 12 in 2 plantation-style villas at beach level, all with ceiling fans and balcony or patio, each with refrigerator, hair dryer, coffeemaker, and personal safe
Meals: Breakfast 7:30–10am, lunch noon–3:30pm (at the beachside bar/restaurant, Trou-au-Diable), dinner 7:30–9:30pm (about $90 for nonguests), in the hillside Piti Piton; informal dress; coal-pot barbecues Fri evenings, Creole buffet Tues; room service for breakfast only $1 extra
Entertainment: Live entertainment most evenings (dancing, local "shak-shak" band, steel band), library
Sports: Beach (volcanic sand), snorkeling gear and snorkeling trips, windsurfing, ocean kayaking, Sunfish sailing, pirogue trips to the Pitons, tennis (1 court, no lights), escorted nature walks and hikes on adjoining estate — all free; small Kai Belte (Home of Beauty, in Creole) Spa with an interesting menu of massage and beauty treatments, new Bike St. Lucia's Team Volvo Cannondale 800s, and complete PADI scuba facility with 3 dive boats and photo lab — extra charge (no spearguns — the sea around here is a designated marine reserve, and the entire bay has been buoyed off to limit boat traffic)
PS: No children under 4, given the hilly terrain; open year-round

Ladera Resort

ST. LUCIA

☆ ☆ ☆ ☆ ☆   Y Y Y   🎱 $ $ $ $
ATMOSPHERE   **DINING**   **SPORTS**   **RATES**

Waking up here is like being present at the Creation. Immediately below, an amphitheater of hillside thick with tropical greenery drops off precipitously to a coconut plantation. Beyond it, the Caribbean glistens, glitters, and shimmers all the way to the horizon. And framing the entire view: the famed Pitons, those postcard-perfect twin volcanic cones soaring straight from the sea to more than double the height of 1,000-foot-high Ladera.

And it's all right there before your dazzled eyes, without the effort of opening the windows or pushing back the shutters, because your hilltop aerie has no west wall. In fact, in some of the suites, you can ooh and aah at the panorama without even getting out of bed. This most unusual inn, part Big Sur, part Bali Ha'i, sits atop the ridge of an extinct volcano (which you would never guess in a thousand nights was a volcano, given the dense foliage), a 4-acre plot in a 200-year-old working plantation that still produces cocoa, coffee, and copra. Conceived by an American interior designer back in the days before too many people worried about the environment (say, the 1960s), Ladera's villas and public spaces are constructed of hardwoods and native stone, camouflaged by flowering shrubs, all with that "invisible" west wall. (Panic not: The villas are designed in such a way that no one can see in, but if you see a helicopter hovering around longer than usual, maybe you'd better slip into the kimono the resort provides for just such moments. Likewise, you don't have to worry about being rained on because the roofs project far enough.)

The resort (at that time known as Dasheene) closed for several years in the 1980s because of some legal wrangling among the major shareholder and the people who own the individual suites; but late in 1992, it reopened with a single owner, $1 million worth of renovations, a new name, and a new team of eager beavers in charge, and, as of 1998, five new villas, all with touches of whimsy. If all continues to go well, romantics can once more frolic in one of the loveliest, most idyllic spots in the Caribbean.

You enter via a gatehouse that still sports the former name, go up a narrow, steep driveway, surrounded by more of that luxuriant foliage, to the main building — a series of terraces and decks with a tiny rock pool that seems to spill over the side of the hill. (If it all seems familiar, it's probably because you saw Superman II — this is the spot, I'm told, where Christopher Reeve landed bearing flowers for the lovely Lois, played by Margot Kidder.)

Each of the wood-framed villas is different in layout and decor, each a designer's fantasy with splashes of color to enliven the stone and tile, wicker and bamboo. Some of the furniture is 19th-century French; some was crafted right in Soufrière by local craftsmen. In one villa, there's a gallery bedroom with open shower, in another, the bathroom is in the style of a Polynesian

grass hut, while some of the bedrooms sport mahogany four-posters or double beds posed on platforms beneath clouds of mosquito netting.

For sure, Ladera is not for everyone. The fitted-carpet brigade and people
who insist on air-conditioning will balk at the plank floors and missing wall;
others may quibble about the absence of tubs or telephones and the trek to
the beach; some may not find it amusing that your waiter offers you a water
pistol to keep the cheeky birds from your croissants. Let me repeat: There's no
fourth wall. Some people love the idea, but then get upset if a tiny bat flutters by. If one of nature's little visitors startles you, leap into each other's
arms — that's what you're here for in the first place. But I can't imagine that
too many guests will complain about the sheer romance of the terrace restaurant by candlelight, or, after dinner, the other pleasure waiting: lying in bed
looking out beyond the Pitons to the moonlight shimmering and glistening
and gleaming on the sea.

Name: Ladera Resort
Manager: Magnus Alnebeck
Address: P.O. Box 225, Soufrière, St. Lucia, West Indies
Location: In the hills south of Soufrière, about 90 min. and $45 by taxi from
    Hewanorra International Airport and 1 hr. 45 min. and $75 by taxi from
    George F. L. Charles Airport
Telephone: 758/459-7323
Fax: 758/459-5156
E-mail: ladera@candw.lc
Web: www.ladera-stlucia.com
Reservations: 800/738-4752, Karen Bull Associates
Credit Cards: All major cards
Rates: $360–$745 EP (Dec 18–Mar 31); 8% tax and 10% service charge extra;
    off-season 30% less
Rooms: 25, 19 one- or two-story suites and 6 three-story villas, all different,
    all open to the breezes, most with shower only (no phones, TV, or other
    distractions), all villas have kitchenettes, some with private plunge pool,
    refrigerator, and coffeemaker
Meals: Breakfast 7:30–10am, lunch 11:30am–2:30pm, dinner 6–9:30pm in
    the covered but breeze-cooled Dasheene Restaurant (about $100); dress is
    "smart casual"; room service for breakfast with plenty of notice, $5 per
    person
Entertainment: Live reggae music Mon; the bar, the guests, the view, lectures
    on the environment, the moon and Venus through powerful telescopes,
    Internet access; shuttle bus to Soufrière and water taxi to Anse Chastanet
    several times per week
Sports: Small pool; watersports and tennis nearby; hikes in the hills to sulfur
    springs and botanical gardens; shuttle buses twice daily to nearby beach
PS: Because of the layout, not really suitable for young children; "no cellphone
    coverage here for at least 3 years — and we hope 5"; open year-round

Jalousie Hilton Resort & Spa

ST. LUCIA

☆☆☆	ΨΨ	❸❸❸	$ $ $ $
ATMOSPHERE	**DINING**	**SPORTS**	**RATES**

Settings don't come much more Edenic than this: a luxuriant coconut plantation beside a curve of beach between those two glorious peaks, the Pitons, which leap from the sea into the sky practically from your doorstep.

Many St. Lucians, including local Nobelist Derek Walcott, campaigned to have the plantation become a national park, and it certainly has all the attributes; instead, it became a resort development at the urging of Lord Glenconner, the former Colin Tennant, who put the island of Mustique on the celebrity map (see the next chapter). Disenchanted with that island, he turned his formidable powers of persuasion on St. Lucia, where he planned to build luxury retreats for his aristocratic chums. But first he parceled out this 375-acre plot to an Iranian-American entrepreneur who would build a resort to attract potential homeowners, while Glenconner kept a home next door, beside his barefoot beachside restaurant, the whimsical Bang Between the Pitons.

Like Bang Between the Pitons, Jalousie is defined by its location. Hilly and lush, the property spreads out across ¼ mile of beachfront and then several hundred feet up the mountainside. You enter through a gatepost at the top of the hill and spiral down a steep driveway, first passing the sports complex (spa, tennis, executive golf course) and then the clusters of cottages one by one until you reach the Great House. From there you can survey the entire scene — the manicured grounds (easy to see why they need 36 gardeners), the swimming pool, the Sugar Mill complex, the beach, the peaks.

Jalousie's cottages, all 102 of them, are designed with wooden exteriors, pitched shingle roofs, and tiny windows. Not very inspired — the architect seems to have missed a once-in-a-lifetime opportunity in a one-of-a-kind location to design something truly inspired. (Ah, if only the folks who put together Jamaica's Strawberry Hill could have had a crack at this spot!) The interiors, too, started out dreary, but the Hilton people, to their credit, have brightened the exteriors and lightened the decor with pastel shades of coral and lemon. For some guests, the decor's baldachins and valances may be a bit too boudoir-ish for the setting, and others will long for screens and louvers; but they'll be comfortable nonetheless. The great feature of these cottages is their private patios with refrigerators and private plunge pools, shaded by pergolas and screened by tropical shrubbery.

The cottages are grouped in clusters with names like Coffee Bean Bend and Passion Fruit Hamlet, spread out around the hillside so that it's difficult to navigate the distances from your room to the beach and restaurant and elsewhere without the ubiquitous jitneys. I stayed in Coconut Grove, over near the Pier Restaurant, an easy walk from the action along a pathway skirting the beach. By day, that is. In the evening, it was easier to pick up the phone and call for a jitney. The most convenient lodgings are designated Sugar Mill, with 12 suites in two two-story cream-colored villas, an easy shuffle to either the beach or the Great House. They don't have plunge pools and the calm may sometimes be shattered by guests arriving by helicopter to avoid the roadwork, but they do have terraces with awesome views.

The beach is in better shape than it was when the resort first opened, thanks to the barges of white sand imported from Trinidad or Guyana to cover the neutral, lava-gray grains beneath. Jalousie's public rooms are generally impressive, the service is gracious if tentative, but the meals are unexceptional and outclassed by the settings — four restaurants, indoors and outdoors, for just over 200 guests.

Besides the setting, what sets this resort off from its neighbors is its full-scale spa with gym and beauty facilities, where you can revel in sulfur spring mud baths (there's a volcano just up the road) and purity and tranquility seaweed wraps.

The truth is, you really don't need a restorative spa here: The very setting — those awesome soaring mountains, the lushly languorous scenery — refreshes, rejuvenates, and calms the soul and does all the other things spas are supposed to do.

Name: Jalousie Hilton Resort and Spa
Manager: Rui Dominigues
Address: P.O. Box 251, Soufrière, St. Lucia, West Indies
Location: On the southwest coast near Soufrière, about 90 min. and $55 by taxi from Hewanorra Airport, 90 min. and $80 from George F. L. Charles Airport
Telephone: 758/456-8000
Fax: 758/459-7667
E-mail: jhr_sales&mkt@candw.lc
Web: www.jalousie-hilton.com
Reservations: 888/744-5262, toll-free direct or 800/445-8667, Hilton Reservations
Credit Cards: All major cards
Rates: $554–$1,080 EP (Dec 19–Apr 30); 8% tax and 10% service charge extra; off-season, 40% less
Rooms: 112 rooms and suites, all with patios or terraces, air-conditioning and ceiling fans, minibars, satellite TV/VCR, clock radio, hair dryer, bathrobes, personal safes, coffeemakers, umbrellas; 102 cottages have private plunge pools
Meals: Breakfast 7–11am, lunch 11:30am–3pm, dinner 6:30–10pm (about $80–$100) outdoor at the beach or indoor in the air-conditioned Great House; recorded music, occasional live music in beachside restaurants; 24-hr. room service at extra charge
Entertainment: 4 bars, special theme evenings in beachside restaurants; although you won't find any reference to it in any of the resort's literature, Bang

Between the Pitons is right next door and it's fun to walk there (4 min.) for a nightcap and the plaintive sounds of an unamplified native band

Sports: Beach, large freshwater pool, 102 private pools, snorkeling, sailing, windsurfing, catamarans, kayaks, paddleboats, aquacycles, kneeboards, tennis (4 courts, with lights, pro), squash court and racquet ball court, gym (breeze cooled), sauna, Jacuzzi, 3-hole/par-3 executive golf course — all free; full-scale spa facilities, scuba (dive shop on site) at extra charge; horseback riding and rainforest tours can be arranged

PS: Some children (they have their own playroom); forget about cellphones in this hemmed-in location; open year-round

Coral Reef Club

BARBADOS

☆☆☆☆☆   ♈♈♈   ❻❻ $ $ $ $
ATMOSPHERE   **DINING**   **SPORTS**   **RATES**

You stay in villas with names like Petrea, Allamanda, and Cordia, and you walk to the beach past splashes of . . . blue petrea and yellow allamanda and orange cordia.

You swim a few leisurely strokes to the coral reef offshore. You dine at a leisurely pace, your lunch and dinner accented with such novel dishes as marlin paté, flying-fish mousse, and tipsy trifle.

Above all, you relax.

The Coral Reef Club is the sort of place where people go to wind down rather than dress up, where entertainers and celebrities go to find undisturbed seclusion. This clubby but unstuffy inn has been a standard-bearer among Barbados resorts for over 40 years, a prototype of the small beachside retreat built around a coral-stone villa. Because it was there before the others, it managed to snare some prize beachfront acreage — more than a dozen acres shaded by mango, mahogany, and cannonball trees.

Not least of Coral Reef's enduring attractions has been its friendly family ambience, with the warm welcomes now extended by the second generation of O'Haras — Patrick, Mark, and Karen (whose husband, Wayne Capaldi, runs The Sandpiper, the sister hotel just down the road). A few years ago, the new regime (under the guidance of Cynthia, their ever-watchful mother) inaugurated a few changes, including the addition of a two-story wing to augment the bungalows, which are artfully designed in a plantation-house style with verandas and gingerbread trim. Its 10 rooms and suites are slightly larger and slightly plusher, with sumptuous rattan-and-wicker furniture, plumper fabrics, and 12 × 16-foot verandas furnished for indoor-outdoor living. The sleek bathrooms, with black tile floors and white tile shower/tubs, have proved so popular that the bathrooms in the original bungalows have been enlarged and redecorated to match. Guests liked the changes so much, in 1999, the O'Haras leapfrogged into the super luxury class with the addition of four Luxury Plantation Suites with private pools. They're part of a new colonial-style wing with 17 rooms and suites built around a new 60×30-foot swimming pool, new landscaping with gazebos, and a new boutique in the style of a Barbados chattel house. The second floor of each of the exquisitely decorated luxury suites (actually, the loveliest rooms on Barbados), comes with a four-poster bed, complimentary starter bar, and — a major novelty for Coral Reef that may or may not sit well with the old-timers — satellite TV/VCR, stereo, and fax machine. But the pièce de résistance is the private 12 × 9-foot pool on the private sun deck. Now, in case any of these longtime Coral Reefers are also worrying about the resort's mature trees and other botanical riches, the O'Haras are quick to point out that "only one tree has been felled in order to carry out the project." These suites in turn became so popular that all the original bungalows were replaced by spanking new one- and two-story cottages with spacious verandas and patios, sumptuous marble-clad bathrooms and, in some cases, private plunge pools (which will be even more private a year from now when the plantings reach maturity). Like the earlier rooms, they are all surrounded by meticulously landscaped gardens.

All the rooms retain the usual homelike O'Hara touches — individual toasters so you get your breakfast toast crisp and fresh, shelves of paperbacks in each room, and refrigerators for easy access to thirst-quenchers. At the moment, only the Luxury Plantation Suites have TV — the verdict is still out on the subject because, with all the french doors and louvers in the rooms, blaring TVs could be intrusive (there's a communal set in the air-conditioned computer room). The O'Hara family has also added a smart 10-station, air-conditioned exercise room and a billiards room; the coral-stone dining pavilion has been livened up with ceiling murals with tropical motifs, and the beam-and-bamboo bar is an even more inviting venue than it was before, with views of the sea from three sides, cooled by 30 slowly turning ceiling fans, and decorated with pleasing island flair (note the hanging planters/lights — in another incarnation they were farmers' dung baskets). Despite all the changes, by the way, the 33-chef brigade forges ahead under executive Graham Licorish, still crafting the kinds of dishes — continental and Bajan and yummy pastries — that encourage most Coral Reef guests to opt for the MAP plan and skip the trendy, reservations-only restaurants nearby.

For Coral Reef habitués (and they are legion), the best news may be that the grounds are as lovely as ever, with the usual brigade of 15 gardeners tending the lawns and every last petal of the petrea, cordia, and allamanda.

Name: Coral Reef Club
Owners/Managers: The O'Hara family
Address: St. James, Barbados, West Indies
Location: On the west coast, 40 min. and $30 by taxi from the airport, 20 min. and $22 from Bridgetown (free shuttle to town weekdays at 9:30am)
Telephone: 246/422-2372
Fax: 246/422-1776

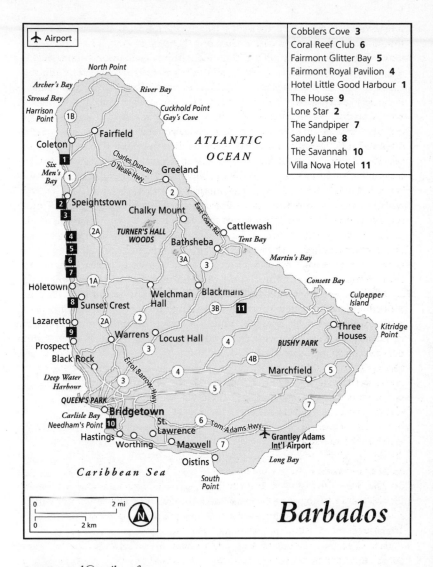

Cobblers Cove **3**
Coral Reef Club **6**
Fairmont Glitter Bay **5**
Fairmont Royal Pavilion **4**
Hotel Little Good Harbour **1**
The House **9**
Lone Star **2**
The Sandpiper **7**
Sandy Lane **8**
The Savannah **10**
Villa Nova Hotel **11**

E-mail: coral@caribsurf.com

Web: www.coralreefbarbados.com

Reservations: 800/223-1108, Ralph Locke Islands

Credit Cards: All major cards

Rates: $375–$2,035 EP (Dec 15–Apr 15); service charge and taxes included in rates; off-season approximately 50% less

Rooms: 88 rooms and suites, in 6 categories, in the clubhouse and various cottages throughout the gardens, all with patios or balconies, air-conditioning and ceiling fans, refrigerators, toasters, direct-dial telephones, personal safes, bathrobes, hair dryers; 5 Luxury Plantation Suites have sun decks with pools, wetbars, TV/VCR, fax machines, CD players

Meals: Breakfast 7:30–10:30am, continental breakfast until noon, lunch 1–2:30pm, afternoon tea 4–5pm, dinner 7:30–9:30pm (about $120) in the breeze-cooled beachside pavilion; Mon evening Bajan buffet, Sun brunch buffet; optional jacket and tie in winter (jacket and tie or black tie required on Christmas night and New Year's Eve), elegantly informal the remainder of the year; 24-hr. room service (but not necessarily full meals) at no extra charge; dine-around program with 3 other hotels; nearby entertainment: live music and dancing 7 evenings a week in season, 4 evenings off-season (amplified "but not loud"), weekly folklore show and beach barbecue, parlor games, TV and computer room, billiards room

Sports: Good beach, good swimming and snorkeling, freshwater pool plus individual plunge pools, tennis (2 all-weather courts, with lights), Sunfish sailing, windsurfing, water-skiing, cocktail cruises, snorkeling gear, Hobie Cat, fitness center — all free; spa treatments extra; catamaran cruises, scuba diving, deep-sea fishing, horseback riding nearby at extra charge; golf can be arranged at nearby Sandy Lane or the Royal Westmoreland Golf Club

PS: "Children welcome except during Feb, when those under 12 years cannot be accommodated" (and they now have their own playground), and "no children under 5 in the dining room after 7pm"; no cellphones allowed in the bar or restaurant, and acceptable elsewhere if used "with discretion"; open year-round

Fairmont Glitter Bay

BARBADOS

☆☆☆	ΥΥ	❻❻	$ $ $ $
ATMOSPHERE	DINING	SPORTS	RATES

The glitter comes from the play of sun on sea, but when the Cunard family (of steamship fame) took over the estate in the 1930s, the guests also provided the glitter — Noël Coward and Anthony Eden, assorted lords and ladies, and merchant princes. Oceangoing Cunarders putting into Bridgetown often found their ships' orchestras shanghaied to play for Sir Edward Cunard's garden parties. All very romantic.

Today, the sea still glitters, lords and ladies still winter here, and at least one Arab prince (accompanied by an entourage of 25) has settled in for 6 weeks on more than one occasion. But Sir Edward's original coral-stone Great House is now the centerpiece of a small resort, in the style of Andalusia rather than the Antilles — white-stucco buildings rising three or four stories above the lawns, their ocher-tiled rooftops eye to eye with the coconut palms, their balconies and terraces angled for sea views. By confining the rooms to one side of the garden and by building up rather than out, Glitter Bay avoids that pitfall of so many of the newer beachside resorts in Barbados — rooms looking into rooms.

The decor is attractively tropical, with Mediterranean overtones: scatter rugs to brighten the quarry-tile floors and — a nice touch — cushioned banquettes on the stucco balconies. Since the resort was conceived originally as a condo operation, most of the accommodations are suites with kitchenettes, in versatile configurations of duplex suites, penthouse suites, and nests with one to three bedrooms.

But Glitter Bay is almost two distinct resorts because the most appealing rooms, for my money, are located not in the Andalusian-style wings but in the beachside villa known as Beach House, a coral-stone replica of the former Cunard palazzo in Venice, with five luxury suites.

Glitter Bay also gives you a sense of space rare in Barbados — 30 acres of tended lawns shaded by royal palms and cannonball trees, pathways lined by frangipani and lady-of-the-night, sturdy saman trees embraced and entwined by traceries of wild orchids, plus another 8 acres from its sister resort next door, Royal Pavilion. (As of 2000, all 38 acres are now under the aegis of Fairmont Hotels.) The old Estate Great House sits well back from the beach, and the remaining structures are grouped around a split-level swimming pool with a wooden footbridge and waterfall. Down by the beach, guests in the Piperade enjoy fresh sea breezes, attentive service, and reasonable prices on a menu that runs the gamut from filet of flying fish or jumbo coconut prawns to citrus roasted chicken.

Name: Glitter Bay
Manager: Roger Soane
Address: St. James, Barbados, West Indies
Location: On the northwest coast, 30-40 min. and $30 by taxi from the airport (you can also arrange to have one of the resort's limos collect you for $100), 20 min. and $22 from Bridgetown
Telephone: 246/422-4111
Fax: 246/422-3940
E-mail: reservations@fairmont.com
Web: www.fairmont.com
Reservations: 800/866-5577, Fairmont Hotels
Credit Cards: All major cards
Rates: $479–$779 EP (Dec 21–Apr 21); service charge 10%; off-season 50% less
Rooms: 67, in three- and four-story wings or beachside villas, all with air-conditioning and ceiling fans, terrace or patio, refrigerator, stocked minibar, television, direct-dial telephones, seersucker bathrobes, coffeemaker, hair dryer, radio; suites also have kitchenettes
Meals: Breakfast 7:30–11am, lunch 11:30am–6:30pm, complimentary afternoon tea 3:30–5pm in Piperade, dinner 7–9:45pm, in the breeze-cooled, beachside restaurant (about $120); informal dress (but no shorts or T-shirts in the evening), Tues buffet dinner, with live entertainment, open to nonguests; Fri-night barbecue; 24-hr. room service; meals can also be charged at Royal Pavilion (see below)

Entertainment: Beachside bar, live amplified music for dancing, some folklore shows

Sports: ½-mile beach, raft, 2-tiered free-form freshwater pool, windsurfing, snorkeling masks, Hobie 16s, water-skiing, tennis (4 courts, with lights), fitness center — all free (shared with Royal Pavilion guests); sailboat cruises and scuba can be arranged at the beach hut, horseback riding 10 min. away, golf on the Royal Westmoreland or Sandy Lane courses

PS: Expect lots of children during holidays (but the young ones have their own planned activities) and a few seminar groups in the off-season; open year-round

Fairmont Royal Pavilion

BARBADOS

☆☆☆	♈♈♈	◐◐	$ $ $ $
ATMOSPHERE	DINING	SPORTS	RATES

The pièce de résistance at this coral-pink palazzo is the Palm Terrace, a capacious beachfront salon for lounging, sipping, chatting, and dining; it's about as elegant, comfortable, and eye-pleasing as any room in the islands. Its two-story vaulted ceiling of pickled pine is specially designed to let in the 20% of sunlight needed for the nourishment of the 20-foot McCarthy palms and other plants that turn the terrace into a mini-conservatory. Five pink stucco archways along the front of the room open to the sea, with graceful arches along the sides encasing Renaissance-paned windows. On the pink marble floors sit natural-stained wicker furniture plump with cushions and pillows covered in a striking water-splashed, gray-and-pink fabric. Even the lighting is artfully contrived, with some bulbs reflecting up pink stucco columns, others focusing downward from the eaves. Ceiling fans add the right tropical touch, and yet the overall elegance of the room allows the grand piano to seem very much in its rightful place beside the sea. The three-tiered afternoon tea served here (complimentary to guests here and from Glitter Bay) is alone almost worth the price of admission.

The entrance to all this elegance is equally impressive: several plant-filled patios with crested tiles on the walkways and gouaches by an Englishman named Adam Smith on the walls, with very fancy boutiques. There's a gigantic travelers' palm beside the pool (artfully lit at night), an amazing bearded fig tree behind the north wing, and hardly a vista or nook that is not accented by flowering flourishes.

The guest rooms come with oversize terraces facing the beach — in fact this is the only resort along the coast with all its rooms right on the beach.

Because the guest rooms are all essentially identical, the choice is in location. Those on the third floor not only are the most private but also have higher pickled-pine ceilings with beams that add a nice sense of space and warmth. Those on the first floor, though, score by having a garden patio in addition to a large terrace — a semiprivate front yard, as it were, with a low wall separating it from the beach — but you'll probably have to lock your doors and therefore sleep with the air-conditioning on. Top or bottom, though, a room in the north wing offers the most privacy. As of spring 2003, the resort is closing for 6 months for a major, badly needed overhaul. I've seen the mockup rooms and they are light years better (especially the bathrooms) than what's there now.

The resort's Café Taboras serves light fare for breakfast and lunches that last until 7pm or thereabouts; at the more ambitious Palm Terrace, the food is probably overpriced but the setting is among the most romantic in the Caribbean.

Like Glitter Bay, Royal Pavilion is now managed by Fairmont Hotels (in fact, the two hotels share the same manager).

Name: Royal Pavilion

Manager: Roger Soane

Address: Porters, St. James, Barbados, West Indies

Location: On the northwest coast, 20 min. and $30 by taxi from Bridgetown, 30–40 min. and $30 by taxi from the airport (you can also have a limo meet you at the airport, about $100 one-way)

Telephone: 246/422-5555

Fax: 246/422-3940

E-mail: reservations@fairmont.com

Web: www.fairmont.com

Reservations: 800/866-5577, Fairmont Hotels

Credit Cards: All major cards

Rates: $579–$829 EP (Dec 21–Apr 21); service charge 10%; off-season 50% less

Rooms: 72 deluxe rooms, all beachfront, all with air-conditioning, balcony or patio, direct-dial telephones, clock radio, TV, seersucker bathrobes, coffeemaker, hair dryer, stocked minibar, in-room safe; plus 1 three-bedroom villa for 6

Meals: Breakfast 7:30–11.30am, lunch and dinner 11:30am–11pm, both in Café Taboras, the casual beachfront dining pavilion; afternoon tea 3:30–5pm, dinner 7–9:45pm in the Palm Terrace (about $130); informal dress (but no shorts or T-shirts in the evening); Italian buffet Wed in Palm Terrace; 24-hr. room service at extra charge; guests can also charge meals in Piperade at Glitter Bay (see above)

Entertainment: Some form of live music most evenings

Sports: See Glitter Bay, above

PS: No children under 13 during Mar–May, Oct–Nov, and half of Dec (you figure that one out); open year-round

Cobblers Cove

BARBADOS

☆☆☆	ΥΥΥ	◉◉	$ $ $ $
ATMOSPHERE	DINING	SPORTS	RATES

Just 40 suites, and 80 guests. A stately drawing room. A charmer of a wood-framed dining pavilion beside the beach. A mini–swimming pool and ¼ mile of unspoiled palm-fringed cove, with just the resort at one end, a fleet of fishing boats at the other, and luxury villas in the middle, screened by masses of seagrapes.

The most northerly of Barbados's small hideaways, Cobblers is a world apart, the unsung rendezvous of actors from the United Kingdom, CEOs from the United States, professionals, and romantics from hither and yon. For some it may be too small — 3 acres of densely green garden with 10 two-story shingle-roofed cottages, four suites to a cottage, arranged in a V around a 50-year-old castellated folly that looks like a setting for a Gilbert and Sullivan opera.

If the property is a tad cramped, the suites are not — big, hardwood balcony or patio with loungers, living room with a wall of louvered shutters that fold right back to make the room and balcony one large space, air-conditioned bedroom, and bathrooms that have just been restyled and spiffed up. The prime locations are those facing the beach (suite numbers 1 through 8 and 33 through 36), but try for one of the upper-level suites — they have higher ceilings, more ventilation, and more privacy (and you don't have the security patrol asking you to close and lock your shutters and windows).

Cobblers Cove's most sumptuous, most spectacular suites are both additions to the classic Great House, both very spacious, very private, very sybaritic. In the Camelot Suite, you can romp in a king-size four-poster canopy bed or a bathtub with whirlpool, serve yourself drinks from the wet bar in the large living room, or climb the stairs to your own secluded rooftop deck with private plunge pool and a second wet bar. Likewise, the Colleton Suite is dominated by an even more massive canopy bed that actually has an ocean view. Other luxuries include a double-headed shower and yet another whirlpool tub, a plunge pool, and loungers on the immense private patio. At around $1,000 a night even in summer you might think these suites had few takers, but don't count on snaring one at the last minute — they're booked up months in advance for weeks at a time, at all seasons of the year. It's these speciality suites rather than the regular lodgings that probably rate Cobbler Cove's appearance in the Relais & Châteaux roster. And the dining.

New chef Michael Taylor orchestrates a brigade of French-trained Barbadian chefs in creating the kind of refined cuisine you expect to find on St. Barths rather than Barbados — fish bouillabaisse garnished with tortellinis of salt cod and braised shank of lamb with eggplant caviar and spiced couscous.

Where once there was this nice little hotel with a fine kitchen, there is now this great little restaurant with a nifty little hotel attached. And since the longtime guests always get their way here, it's likely to stay that way although the long-serving Hamish Watson (Mr. Cobblers Cove, to many) has moved on to another hotel and has been replaced by another seasoned general manager, Ross Stevenson, who comes to this charmed corner of Barbados via Gleneagles Hotel, Cliveden, and the Royal St. Lucian.

Name: Cobblers Cove
Manager: Ross Stevenson
Address: St. Peter, Barbados, West Indies
Location: On the sheltered northwest coast, adjoining the village of Speightstown (pronounced "Spites-ton"), 45 min. and $32 by taxi from the airport, 15 min. and $22 by taxi from Bridgetown
Telephone: 246/422-2291
Fax: 246/422-1460
E-mail: reservations@cobblerscove.com
Web: www.cobblerscove.com
Reservations: 800/890-6060, toll-free direct or 800/735-2478, Relais & Châteaux
Credit Cards: MasterCard, Visa
Rates: $552–$2,336 EP (Dec 21–Mar 29); service charge and taxes included; off-season 35% less
Rooms: 36 one-bedroom and 2 two-bedroom suites, with private bathroom, air-conditioning and ceiling fans, louvered doors, kitchenette, stocked minibar, hair dryer, English bathing amenities, bathrobes, minisafe, balcony or patio, direct-dial telephones; plus the stunning Camelot and Colleton suites
Meals: Breakfast 8–10am, lunch 12:30–2:30pm, snack menu 2:30–4pm, afternoon tea 4–5pm, dinner 7–9pm (about $120), in the beachside pavilion; traditional curry lunch Sun, open to nonguests; barbecue buffet Tues; "elegantly casual" dress; room service 8am–9pm at no extra charge; dine-around plan with nearby resorts
Entertainment: Lounge/bar, occasional live music (not too loud, but not exactly pianissimo either), radio or TV for rooms on request only
Sports: Lovely beach and lagoon-smooth bay, small freshwater pool, snorkeling gear, water-skiing, windsurfing, Sunfish sailing, Omni tennis court (with lights), and air-conditioned fitness center across the street — all free; scuba diving, picnic cruises, golf at the Royal Westmoreland or Sandy Lane at extra charge
PS: No children from mid-Jan to mid-Mar; open year-round; guidelines regarding cellphones? "I run them into the sea — unless my guests have beaten me to it"

The Sandpiper

BARBADOS

☆☆☆☆   ♈♈♈   ◑◑ $ $ $ $
ATMOSPHERE   DINING   SPORTS   RATES

Owned by the O'Hara family of the esteemed Coral Reef Club and located just a few miles south along the beach, The Sandpiper is run by Wayne Capaldi, husband of Karen O'Hara, with the same kind of dedication to guests and their comfort. Its two-story wings house 45 rooms and suites embracing a trim and tidy garden with a free-form swimming pool beside an inviting thatched-roof, beam-and-latticework bar/restaurant cooled by 12 ceiling fans, decorated with vines and ginger lilies, and surrounded by mother-in-law tongue and banana trees.

All lodgings now have large living rooms and bedrooms with white ceramic-tile floors and rattan-and-wicker furniture, and kitchens equipped with ovens, four-ring burners, and refrigerators (but please note, dishwashing is not part of the maids' regular duties). As comfortable and relaxing as these rooms may be, I still prefer the two wings of older lodgings, which have more of an island flavor and happen to be closer to the relatively uncrowded white sand beach — and which have just been restyled and upgraded, without detracting one whit from their island flavor.

Wednesday night is the managers' cocktail party and buffet, and Sunday is barbecue night; but the other days of the week the restaurant is busy with Bajans and vacationers from other hotels. They come to sample Scott Williams' tempura shrimp in banana batter and seared duck filet with maple-glazed plums.

But what appeals above all to the well-to-do, well-traveled Europeans who gather here every winter are the gracious welcome and the attentive service — even with just 45 rooms, The Sandpiper offers bar service to guests sunbathing on the beach.

Name: The Sandpiper
Owners/Managers: Karen O'Hara and Wayne Capaldi
Address: St. James, Barbados, West Indies
Location: On St. James Beach, 35 min. and $30 from the airport, 20 min. and $22 from Bridgetown
Telephone: 246/422-2251
Fax: 246/422-0900
E-mail: coral@caribsurf.com
Web: www.sandpiperbarbados.com
Reservations: 800/223-1108, Ralph Locke Islands
Credit Cards: American Express, MasterCard, Visa
Rates: $480–$895 BP (Dec 15–Apr 23); service charge and taxes included; off-season about 50% less
Rooms: 45 rooms, including one- and two-bedroom suites with living rooms and kitchens, refrigerator, all with terrace, toaster, direct-dial telephones,

shelves of paperbacks, air-conditioning, ceiling fans, hair dryer, personal safe, TV on request

Meals: Breakfast 7:30–10:30am, continental breakfast 7am–noon, lunch noon–2:30pm, afternoon tea 3–5pm, dinner 7–9:30pm (about $110); "elegantly informal" dress, but no T-shirts or shorts in the bar or restaurant after 7pm (on Christmas night and New Year's Eve, black tie or jacket and tie is requested); room service during restaurant hours at no extra charge; dine-around plan with other hotels nearby

Entertainment: Bar, low-key live entertainment nightly in season (4 evenings a week out of season), Wed managers' cocktail party, Sun barbecue

Sports: White sand beach, tennis (2 courts, with lights, across the street), windsurfing, water-skiing, snorkeling, sailing — all free; scuba diving at extra charge; golf privileges at Sandy Lane and Royal Westmoreland Golf Club

PS: Children under 12 not allowed in Feb, children under 5 not allowed in the restaurant or lounge after 7pm; open year-round

Sandy Lane

BARBADOS

☆☆☆☆   ⓎⓎⓎ   ❻❻❻❻ $ $ $ $ $
ATMOSPHERE   **DINING**   **SPORTS**   **RATES**

Physically, Sandy Lane is one of the class acts. Beyond the decorative gatehouse, an imposing driveway curves beneath massive mahogany and tamarind trees, past terraced gardens with cherub fountains and flowerbeds, down to the Palladian porte-cochere and main lodge, built of native, pink-gray, handcut coral stone.

That description, from the 9th edition of this guidebook, holds good today — but it doesn't convey any idea that in the interim that Palladian entranceway has been leveled by demolition hammers and the lovely gardens have been trampled by bulldozers and backhoes paving the way for a complete rebuilding of the hotel.

But walk through the marble-floored lobby with its dazzling view of beach and sea beyond the balustrade and you'd swear the place was exactly the same. In fact, the dimensions have been enlarged by a few inches here and there, but you'd never notice. The reason for all this architectural sleight of hand was that the original building was 40 years old and beginning to show its age; the coral stone was chipped away each time some fancy modern gadgetry was installed. When new owners, a group of Irish entrepreneurs with regal aspirations and seemingly bottomless wallets, took over in 1998, they decided the best way to save Sandy Lane and bring it into the 21st century was to knock the whole thing down and re-create it. First step: Go out and buy the quarry to ensure a bottomless supply of coral stone. Next, buy up a few plantations in the hills behind the resort's existing golf course and build another even more challenging course incorporating the quarry. Finally, build a spa; everyone has to

have a spa these days, but Sandy Lanes' had to be bigger and grander than any
other in the islands. In between, there was much changing of minds, pulling
down of replacements, and starting over from scratch. Some $500 million later,
Sandy Lane reopened last year — over-hyped and overpriced. Since then,
everyone has come to their senses — the owners have acquired a hint of mod-
esty and the prices are more in line with other "world-class" hotels, and you
can eat here for no more than you'd pay at the island's finer restaurants.

The owners wanted Sandy Lane to rank with, if not outstrip, the greatest
resorts elsewhere in the world, so it had to have all the latest bells and whis-
tles. So, sure enough, walk into your room and you're confronted with push-
button panels for operating all the *de rigueur* devices — air-conditioning,
window shades, lights, shutters, wall-mounted plasma-screen TV. Open the
glass sliders and the air-conditioning switches itself off. The attention to detail
is remarkable — you'd be hard pressed to find such meticulous craftsmanship
in a palace, never mind a resort, anywhere in the world. The waiters' stations
in the restaurants are like pieces of furniture from a mansion, the breakfast
buffet is arrayed on marble stands with engraved name tags for each dish
(none of your little hand-lettered scribbles here). Even the toilets (not the private bathrooms, the toilets) have commissioned artworks. The vast new spa,
with its cherry paneling, marble and honed granite, a spa garden with ice cave
and crystal laconium looks like the pleasure palace of an oil sheik. The 200 or
so guests are attended by a staff of 650. Over at the new Tom Fazio–designed
golf course, the clubhouse alone cost $50 million and comes with Waterford
crystal and stylish Mobilia furniture. The new water desalination plant for the
golf course turns out 1½ million gallons of water a day. But there are also lots
of little welcome touches in the rooms: pullout shelves for suitcases, night
lights, laundry hampers, Porthault towels, six-nozzle showers, and not the
usual two but four bath mats — and so it goes on.

It's all very high-end impressive, and maybe when they eliminate some of
the kinks (service in the restaurants was way below par six months after the
hotel reopened) it really will be a match for the grandest hotels anywhere.
And there's the rub: The original rooms had some hint of Caribbean style, but
when you wake up in these new rooms, you might think you're in London
or Dubai or Singapore. To be fair, you'll be wonderfully comfortable and well
looked after (there's a beach lounger, for example, for every single guest —
not all the grand resorts can make that claim), but if you want a more
Caribbean experience, you should probably try some of the other resorts up
and down the coast.

Name: Sandy Lane Hotel
Manager: Colm Hannon
Address: St. James, Barbados, West Indies
Location: On the west coast, about 35 min. from the airport, about $30 by taxi
and much more in the resort's private limos
Telephone: 246/444-2000
Fax: 246/444-2222

E-mail: mail@sandylane.com
Web: www.sandylane.com
Reservations: Direct
Credit Cards: All major cards
Rates: $900–$6,000 CP (but most are in the $900–$1,200 range); tax included, 10% service charge extra; off-season, 55% less
Rooms: 100 rooms and suites, some with garden views, all with air-conditioning, ceiling fans, direct-dial telephones with Internet access, plasma TV screens, VCR, CD players, remote controls for lights etc., huge balconies/lanais (with sofas, chairs, tables), bathrooms with separate tub, separate shower, separate toilet, electronic scales, bathrobes, twin vanities
Meals: Breakfast 7:30–10:30am, lunch noon–3pm in one of several restaurants, afternoon tea 3–5:30pm, dinner 6:30–10:30pm in the Bajamn Blue and L'Acajou restaurants (1 alfresco, 1 air-conditioned; from $60–$140); casual elegant (long trousers for men, no shorts, no T-shirts, no tank tops); 24-hr. room service at extra charge; some recorded music in the restaurants
Entertainment: Live music most nights in season, dancing under the stars
Sports: Beach (miles of it), free-form freshwater pool in the garden, fitness center — all free; Sunfish sailing, water-skiing, windsurfing, snorkeling gear, tennis (9 courts, with lights, pro shop, across the roadway), golf (45 holes, across the roadway, including the brand-new Green Monkey course available to hotel guests only), spa treatments (some quite exotic) at extra charge; scuba diving nearby
PS: Children welcome (they have a playhouse); no rules regarding cellphones; open year-round

The House

BARBADOS

ATMOSPHERE

SPORTS

$ $ $ $
RATES

These days, "design hotels" turn up in the most unlikely places. The House is one wing of a larger hotel dating from the Sixties, Tamarind Cove, but restyled in such a distinctive way as to be virtually a new hotel. Almost. But there are enough nice touches to set The House apart from its uninspired neighbors.

The owners — a multinational family representing Italy, Venezuela, and Switzerland — like to think of The House as an "overall experience" that begins before you leave home. One of their Personal Ambassadors will call to find out what you'd like to have in the way of drinks in the refrigerator (you pay for them, of course), what sports activities you'd like to pursue, what tours you might like to take, and above all, when you arrive at the airport. If you're on the right rate and book online, you qualify for the Meet & Greet service: You'll be met at the tarmac, escorted through immigration and Customs, then conveyed in a late-model BMW (sunscreens on the rear windows, a cooler with chilled water) and driven to a "secret" driveway behind high walls and heavy wooden electric gates (it works like clockwork, I've tried it). There you'll be greeted by your ambassador, offered fruit punches, and escorted through the portcullis-like doorway to a patio and fountain beneath two large Mediterranean blue canvas "sails," with instant views of the beach and sea beyond the contemporary furnishings of the lobby-lounge.

Even the view is artfully "designed": white-trellised bar on the right, facing large canvases of thick-textured blue to match the blues of the sea and more blue "sail" sunshades; low chunky wooden tables are lined with banquettes and armchairs upholstered in white cotton, with oversize board games and bowls strewn around the table tops; just beyond the lounge, tables beneath the canvas sunshades function as an alfresco breakfast room. At night, the setting becomes quite theatrical with a parade of torches, candles, and recessed spotlights leading the eyes to the sea. Even the wooden tables are contrived in such a way — each one a shade narrower at the sea end — as to form a line of perspective that leads the eye seaward. Another refreshing touch is a wall of louvered shutters in the entryway courtyard, opening up to reveal a library of some three hundred books in assorted languages.

These public areas are the most appealing part of the hotel. The qualifying "almost" above is the fact that the rooms are hemmed in by the dimensions of the original hotel, except when two are opened up to become a one-bedroom suite, and dulled by the ever-present sliders to the balcony, rather than sexy, romantic louvers. But they've been jazzed up with a few decorative flourishes such as white bedspreads backed by Mediterranean blue padded headboards, planters' chairs on the balconies (although there may not always be room to open the extension armrests), high-end toiletries in the bathrooms, padded hangers in the closets, and espresso machines in the refreshment niches. Four of the rooms have "private" Jacuzzis on patios that are not too private, at least until the foliage has had a chance to flourish (the hotel opened only in late 2002). The staff, dressed in chic billowing white cotton, is pleasant and helpful (you get spritzed regularly and served fresh fruit frequently on the beach), and the ubiquitous young ambassadors are always eager to be of service.

The House has charge arrangements with the separately owned restaurant next door, the serenely designed wood-and-lattice Daphne's Barbados, an associate of London's Daphne's, with a crackerjack chef and manager from England who produce some of the best dining (try the grilled mahimahi with marsala, peperonata, and zucchini and see if you don't agree) and run one of the most polished restaurants on the island.

Oh, the other thing about your welcome: The room rate includes a 30-minute Jet Lag Massage on arrival — either in your room or on the lawn beside the beach beneath a shady tree. It's so relaxing and beguiling you don't even notice until later that you didn't really have to enter The House via its big wooden gates and private drive — you could have walked from the parking lot along the covered walkway and straight into the lobby. And that may be the drawback to The House: In another more private, more oasis-like setting, it would be a *really* special hideaway.

Name: The House
Owner/Manager: Marcello Pigozzo
Address: Paynes Bay, St. James, Barbados, West Indies
Location: On the west coast, 35 min. and $30 by taxi (unless you have the Meet & Greet package), 15 min. and $20 from Bridgetown
Telephone: 246/432-5525
Fax: 246/432-5255
E-mail: thehouse@eleganthotels.com
Web: www.eleganthotels.com
Reservations: Direct or 800/326-6898, Elegant Hotels of Barbados
Credit Cards: All major cards
Rates: $776–$1,452 CP (Dec 19–April 15); service charge and taxes included; off-season, 30% less
Rooms: 31 rooms and suites, including 9 one-bedroom suites, 17 Junior Suites, and 4 garden-view suites with private plunge pools, all with air-conditioning, minibar, 25-channel TV, hair dryers, bathrobes, safes, direct-dial telephones, espresso coffee machines, tea/coffeemakers
Meals: Buffet breakfast anytime, lunch noon–3pm (light meals on the terrace, full meals in Daphne's), dinner 6–10pm in Daphne's (about $80); private dinners in tented cabanas on the beach; limited room service; casual but stylish dress ("no sneakers, caps, or T-shirts in the restaurant after 6"), quiet but incessant live or recorded background music
Entertainment: The library, board games, and conversation in the lounge
Sports: Pool and whirlpool, 4 private plunge pools, water-skiing, kayaks, boogie boards, snorkeling gear, Sunfish sailing, windsurfing, crewed Hobie Cats — all free; massages (apart from the Jet Lag version) at extra charge; golf, scuba, tennis nearby
PS: "To maintain a tranquil atmosphere, The House only welcomes adults (12 years and over)," and those over 12 are charged at the full adult rate, so you're not likely to be overwhelmed by kids; open year-round

Villa Nova Hotel

BARBADOS

☆ ☆ ☆ ☆	♈ ♈ ♈	❻	$ $ $ $
ATMOSPHERE	DINING	SPORTS	RATES

Ah, the peace of it all. The hush and tranquility. A purple-flowered tree subs in for a lifeguard at the blue-tiled patio swimming pool. An oversize wedding gazebo nestles beneath mahogany and yellow poui trees. Weathered stone steps lead down to a terrace and fountain where romantic couples like to have breakfast (the staff say they'll set up tables for any meal, anywhere in the gardens). And what gardens!

In fact, Villa Nova could almost be called Garden Nova, as it is a 15-acre oasis of greenery and flowers on a knoll 960 feet above sea level and overlooking miles of pastureland and acres of sugarcane. The cool elevation, the fragrance of the flowers, the serenade of birdsong, the chirruping of tree frogs, the frolics of monkeys swinging in the trees — these become your consolation prize for not having a beach on your doorstep. You can do your daily dose of tanning a few paces from your room around a lovely, Beverly Hills–like pool.

This is the perfect setting for lovers who want to unwind and slow down and while away their hours with long, lazy breakfasts on the balcony, hours by the pool beneath the white sunshades, leisurely lunches on the dining terrace beneath a shady ramada, maybe an occasional game of tennis. Follow one of the nine gardeners (some have been around for 30 years) on a horticultural tour, spend some time admiring the antiques and artworks. Evenings begin with cocktails on the wraparound veranda or among the black-and-white photos of celebrity tipplers in the burgundy-draped bar. Dinners unfold on the candlelit garden terrace — people drive from all over the island for the pistachio-crusted rack of lamb with Bajan-steamed pudding, *mille-feuille* of veal escalope with roasted vegetables, mango tatin with passion fruit ice cream.

This place of serenity and seclusion was, from 1965 to 1971, the retreat of Lord Avon, better known as Churchill's wartime aid, Sir Anthony Eden. Here the Edens entertained a steady stream of distinguished guests, including Queen Elizabeth and Prince Philip. It's a bulbous-shaped villa designed for gracious, aristocratic living. There's a music room with a Bechstein grand, a private dining room with a grand mahogany table from the officers' mess of the former British garrison. Light filters through fanlights and architraves, through louvered doors and demerara shutters, and the lounge has no fewer than 10 doorways to keep the rooms cool.

A few years ago Villa Nova was taken over by an English lady, Lynne Pemberton, who had racked up some experience in the hotel business when she helped her ex-husband, Michael Pemberton, put together the Royal Pavilion and Glitter Bay hotels on the West Coast, and she completed Villa Nova's conversion to an inn in the spring of 2001. She has put heart and soul (and, one surmises, a small fortune) into this country inn, filling its gracious rooms with original, sometimes quirky, artwork, Chinese Chippendale and Virginia spoon-back chairs, Murano glass lamps, and a few items from the Avon years, including his lordship's butler's table.

The original guest suites have been stylishly redesigned by noted British decorator Nina Campbell. The Eden Suite, with its seven-door closets and a 20 × 6-foot terrace, is the prime choice of honeymooners, but I prefer the regular Campbell-designed suites in a new wing tacked on in 2001. My favorite would probably be number 11, with a large foyer, dark-stained hardwood floors, and high ceilings with crown moldings. French doors lead to a roomy balcony with a sea-green balustrade. The sumptuous white-tiled bathroom showcases a claw-footed tub, a toilet with a wooden seat, separate tiled shower stall, double vanity, Aqua Di Palma and Philip Kingsley toiletries, and ribbed Frette towels.

But as with all country inns, it's the little touches that count. When the Land Rover Discovery picks you up at the airport, the driver will offer you a drink of water. No big deal. But here, the water is served with linen napkins and you drink from glasses, not bottles. There are CDs beside the JVC player. The votive candles in your room are lighted at turndown. Attendants bring your drinks to the pool, cool you off with spritzers, unpack and pack your suitcases, and steam your clothes. You get to use the executive lounge at the airport on your way home. You may begin to feel a bit like an earl or countess.

And when you feel like having the sand between your feet, the Land Rover will drive you to the Coral Reef Club, 30 minutes away on the west coast (see above), where you'll have a day room, lunch, and use of the watersports facilities — for $100 a day or thereabouts.

Name: Villa Nova Hotel

Manager: Trevor Vels

Address: St.John, Barbados, West Indies

Location: In the hinterlands, 30 min. from the airport, 20 min. from the west coast beaches; $20–$25 from the airport by taxi, $40 by private Land Rover

Telephone: 246/433-1524

Fax: 246/433-6363

E-mail: villanova@sunbeach.net

Web: www.villanovabarbados.com

Reservations: Direct

Credit Cards: American Express, MasterCard, Visa

Rates: $650–$950 CP; 7.5% tax and 10% service charge extra; off-season, 30% less

Rooms: 27, including 8 one-bedroom suites, all with air-conditioning and ceiling fans, umbrellas, safes, bathrobes, hair dryers, direct-dial telephones, wide-screen television, CD player with a selection of CDs

Meals: Breakfast 7–11am, lunch 12:30–3pm on the terrace or anywhere in the gardens, afternoon tea 3–5pm, dinner 7:30–10pm (about $100); casual but elegant dress, "no shorts in the public areas after 7pm"; room service during dining room hours; quiet background music in the bar and restaurant

Entertainment: The bar, games room, library of DVDs

Sports: Pool, fitness center (a spa with water garden to come in 2003–04), tennis (2 courts, with lights) — all free; in-room spa treatments at extra charge; guests can use the beach and facilities at Coral Reef Club, and there's a public golf course a few minutes away

PS: Not suitable for children; open year-round

Hotel Little Good Harbour

BARBADOS

☆☆   Y Y Y   ❻ $ $ $
ATMOSPHERE   **DINING**   **SPORTS**   **RATES**

Here's another hideaway for lovers of the offbeat. You drive past the grand hotels, the mansions almost as grand as the hotels, the shopping centers, then turn onto the sort of road that makes you wonder where the taxi driver is taking you, skirting the shore and the colorful fishing boats hauled up on the beach beneath the palm trees. It's a slightly ramshackle corner of the island — until you arrive at a sturdy gray stone building that looks something like the remains of a fort with a cottage on top. Which is more or less exactly what it is. Across the street, above another gray stone wall, a steep little hillside sprouts traditional peaked cottages in tropical-fish colors with white gingerbread trim. Little Good Harbour is a little world unto itself.

The rooms in this family-owned, family-run inn are more stylish than you might expect to find out here, part Indonesian, part Caribbean, with lots of shutters and louvers, lots of wicker and rattan, wood-plank floors, and beds draped in muslin netting. Each cottage has small balconies, well-equipped kitchens, living rooms on the lower floor, bedrooms up a few steps, and ship-shape bathrooms with glass-enclosed shower stalls. The only hint of resort is a small swimming pool ringed with cushioned loungers and sun umbrellas.

Don't expect any excitement here (unless you head for the weekend fish fries at Six Men's Bay, but check the front desk for a briefing on the modus operandi). This is strictly back-of-beyond, local-color Caribbean, except that the old fort across the street is now one of the hottest restaurants on the island; and foodies drive all the way up here to sample Trevor Bye's crispy fried duck wontons and tomato risotto with toasted pine nuts and pesto, say, or seafood crepe and sautéed Caribbean shrimp with Thai broth and basmati rice, or Thai greentiger-prawn curry. Louvered doors fill one wall, mirrors reflect the beach and sea, and soft background music vies with the steady rumble of surf.

Name: Little Good Harbour Hotel
Manager: Andrew Warden
Address: Shermans, St.Peters, Barbados, West Indies
Location: Way up north, beyond Speightstown, on the west coast, about 18 miles or an hour and $35 by taxi from the airport
Telephone: 246/439-3000
Fax: 246/439-2020
E-mail: Littlegoodharbour@sunbeach.net
Web: www.littlegoodharbourbarbados.com
Reservations: Direct
Credit Cards: MasterCard, Visa
Rates: $302–$362 EP (Dec 16–Apr 15); plus service charge 10% and 7.5% tax; off-season 30% less

Rooms: 15 cottages, including 10 with 1 bedroom, all with private balcony, queen-size bed and decorative netting, air-conditioning and ceiling fans, showers only, seersucker bathrobes, hair dryer, cable TV/VCR, CD player, direct-dial telephone, tea/coffeemaker, safe, kitchen/pantry
Meals: Breakfast 8–10am, lunch noon–2:30pm, dinner 7–9:30pm, all at the Fish Pot ($70–$90); casual dress; no room service; mild background music
Entertainment: Alleyne's Bar in the Fish Pot, library of CDs and videos
Sports: Beach, small pool; watersports nearby
PS: Some children; open year-round

Mount Irvine Bay Hotel & Golf Club

TOBAGO

☆☆☆	⅋ ⅋	❻❻❻❻	$ $ $
ATMOSPHERE	DINING	SPORTS	RATES

The centerpiece is an old sugar mill, fitted with a shingle-roofed ramada, and stylishly transformed into an open bar and dining terrace.

A two-story wing of balconied guest rooms overlooks a big blue-tiled swimming pool with a swim-up bar; other rooms (46 out of 105) are housed in little square bungalows engulfed in heliconia and thumbergia. Now the resort has sprouted a new lobby to rival the sugar mill, a tall timber octagon with a skylight filtering the sun onto desks and chairs and sofas where guests sign in and relax. But what makes this 1970s resort so attractive is still the setting: 27 acres of tropical flora surrounded by 130 acres of fairways and coconut palms, laid out on a bluff above the curve of Mount Irvine Bay, with the famed Buccoo Reef breaking the sea just beyond the headland.

Most of the balconies and loggias are placed to make the most of these views — which is just as well, because without the views the rooms would be fairly dull and uninspired. With the exception of the standards, the rooms are quite large, with twice the usual closet space. The best of the bungalows, the priciest accommodations, have large loggias that are virtually outdoor living rooms with terrazzo floors and khus khus rugs; the bedrooms are smaller, so they really need the air-conditioning units that are stuck in the walls.

The pièce de résistance of Mount Irvine is its Sugar Mill Restaurant, especially in the evening, with the candlelight flickering, with soft lighting accenting its gray stone walls and raftered ceiling, and the scent of jasmine wafting in from the garden. (There's also a second air-conditioned restaurant, the Jacaranda, for "gourmet dining," but my guess is you'll prefer the open terrace.)

For guests who enjoy a round of golf, earnest or casual, the Mount Irvine should rate highly. Not just because its lovely, rolling fairways are a challenge for players of all handicaps, but also because any time I've been there I've had the fairways and greens almost to myself, and because it's one of the biggest bargains around — $41 for 18 holes, less with a weekly ticket.

Even if you're not a golfer, take a walk or bike ride along the course's winding pathways to enjoy the views of the tropical greenery, the bay, and that spectacular reef.

Name: Mount Irvine Bay Hotel & Golf Club
Manager: Carlos B. Dillon
Address: P.O. Box 222, Scarborough, Tobago, Trinidad & Tobago, West Indies
Location: 10–15 min. and $12 by taxi from the airport
Telephone: 868/639-8871, 868/639-8872, or 868/639-8873
Fax: 868/639-8800
E-mail: mtirvine@tstt.net.tt
Web: www.mtirvine.com
Reservations: 800/742-4276, Charms
Credit Cards: American Express, Diners Club, MasterCard, Visa
Rates: $255–$595 EP (Dec 17–Apr 15); service charge 10%; off-season 30% less
Rooms: 105, including 52 superior rooms and 6 suites in the main building; the remainder in two-room bungalows; all with private bathroom (tub and shower), air-conditioning (cross-ventilation in bungalows only), balcony or loggia, direct-dial telephones, cable TV; wet bar and refrigerator in bungalows
Meals: Breakfast 7–10am (continental breakfast to 10:30am), lunch noon–3pm (the quietest spot is the golf-course clubhouse), snacks at the beach pavilion all day, dinner 7–10pm at the open-air Sugar Mill Restaurant, the air-conditioned Jacaranda Room, or Le Beau Rivage at the Golf Club (about $80); elegantly casual in the Jacaranda and Le Beau Rivage, informal on the terrace, but "we do believe that informality has its acceptable limits within a hotel, and house rules do not permit T-shirts or sleeveless vests in the public areas after 6pm"; room service 7am–10pm, $3 extra; recorded music or radio on terrace, possibly live music in the Jacaranda Room and beside the pool
Entertainment: Steel bands, calypso and limbo shows, live entertainment in the Jacaranda Room and Le Beau Rivage
Sports: Quaint beach across the road, with beach bar, snack bar, chaise lounges, changing rooms, and local fishermen and their boats (there are better beaches nearby), freshwater pool with swim-up bar, tennis (2 courts, with lights), sauna — all free, except for evening tennis; snorkeling gear, bikes and scooters for rent, golf (18 holes, reduced fees for guests); excursions (to Buccoo Reef to watch the fish, to Grafton's estate to watch the birds) can be arranged
PS: The hotel can handle groups of up to 200, but they are usually low-key; some, but not many, children; open year-round

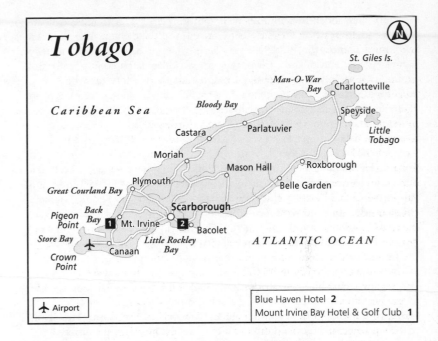

Tobago

St. Giles Is.

Man-O-War Bay — Charlotteville

Caribbean Sea

Bloody Bay

Speyside

Castara — Parlatuvier

Little Tobago

Moriah

Mason Hall — Roxborough

Plymouth

Great Courland Bay

Belle Garden

Back Bay

Scarborough

Pigeon Point

Mt. Irvine

1 **2**

Bacolet

Store Bay

Little Rockley Bay

ATLANTIC OCEAN

Crown Point

Canaan

✈ Airport

Blue Haven Hotel **2**
Mount Irvine Bay Hotel & Golf Club **1**

Blue Haven Hotel

TOBAGO

☆☆☆ **ATMOSPHERE**   ♈ ♈ ♈ **DINING**   😊😊 **SPORTS** $ $ $ **RATES**

Let's begin with a dash of history: Its underpinnings are the outworks of 18th-century Fort King George, and the secluded beach below its cliff is said to be the very spot where Robinson Crusoe was cast ashore on September 30, 1659 (check your Defoe).

Add a soupçon of celebrity: The honeymooning Princess Margaret stayed here, and during the 1950s and 1960s, Blue Haven was the haunt of Hollywood sex symbols like Rita Hayworth and Robert Mitchum ("That man likes to move his fists fast," said my cab driver, who had been a policeman during the Mitchum era, "especially when someone talks to his woman").

Now tack on a fairy-tale ending: After years of neglect and decay, the storied hotel was brought back to life in 2000 by an Austrian-Trinidadian couple, Karl and Marilyn Pilstl, one a techie, the other an interior designer. What they've done is restore and embellish the original Hollywood-meets-the-tropics building, retaining its whimsical arches and outside corridors, livening up the facade with fresh coats of coral pink and white trim, and enhancing the octagonal lobby with original paintings.

Then they added two annexes with additional rooms, with curious floating roofs that create an air space between the roofs and the ceilings to keep the rooms cooler (the Pilstls are very serious about being environmentally savvy). At one end of the garden, they took a dilapidated colonial villa and revamped it as Shutters by the Bay Restaurant, an airy, white-on-white space with three walls of white demerara shutters, fine crystal, and custom-designed chairs finished with woven water hyacinth.

Another Austrian, chef Richard Goetzendorfer (formerly of Kempinski in Munich and Hilton in Vienna) clearly relishes the chance to spread his culinary wings, larding his menus with imaginative dishes that wed Europe and Tobago. Each dinner begins with a "welcome," an amuse-gueule, served in a dainty lidded tureen — cold melon soup one evening, hot callaloo soup another — refined little preludes to a meal that might proceed to Trinbago chicken pelau and end with piña colada rolls and calypso banana cream cake.

Apart from dimensions (370 sq. ft.–1,300 sq. ft.) and view (sunrise or sunset), the rooms are all similar — and all distinguished by a wall-to-wall, waist-high window between the tub and the living room, giving guests a glimpse of the sea while they shower (folks who are touchy about these things can lower blue-striped roman shades and make the window disappear). The rooms are full of refined touches, including spindly halogen lamps above the bathroom mirrors, antique bottles and vials above the washbasin, blue duvets and colorful Egyptian cotton throw pillows on custom-made mahogany beds, blue trim on the drinking glasses, and blue canvas for balcony dividers and directors' chairs.

The lore of Blue Haven still lures visitors — rooms 30 and 20 are scooped up by nostalgia buffs because that's where the stars stayed. And one British couple settled into the corner table of the broad terrace every afternoon at 4pm because they'd seen a photograph of Princess Margaret and Tony Amstrong-Jones having afternoon tea in that same spot.

And it's quite a spot. The hotel sits on a headland with churning surf on three sides; half of the 15 acres are unspoiled nature. Unspoiled but not unplucked — the fruit trees supply the oranges, papayas, bananas, and tamarinds for the kitchen.

Name: Blue Haven Hotel
Owners/Managers: Karl and Marilyn Pilstl
Address: Bacolet Bay, Scarborough, Tobago, West Indies
Location: In a smart residential quarter just outside the capital, Scarborough, about 20 min. and $15 from the airport
Telephone: 868/660-7400
Fax: 868/660-7900
E-mail: bluehaven@bluehavenhotel.com
Web: www.bluehavenhotel.com
Reservations: 800/237-3237, Elegant Resorts International
Credit Cards: American Express, MasterCard, Visa
Rates: $250–$605 (Dec 16–Apr 15); plus 15% for service charge and taxes; off-season 30% less

Rooms: 55, including 10 suites, all with air-conditioning and ceiling fans, private balconies, cable TV, direct-dial telephones with dataports, in-room safes, minibars

Meals: Breakfast (buffet) 7–10am, lunch at the beach bar 11:30am–4pm, dinner 7–10pm in Shutters ($80–$90); elegantly casual dress (long trousers for men); room service all meals, $3 per tray

Entertainment: Steel band on the beach Sun, live music with managers' cocktail party Thurs, Latin Night Sat, poolside

Sports: Cliffside pool, beach — free; tennis (1 court, with lights), 4-station gym, massages in the small spa, kayaks, windsurfing, scuba diving and snorkeling gear, Hobie Cats at extra charge

PS: Children welcome but you're unlikely to be overrun by them; open year-round

OTHER CHOICES

Exotica

DOMINICA

It's a mere 6 miles or so south of Roseau, the island capital, but brace yourself for one final winding, bone-shaking, axle-breaking mile from the main road before you reach serenity, birdsong, and more serenity. Exotica is 4 acres of organic farm with six cottages in a precipitous garden filled with plumbago, allamanda, and Jerusalem thorn (you don't have to ask the name of the fruit tree beyond your veranda — it's the same name as your cottage). What you're looking at here is what owners Athie and Fae Martin call an "eco-agro resort." You're surrounded with nature and the kitchen is well stocked with fresh produce — but it's hardly a place for roughing it. One louvered wall of your wood-and-stone cottage opens back, turning your sitting room and veranda into an indoor/outdoor lounge with kitchenette (4-ring burner) and, surprisingly, TV (40 channels). Bedrooms easily accommodate 6-foot-long beds, the bathrooms are tiled and airy, and everything is designed to harmonize with the environment and capture the breezes. At this elevation (1,300 ft.), there's no need for air-conditioning — all you need is time to enjoy the views of the sea and the foothills of Morne Anglais and Morne Canot. If you don't feel like preparing your own meals, you can enjoy simple island dinners in the 20-seater cottage known as Sugar Apple Café (say, christophene celery soup, snapper in lemon sauce with breadfruit and cheese soufflé, banana in butter rum sauce, all prepared with fresh organic produce from the farm or fish from the sea 6 miles away). 6 cottages. Doubles: $150 CP, winter 2002–03. *Exotica, P.O. Box 109, Roseau, Dominica, West Indies. Telephone: 767/448-8839; fax: 767/448-8829; e-mail: exotica@cwdom.dm.*

Fort Young

DOMINICA

The fort was built in the 1700s to protect the entrance to Roseau harbor, the hotel came along in the 1960s, and after various rehabs and renovations the 2001 version is twice the size of the original and enhanced with a spa, waterfront restaurant, and watersports facility. The original guest rooms, built into the parapets facing the sea, are perfectly adequate; the newest rooms and suites fill a new wing beside the sea with fancier quarters featuring spacious suites with whirlpool tubs and kitchen facilities. The central courtyard (presumably the parade ground in days gone by) is taken over by a swimming pool, sunning terrace, and open bar/pavilion. The main restaurant, the grandly named Marquis de Bouille, is in a large, somewhat somber but cool stone-walled hall adjoining the lobby; the new Waterfront Restaurant offers air-conditioned dining with sea views. Since Fort Young is right on the edge of downtown, convenient to everything (the main government building is just across the street), the folks at the next table in the bar are likely to be business travelers; but for vacationers who want to enjoy Antillean atmosphere, it's still a romantic spot — despite the cannon at the ironwork entrance. And, it's good value. 53 rooms and suites. Doubles: $100–$250 EP year-round. *Fort Young, P.O. Box 519, Roseau, Dominica, West Indies. Telephone: 767/448-5000; fax: 767/448-8065; e-mail: fortyoung@cwdom.dm; Web: www.fortyounghotel.com.*

The Royal St. Lucian Hotel

ST. LUCIA

Yet another luxury resort with acres of marble, fountains, satellite television, air-conditioning, bathrobes, lavish pool — everything but personality (even lavish landscaping is unlikely to disguise the cookie-cutter, three-story architecture). It happens to be on the island's grandest expanse of beach, which it shares with its sister hotel, the St. Lucian (popular with package groups), but only a few of its suites — your best bet — actually face directly across the beach to the sea, and fewer still have enormous terraces. All the rooms are comfortable and thoughtfully designed. The Royal St. Lucian could be anywhere — but it is right on the island's best beach and it now has its own spa. 96 suites. Doubles: $500–$870, winter 2002–03. *The Royal St. Lucian Hotel, P.O. Box 977, Reduit Beach, Castries, St. Lucia, West Indies. Telephone: 758/452-9999 or 800/255-3859; fax: 758452-9639; e-mail: royal@candw.lc; Web: www.travelhop.com/stlucia/royalst lucian.html.*

0 5 mi
0 5 km
N

Douglas Bay
CABRITS NATIONAL PARK
Marigot
Prince Rupert's Bay
Portsmouth

ATLANTIC OCEAN

CARIB TERRITORY

Caribbean Sea

Layou R.

MORNE TROIS PITONS NATIONAL PARK

Dominica

Trafalgar Falls

Roseau R.

Boiling Lake

Roseau **1**

2

Exotica **2**
Fort Young **1**

The Savannah

BARBADOS

The south coast of Barbados has some of the island's liveliest bars and best restaurants, but there hasn't been a decent hotel in this area, other than some all-inclusives. Now there is, an old-timer rehabbed with a smart new beachside wing added. From the street, the original has something of the air of a New Orleans mansion with wrought-iron balustrades around the second-floor veranda, sitting at a right angle to the main road behind a circular drive-way. It was taken in hand a few years ago by a group known as Gems of Barbados, dedicated to resurrecting, upgrading, modernizing, and generally preserving the island's older, unsung hotels. They've gone about it the right way in this case — an airy, breeze-cooled lobby with marble floor and coral-stone reception desk, period pieces from local plantations, and sepia prints of old Barbados on the walls. Rooms in the original building still have their wood-plank floors and tall louvered doors (the louvers now "sealed" because of the air-conditioning). It has the air of a well-tended private manor — albeit a manor with TV and faxes in every room. Then you walk through the inviting new Boucan Wine Bar and Restaurant and come to what appears to be a completely different establishment — two wings of contemporary white trimmed with blue balustrades, lining an impressive series of pools and cascades running all the way to the sand. Fitness center and day spa. 101 rooms and suites. Doubles: $230–$460 EP, winter 2002–03. *The Savannah, The Garrison, near Bridgetown, Barbados, West Indies. Telephone: 246/228-3800; fax: 246/228-4385; e-mail: savannah@gemsbarbados.com; Web: http://gemsbarbados.com.*

Lone Star

BARBADOS

Odd name, odd spot. Well, it's not every day you find a restaurant/hotel created from a gas station (or, this being Barbados, garage), the first one on Barbados to feature an automatic pump. After lying derelict for several years, the beachside gas station was bought by a group of English restaurateurs (Prego and Ocean in Richmond, The Wharf in Teddington) and converted into a beachside bistro. It turned out to be such a hit (especially with the celebrities who vacation in nearby villas) that the owners bought up an adjoining block of apartments and added four suites to their roadside eatery — Lincoln, Studebaker, Buick, and Cord. The spacious suites are rather dashing, decorated in a nautical manner with white-on-white upholstery set off by polished mahogany headboards and floors of polished purpleheart. White muslin drapes on the verandas represent sails, the lamps come from a fishing trawler, and the compact bathrooms could be on a classy motor yacht. The suites also come with wet bars, satellite TV, stereo, and individual printer/ fax units. The problem is, the lodgings are right on the beach, so guests are going to have to close and lock their sliding-glass doors and switch on the air-conditioning before turning in for the night — or before heading for the dining terrace for chicken tandoori masala or tiger prawns from the chilled seafood bar. But Lone Star has a funkiness, a sense of fun and informality, that will appeal to many escapists; and there's always something to be said for being able to step directly from sand to sophistication. 4 suites. Doubles $585–$690 CP, winter 2002–03. *Lone Star Restaurant & Hotel, Mount Standfast, St. James, Barbados, West Indies. Telephone: 246/419-0599; fax: 246/419-0597; e-mail: lonestargarage@caribsurf.com; Web: www.thelonestar.com.*

St. Vincent–Grenadines & Grenada

*T*he most desirable islands, like

the most desirable lovers, make extra demands. That's how it

is with the Grenadines: They'll reward you with seclusion,

serenity, and privac; but you first have to get there, switching

planes at least once, maybe twice. These islands are really part

of the British Windwards, but they're so special, so totally

Caribbean, that they deserve a category all to themselves.

They are, in fact, two quite separate and independent

nations: Grenada and St. Vincent–Grenadines (consisting of,

for the purposes of this guide, St. Vincent, Young Island,

Bequia, Mustique, Canouan, Mayreau, Palm Island, Petit St. Vincent, and Union, which is the transit airstrip for Mayreau, Palm, and PSV).

St. Vincent is a mountainous island, lushly forested, incredibly fertile, and brimming with papaws, mangoes, and breadfruit. The bustling capital, Kingstown, is in the south, surrounded by towering hills, but the main scenic attractions are daylong excursions along the Leeward Highway to the foothills of 4,000-foot-plus Mount Soufrière or via the Windward Highway to Mesopotamia and Montreal — all very picturesque.

Bequia is a dream. The most romantic way to get there is by boat. Not a big, powerful cabin cruiser or twin-hulled ferry, but a cargo/passenger ferryboat stacked with chickens, toilet paper, kerosene, Guinness stout, Heineken beer, bags of cement, a carburetor, more Guinness, and more Heineken. If you see a man get aboard carrying bags of money accompanied by a guard with a discreet gun, you know you're on the "bank boat." The trip takes about an hour, and you arrive in one of the most beautiful and most sheltered harbors in the Caribbee, in the town of Port Elizabeth. There's not much more to Bequia than the hills you pass on the way into the harbor, but it's one of the most charming, most idyllic islands of all. Nothing much happens here, except once or twice a year when whales are spotted, and the men go out in their small boats armed only with hand harpoons — one of the few remaining teams of hand harpooners in the world. The island acquired an airfield in 1993 or thereabouts, but for true Bequia lovers the only way is by boat.

Mustique, Palm Island, and Petit St. Vincent are privately owned, and when you read about their hotels, you're more or less reading about the islands themselves.

Canouan is a tiny (3½ × 1½ miles) island where electricity was installed as recently as 12 years ago. Yet it was about to lay claim to being the next hot Caribbean destination by having an Italian-Swiss consortium build an expansive resort with a golf course and small casino and then turn the management over to the Rosewood people, only to have the deal fall apart, closing the resort for "renovations." As of this writing, word is that the resort will be back in action for the winter season, with a new management company running things. Canouan is, of course, part of St. Vincent, while Carriacou (a constant source of confusion) is to the south and part of Grenada.

Grenada, like St. Vincent a lush volcanic island, is the largest of the group (21 × 12 miles) and is scenically still one of the most beautiful of all the Antilles — despite the efforts of modern firepower to wipe the island off the charts. You remember the events of October 1983? Some people called it an invasion, others a rescue mission. The official island description is a diplomatic "United States/Eastern Caribbean Intervention." Not much has changed since then, give or take a shopping mall or two. The Grenadians are pro-American (they always have been); some of the roads have been resurfaced, mostly those between Government House and the new airport. The major improvement these days is the airport that started it all, Point Salines International. It's located in the southwest, near the hotels, thus eliminating the hour-long drive from the old Pearls Airport.

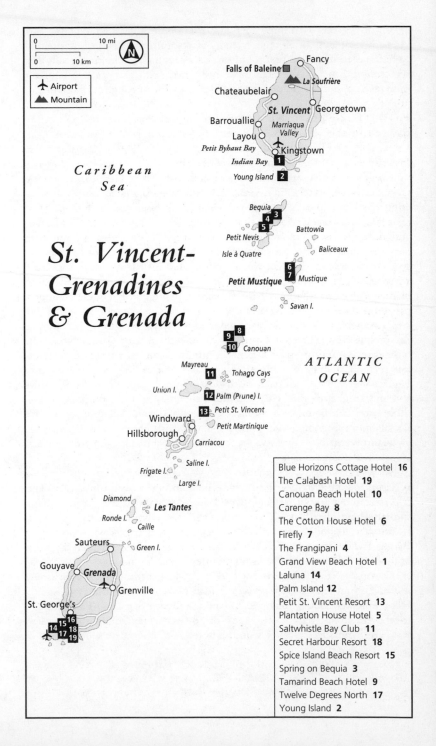

0 10 mi
0 10 km

✈ Airport
▲ Mountain

Falls of Baleine
Fancy
La Soufrière
Chateaubelair
St. Vincent Georgetown
Barrouallie
Marriaqua Valley
Layou
Petit Byhaut Bay
✈ Kingstown
Indian Bay
1
Young Island **2**

Caribbean Sea

Bequia
4 **3**
5
Battowia
Petit Nevis
Baliceaux
Isle à Quatre
6
7 *Mustique*
Petit Mustique
Savan I.

St. Vincent-Grenadines & Grenada

9 **8**
10 *Canouan*

ATLANTIC OCEAN

Mayreau
11 *Tobago Cays*
Union I.
12 *Palm (Prune) I.*
13 *Petit St. Vincent*
Windward
Petit Martinique
Hillsborough
Carriacou

Frigate I.
Saline I.
Large I.

Diamond
Les Tantes
Ronde I.
Caille
Sauteurs
Green I.
Gouyave
Grenada
✈ Grenville
St. George's
15 **16**
14 **18**
✈ **17** **19**

Blue Horizons Cottage Hotel	**16**
The Calabash Hotel	**19**
Canouan Beach Hotel	**10**
Carenge Bay	**8**
The Cotton House Hotel	**6**
Firefly	**7**
The Frangipani	**4**
Grand View Beach Hotel	**1**
Laluna	**14**
Palm Island	**12**
Petit St. Vincent Resort	**13**
Plantation House Hotel	**5**
Saltwhistle Bay Club	**11**
Secret Harbour Resort	**18**
Spice Island Beach Resort	**15**
Spring on Bequia	**3**
Tamarind Beach Hotel	**9**
Twelve Degrees North	**17**
Young Island	**2**

If you're simply planning to find a great little hideaway and flake out, Grenada has plenty of pleasant, friendly places for doing just that. In the bargain, to try to lure back their old North American clientele (the British kept on coming), the local hotels have been raising their rates by miniscule smidgens, so you may find that your vacation dollars will go further here.

HOW TO GET THERE   To get to most of these islands, you have to travel to another island first — Barbados (American, BWIA, Air Jamaica, Air Canada), Puerto Rico (almost everyone), or St. Lucia (BWIA, Air Jamaica), in that order of convenience — with connections on a veritable air force of small airlines, such as Mustique Airways, SVG Air, TIA, LIAT, BWIA, Caribbean Star, American Eagle, and Grenadines Air, all flying small twin-engine aircraft that carry anywhere from 4 to 20 passengers. With their shared charter and air-taxi services, they've become a sort of bus service for islanders and visitors. Mustique Airways has the largest fleet of aircraft, and I find them very dependable; but your best bet is to ask your travel agent or resort to make plans in advance to get you to your final island. Many visitors, especially when traveling as foursomes, find it costs about the same to charter a small plane and have it waiting for their international flight. For some additional pointers on this subject, log on to www.Grenadines.net.

Passengers flying into Barbados will find representatives from, say, Mustique Airways waiting to greet and escort them directly to their planes without the business of going through Customs and immigration at Barbados. Likewise, luggage goes straight to the inter-island plane. Not so, however, on the return flight, when you have to "site" Barbados, then walk around to the departure hall and stand in line to check in and clear immigration. Southbound, you should arrive in Barbados by 4pm, since most of the Grenadines airports have no facilities for landing after dark and the out islands are 35 to 55 minutes away; the alternative is that you spend the night in Barbados and catch the first flight out the next morning.

You can also get to Bequia from St. Vincent by ferryboat, sturdy motor vessels that shuttle freight and passengers to and fro several times a day. This trip takes about 1 hour, depending on how heavily the Atlantic comes rolling through the passage between the two islands. The advantage of the ferryboats is that there is one departure in the evening, so passengers who can't fly to Bequia (where there's no nighttime landing) can at least get there by boat, even if the difference in time is 60 minutes versus 5 minutes.

Currently, Grenada can be reached by Air Jamaica from New York (some nonstop, some via St. Lucia), via San Juan on American Airlines (a slightly inconvenient schedule), or by LIAT and Caribbean Star from Barbados. Go for the Air Jamaica flights, which get you to Grenada around lunchtime — so you can spend a full afternoon on the beach.

For information on St. Vincent-Grenadines,
call 800/729-1726 or 212/687-4981 or visit www.svgtourism.com;
for Grenada, call 212/286-9339 or visit www.grenada.org.

Young Island

ST. VINCENT

☆ ☆ ☆ ☆ ☆   𝚼 𝚼   ➏ ➏ $ $ $ $
ATMOSPHERE   **DINING**   **SPORTS**   **RATES**

A Carib Indian chieftain, they say, once kept his harem on this islet, and generations of Vincentians used it as their vacation escape from the "mainland," a couple of hundred yards away across the lagoon. Now, Young Island is 35 acres of Polynesian petals. Half a million plants clamber up the hillsides. It took almost as long to landscape the grounds as it did to build the cottages and pavilions; but that was almost 30 years ago, and now the island garden luxuriates. Ginger lilies and giant almond trees soften the sun's rays as you stroll along stone pathways to quiet benches where twosomes can enjoy the breezes and sunsets. Swimming in the free-form pool, canopied by bamboo and fern, you half expect Lamour and Hope to go floating by. And you're still shrouded by shrubbery and flowers when you rinse the sand off because each room has an open patio shower screened by neck-high bamboo fences.

Two hundred yards may not sound like much of a journey, but once you board the dinky launch for the 3-minute voyage, you could be on your way to Bali Ha'i. Once guests step ashore and sip the zingy Hibiscus Special that's waiting for them on the dock, they usually find there's no compelling reason — not even the 200-year-old botanical garden, not the oddball 150-year-old cathedral — to board that launch again until it's time to head for home. (Actually, if they sip more than half of their Hibiscus Special, they probably *will* see Lamour and Hope.)

Why escape tranquility? There are so many ways to enjoy the barefoot euphoria of Young Island when you put what's left of your mind to it. At the Coconut Bar, lounge in a thatched bohio on pilings that rests about six strokes from the shore. Curl up in a bohio-shaded hammock, within semaphore distance of the shore-bound bar. Flatten out on the sand. Climb the hundred-odd steps to the peak of the island for an isolated stroll in one direction or the tennis court in another.

But maybe the most sensuous way to enjoy the serenity of Young Island is to stay put in your own wicker wonderland. Guest rooms feature lots of rush matting, native fabrics, terrazzo and shell floors, screened windows with jalousies, and hardwood louvers. For anyone who has been to Young Island in the past, the rooms have been refurbished, and although the overall Polynesian ambience remains, they're brighter and more inviting. The cottages are located on the beach and at various elevations up the jungly hillside, accessible by stone steps; the higher the cottage, the cooler the air but the wider the panorama.

Three hilltop cottages, each a spacious luxury suite, come with a huge semicircular deck/terrace with loungers and hammock, a living room with rattan sofa and swivel chairs, a refrigerator, a toaster, a kettle, and the makings for a pot of coffee or tea. Each louvered bedroom, recently refurbished, has two queen-size beds and a separate dressing room paneled with greenheart, with bathrobes and amenities, twin vanities, and open-to-the-breezes shower stall. The views are eye filling, the breezes rejuvenating, and the solitude complete.

Just how far you've gotten away from it all is brought home to you when, thumbing through the welcome booklet, you come across this sentence: "Keys for the cottages are available at the front desk, if this is considered necessary."

Name: Young Island
Manager: Bianca Williams Porter
Address: P.O. Box 211, St. Vincent–Grenadines, West Indies
Location: Just east of Kingstown, 200 yd. offshore, about 10 min. and $8 by taxi from the airport, shuttle launch to the resort free at all times; the hotel can arrange a "shared seat" charter flight from Barbados to St. Vincent for a few dollars more than the scheduled one-way fare, if you give them advance warning
Telephone: 784/458-4826
Fax: 784/457-4567
E-mail: y-island@caribsurf.com
Web: www.youngisland.com
Reservations: 800/223-1108, Ralph Locke Islands
Credit Cards: American Express, MasterCard, Visa
Rates: $390–$710 MAP (Dec 16–Mar 31); tax and service charge 17%; off-season 20% less
Rooms: 30, all cottages, some beside the beach, others on the hillside, 1 with air-conditioning, all with ceiling fans, patio or veranda, indoor/outdoor shower (no phones, but there is now a comfy phone booth in the new lobby)
Meals: Breakfast 7:30–10am, lunch 12:30–2:30pm, dinner 7:30–9:30pm (about $86 for nonguests) in one of the breeze-cooled beachside pavilions; informal dress; room service for breakfast only at no extra charge
Entertainment: Live music 3 nights a week — steel band and barbecue on Sat, Bamboo Melodion Band on Fri, live band on Wed in season
Sports: Beach with offshore Coconut Bar, saltwater lagoon pool in the garden, tennis (1 court, no lights), snorkeling, Sunfish sailing, glass-bottom boat trips, windsurfing — all free; scuba, water-skiing, and occasional day cruises (to Bequia, Mustique) on the resort's 44-ft. yacht at extra charge; sail-away packages let you combine a stay on the island with a 3- or 4-day cruise aboard one of the resort's sailboats
PS: A few day-trippers on weekends, very few children (except maybe in summer when the resort promotes special family packages); "no cell-phones in restaurant"; open year-round

Grand View Beach Hotel

ST. VINCENT

☆☆　　　　　　　Y　　　　　　　❻❻　　　　　　$ $ $
ATMOSPHERE　　　DINING　　　　　SPORTS　　　　RATES

Your Grand View grand view is made up of islands, lagoons, bays, sailboats, Young Island, a fort, mountains, headlands, and the dazzling sea that turns into dazzling sky somewhere beyond Bequia. The hotel itself is a big, white, rather ungainly two-story mansion on top of a bluff (not on the beach, despite its name) between two bays and surrounded by 8 acres of bougainvillea, frangipani, palms, and terraced gardens. It's a beautiful location if you don't mind climbing up and down to the beach. About 150 years ago it was a cotton-drying house, the private home of the Sardines, whose ancestors came over from Portugal; Frank Sardine, Sr., converted it into a hotel almost 35 years ago, and despite its longevity, it's in spanking fresh condition. It's homey, pleasant, very friendly, and very relaxed, like the sort of small hotel Europeans would flock to on the less chic villages of the French Riviera (and, in fact, the hotel gets lots of visitors from Europe judging from the German and Italian paperbacks in the lounge library). Most of the guest rooms are plain and unadorned, although the deluxe rooms have been spruced up with friezes of flowers to match the room names; the friezes were hand-painted by the Sardines' daughter. The two prime suites come with whirlpool tub. But who needs decor when you have a view like this?

Added bonuses are the Grand View Club, a racket and fitness center that offers aerobics classes and equipment, a sauna, and massage, as well as a beach bar, Surfside, so you don't have to climb the terraced hillside when you're thirsty.

Name: Grand View Beach Hotel
Owners/Managers: Tony and Heather Sardine
Address: P.O. Box 173, Villa Point, St. Vincent–Grenadines, West Indies
Location: At Villa Point, 5 min. and $9 by taxi from the airport, 10 min. from town
Telephone: 784/458-4811
Fax: 784/457-4174
E-mail: grandview@caribsurf.com
Web: www.grandviewhotel.com
Reservations: 800/633-7411, Caribbean Inns Ltd.
Credit Cards: American Express, MasterCard, Visa
Rates: $185–$220 CP (Dec 15–Apr 15); service charge 10%; off-season 40% less
Rooms: 20 rooms, with air-conditioning, TV, direct-dial phone, some with minibar; 2 suites with whirlpool bathtubs

Meals: Breakfast 7:15–9am, lunch noon–3pm, afternoon tea 4:30–5:30pm, dinner 7:30–8:30pm (about $56), casual dress; limited room service at no extra charge

Entertainment: Pleasant lounge with wicker armchairs, a vintage radio, a few books; live music on Mon, maybe a cocktail party once a week in season, depending on the guests

Sports: Beach at the base of the cliff, swimming pool on top — all free; snorkeling gear for rent; tennis court (1 court, with lights at extra charge at night), 31-ft. fishing boat, squash court, windsurfing, plus exercise classes, aerobic machines, sauna, and massage at the fitness center (shared with local members but rarely crowded); sailing and scuba by arrangement at extra charge

PS: A few children; open year-round

Spring on Bequia

BEQUIA

☆ ☆ ☆   Υ Υ   😖 😖 $ $
ATMOSPHERE   DINING   SPORTS   RATES

You're sitting on the terrace of your room, maybe lounging in a hammock, and looking across a valley of coconut palms toward a bay, a pair of headlands, and a sheltering reef. What you see is a working plantation that produces mangoes, avocados, plums, and melons — to say nothing of all those coconuts; and what you are staying in is a 10-room jewel on a very quiet hillside in a very quiet corner of a very quiet island.

The 250-year-old Spring Plantation was bought about 30 years ago by an Iowa lawyer, who planned to build a few unobtrusive homes among the trees of the hillsides (they're there, but you may not see them!) and a small inn to house prospective buyers and visitors. Part Japanese, part Finnish, part Caribbean, the hotel's clean, contemporary lines enclose large open-plan rooms with native-stone walls, stone floors, furniture fashioned from wood right there on the plantation, khus khus rugs, and whole walls of purpleheart louvers that push back to bring the outdoors right inside. When I first went there more than 20 years ago, Spring had no electricity and no hot water, and guests got around with the help of kerosene lamps. But Spring now has electricity, so there are lights for reading in bed; and the stone-wall shower stalls gush hot water.

All the guest rooms are rustic, charmingly so. The four rooms in the old plantation Great House, draped in frangipani and cordia, are close to the swimming pool and tennis court, but since they're also next to the kitchen, some guests prefer to be higher up the hill in one of two cantilevered wings: Gull, with four rooms, halfway up the hill, or the Fort, with two and higher still. They're a stiff climb from the dining room, even more so from the beach;

but if you've come here for seclusion, this is Seclusion with a capital S, with a beautiful view thrown in for good measure.

Spring's lobby/bar/dining room, attached to the old Great House, is open on two sides and overlooks the old syrup mill and slave quarters, a pleasant, breezy gathering place with a rustic roof of beams and planks, walls of canvas, and matted bamboo screens. The bar stools are the stumps of coconut palms with purpleheart seats; the native-stone walls are covered with vines and planters that are decorated with turtle shells and anchor chains. But mostly the decor is the trees and the flowers, and you're more aware of plantation than inn. Having dinner here is a bit like dining out in a cage of tree frogs and crickets — this is the real Caribbean flavor. The home-cooked meals are no letdown, either, especially the curry brunch on Sundays.

The pride of the Rudolf family (who attribute their fascination with innkeeping to an earlier edition of this guidebook), Spring is still a working plantation, with 200 young citrus trees and some grapevines, still one of the quietest, most romantic tiny inns in the islands — and daughter Candy may be the only innkeeper in the Caribbean who speaks fluent Chinese.

Name: Spring on Bequia
Manager: Candy Leslie
Address: Bequia, St. Vincent–Grenadines, West Indies
Location: On the southeast coast, but just 1 mile over the hill from Port Elizabeth; the inn will pick you up at the dock or airport; for some guests, the inn is a pleasant 30-min. walk from town on a resurfaced road
Telephone: 784/458-3414
Fax: 784/457-3305
E-mail: candy@springonbequia.com
Web: www.springonbequia.com
Reservations: 612/823-1202, the inn's U.S. office
Credit Cards: All major cards
Rates: $140–$220 EP (Dec 15–Apr 14); service charge 10%; off-season 30% less
Rooms: 10, 4 in the main lodge, 6 in two hillside units with private bathroom (shower only), breeze cooled (ceiling fans in some rooms), most with balcony
Meals: Breakfast 7:30am–noon, lunch noon–2pm, dinner 7:30pm (about $60); informal; no room service
Entertainment: Parlor games, conversation around the bar
Sports: 500 feet of virtually solitary sandy beach (about 5 min. away along a pathway through the coconut palms, the pride of Barbados), freshwater pool, tennis (1 court, no lights, rackets available), walking and hiking trails, snorkeling gear — all free; sailing trips to Mustique and the Tobago Cays
PS: "Not really suitable for children"; closed mid-June through Oct

Plantation House Hotel

BEQUIA

☆ ☆ ☆	⅂	🟠 🟠	$ $ $ $
ATMOSPHERE	DINING	SPORTS	RATES

If you make landfall on Bequia by boat and you're toting just one carry-all (all you ever need on this island unless you bring your own dive gear), you can walk to the hotel from the dock. Stroll along the main street beside the beach where they build wooden schooners, past the big tree with the wooden benches, through the garden of The Frangipani hotel, and past Gingerbread House and a couple of private homes until you arrive at this two-story, plantation-style house with a broad veranda on three sides, framed by sea-grape trees and clumps of bougainvillea.

If you've ever been to Bequia before, you'll recognize it as the old Sunny Caribbee. Now the main house has been rebuilt (concrete rather than wood, after the original burned down) and modernized; the once-gloomy wooden cabins have been freshly painted, enlarged, and primped up with brighter colors on the walls, decorative netting over the beds, and smart new bathrooms. Very attractive — but a tad overpriced. They've been augmented with a three-bedroom cottage by the edge of the beach, and the 10 acres of garden are in better shape than ever — trim lawns, splashes of oleander, hibiscus, and fragrant frangipani.

The main lodge is a pleasant surprise, just the right balance between tradition and sophisticated comfort. There's that shady wraparound veranda, one side of it the dining terrace, the other side the lounge with comfy upholstered armchairs and sofas that are perfect for relaxing and reading at teatime.

There's a pleasant, beachy, laid-back feel to the place, with just the right touch of sophistication — but again, a tad overpriced, even with constant refurbishing. Because the roadway winds into the foothills before dipping down to the hotel, there's little traffic and no crowds. In the evening you can just sit there and watch the occasional dinghy drifting ashore with thirsty voyagers — or you can amble back along that beachside path to see what the rest of the world is up to. Fortunately, not much — Bequia is about as slow-poke as an island can be, even if someone did tack on a landing strip.

Name: Plantation House Hotel
Owner/Manager: Alena Rizza
Address: P.O. Box 16, Bequia, St. Vincent–Grenadines, West Indies
Location: On the edge of town, about 5 min. by taxi from the ferry dock, 10 min. and $10 from the airport
Telephone: 784/458-3425
Fax: 784/458-3612
E-mail: planthouse@caribsurf.com

Reservations: Direct

Credit Cards: American Express, MasterCard, Visa

Rates: $353–$564 EP (Dec 15–Apr 14); service charge 10%; off-season 50% less

Rooms: 27 rooms, 5 upstairs in the main lodge, 17 in individual guest bungalows, 3 in a three-room cottage, all with air-conditioning, direct-dial telephones, TV, closet safe, minibar, shower only; ceiling fans and mosquito nets in cottages

Meals: Breakfast 7:30–10am, lunch noon–2:30pm, afternoon tea 3–4pm, dinner 7:30–9:30pm on the veranda or beside the beach (about $70); informal dress; limited room service at no extra charge

Entertainment: Veranda bar, live music and barbecue every Tues at Greenflash, the beach bar; other bars and restaurants a short walk away along the beachside path

Sports: Freshwater pool, tennis (1 court, with lights), windsurfing, bicycles, Hobie Cat, snorkeling gear — all free; Sail-Away package with crewed CSY 44-ft. yacht; water taxi to Princess Margaret Bay, free to hotel guests

PS: "We love children" — but not under 3 years old; some small groups from cruise ships

The Frangipani

BEQUIA

☆☆	ΥΥ	❻	$
ATMOSPHERE	DINING	SPORTS	RATES

They used to build island schooners in the front yard here, the lounge was a ships' chandlery back in the 1930s, and the sea captain who built it disappeared with his crew in the Bermuda Triangle — while his schooner sailed on. His son, recently retired as prime minister of St. Vincent and the Grenadines, turned this white-walled, red-roofed family home into an inn in the 1960s, and it's now one of the most popular watering places in the Grenadines. It hasn't lost touch with its nautical heritage, either: Antique charts and seascapes decorate the lounge; the jetty at the bottom of the garden welcomes fleets of dinghies from the yachts moored just offshore; and sooner or later everyone who sails the Grenadines stops off at the Frangipani beach bar to greet old friends they last saw beating toward the Tobago Cays.

The Frangi, as it's known among sea dogs, is a real wicker-decked West Indies inn. The rooms upstairs are scantily furnished, with mosquito nets, partition walls, and a couple of shared bathrooms down the hall — like the deck of a schooner, it's functional rather than frilly. If you prefer bunking down in something more substantial, ask for one of the rooms in the stone-and-timber garden cottages, which are big, comfortable cabins with spacious bathrooms, dressing rooms, khus khus rugs, and louvers. Each of these 10 rooms has beams and furniture crafted from local hardwood; each has its own sun deck or covered veranda overlooking the anchorage.

There's little to do here besides unwind. Evenings, you can nibble fresh seafood on the veranda (the cooking is much improved) or sit on the seawall and listen to rigging; you can swap a few fancy tales with yachters, listen to a folk singer, or have another beer and watch the last sailors row off in zigzags to their yachts. In the morning, grab a cup of coffee and settle into a large, purpleheart armchair beside the beach. Watch the schooners and ketches weigh anchor for the Tobago Cays or Martinique. Don't bother waving good-bye — they'll soon be back at Frangi.

Name: The Frangipani
Owners/Managers: Sabrina Mitchell
Address: P.O. Box 1, Bequia, St. Vincent–Grenadines, West Indies
Location: On the waterfront, a 3-min. walk from the schooner jetty, 15 min. and $12 from the airport by taxi
Telephone: 784/458-3255
Fax: 784/458-3824
E-mail: frangi@caribsurf.com
Web: www.frangipanibequia.com
Reservations: Direct
Credit Cards: American Express, MasterCard, Visa
Rates: $65–$175 EP (Dec 15–Apr 14); service charge 10%; off-season 30% less
Rooms: 10 with private bathrooms and balconies in the garden cottages; plus 4 in the main house sharing bathrooms (cold water only); mosquito nets and ceiling fans throughout (no phones, no TV)
Meals: Breakfast 7:30–10am (served on verandas of the garden units), lunch all afternoon, dinner 7–10pm (about $50–$60), served in the beachside patio bar/restaurant with harbor view; casual dress; room service for breakfast only
Entertainment: Barbecue and "jump-up" every Thurs year-round, live music every Mon in season
Sports: Tennis (1 court, no lights) — free; Mistral windsurfers, NAUI and PADI scuba, Sunfish sailing at extra charge, with a discount for Frangi guests; 45-ft. yacht available for day trips or special 3-day charters to Tobago Cays
PS: Lots of yachters, castaways, and beachcombers (and forget the few days around the Easter Regatta); no cellphones allowed in rooms, bar, or restaurant; not many children; closed Sept; the inn also rents 3 cottages nearby

The Cotton House Hotel

MUSTIQUE

☆☆☆☆☆	♈ ♈ ♈	❻❻	$ $ $ $ $
ATMOSPHERE	DINING	SPORTS	RATES

It's that rare combination of informality and elegance, of unspoiled (well, almost unspoiled) surroundings and civilization. Here you are, on a private tropical island with a permanent population of 300, a few coconut and citrus groves, and a half-dozen deserted beaches.

You can spend an entire day here without meeting anyone other than your maid, waiter, or beach attendant; you can disappear to a beach for a picnic lunch with not another soul in sight; you can spend hours snorkeling among fish that rarely, if ever, encounter Homo sapiens. Then, in the evening you might mingle with escapists who turn out to be cosmopolitan, urbane, world-traveled — maybe even celebrated.

Mustique, unique Mustique, is small (just 3 miles long and 1½ miles wide) and flat (about 400 ft. at its highest point). You arrive by air in a seven-seater that sweeps in between a pair of hills, then nose-dives to touch down in what is basically a pasture with a runway and tiny thatch-and-bamboo terminal. When Bopsin, aka Gideon Gabriel, the hotel driver/greeter/chauffeur, sees the plane coming, he hops into his minivan, and by the time you've taxied to the terminal and cleared immigration, he's waiting there to convey you to the hotel.

And what a hotel! The Cotton House itself is an 18th-century storage house of handsome proportions: two floors of mellowed coral stone rimmed by a deep veranda and accented by louvered doors. A few yards away, atop a knoll, the great British designer Oliver Messel created a swimming pool known as Messel's Folly, the sort of romantic setting he might have designed for a Gluck opera at Covent Garden. Beyond the stone stump of the original windmill, a pair of stately, two-story Georgian Colonial–style villas house one-third of the guest rooms, each with a different color scheme and decorations; other guest rooms are in three cottages fashioned in vaguely "island cottage" style, and another five "beachfront-front" suites are housed in Messel's Coutinot House, a former private villa. With their Messel designs, the original lodgings were visual delights, but subsequent renovations slowly mussed up their good looks. Then, hurrah, a 1999 rehab restored them to something like their original refinement and added the five new top-of-the-line suites in Messel's Coutinot House. Pickle-pine furniture adds a light tropical touch, four-poster and pencil-post beds are artfully draped with netting bunched into rosettes, the bathrooms are marbled and luxurious, and the toiletries are by Contemporel. Contemporary touches include CD players (playing quietly when you arrive), direct-dial telephones, and minibars. Most rooms and suites have a properly outfitted balcony or terrace, which are perfectly secluded spots for breakfast or afternoon tea — or, for that matter, lunch or dinner.

The original Great Room of The Cotton House had likewise been denuded of many of its outstanding antiques, but is once more a gathering place of charm and style; the veranda is still a magical place for candlelit, tree frog–serenaded dinners, especially now that the resort has a chef to match the setting. The most recent addition to the pampering is a beachfront spa with four treatment rooms. Louvered doors open to the breezes and the relaxing sound of gentle surf; the featured products are by E'spa and Decleor.

The Cotton House, now owned by the Mustique Company (all the villa owners plus a few others), is currently managed by a Paris-based company called GLA International, whose classy president, Grace Leo-Andrieu, was involved in setting up Le Toiny on St. Barthélemy and the much-admired hotels Montalembert and Lancaster in Paris. A French-born manager and a French chef, Oliver Sevestre and Emmanuel Guemon (the latter from Sandy Lane Hotel), respectively, are adding a *soupçon* of Gallic style to an island that has always been quintessentially English. In return for the hefty price tag, Cotton House gives you a degree of personal service that goes well beyond the basics. A menu of pillows will ensure a good night's sleep. The maid will unpack your luggage and press whatever you plan to wear during your first evening and have it back to you before dinner. You can discuss the evening's menu with Chef Guemon for special dishes. You can have your fresh Mustiquean lobster and pink prawns with sweet pickled ginger served in "a romantic location of your choice" at no extra charge. When I sat down on the veranda of The Cotton House for afternoon tea overlooking the lily pond, I noticed that my waiter remained hovering beside my tray while I shot a few photographs. Since there was no check to sign, I couldn't figure out what he wanted — until I realized he was voluntarily standing guard to chase the birds away from my scones and cake.

Mustique may be too quiet for some restless souls (oh, the serenity of it!), yet for all its isolation, it can plunge its guests into the sort of belting nightlife that larger islands envy. For a start, there's Basil's Bar, that rollicking, world-famed wood-and-wicker deck on Britannia Beach, where you might find yourselves at 3:30 some morning, beneath a full moon and myriad stars, listening to bamboo flute and "shak-shak" music, and mingling with princesses and viscounts, rock stars and fishermen, and CEOs masquerading as swingers.

Name: The Cotton House Hotel
Manager: Oliver Sevestre
Address: P.O. Box 349, Mustique, St. Vincent–Grenadines, West Indies
Location: On a private island, 45 min. by twin-engine plane from Barbados (with advance warning, the hotel will arrange seats on a shared charter flight, about $280 per person, round-trip)
Telephone: 784/456-4777
Fax: 784/456-5887
E-mail: cottonhouse@caribsurf.com

Web: www.cottonhouse.net

Reservations: 877/240-9945 (toll-free direct), or 800/223-1108 (Ralph Locke Islands)

Credit Cards: All major cards

Rates: $790–$1,250 (Dec 20–Apr 4); service charge 10%; off-season 25% less

Rooms: 20, including 5 suites, in various one- and two-story cottages, all with air-conditioning and ceiling fans, direct-dial telephones, stocked minibar, CD player (library of CDs at reception), marble bathroom (robes, hair dryer), balcony or patio; fax machine and TV/VCR on request

Meals: Breakfast 7:30–10am, lunch 12:30–2:30pm beside the pool or in a picnic hamper delivered to any of the 12 beaches, afternoon tea 3:30–5:30pm on the veranda, dinner 7–9:30pm in the Great House (about $90 for nonguests); casual but "island elegant" dress ("jackets or ties not required"); room service for all meals at no extra charge; some recorded background music

Entertainment: Parlor games, 2 weekly cocktail parties (1 with the manager and staff, 1 where you usually get to mingle with villa owners), jump-up at Basil's Bar every Wed, occasional live music at the lounge/bar of Firefly hotel (see below)

Sports: 6 beaches, freshwater pool, tennis (2 courts, no lights), snorkeling gear, windsurfing, Sunfish sailing, kayaks, fitness center — all free; minispa beside the beach, horseback riding, scuba, cruise by sailboat or speedboat to Tobago Cays and Bequia, treatments in the new beachside spa at extra charge

PS: "No cruise ships with more than 25 passengers"; few children in the hotel, the kids on the beach are probably staying in villas; cellphones available for rent; open year-round

PPS: In addition to The Cotton House, Mustique has 90-odd one-of-a-kind luxury villas for rent, some perched on hillsides, some beside the beach. None of them is designed specifically for twosomes, but if you decide to junket with friends, this could be a memorable way to spend a vacation a la jet set. Mick Jagger's wood-and-bamboo home may or may not be on the list of rentals, but Viscount Linley's is (although it's quite modest compared to some of the others). Among the most attractive two-bedroom villas: Blue Waters, Ultramarine, Jacaranda, and Pelican Beach (all on the water), and the lovely Yellowbird (in the hills). In 2000–01, two-bedroom villas cost about $6,500–$8,800 a week in winter and $3,500–$6,000 in summer, in each case with full staff, Jeep, and laundry. Or, in other words, from just over $200 per day for two couples sharing. For details, contact Mustique Villas, Sanctuare, at 800/225-4255, or The Mustique Company at 784/458-4621; or check out the website at www.mustique-island.com.

Firefly

MUSTIQUE

☆ ☆ ☆	⚲ ⚲	❻	$ $ $ $
ATMOSPHERE	DINING	SPORTS	RATES

Firefly was one of the original private villas on the island, built in the early 1970s, before becoming a low-key, low-priced B&B. Four years ago it was bought by Stan Clayton, an English nightclub impresario, who had retired and settled in Grenada because he and his wife "have been coming to the Caribbean for 30 years." But he decided he needed something to occupy his energy and attention, so he acquired Firefly sight unseen, moved to Mustique, and immediately set about upgrading its facilities — like terracing the precipitous hillside to accommodate a multilevel bar and thatch-topped barbecue, a couple of dining terraces, a duo of stunning lip-high swimming pools joined by a cascade, and a separate sunning terrace for overnight guests — all surrounded by frangipani and flamboyant trees and with mesmerizing views across the trees to the sailboat-studded bay. This is a particularly beguiling spot for lunch because the English chef Kevin Snook serves locally caught fish as well as meat dishes such as samosas and rotis — almost like lunching in your own staffed villa, but with everyone seated at different tables. Dinner is served on the recently built dining terrace overlooking the ocean; after-dinner drinks, in the lounge/bar where Broadway producers and folks like Phil Collins have been known to sit down at the grand piano and entertain one and all.

From the lounge, on the topmost floor, a spiral staircase leads down to the "second" floor with four bedrooms, each designed with vertical louvers and one wall open to the trees and sunsets. Bathrooms come with solid brass fixtures, two with stone shower stalls, one of which is half outdoors so that you bathe practically among the branches of the trees (oh, all right then, there's a filmy curtain you can draw so the hummingbirds won't see you). Another room has its own whirlpool on a private sun deck — and a bathtub made from beach pebbles. The beds are inviting, queen-size four-posters draped with decorative netting. Very charming, very romantic. As it says in the brochure, "Not a hotel — an experience. . . Not for the pretentious or the stuffy."

But I can't guarantee your serenity here — Firefly has a reputation for impromptu cavorting and house parties, which is part of its unique appeal.

Name: Firefly
Owners/Managers: Stan and Elizabeth Clayton
Address: Mustique, St. Vincent–Grenadines
Location: About 5 min. from the airport; the owners will collect you (for information on getting to Mustique, see "The Cotton House Hotel," above)

Telephone: 784/488-8414
Fax: 784/488-8514
E-mail: enquiries@mustiquefirefly.com
Web: www.mustiquefirefly.com
Reservations: Direct
Credit Cards: American Express, MasterCard, Visa
Rates: $650–$750 MAP plus the use of a "mule" runaround (Jan 5–Dec 21); service charge 15%; lower by a few dollars in the off-season (stay 7 nights and the rate will include your airfare from and to Barbados, with entrance to the executive lounge at Barbados airport on the way home)
Rooms: 4 with ceiling fans (and lots of louvers), 2 with air-conditioning, 3 with shower only, 1 with bathtub; hair dryer, direct-dial telephone, terrace or deck, CD player, minibar, bathrobes
Meals: Breakfast 8–10am, lunch noon–4pm, afternoon tea 4–5pm, dinner 7–11pm (about $75 for nonguests); "Mustique casual" dress; limited room service at no extra charge; background music (mostly quiet, recorded jazz)
Entertainment: Occasional impromptu recitals on grand piano ("often the bar is lively, noisy, and open late"); otherwise, Basil's Bar, 5 min. away
Sports: Pool only — but other activities on land and sea can be organized
PS: No children under 12; "We don't want your cellphones or your computers here. We don't want you receiving or sending a constant stream of telephone calls, faxes, or e-mails;" open year-round

Saltwhistle Bay Club

MAYREAU

☆☆☆☆	YY	⚽⚽	$ $ $ $
ATMOSPHERE	DINING	SPORTS	RATES

Real barefoot, flake-out, crash territory — an unspoiled bay on an unspoiled cay in the unspoiled Grenadines. To get there you first fly to Union Island, where you'll be met by the resort's launch, which will skim you across the channel past Saline Bay, then finally around a headland and into Saltwhistle Bay.

Tom and Undine Potter, a Canadian/German couple, settled here 16 years ago and built a beachside restaurant catering to passing yachts, then opened their hotel a decade ago. When you sail into the bay, with its glistening semicircle of sand, and beyond the beach, where dwarf palms and seagrape trees part to reveal glimpses of another shining sea beyond, you may well wonder, "Where did they build their hotel?" Go in a bit farther; it's all there nestled into 22 acres of coconut palms, more seagrapes, clusters of oleander and flamboyant, that great curve of soft white sand, and a windward beach that's pure Robinson Crusoe.

There's nothing plush or luxurious about the Saltwhistle's accommodations — but there's nothing spartan about them either. The guest quarters are

CARENAGE BAY, CANOUAN

Here's an island that has little going for it — no rain, no forest, certainly nothing like the "magnificent lushness" promised by the resort's brochure — other than some lovely bays with ribbons of white sand and protective reefs that turn the water every razzle-dazzle shade of blue. It didn't have electricity until 10 years ago. Most of its 200 households don't even have running water.

Now, behold! A 155-room resort that looks a bit like Costa Smeralda on Sardinia (same architect) and a golf course. "We're the new Mustique," I was told by a representative of the developers (an Italian tycoon with Swiss banks). Forget it! There can never be another Mustique. Though its plans incorporate private luxury villas for the Euro-rich — some of which will ultimately be for rent, a la Mustique — the Carenage is something completely different.

The resort covers the entire northern third of the 4-square-mile island, the three-story core in a bowl-like valley rising from a reef-sheltered bay. The lodgings are mostly one-story, villa-style structures arranged in an arc around the valley, with the golf course to the north, restaurants and bars adjoining one of the two beaches, and a small casino and restaurant sprouting from a hilltop. The colors are eye-catching — too eye-catching, maybe, although the tropical sun and the lavish plantings have toned the colors down to a pleasantly weathered look. The rooms and suites are larger than usual — about 800 square feet for an executive suite with high chapel-like ceilings. Interiors are painted in offbeat colors — buttercup and pumpkin (or thereabouts) — but too many of the chairs and sofas are oversized and none is too comfortable for sitting upright for any length of time. But

in sturdy native stone and timber cottages, each with hardwood louvers, handcrafted furniture, white clay floors, ceiling fans, and spacious bathrooms with stone shower stalls (and oodles of hot water). Some two-room cottages share a spacious rooftop gallery with loungers, tables, and chairs. The dining room is an ingenious collection of circular stone booths topped by thatched canopies where you can stuff yourselves with such local delicacies as curried conch, turtle steaks, and lobster, all fresh from the surrounding reefs.

There's not much going on at Saltwhistle — delightfully so. Of course, for the truly ambitious there are picnics to the wild and windswept beach with views of Palm Island and Tobago, snorkeling gear, fishing with the locals in their gaff-rigged sloops, a walk up the hill to the village for a warm beer and a sweeping view of all those cays and reefs, or a hike down to Saline Bay to watch the mail boat come in. If any or all of these possibilities (or just the thought of them) exhaust you, there's always the lure of a good book, a rum punch, and a private hammock strung between the cedar and seagrape trees.

you could settle into one of the executive suites nicely for weeks. The living room comes with a kitchenette (two burners, refrigerator, attractive chinaware and cutlery); the bedroom has its own refrigerator; and the bathroom is lavishly accoutered with white tiles and Frette bathrobes and towels. I particularly welcome the window/door treatments of glass and louvers that give you the option of air-conditioning or bug-free natural ventilation. The terraces are spacious and furnished with extravagantly cushioned loungers, but they may not be as private as you would like. True, there are several annoying little oversights here and there (someone should have given more care to the lighting), but the overall effect is much more chic, more stylish, and more Mediterranean than you might expect in this castaway island.

Probably because the owner is Italian, the best features of Carenage Bay are the restaurants: the invitingly louvered pavilion, the Beach Club beside the enormous free-form swimming pool; the Surfside beside the tennis courts at the beach one bay over; the air-conditioned La Piazza in the main building; and, the newest of the bunch, the Bagetelle up at the casino. Four restaurants for 155 rooms and suites might seem ambitious, but usually no more than two of them are open on the same evening. It's a question of giving guests variety and options.

Alas, as of this writing (spring 2003), there are no options: The owners have been having difficulty finding an experienced company to run their resort so it's been closed for more than a year. All the signs and rumors point to it reopening, sometime in 2004, under the flag of an international hotel chain, probably Asian-based. For information, call 784/458-8000.

Name: Saltwhistle Bay Club
Managers: Undine and Tom Potter
Address: Mayreau, St. Vincent–Grenadines, West Indies
Location: South of St. Vincent, a few miles from the islands of Union, Canouan, and Palm; to get there, you fly from Barbados to Union, where the hotel collects you by boat ($50 per person, round-trip), but since the club (with advance notice) will make all the arrangements, all you have to do is get to Barbados
Telephone: 784/458-8444
Fax: 784/458-8944
E-mail: swbreserve@yahoo.com
Web: www.saltwhistlebay.com
Reservations: Direct
Credit Cards: American Express, MasterCard, Visa
Rates: $480 MAP (Dec 20–Mar 2); service charge 10%; off-season 40% less

Rooms: 10, all with ceiling fans (and steady cross-ventilation), queen-size bed, bathrobes, shower only; some with shared rooftop decks

Meals: Breakfast 8–10:30am, lunch noon–2pm, dinner 7–9pm (about $80, for nonguests), all served in beachside booths; occasional beach barbecues; casual dress; recorded music; room service on request at no extra charge

Entertainment: Steel band every Thurs in winter, hammocks strung between the trees, conversation in the bar, darts, backgammon, a moonlit stroll on the beach

Sports: 300–400 yd. of beautiful beach, snorkeling gear, windsurfing — all free; scuba diving, boat trips to Tobago Cays, island picnics, excursions with local fishermen at extra charge

PS: Some children; cellphones don't work here; closed Sept–Oct

Petit St. Vincent Resort

PETIT ST. VINCENT

☆☆☆☆☆   ΥΥΥ   ❻❻ $ $ $ $ $
ATMOSPHERE   DINING   SPORTS   RATES

"Some of our guests never put on any clothes until dinnertime." Not in public, perhaps, but on their private terraces, because all but half a dozen of the rooms here are self-contained cottages, widely dispersed around this 113-acre private out-island. It may well be the most secluded, most private of the Caribbean's luxury hideaways.

It's certainly one of the most consistently dependable. PSV has no problems with revolving-door management. Any good resort manager knows where the pipes and power cables are, but in the case of Haze Richardson, he doesn't just know where they are — he put them there in the first place. He helped lay the cables and the pipes, helped quarry the stones for the cottages, installed the refrigeration in the kitchen, built a desalination plant, and planted the fruit trees. Now the resort even makes its own fiberglass Jeep-like Minimokes. Richardson came to the island by way of a 77-foot staysail schooner, *Jacinta,* which he skippered. One of his charterers was the late H.W. Nichols, Jr., then the top man at a big corporation in Cincinnati, who bought this dinky Grenadine from a little old lady in Petit Martinique, the island just across the channel. Richardson and his team started building in 1966 and worked hard for 3 years, working with whatever was available (mostly bluebitch stone and hardwood) and planning the location of the individual cottages to make the most of the breezes and vistas.

It may sound simple and rustic, but it's really quite lavish in terms of solitude and seclusion — all that space for only 44 guests (and a staff of 75 to boot). The cottages follow a basic U-shaped pattern: big open sun deck, big shaded breakfast patio, big glass-enclosed lounge separated by a wall of bluebitch from a big sleeping area with twin queen-size beds, separated in turn from a stone-walled dressing room and bathroom with curtain-enclosed shower. Guest room interiors follow a basic style of bluebitch walls, purple-heart louvers, khus khus rugs on red-tile floors, seersucker bathrobes, baskets of toiletries, and sprightly fabrics in soft islandy shades of yellow, turquoise, and terra-cotta. There are no newfangled gadgets like televisions or telephones.

For room service, there's the unique PSV semaphore system: a bamboo pole with a notch for written messages (for example, "two piña coladas fast," "afternoon tea for two") and two flags — red for "Do Not Disturb," yellow for "Come In." But the tactful maids and room-service waiters first ring the little brass bell at the entrance — just in case you want to slip into your fluffy PSV-crested bathrobes.

Where the rooms differ is in location: up on the bluff for the best breezes and views, down on the beach by the lagoon, or on the beach beyond the dock. Cottage 1, on the bluff, is one of the most secluded, with a big deck overlooking a dazzling sea and the craggy silhouette of Union Island. If you want a beach right on your doorstep, cottages 6 through 11 are for you; they look out on unspoiled castaway beach. For total detachment, turn your back on the entire resort and check into cottage 18, where a few stone steps lead to a private patch of beach, and beyond that nothing but ocean — all the way to Guinea-Bissau or thereabouts. Some of the cottages are what pass in these lazy climes as a stiff hike (all of 5 min.) to the dining pavilion, but you can always arrange to be picked up by one of the ubiquitous "mokes."

This hilltop bar/dining pavilion is the focal point of the resort, with soaring hardwood roof and indoor/outdoor patios and gazebos overlooking the anchorage and Petit Martinique. It's a beautiful place to sit and savor the twilight while sipping a Banana Touch or mango daiquiri. PSV meals are well above average for these parts (meats, for example, are personally selected by Julia Child's butcher, a regular PSV guest, and flown in specially for the resort); the dining-room staff is particularly attentive.

Indeed, one of the main attractions of PSV, a feature that sets it apart from many of its peers, is its long-serving staff. They seem to genuinely care about making your vacation perfect. More often than not, owner Haze Richardson is at the dock to greet you with a piña colada when you arrive. The staff is solicitous about getting you back to Union on time for your plane. There are beach chairs in your room in case you want to tote one to a nearby beach, but if you want to cart your lounger along, one of the roving stewards will pick you up in his Minimoke and transport you and a cooler to whichever beach you choose (the one at the west end is particularly tranquil, with hammocks strung beneath thatch bohios, woven bamboo fences to preserve your privacy, and a "birdcage" filled with St. Vincent bananas in case you get peckish). If you're bored with that, you can even have one of the boatmen transport you to PSR (Petit St. Richardson), a minuscule offshore cay with lots of sand and a solitary bohio.

But why quit your own private deck in the first place — with or without swimsuits?

PSV may not be for everyone. You have to be your own entertainment. You have to forgo the plushest amenities. You have to dine in the same dining room every evening, except for the beach barbecue. But for anyone who genuinely wants a castaway setting with civilized comforts and refined service, who wants to get as far as possible from the everyday world without taking forever getting there, Petit St. Vincent is a beautiful, enchanting hideaway.

Name: Petit St. Vincent Resort

Owners/Managers: Haze and Lynn Richardson

Address: Petit St. Vincent, St. Vincent–Grenadines, West Indies

Location: An inkblot on the charts, just 40 miles south of St. Vincent and 20 min. from Union Island, the nearest airstrip, by one of PSV's 42-ft. launches (the ride is free); the easiest way to get to Union is by shared-seat charter from Barbados (about $120 each way per passenger), which can be arranged in advance by PSV

Telephone: 784/458-8801

Fax: 784/458-8428

E-mail: info@psvresort.com

Web: www.psvresort.com

Reservations: 800/654-9326 or 513/242-1333, fax 513/242-6951, the resort's U.S. office; or 800/223-6800, Leading Hotels of the World

Credit Cards: American Express, MasterCard, Visa

Rates: $910 FAP (Dec 16–Mar 15); service charge 10%; off-season 35% less

Rooms: 22 cottages, all with bedrooms and sitting room, open and shaded patio or terrace, shower only, amenities trays, bathrobes, hammocks, ceiling fans (otherwise acres of louvers take care of the cooling)

Meals: Breakfast 7:30–10am, buffet lunch 12:30–2pm, afternoon tea 4–5pm, dinner 7:30–9:30pm (all in the hilltop dining pavilion); Sat barbecue with Grenadine steel band; dress informal but stylish (cover-ups required at lunchtime); room service all meals (including early-morning coffee service and "flagpole" lunch at the West End Beach) at no extra charge

Entertainment: Bar, occasional live music, manager's cocktail party, backgammon and other parlor pastimes

Sports: Virtually continuous beach (plus the offshore cay), snorkeling, Sunfish sailing, Hobie Cats, windsurfing (with instruction by shore simulator), tennis (1 Omnicourt, with lights), croquet, fitness trail, footpath up 275-ft. Mt. Marni (great view), snorkeling off 20-ft. island boat built from island cedar — all free; water-skiing, scuba diving, and day trips on a powerboat or sailboat trips to Tobago Cays and Mayreau at extra charge

PS: Few children, no groups except maybe the crew from a passing yacht who stop by the bar for a drink; "cellphones are discouraged"; closed Sept–Oct

The Calabash Hotel

GRENADA

☆☆☆☆	♈♈♈	❻❻	$ $ $ $
ATMOSPHERE	DINING	SPORTS	RATES

You never have to worry about making it to the dining room in time for breakfast because your maid has her own pantry adjoining your room. So leave your order the night before, and whenever you wake up and feel like breakfast, let the maid know. She'll serve it to you in bed, in the sitting room, on your private patio, or, depending on your room, beside your private pool. Talk about service! And when you finally make it to the beach, the staff brings you fresh fruit to brighten your morning; in the afternoon they set up complimentary tea in the bar; and in the evening they serve complimentary canapés before dinner. That's the sort of service you get in a hotel where the number of staff matches exactly the number of guests.

The Calabash is an old Grenada favorite — the British in particular have been wintering here loyally since it opened in the 1960s. The intimate little resort circles 8 beachside acres, a manicured "village green" dotted with lofty trees and fragrant shrubbery. The 30 suites perfectly capture island atmosphere: comfortable but not plush, rustic but snug. All the suites (which are named after flowers) are in two-story cottages arranged in a horseshoe around the lawn, all facing the beach. I particularly like those on the west side, especially the higher-ceiling units on the second floor. My favorite, cottage number 1, nearest the water, has the largest and most romantic terrace, although the Thorneycroft Suite, with a private swimming pool and double Jacuzzi, ranks up there with the loveliest suites in the Caribbean.

Eating is one of the prime pleasures at The Calabash. Lunch is served in a breezy gazebo a few paces from the lagoon-like waters of L'Anse aux Epines. The main dining pavilion, Cicely's (one of the island's most acclaimed restaurants, but house guests are guaranteed a table), is an open terrace fashioned from native stone and furnished with chairs and tables of polished saman. Flowering *Thunbergia grandiflora* dangles from overhead vines, threatening, it seems, to reach down and gobble up Cicely Roberts's warm shrimp and callaloo tartlet.

The resort has been steadily upgraded in the past few years, but what brings the British and others back year after year is the long-serving staff — friendly, willing, and attentive but unobtrusive. They make The Calabash an inviting, low-key, very relaxed hideaway.

Name: The Calabash Hotel
Manager: Clive Barnes
Address: P.O. Box 382, St. George's, Grenada, West Indies

Location: At L'Anse aux Epines (Prickley Bay) on the south coast, about
10 min. and $16 by taxi from the airport
Telephone: 473/444-4234 or 473/444-4334
Fax: 473/444-5050
E-mail: calabash@caribsurf.com
Web: www.calabashhotel.com
Reservations: 800/528-5835, toll-free direct
Credit Cards: American Express, MasterCard, Visa
Rates: $430–$886 CP (Dec 29–Apr 3); service charge 10%; off-season
40% less
Rooms: 30 suites, all with bathrooms and showers, porches, air-conditioning
and ceiling fans, minibars, safes, tea or coffeemakers, CD players, clock
radios, hair dryers; 22 suites have whirlpools or whirlpool bathtubs, 7 have
private plunge pools, the Thorneycroft Suite has a private swimming pool
Meals: Breakfast anytime on your porch, lunch noon–2:30pm in the beach
bar (with recorded music), dinner 7–10pm in the arbor-covered dining
terrace, Cicely's Restaurant (about $100); informal dress (but trousers,
rather than shorts, required in the evening); room service for all meals at
no extra charge
Entertainment: Some recorded music, piano, steel band or country trio several
times a week, TV room/library, billiards room
Sports: Beach, tennis (1 concrete court, with lights), windsurfing, Sunfish sailers, kayaks, snorkeling gear, fitness room — all free; complimentary greens
fees at Grenada Golf Club; new aromatherapy and reflexology center
(treatments at extra charge); scuba and water-skiing can be arranged
PS: Occasional din of planes, rarely after 10pm; no children under 12 mid-Jan
to mid-Mar; closed Sept

Secret Harbour Resort

GRENADA

☆☆	Y	❻	$ $ $
ATMOSPHERE	DINING	SPORTS	RATES

For lovers, the secret harbors at Secret Harbour may be the bathtubs —
sunken, free-form masses of colorful Italian tiles, potted plants, and an
unglazed "wagon wheel" window that lets you listen to the lapping of the
water below as you lazily lap the water on each other's backs.

This Secret Harbour is a Spanish-Mediterranean village on a terraced hillside of gardens and greenery: a splash of red-tiled roofs, white stucco arches,
stained glass, and hand-hewn beams among lime and papaw trees, frangipani,
and triple bougainvillea. At the top of the hill are the lobby/lounge and
restaurant; the guest bungalows are a few feet above the water, and between
top and bottom there's a big, tiled free-form pool as colorful as your bathtub.

Secret Harbour, owned by The Moorings, the yacht-charter company, welcomes you with low-key luxury in keeping with the Spanish-Mediterranean theme: a big, semicircular balcony overlooking the bay, with padded loungers and enough room for a dinner party; arched glass-paneled doors leading into a small, sunny lounge foyer with bright two-toned banquettes; a pair of authentic four-poster double beds from island plantations; and stained-glass windows to cast spangled light for just the right romantic mood. To say nothing of your sexy bathroom.

Name: Secret Harbour Resort
Manager: Esther Neptune
Address: P.O. Box 11, St. George's, Grenada, West Indies
Location: On a quiet bay (Mt. Hartman) on the south shore of the island, a few miles from the resort hotels along Grand Anse Beach, 10–15 min. and $16 from St. George's $16 by taxi, 10 min. and $16 from the airport by taxi
Telephone: 473/444-4439
Fax: 473/444-4819
E-mail: secretharbour@caribbeanhighlights.com
Web: www.secretharbour.com
Reservations: Direct
Credit Cards: American Express, MasterCard, Visa
Rates: $240 EP (Dec 20–Apr 14); service charge 10%; off-season 45% less
Rooms: 20 suites in 10 cottages, all with air-conditioning, ceiling fan, refrigerator, four-poster bed, hair dryer, radio, and large verandas
Meals: Breakfast 7:30–10:30am, lunch noon–2pm, afternoon tea 4pm, dinner 7:30–10pm (about $60) in an open-air terrace overlooking the water; limited room service at no extra charge; informal dress (but slacks rather than shorts at dinner)
Entertainment: Steel bands occasionally
Sports: Small (private) beach, sunbathing terrace, freshwater pool, Sunfish sailing, windsurfing, snorkeling, tennis, boat trips — all free; skippered yachts and scuba can be arranged to nearby Hog and Calivigny Islands
PS: No children under 12; open year-round

Spice Island Beach Resort

GRENADA

☆☆☆☆   ΥΥ   ❻❺ $ $ $ $
ATMOSPHERE   **DINING**   **SPORTS**   **RATES**

Begin the day by slipping out of bed, sliding back the screens, and plopping straight into your private plunge pool. When you hear a rap on the garden gate, it means the waiter has arrived with your breakfast, which he'll set up on your private, shaded breakfast patio. Dawdle over the fresh island fruits and nutmeg jam. After breakfast, step down onto your private sunning patio and spread out on a lounger — the garden wall screens you from passersby, and the garden door locks; so you can shuck your bikini or robe or whatever you have half on, half off. Spend the entire day here — sunning, dipping, eating, loving, dipping, sunning, all in your own private little sun-bright world.

Your Pool Suite, if you take time to notice, is craftily designed: The sun deck is in the sun all day; the breakfast patio is in the shade all day. In addition to your tiny garden and freshwater pool, your suite has white tiled floors with soft scatter rugs, wicker chairs, and fitted dressers crafted from local hardwoods. If you're in one of the new Royal Pool Suites, you'll also have your own private wood sauna, an all-marble bathroom, and a separate small living room with cable TV. The beach suites — with sliding-glass doors and patios leading directly onto the beach — are less opulent and afford less privacy since the beach is public — but they have whirlpool tubs with skylights. All of Spice Island's rooms and suites — beach or poolside — have air-conditioning and louvers for cooling and individual solar water heaters for reliable supplies of hot water. All the rooms also feature Jacuzzis or whirlpool spas, some double-sized.

Longtime Spice Island fans might be taken aback when their taxis pull up to the front door — now with a porte-cochère and a broad terrace with boutiques greeting them before they reach the reception desks, where they can sit down and register and look around at all the changes. The dining room (now named Oliver's) has been enhanced with coral-pink pillars and comfy new chairs, and the Sea & Surf bar-lounge is now on two levels with a shaded section for lunchtime snacks. Just beyond the bar is a first for Spice: a swimming pool (pretty as a picture, but when I was there, most guests were lounging around the beach rather than the pool).

When you get curious about the rest of the world, stroll a few yards across the lawn, among the coconut palms and flowering shrubs, to Grand Anse Beach, with over 2½ miles of fine white sand. Jog. Walk. Work up an appetite or thirst, both of which you can satisfy in pleasant surroundings in the inn's beachside pavilions (which have menus that cleverly blend international and local cuisines, including callaloo crepes, grilled medallions of pork tenderloin with creamed dasheen and fresh tamarind sauce, breaded flying fish with fried bananas and mango chutney). But no matter how tasty the breadfruit vichyssoise or nutmeg ice cream, no matter how jolly the music of the folk trio that serenades you, it's always a delight to slip off to your private patio and your private pool for a midnight swim beneath your private stars. Despite what you may have heard about all the renovations and enhancements, here beside your private pool you realize that Spice Island hasn't really changed. It's just better than ever. And given the fact that the rates ($515 and up for two) include all meals, beverages, and house wines, this has to be one of the best values in the Caribbean.

Name: Spice Island Beach Resort
Owner/Manager: Royston Hopkins

Address: P.O. Box 6, Grand Anse, St. George's, Grenada, West Indies

Location: On Grand Anse Beach, 10 min. and $10 by taxi from St. George's, 15 min. and $15 by taxi from the airport

Telephone: 473/444-4258 or 473/444-4423

Fax: 473/444-4807

E-mail: spiceisl@caribsurf.com

Web: www.spicebeachresort.com

Reservations: 800/223-9815, International Travel & Resorts

Credit Cards: American Express, Discover, MasterCard, Visa

Rates: $515–$896 FAP, including beverages and house wines (Dec 15– Apr 15); service charge 10%; off-season 20% less

Rooms: 66, in 6 categories, all with whirlpool, air-conditioning, ceiling fans, louvers, patio or lanai, safe, minibar, clock radio, telephones, bathrobes, hair dryers; Private Pool Suites have plunge pools, the Royal Private Pool Suites include all the above plus a redwood sauna and stereo CD player

Meals: Breakfast 7–10am, lunch 12:30–2:30pm, afternoon tea 4pm, dinner 7–10pm (about $90 for nonguests); limited room service at no extra charge; elegantly casual dress (no shorts); some live music, otherwise low-key recorded music

Entertainment: Barbecues, steel bands, and local bands several nights a week in season

Sports: 2½-mile beach (hotel's frontage about 1,600 ft., with, alas, some vendors), freshwater pool plus 24 private pools; small fitness center, bicycles, tennis (1 court, with lights), snorkeling gear, Hobie Cats and kayaks — all free; new spa with massage and hydrotherapy treatments, scuba diving, water-skiing at extra charge; complimentary greens fees at Grenada Golf Club (but you need your own clubs)

PS: No children under 5 during the high season; no children under 12 in Pool Suites; open year-round

Laluna

GRENADA

☆☆☆	☷	➒	$ $ $ $
ATMOSPHERE	DINING	SPORTS	RATES

Given the gnarled coastline of southern Grenada, Morne Rouge Bay is just around the corner from Grand Anse Beach as the pelican flies, but given the hilliness of the island, the two bays seem to be miles apart, up and around and around and down a lot of bumpy unpaved roadway.

That's appropriate, because the new Laluna is far removed in style and attitude from any other resort on the island; it's part Bali, part Fantasy Island, part South Beach Miami. It sits on a pretty little beach even most Grenadians have overlooked. Now an Italian fashion guru, Bernardo Bertucci, is hoping it will stay that way so that the 30-odd guests at his funky new hideaway will be able to enjoy unalloyed peace and solitude.

Your first sight of Laluna is startling: a tree-filled hillside falling off to the beach and terraced with clusters of thatch-roofed, splashily colored cottages. But don't ask what colors. The cottages are finished, inside and out, in "an ancient Mediterranean" technique that impregnates the colors into the cement — "blue" becomes cobalt and mauve and lavender all in one wall; "pink" nudges red, coral, cantaloupe, and salmon. The result is slightly disheveled, a look wholly in harmony with Laluna's sandals-and-shorts ambience.

The same kaleidoscope color schemes follow you indoors. These rooms are made for romance, with soft lights, white-netted king-size beds, stereo CD for your own mood music, and indoor/outdoor showers. It's all very "designy" — a wood-framed mirror leans casually against a wall, plump over-sized cushions cover a concrete banquette, and there are teak loungers and Balinese daybeds on the veranda — a mélange of Caribbean, Mediterranean, and Balinese styles (one of the Italian architect-designer team designed Giorgio Armani's home on the island of Pantelleria). Each cottage has its own plunge pool (by the time you get there the new plantings should be full-grown, and it might be really private), which is just as well because apart from the single guest cottage smack dab on the beach, the others are a stiff climb from the beach back up that steep hillside. It's simpler here to tumble back into bed than to go swimming.

Rounding out Laluna's Italian colony is Chef Bernadetto, who sprinkles his lunchtime menu with vegetable burgers and pizzas and his dinners with penne *amatriciana,* seafood Benedetto, and spicy Thai peanut chicken curry. The inn promises Italian vintages from small, undiscovered wineries, but other than a Fantinel Borgo Tesis and an Allegrini Amarone, the curios are more likely to hail from Oregon or New Zealand. If not every evening turns out to be a culinary triumph, all is not lost: You can always walk a few yards along the sand to the Beach House, one of the island's best restaurants.

If peace and solitude are not what you have in mind, give Laluna a pass; if traditional hotel rooms are your idea of bliss, bliss out elsewhere. But for people who appreciate the offbeat and the original, the hip and the chic, here's the hippest, chicest spot on the island. Jot down Laluna as the sort of tucked-away, stylized enclave sought out by lovers willing to sacrifice luxury for chic, or by reclusive celebrities craving solitude, like the English rock star who checked in last winter for 7 days, taking three cottages — one for him, one for the nanny and child, one for the bodyguard.

Name: Laluna
Manager: Charles Hossle
Address: Morne Rouge, P.O. Box 1500, St. George's, Grenada, West Indies
Location: On the southwest corner of the island, about 10 min. and $10 from the airport
Telephone: 473/439-0001
Fax: 473/439-0600
E-mail: info@laluna.com
Web: www.laluna.com

Reservations: 866/452-5862, toll-free direct
Credit Cards: American Express, MasterCard,Visa
Rates: $480–$960 CP (Dec 20–Apr 15); service charge 10%; off season 50% less
Rooms: 16 rooms in 12 cottages, all with air-conditioning and ceiling fans, stereo CD player, minibar, TV/VCR, coffeemaker, direct-dial phone, modem outlet, in-wall safe, indoor/outdoor shower, hair dryer, bathrobe, veranda, and private plunge pool
Meals: Breakfast 7:30am to whenever, lunch noon to whenever, dinner 7–11pm ($80–$100); no dress code ("come barefoot if you like"); quiet recorded jazz or pop music; room service for breakfast only
Entertainment: Library of paperbacks, CDs, and cassettes
Sports: Beach, large freshwater pool, 16 private plunge pools, kayaks, Hobie Cats, windsurfing, snorkeling gear, mountain bikes — all free; in-room massage at extra charge; everything on Grand Anse beach
PS: No children under 10 (except by special request — it might help to be a rock star with a nanny and a bodyguard); cellphones don't work in this hemmed-in location; open year-round

OTHER CHOICES

Twelve Degrees North

GRENADA

Another spot worth looking into, although it's not a full-service hotel, is Twelve Degrees North, a group of eight self-contained apartments (6 with one bedroom, 2 with two bedrooms), each with its own maid who prepares breakfast and lunch, fixes the beds, tidies up, and does your personal laundry, but leaves discreetly at 3pm so that you can have some post-lunch privacy. The apartments are immaculate, attractively decorated with simple island-style furnishings, cooled by ceiling fans rather than air-conditioning, and each has a large dining balcony or patio overlooking L'Anse aux Epines. Your fridge will be stocked for your arrival — anything you don't want you can return the next day. On the beach, at the foot of the hill, you'll find an honor bar, two Sunfishes, a 23-foot launch, two windsurfers, kayaks, a freshwater pool, and a 130-foot pier with four park benches; up top there's a Plexipave tennis court in tip-top condition (but bring your own rackets and tennis balls). Twelve Degrees North, owned and operated by Joe Gaylord, the American who built it and keeps everything running like clockwork, is in the residential area of L'Anse aux Epines, a short taxi ride from several good restaurants for dinner. No children under 15 years old. 8 apartments. Doubles: $230, winter 2002–03 (no credit cards, 1 week minimum stay). *Twelve Degrees North, P.O. Box 241, St. George's, Grenada, West Indies. Telephone and fax: 473/444-4580; e-mail: 12degrsn@caribsurf.com; Web: www.twelvedegreesnorth.com.*

Blue Horizons Cottage Hotel

GRENADA

For many visitors to Grenada, this is simply the garden they pass through on the way to one of the island's finest restaurants, La Belle Créole. Diners have a hillside view over the bay as they sit down to conch scram, Grenadian caviar, and deviled langouste; but lower down, hidden among the saman and cassia trees and coral plants, are 16 unadorned cottages housing 12 no-frills suites and 22 deluxe rooms, all spiffed up with mahogany furniture, new kitchenettes, new beds, even new hair dryers. Gathering spots for guests are the pavilion lounge (TV, parlor games) and the pool bar, shaded by a tall Barringtonia that blossoms for 2 hours every evening at twilight. A short walk from Grand Anse Beach and the shared sports facilities at Spice Island Inn (a sister hotel), Blue Horizons is ideal for lovers on a tight budget; La Belle Créole may not be inexpensive, but lunch around the pool is moderately priced and there are several restaurants within walking distance. 32 air-conditioned rooms and suites. Doubles: $170–$190 EP, winter 2002–03. *Blue Horizons, P.O. Box 41, St. George's, Grenada, West Indies. Telephone: 473/444-4316; fax: 473/444-2815; e-mail: blue@caribsurf.com; Web: www.grenada bluehorizons.com.*

Canouan Beach Hotel

ST. VINCENT-GRENADINES

The beach is the grabber here: about ¼ mile of white palm trees sprouting up at strategic spots for shade, loungers awaiting beneath the fronds, and beyond the gently rolling surf and reef the kind of view that dreams are made of. A grab bag of Grenadines is on the horizon — Mayreau, Union, Palm, the Tobago Cays, even Carriacou. There's another beach to windward on the other side of the property, perfect for long walks at sunset. The inn itself has just the right castaway feel to it — low bungalows with pairs of rooms, simply furnished in French style with wood-framed cot beds, desk/dresser, and chair. There's only air-conditioning, alas, except in the three "Privilege" rooms, which also have paddle fans. For active guests, there's a watersports shack (windsurfing, Hobie Cats, snorkeling, day trips to the Tobago Cays aboard the resort's catamaran), a tennis court with lights, and, for some inexplicable reason, a golf driving range. I didn't see too many active guests, though, and I suspect that most people who come here (Europeans, mostly) spend most of their days lounging around on their patios or on the beach, their evenings lounging around drinking the bartender's ominous specialties — "sex on the beach," "earthquake," or "Long Island iced tea" (vodka, rum, tequila, and triple sec in unspecified quantities). The joy of dining on freshly caught grilled snapper and the castaway ambience of the beachside dining pavilion are flawed by the blaring music — nothing that a couple of Long Island iced teas won't help you ignore. 32 bungalows. Doubles: $400–$460 FAP, winter 2002–03. *Canouan Beach Hotel, South Glossy Bay, Canouan, St. Vincent–Grenadines, West Indies. Telephone: 784/458-8901; fax: 784/458-8875; e-mail: cbh@grenadines.net; Web: www.grenadines.net/canouan/ canouanbeachhotelhomepage.htm.*

Tamarind Beach Hotel

ST. VINCENT-GRENADINES

The resort's centerpiece is a dramatic Amazon-style pavilion with a palapa-thatch roof soaring 30 feet or so above eight ocher columns. A smaller rattan-furnished pavilion houses the open lobby; masses of bougainvillea, palms, and ferns lend their shade to paths leading to the two three-story wings of Brazilian ipe hardwood, with their balconies decorated with gingerbread trim and carved balustrades. The guest rooms are vaguely reminiscent of large state-rooms on classic private yachts — paneled and trimmed in two tones of hard-wood, with lush rugs on hardwood floors and white wicker adding splashes of tropical style. They're simple and tasteful but they come with perks like ceiling fans (some rooms are also air-conditioned), minibars, Internet access, and private safes. Two more thatch pavilions are given over to alfresco dining beside the bay, where the hotel lays Sunfish sailers, hydrobikes, and snorkeling gear. Tamarind Beach is an offshoot of the posh Carenage Bay Resort (see above) and a pleasant option until the main resort is up and running once more — and for people looking to count their pennies a worthwhile alternative at any time. 44 rooms and suites. Doubles: $240–$440 EP, winter 2002–03. *Tamarind Beach Hotel, Charlestown, Canouan, St. Vincent Grenadines, West Indies. Telephone: 877/707-6571 or 784/458-8044; fax: 784/458-8851; e-mail: info@tamarind.us; Web: www.tamarindbeachhotel.com.*

Palm Island

ST. VINCENT-GRENADINES

I loved this place when it was owned by the Caldwell family (or at least before it started to decline), and now it has been resurrected by Rob Barrett, the man who runs Antigua Resorts, including Galley Bay and St. James's Club. The new Palm Island is an all-inclusive, but since there are no other bars or restaurants on this private 135-acre island, that arrangement makes sense. And, like Galley Bay, it doesn't succumb to the pell-mell pleasure-at-all-cost aura of other all-inclusives. The original Palm Island feel is still there: a grand main pavilion in soaring Polynesian style, a collection of islandy bungalows in stone and timber scattered among the casuarina trees that line a breathtaking beach. The cottages have been livened with brighter decor and a few extra amenities (like air-conditioning, but still no TV or telephones), and augmented by new two-story bungalows a few paces from the beach. Another addition is a swimming pool with cascades, but why anyone would want one here, where the water is gorgeously inviting, is a question for another time. Plenty of watersports and trips to surrounding islands. 40 rooms. Doubles: $580–$700, all inclusive, winter 2002–03. *Palm Island, St. Vincent–Grenadines, West Indies. Telephone: 954/481-878; fax: 954/481-1661; e-mail: reservations@ palmislandresorts.com; Web: www.palmislandresorts.com.*

The Dutch Leewards

They're ledges of coral rather than volcanic peaks, they're covered with cacti rather than jungle plants, and they have a personality all their own — part Dutch, part Indian, part Spanish, part just about everything else. They even have their own language, Papiamento, which grabs a few words from any language that happens to come along, shakes them around like a rum punch, and comes up with something as infectiously charming as the people themselves. Thus, *Carne ta camna cabes abou, ma e sa cuant' or tin* means, "He is as innocent as the babe unborn," although the literal translation is, "The sheep walks with its head down, but it knows what time it is"; or *stropi cacalaca,* which means "sweetheart" or "darling," although its literal translation is something quite unsuspected.

Bonaire is the loveliest of the trio, a coral boomerang 24 miles long and 5 miles wide, a world all its own, a world so bright, so luminous from coral and sand that you practically get a suntan just crossing the street. It has more goats than cars, and almost as many flamingos as people; one-third of the island is national park, and another large chunk is salt flats cultivated by Dutch seafarers a couple of centuries ago.

Curaçao is the largest of the three, and its main city, Willemstad, is the capital of all the Netherlands Antilles. Willemstad is utterly unique, almost a miniature Caribbean Amsterdam with gingerbread houses the colors of a coral reef; the historic buildings are being vigorously restored (see Hotel Kura Hulanda, below), and the area around its waterfront is now a UNESCO World Heritage Site.

Aruba is all beach but is unsurpassed by any other island, with mile after mile of some of the whitest sand in the Caribbean. It's the smallest but the liveliest of the Dutch Leewards, with high-rise hotels, nightclubs, casinos, and lots of restaurants to keep you from enjoying the moon and the stars — but, alas, no romantic hideaways.

HOW TO GET THERE Since Aruba is the biggie here, most flights head there first — on American, Continental, Delta, and US Airways, among others. American Eagle recently inaugurated nonstop service between San Juan and Curaçao to augment direct flights from Miami on American, and there are now direct flights to Curaçao on Delta from Atlanta, DCA (the islands' own airline) from St. Maarten, and Air Jamaica via Montego Bay. Bonaire, hitherto the poor relative that always involved a change of plane, now has direct flights on American Eagle from San Juan and on Air Jamaica via Montego Bay. However, one advantage of flying back to the U.S. via Aruba is that you clear U.S. Customs at Aruba before you leave, so there are no hassles when you arrive home. Getting from one island to the next is a cinch — DiviDivi Airlines, for example, flies six-seaters between Bonaire and Curaçao just about every half hour. "They're so reliable," one local tells me, "you can set your watch by them."

For information on Aruba, call 800/862-7822 or visit www.aruba.com; Bonaire, 800/266-2473 or www.infobonaire.com; Curaçao, 800/270-350 or www.curacao-tourism.com.

Avila Beach Hotel **4**
Curaçao Marriott Beach Resort & Emerald Casino **2**
Floris Suite Hotel **1**
Hotel Kurá Hulanda **3**

Hotel Kurá Hulanda

CURAÇAO

☆☆☆
ATMOSPHERE

ᚔ ᚔ ᚔ
DINING

◉
SPORTS

$ $ $
RATES

Every so often (but not nearly often enough) something truly exceptional appears on the scene. Here's a dazzler. And in Curaçao, of all places.

On reflection, why not? Most of the island capital, Willemstad, as I mentioned earlier, is a World Heritage Site, which in itself sets it apart, and its combination of history and charm is just right for a hotel that is also a restoration, a cultural center, and, if one wants to get slightly philosophical about it, a celebration of the human spirit. It's also very romantic.

If you know Willemstad, you know how the city is split in two by the channel leading to the inner harbor, with Punda on one side, and Otrabanda on the other side, with the famous old swing bridge connecting the two. Punda has been well and truly spruced up, with its former Dutch-style warehouses and town houses converted into tax-free stores, fashion boutiques, and smart restaurants; Otrabanda, on the other hand, was falling into decay, except around the cruise-ship pier. Then in 1998, an extraordinary Dutch entrepreneur named Jacob Gelt Dekker came along and bought up a tract of the old district, restored it, and turned it into a complex with a 100-room first-class hotel, three restaurants and three museums, a village square with wooden cafe tables beneath a neem tree — and a dash of magic. All with his own cash, estimated at somewhere between $30 and $40 million — and all within 2½ years.

The 100 or so restored buildings are typically Dutch Colonial — tall facades of yellow and ocher, coral and mustard with contrasting two-tone shutters, lining narrow alleyways paved with *labrilla* tiles from Colombia and custom-designed cobblestones imported by the container-load from Rajasthan, graced with neem and mango trees, filled with statuary and whimsical figurines. Walk this way and you're in a sculpture garden with figures by Peter Chikumbiriki; step into the museum and you move through rooms filled with African art and Mesopotamian artifacts, through a museum recounting the history of slavery and another dedicated to Anne Frank. It's all top-quality stuff, priceless probably, and all the personal property of Mijnheer Dekker.

All of which would be rewarding even if the hotel were a mere youth hostel. It isn't. It's put together with great style and charm and care, with oodles of antiques and artworks. You enter through an elegant lobby furnished with black-and-silver sofas from India and decorated with an antique horse from ancient China and a West Indian woman's head in alabaster. The 100 rooms and suites are all different, nicely combining a sense of place with contemporary perks. Nothing stuffy and historic here: Number 107 is a Spa Loft with a whirlpool tub and a 12-headed shower and TV/VCR in the bathroom; number 118 has terra-cotta floors and Indonesian armchairs and sofas; in number 153 you'll bunk down in a sleigh bed and bathe in a black marble bathroom; another four rooms are lodged in a dainty building in lime-green trimmed with white and set right on the village square. The top-of-the-line Indian Bridal Suite sports a massive maharajah-style, canopy four-poster and hammered sterling handcrafted furniture. The rooms are deployed among several courtyards with statuary and swimming pools that give you the choice of being in the thick of things or tucked away in your own little enclave — if you want quiet, opt for rooms around the Curaçao Garden or Bolivar Pool.

Willemstad is not without interesting restaurants, but I suspect that if I were in town for just two or three nights, I'd take all my meals at Kurá

Hulanda — breakfast in the News Café on the village square, lunch in the patio of the Museum Restaurant, dinners in the jaunty Jaipur with its Rajasthan red decor and open kitchen with an authentic tandoori oven, or in the refined Astrolab Observatory Restaurant with its vitrines of antique navigational instruments and its inviting courtyard terrace beneath a spreading ficus tree.

Kurá Hulanda is one of those enclaves worth the trip in itself. True, there might be times when the alleyways and museums might be awash with schoolchildren or cruise-ship passengers, but they usually leave by early afternoon when you can stroll undisturbed among the Mesopotamian prayer cones and Dogon dancing masks and the pair of canvases from the atelier of Rubens. The great thing about these museums, this heritage site — when you get tired you simply slip off to bed.

Name: Hotel Kurá Hulanda
Manager: Eric Bettelheim
Address: Klipstraat 9, Willemstad, Curaçao, Netherlands Antilles
Location: In Otrabanda, 5 min. on foot from the town center, 15 min. and $16 from the airport by taxi
Tel: 5999/434-7700
Fax: 5999/434-7701
E-mail: kurahulanda@interneeds.net
Web: www.kurahulanda.com
Reservations: Direct
Credit Cards: All major cards
Rates: $199–$1,000 EP (Dec 21–Apr 20); 7% tax and 12% service charge extra; off-season, 10% less
Rooms: 100 in several buildings, all different, some split loft, all with Indian marble bathrooms, air-conditioning (some also with ceiling fans), bathtubs/showers, hair dryers, bathrobes, minibars, direct-dial telephones with Internet access, radio/alarm/CD players, cable TV, safes
Meals: Breakfast 7–11am, lunch 11am–3pm, dinner 6–11pm in a choice of 3 indoor/outdoor restaurants and 1 cafe ($50–$80), room service 7am–11pm, recorded background music in Jaipur, casual dress but "collared shirts and long trousers in Astrolab"
Entertainment: The immediate surroundings, happy hour in Jacob's Bar on the village square, live music somewhere on the property every Wed evening; plus lots of cafes and bars within walking distance
Sports: 3 small swimming pools, fitness center — free; shuttle to Kon-Tiki Beach (with facilities); watersports and golf nearby
PS: Some children; open year-round

Avila Beach Hotel

CURAÇAO

☆☆☆	ΥΥΥ	⑥	$ $
ATMOSPHERE	**DINING**	**SPORTS**	**RATES**

With its jungle greenery and glimpses of sun-dappled patio, this driveway spells "tropics" even before you step inside. "I like to give my guests a feeling of the tropics; I like to find things to make it interesting," says owner Nic Møller. "It" being a four-story colonial governor's mansion built in a time (early 19th c.) when ships had to fire gun salutes for the mansion as they bobbed and tacked down the coast to the great harbor of Curaçao. The impeccably kept mansion — sunburst yellow with white trim and a red-tiled roof — stands next to the octagon-shaped home where Simón Bolívar used to visit his sisters (now beautifully restored by Møller, it could still receive a liberator or governor at a moment's notice). It certainly is interesting.

The lobby area has been brightened with a cultivated Euro-Caribbean air — pastel colors replacing the heavy wood paneling, Oriental rugs blending with smart cane furniture, and a grand piano standing ready for the occasional recital. Wood beams decorate the ceilings; large mirrors are guarded by life-size ceramic hounds.

Follow the sun through this pleasant lobby and you come to a breezy patio-terrace with flagstones and ceramic lamps, a sunshade of twining palms and flamboyant trees, cacti and rubber plants, and white wooden chairs grouped around tables. Farther down, there's a second arbor shading rustic lounging chairs and the inn's signature Schooner Bar, shaped like a ship's prow with a sail projecting from the mast.

Then comes the beach. Here's where a little ingenuity came in: The Avila is indeed on the ocean; but on this stretch of the coastline there's precious little natural beach, so someone fashioned two breakwaters to create two small lagoons, each with a sandy beach. Between the lagoons, a pier leads out to the Blues restaurant and cocktail lounge, perched on stilts over the water. It's a great place to watch sunsets and listen to live jazz. One beach is ringed by a sunbathing terrace and shaded by half a dozen *bohios* (huts); the other is bordered by a promenade lined with benches and tall, iron-poled, orange-capped lanterns that guide you to the edge of the property — perfect for private stargazing and surf listening.

The Danish-descended Møller family, owners of the Avila since 1977, doubled the size of their inn in 1992 with the opening of a completely new wing, La Belle Alliance, which dramatically upgraded the personality of the hotel without destroying the style of the original, now known as Classic Avila. Classic Avila's rooms were refurbished around the same time with striped fabric blinds, wooden beds and couches, framed antique maps, or pretty watercolors. The 30 "standard" rooms in the Classic Avila are fairly small and sunless, in traditional island style; favorite rooms here are the "preferred" rooms on the upper floors, such as rooms 344 and 345, which have terraces for afternoon sunning; and since they're still hitched to the public water supply, the showers

are heated by the sun (don't wait too late in the day to freshen up). In the Belle
Alliance, all 40 deluxe rooms have terraces facing the water; they are pleasantly
designed in tropical fabrics and rattan furniture, and they catch cross breezes
(at least on the upper floors). A few of these rooms and all of the one- and
two-bedroom suites have kitchenettes. There are 20 more suites in the Blues
Wing ("blues" as in jazz, hence the saxophonist motif on each door), which
opened in winter 1996–97 on the western pier. This two-story, all-wood structure offers 20 distinctive deluxe rooms with ocean views, private terraces,
ceramic tile floors, and kitchenettes (I'd opt for rooms number 290 and number 291 at the end of each wing, for the best views). With the new rooms came
two new restaurants, one of them a combination restaurant/jazz bar with live
blues music.

The Avila in any of its incarnations is by no means a grand luxe hotel
(who would believe that the funky little hotel of the '70s now has high-speed
Internet access?), but it's lovely and welcoming, comfortable and efficient,
with more colonial charm than any other hotel on the island. Especially in
the evening, when you sit around the Schooner Bar sipping an Amstel and
the pelicans dive for their supper or a cruise ship passes like a wall of lights.
You'll soon be sitting down on the adjoining Belle Terrace Restaurant to a
dinner of medallions of yellowfin tuna on a fennel fricassee or saffron-
poached red snapper served on spinach fettuccini, beneath an extraordinary
"thatch" roof that's fashioned from a single flamboyant tree. This is classic
Caribbean.

Name: Avila Beach Hotel
Owners/Managers: The Møller Family
Address: P.O. Box 791, Willemstad, Curaçao, Netherlands Antilles
Location: On the outskirts of Willemstad, about 15 min. and $18 from the
airport
Telephone: 5999/461-4377
Fax: 5999/461-1493
E-mail: info@avilahotel.com
Web: www.avilahotel.com
Reservations: 800/747-8162, toll-free direct
Credit Cards: All major cards
Rates: $242–$270 EP (Dec 16–Apr 15); service charge 12%; 7% government
tax, off-season 20% less
Rooms: 100 rooms, including 8 suites; all with air-conditioning, direct-dial
telephones, TV, radios, hair dryers, bathrobes; some deluxe rooms and suites
also have refrigerators, kitchenettes, and Jacuzzi tubs
Meals: Breakfast 7–10am, lunch noon–2pm, dinner 7–10pm at the Belle
Terrace restaurant, beside the beach (about $80) or at the Blues restaurant
on the pier (about $60); casual dress; live music in Blues; room service for
breakfast only at extra charge
Entertainment: Schooner Bar near the beach, Antillean night on Wed, barbecue on Sat with mariachi or steel band, blues band 7–10pm Thurs; music

can sometimes be heard in the guest rooms and on terraces and might disturb your reveries; free shuttle bus to Willemstad on weekdays
Sports: 2 small, pleasant beaches, tennis (1 court, with lights) — free; snorkeling off the beach (bring your own equipment)
PS: Some families on weekends; open year-round

Floris Suite Hotel

CURAÇAO

☆☆	⅄	❻❻	$ $ $
ATMOSPHERE	DINING	SPORTS	RATES

Coming up the flower-decked driveway, swinging into the courtyard, stepping into the spacious, open lobby with its battery of sofas and chairs and colorful cushions, you'd never believe that this place began its career as an Arthur ($5-A-Day) Frommer's hotel, back in the early '70s. A few years ago it was acquired by a wealthy Dutch entrepreneur, and last year it opened as the island's first boutique design hotel, transformed from Cinderella to Princess (well, let's say baroness) by one of Holland's leading designers, Jan de Bouvrie.

Most of the rooms face gardens, but those facing the pool probably have the prettiest views. If you opt for a Loft Suite (the least expensive digs), be aware that the steps to the bedroom are very steep, in the style of Amsterdam town houses — and the bathroom is on the lower floor. Trouble is, for my money the design is dated, without the panache of Soho or South Beach. There's lots of mahogany paneling, which is appropriate for the Caribbean, but Jan des Bouvrie seems to be a lover of rectangles — it's almost like living in a brown-and-white painting by Mondrian. There are plenty of nice touches (pantries, full-size fridges and freezers, ingenious Bouvrie-designed cups and saucers, the Duscholux shower stalls); the gardens have never looked so welcoming, and the new free-form pool is a major enhancement; the dining terrace is pleasant even if you might have too much time to watch the chefs preparing your deep-fried *brie de Meaux* and bouillabaisse in the exhibition kitchen (the Tarte-tatin with dulce de leche is worth the wait). But there are also a few oversights: the absence of ceiling fans in some rooms, the lack of toiletry holders in the showers, the single bar of soap in each room, and infelicitous instructions in the guest orientation folder like "Do not hang damp clothes over the lamp shades." Oversights like these are not unexpected when the people who put the place together are financiers and designers rather than hotel pros, but a savvy new manager, Eric Kortenbach, promises to have these shortcomings straightened out by the time you get there.

There's no beach on the premises, but that's canceled out by a pleasant patch of sand with a watersports shack and beachside restaurant, La Plage Hook's Hut, 7 minutes away on foot (there's shuttle service from the hotel); the pool, surrounded as it is with flowers and gentle cascades, is a lovely and relaxing oasis, even if it's a tad too close to the roadway. If you don't mind not being directly on a beach, if you welcome distinctive surroundings, Floris is an appealing alternative to the Marriott and Hilton. The staff is certainly friendly and eager to please — and get your wake-up calls on time.

Name: Floris Suite Hotel
Manager: Eric Kortenbach
Address: Piscadera Bay, Curaçao, Netherlands Antilles
Location: At Piscadera Bay, near the Marriott and Hilton, about 5 min. from Willemstad (free shuttle), 15 min. and $18 from the airport
Telephone: 5999/462-611
Fax: 5999/462-6211
Reservations: Direct, or 800/337-4685, Design Hotels
E-mail: info@florissuitehotel.com
Web: www.florissuitehotel.com
Credit Cards: American Express, MasterCard, Visa
Rates: $180–$280 EP (Dec 15–Apr 14); 7% tax, 12% service charge extra; off-season 25% less
Rooms: 71 suites (although, despite the name, 40 of them are really large rooms), all with air-conditioning (most also with ceiling fans), kitchens, minibars (on order), coffeemakers, cable TV, direct-dial telephones with dataports, safes, bathrobes (awaiting delivery), hair dryers, most with showers only, most with balcony or patio
Meals: Breakfast 7–10am, lunch 11am–3pm at the pool or Hook's Hut, dinner 6–10pm in Sjalotte (about $80); room service during dining hours at extra charge, casual but smart dress ("no shorts in the dining room"), some recorded or piano music evenings
Entertainment: Some live music but plenty of options across the street at the Marriott or Hilton
Sports: Freshwater pool, tennis (1 court, no lights), small fitness room — all free; watersports at Hook's Hut at extra charge; golf 20 min. away
PS: Not many children; open year-round; no rules regarding cellphones

Curaçao Marriott Beach Resort & Emerald Casino

CURAÇAO

☆ ☆	Y Y	😊 😊	$ $ $
ATMOSPHERE	**DINING**	**SPORTS**	**RATES**

On an island where cacti and gravel are more common than palms and bougainvillea, the manicured lawns and fountains at this Marriott make it as welcome as an oasis. A curving driveway winds around the lawns toward a large, open-sided reception hall, ringed by the usual facilities in this kind of resort — boutiques, casino, lounge, and restaurants. Curving steps lead past a cooling waterfall to an informal, open-air cafe; then to a large, sometimes crowded pool area; and finally to a welcome (if gravelly) beach lined with palm trees and dotted with chiki huts. Lined up parallel to the beach and sprawled over several acres are the Marriott's three-story buildings, designed in Dutch-Caribbean style with ocher-yellow stucco and red-tiled roofs.

Marriott is not usually the kind of place that appears in Caribbean Hideaways: This 10-year-old is a bit big (248 rooms and suites), it welcomes groups and conventions, it's run by a chain, and its interior decor is that style best described as "Deluxe Anywhere." But, the exteriors of the Curaçao Marriott have been designed with unusual sensitivity to blend with the island character, its kitchens offer an unusually high level of cuisine and service, and the best of its rooms afford a decent level of comfort and convenience (although the rooms may be upgraded by the time you get there to keep abreast of Hilton, who've just moved into the old Sheraton along the beach). In any case, it has one of the best beaches on the island — so here it is.

Many guest rooms, though, are short on privacy: The beach-level, ocean-view studio suites, for example, are spacious and attractive, and their glass sliders (no screens, alas) lead directly to private patches of grass furnished with chairs and a table. But anyone can walk past those rooms and peek in — which means I'd have to keep my curtains drawn and air-conditioner switched on to avoid being a potential exhibit for gawkers. These rooms are, of course, the most convenient to the sand and the sea, but some guests might sacrifice a little convenience (and pay a few dollars more) for a deluxe ocean-front room on the second or third floor, with private balconies and lovely views.

Better yet, splurge on one of the eight terrace suites — third floor, corner — each with a separate bedroom and living room and huge terraces (of these, suites 384, 350, 334, and 337 are especially attractive). Not only do the bathrooms have whirlpools, but you can also step from your whirlpool, slide open the glass doors, and dry off on your second terrace, which is just big enough for a chaise lounge.

There's a temptation, in pampering quarters like these, just to call down for room service, but the Marriott happens to have three fine restaurants, each with its own chef and style of cuisine. In the evening, when the bustle quiets down and the conventioneers have trooped off to the casino, the Marriott's beach is positively romantic — dozens of small iron lanterns dot the paths, spotlights illuminate the copse of palm trees, and steady trade winds cool the balmy air. You can easily forget how many people you're sharing with and pretend it's all your own.

Name: Curaçao Marriott Beach Resort & Emerald Casino
Manager: Jorge Landa
Address: Piscadera Bay, P.O. Box 6003, Curaçao, Netherlands Antilles

Location: On the southern coast, 3 miles from Willemstad, 15 min. and $18 from the airport
Telephone: 5999/736-8800
Fax: 5999/462-7502
E-mail: res@marriottcuracao.com
Web: www.marriott.com
Reservations: 800/223-6388, the hotel's U.S. office
Credit Cards: All major cards
Rates: $219–$375 (Jan 3–Apr 6); service charge 19.84%; off-season 30% less
Rooms: 247 rooms and suites, all with balcony or patio, minibar, remote-control TV, clock radio, air-conditioning, direct-dial telephone, some with king-size bed, hair dryer, in-room safe
Meals: Breakfast 7–11am; lunch noon–4pm; bar and dinner, indoor and outdoor, 6–11pm (about $60–$70); casual dress; room service 7am–11pm at extra charge
Entertainment: Caribbean limbo show Wed, seafood buffet with live jazz Fri, casino, sunset cruises, shopping arcade
Sports: Beach, free-form swimming pool with swim-up bar, 2 whirlpools, wading pool, 14-station fitness center, steam room, sauna — all free; kayaks, Sunfish sailers, windsurfing, scuba diving at extra charge; 18-hole golf course, deep-sea fishing charters can be arranged
PS: Supervised program for children; open year-round

Harbour Village Beach Resort

BONAIRE

☆☆   ⅋   ❻❻ $ $ $
ATMOSPHERE   **DINING**   **SPORTS**   **RATES**

Harbour Village Beach Resort has a lot going for it, not the least of which is the laid-back island of Bonaire itself. The island's incredibly clear water and protected coral reefs are world-famous dive destinations; even if you're not a diver, you need only walk out from the hotel's private beach, snorkeling gear in hand, to glimpse some of that precious beauty.

The marina and "village" is situated on the western side of the island, facing the tiny islet of Klein Bonaire and the nightly tropical sunsets, only a few minutes' walk from the dollhouse capital town of Kralendijk. Surprisingly, this side of the island — the entire island, in fact — lacks long, beautiful, sandy beaches, but Harbour Village has solved this problem by creating its own horseshoe-shaped stretch of cool white coral sand dotted with palm trees. At one end of the horseshoe is a fully staffed and equipped dive shop; at the other end sits La Balandra Beach Bar and Grill, its terrace jutting out on a schooner-shaped pier over the water just far enough to catch the trade winds that cool the Bonaire coast.

The resort is laid out village-style, with two-story, cantaloupe-colored stucco buildings and sloping Spanish-tile roofs. Some buildings face the ocean; others look out on the 60-slip marina or gardens. Try for one of the oceanfront rooms; for privacy and view, they're worth it.

Rooms, recently refurbished, are now lighter and more comfortable, decorated with nautical motifs including miniature rowboats in the marina rooms and, at least in the suites, equipped with butler trays and, in some cases, microwaves. Number 325, for example, is a one-bedroom oceanfront suite just a few steps from the beach. The full living room has a comfy sofa, armchair and ottoman, dining area, and cable television; the bedroom has a king-size bed and a second television. In addition, there are two large bathrooms, each with tub and abundant towels, and plenty of closet space stocked with more than enough wooden hangers (a rarity in itself in these parts). The terrace overlooks palm trees and the beach beyond.

The rooms lack cross-ventilation or a truly "island" feel, and the terrace doesn't capture any of those pleasant offshore breezes just a few feet away, since they've installed louvers and screens; you may be able to get by with the ceiling fans without the air-conditioning.

Unfortunately, things have not been thriving here: The Kasa Coral Restaurant is closed, the spa has gone, and about half of the rooms are now privately owned second homes. There are plenty of other restaurants nearby, including the Lighthouse at the far end of the marina; but if you're into spas, there's not much choice elsewhere on the island, and you'll just have to spend your time dozing on the sand beneath one of those palm trees or, if you have a balcony, on your new hammock. But Harbour Village is still a godsend for avid divers who want their comforts ashore, where they can think about all the angelfish and sergeant majors.

Name: Harbour Village Beach Resort
Manager: Frank Gonzalez
Address: P.O. Box 312, Kralendijk, Bonaire, Netherlands Antilles
Location: At Playa Lechi, on the edge of town, about 10 min. from the airport (transfers included)
Telephone: 599/717-7500
Fax: 599/717-7507
E-mail: reservations@harbourvillage.com
Web: www.harbourvillage.com
Reservations: 800/424-0004, First Class Resorts
Credit Cards: All major credit cards
Rates: $315–$595 CP (Dec 15–Apr 15); service charge 15%; off-season 20% less
Rooms: 31, including one-bedroom suites, with balcony or terrace, air-conditioning, ceiling fans (some with louvers and screens), telephones, minifridge, hair dryer, terry-cloth bathrobes, cable TV, safe, hammock, some with shower only

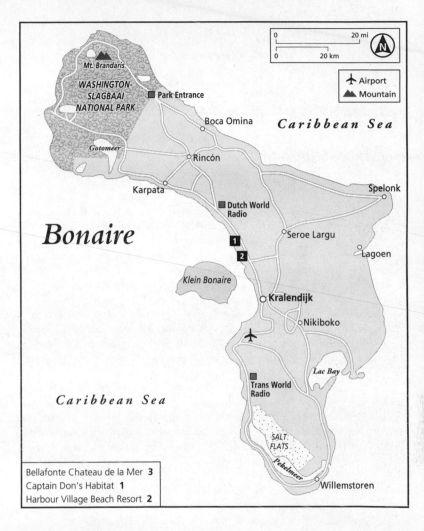

Bellafonte Chateau de la Mer **3**
Captain Don's Habitat **1**
Harbour Village Beach Resort **2**

Meals: Breakfast 7:30–9:30am, lunch noon–3pm, no dinner; informal dress; room service to 3pm at extra charge

Entertainment: Lounge/bar

Sports: Small beach, freshwater pool, fitness center, snorkeling, kayaking, tennis (2 courts, with lights), small-boat sailing — all free; scuba diving (fully equipped dive shop, lessons, 2 scheduled dives daily), deep-sea fishing, powerboat rides, bicycles at extra charge

PS: Some children; cellphones may not be used on diveboats; open year-round

Captain Don's Habitat

BONAIRE

☆	⍦	☉	$
ATMOSPHERE	**DINING**	**SPORTS**	**RATES**

Captain Don's is, first and foremost, top to bottom, a dive resort; and because it happens to be on one of the best dive islands in the world, diving, diving, diving is what all the other guests will be talking about in the bar. But that doesn't mean non-divers will find nothing here to divert them.

On the contrary, as the first dive boat leaves at sunup, non-diving guests will have the pool, vest-pocket beach, and terrace all to themselves for much of the day. Since the main form of nightlife here is night diving, you may well also have the bar and dining terrace to yourself in the evening. If the cuisine is relatively undistinguished, the same can't be said of the lodgings (except for the original Habitat rooms, which should be avoided). Most of the rooms are in contemporary, white stucco, two-story villas spread out along the coral seafront. The best of the bunch are the villa deluxe studios and suites (ground floor, ocean view, with large patios facing the water) and villa superior doubles (second floor, ocean view, many with balconies). Although they lack TV and phones, the rooms do offer space, privacy, and views; the suites and studios have fully equipped kitchens. Room number 601 is particularly appealing: A villa deluxe suite, it has a large bedroom with king-size bed, full living room, dinette, and kitchenette, plus a lovely patio a few steps from the water, but set back just far enough to give you some privacy.

The Captain Don of the title is Don Stewart, a Californian who sailed into Bonaire back in the 1960s. I first met him in the early 1970s when he was moonlighting as bartender at the old Flamingo Beach Hotel. This was no ordinary bar (the Flamingo had functioned as a prisoner-of-war camp during World War II), and Don was the island's leading dive master and raconteur— and conservationist: Long before it was the fashionable thing to do, Don was lobbying Caribbean governments and fellow divers to ban spear guns and the chipping of coral for souvenirs. That Bonaire still has some of the finest reefs and a trendsetting conservation policy is largely due to Don's efforts. If you're a diver, you probably know that; if you're not, go ask Captain Don.

Name: Captain Don's Habitat
Manager: Jack Chalk
Address: P.O. Box 88, Kralendijk, Bonaire, Netherlands Antilles
Location: On the leeward side of the island, about 10 min. and $12 from the airport
Telephone: 599/717-8290
Fax: 599/717-8240
E-mail: bonaire@habitatdiveresort.comb
Web: www.habitatdiveresorts.com
Reservations: 800/327-6709, the hotel's U.S. office
Credit Cards: American Express, Diners Club, MasterCard, Visa

Rates: $180–$210 (Dec 20–Apr 4); service charge included; off-season 20% less

Rooms: 82 rooms and suites, plus full villas, all with air-conditioning, some with ceiling fans, some with balcony or patio, some with kitchenette, some with phones and TV

Meals: Breakfast 7–10am, lunch 11am–2pm, pizzas 3–10pm, dinner 7–10pm at Rum Runners overlooking the water (about $40–$50); casual dress; no room service

Entertainment: Recorded music at dinner, slide shows, theme buffets, and special entertainment nights during the week

Sports: Small beach, pool — free; fully equipped dive facility with scuba and snorkeling equipment for rent or sale, dive certification courses available, fishing charters at extra charge

PS: This hotel is primarily a dive facility that attracts serious divers

OTHER CHOICES

Bellafonte Chateau de la Mer

BONAIRE

"I try to do things differently," says Sjoerd Vanderbrug, co-owner/developer/manager/host of the Mediterranean-style complex that's subtitled Chateau de la Mer. Different because it doesn't have a dive shop (although it does have rinse tanks, outside showers, and secured storage), doesn't have a pool, doesn't have a restaurant. What it does have are 14 spacious, comfortable studios and apartments on three floors (no elevator), all done with a sense of style (pattern Portuguese tile floors, paneled doors, imported mahogany tables from Indonesia, original artwork by a local expat), all with full kitchens, electric barbecues, TVs, phones, and safes. Since the rear rooms are close to the roadway (hardly the NY Thruway) and the airport (hardly JFK), the windows are specially sealed and, despite the ceiling fans, the rooms are designed for air-conditioning. These apartments are the most luxurious lodgings on the island, and reasonably priced because there's only a wooden pier and crystal clear swimming hole substituting for a pool and beach (there are beaches within walking distance) and the nearest dining spots are in town. You'll need a car for a few days at least. The rest of the time, just laze around and read, although Vanderbrug can arrange all sorts of trips by land and sea, tell you where to get your groceries, tell you where to eat out. The name? Apparently Harry Belafonte used to own a chunk of property around here, but by changing the spelling, it's now Beautiful Fountain to match the one in the entranceway. 14 apartments. $150–$365, no meals, winter 2003–04. *Bellafonte Chateau de la Mer, EEG Boulevard 10, Bonaire, Dutch West Indies. Telephone: 599/717-3333; fax: 599/717-8581; e-mail: info@bellafontebonaire.com; Web: www.bellafontebonaire.com.*

All-Inclusive Resorts

A QUICK RUNDOWN OF SOME PLACES YOU WON'T BE EMBARRASSED TO STAY IN

When I set out to research the first edition of this guidebook back in 1972 or thereabouts, I went to Negril in Jamaica to check out the recently launched Hedonism all-inclusive resort. Mistake! It was midday on a Sunday, but it might as well have been midnight, with music blasting and skimpily clad couples gyrating and whooping and nobody paying the slightest attention to the gorgeous beach. Dante's Inferno meets Spring Break. I reeled out and swore off all-inclusives evermore.

But raucous Hedonism wasn't the sole reason I shunned all-inclusives (nothing wrong with a little bit of hedonism now and then, after all). They seemed to me to contradict one of the main reasons for going to the Caribbean in the first place — to get out and about and see something of other peoples and other cultures. Because guests pay for everything up front, there is little incentive to leave the compound because that would mean paying extra for drinks and meals already paid for.

In recent years, the all-inclusive concept has spread briskly ("all-inclusive," by the way, meaning resorts that throw in everything, including wine and liquor for one price), both geographically and demographically. The idea took root in Jamaica, but you'll find such places throughout most of the islands now; they began for couples only, but they now offer special facilities for families, singles, and senior citizens. Some of them do, indeed, now encourage guests to get out and see something of the islands by organizing complimentary sightseeing tours, supplying bikes and picnics, or arranging dine-around plans that allow guests to eat in local restaurants at no extra cost.

Because the basic concept — everything for a fixed price with no surprises, no fussing, no tipping, and so on — seems to have wide appeal, I herewith pass along a few observations on some of the all-inclusives that readers of this guide might like to consider should they decide to sample this kind of vacation. But be warned that "all-inclusive" means different things to different resorts — some include spa treatments, for example, and some do not. I should also mention that several of the Caribbean's traditional resorts have decided either to offer all-inclusive plans along with their regular rates or to go whole hog and eliminate a lot of bookkeeping by offering guests wine, liquor, and sports facilities — in some cases, even laundry. This makes them, in essence, all-inclusive resorts, although they do not necessarily identify themselves as such. A few of them are already discussed in this guide, such as Curtain Bluff on Antigua, to name one standout.

Note: In the following listings, all rates are for peak season, winter 2002–03, for one night unless specified otherwise, although there is usually a 4- to 7-night minimum stay. Most of the resorts also have package plans that include airfare, which will reduce the actual rates listed here.

ST. JAMES'S CLUB, ANTIGUA   It opened to great, celebrity-studded fanfare in 1985 — gratis — but unlike places like La Samanna and Malliouhana, the St. James's Club never really caught on with the celebrities once they had to start paying for their rooms. Now, as part of the all-inclusive empire of Rob Barrett, it offers two beaches, three freshwater pools, gym, watersports, and seven tennis courts. The resort's lodgings include rooms in 3 three-story blocks between the beaches and 73 two-bedroom villas on the hillside above the lagoon. With 100 acres of grounds, there's space for everyone — but don't expect swift service. 200 rooms and suites. Doubles $520–$860, with everything, more or less, included. *St. James's Club, P.O. Box 63, St. John's, Antigua, West Indies. Telephone: 800/858-4618; fax: 268/460-3015; e-mail: reservations@eliteislandresorts.com; Web: www.eliteislandresorts.com.*

GRAND LIDO NEGRIL, NEGRIL, JAMAICA   Probably the most posh of the all-inclusives, owned by SuperClubs, the outfit that started it all. One of its two beaches is reserved for nude sunbathing; hot tubs with bars/cafes are dotted among the trees; air-conditioned guest rooms come with TVs, CD players, and Internet access; guests can take a sundown cruise on the 150-foot yacht on which Prince Rainier and Princess Grace honeymooned. For adults (couples and singles). 210 suites. Doubles $525–$680. *Grand Lido Negril, Norman Manley Boulevard, Negril, Jamaica, West Indies. Telephone: 800/467-8737; fax: 876/957-5517; e-mail: GLN@800gosuper.com; Web: www.superclubs.com.*

COUPLES SWEPT AWAY, NEGRIL, JAMAICA   Swept Away is Grand Lido's near neighbor — for some guests its more appealing neighbor because its guest rooms are designed for the breezes, with fans and lots of louvers looking out on masses of tropical greenery (air-conditioning is there as a backup). The tennis and fitness center across the road is considered one of the finest in the Caribbean (it comes with a fitness center and racquetball and squash courts). Two restaurants, five bars, watersports. 134 rooms. Doubles $765–$1,035. *Couples Swept Away, P.O. Box 37, Long Bay, Negril, Jamaica, West Indies. Telephone: 800/268-7537; fax: 876/957-4060; e-mail: sweptaway@info chan.com; Web: www.couples.com.*

GRAND LIDO SANS SOUCI, OCHO RIOS, JAMAICA There's a Riviera-like quality to this coral-and-white resort, operated by SuperClubs and set among terraced gardens rising above and beside the beach, with a mineral pool at one level, a freshwater pool at another, and a dining terrace up top. Charlie's Spa offers, among other indulgences, alfresco massage in a gazebo beside the sea. Facilities include formal and casual dining, tennis, and assorted watersports. 146 rooms and suites. Doubles from $540. *Grand Lido Sans Souci, P.O. Box 103, Ocho Rios, Jamaica, West Indies. Telephone: 800/467-8737; fax: 876/ 974-2544; e-mail: GLS@800gosuper.com; Web: www.superclubs.com.*

THE BODY HOLIDAY AT LESPORT, ST. LUCIA Located at Cap Estate on the northern tip of the island in a secluded bay, LeSport is dedicated to the "Body Holiday," as they put it, with an imposing hilltop spa, the Oasis, for gosh-that's-nice treatments. To celebrate its 10th anniversary in 2000, the resort added seven Luxury Ocean Front Junior Suites, 18 Luxury Ocean Front Rooms, and a new holistic temple at the Oasis, adding ayurveda, iridology, and advanced reflexology massage, among others, to the repertoire of treatments (one 50-minute treatment per person per day included in the rate). Your personal Body Guide helps you plot strategies for new lifestyle habits (diet, exercise, relaxation, that sort of thing). But for spouses and companions who don't want to be structured, slapped around, or dunked in seaweed, there's also a full roster of watersports, tennis, archery, golf (just 5 minutes away, greens fees and shuttle included), and visits to the fitness center and sauna. And its Tao Restaurant is quickly gaining a reputation as one of the most refined dining spots in the Caribbean. 154 rooms and suites. Doubles $460–$1,156. *LeSport, P.O. Box 437, Castries, St. Lucia, West Indies. Telephone: 800/544-2883; fax: 758/ 450-0368; e-mail: tropichol@aol.com; Web: www.thebodyholiday.com.*

LA SOURCE, GRENADA It's a health-oriented cousin to LeSport in St. Lucia but less formal, more a beach hotel with spa and fitness facilities than a true spa, and, for many, it's also more attractive than LeSport. Opened in 1993 on 40 hilly acres in a lovely cove setting called Pink Gin Beach, La Source is stylishly furnished with four-poster beds and wall-to-wall windows facing the sea. A limo picks you up at the airport, just minutes away; the staff is lively and friendly, the atmosphere informal and fun, and the clientele mostly couples, many of them all the way from Britain. The food, if not truly gourmet, is plentiful, and the terrace of the Great House restaurant, overlooking the water, is appropriately romantic. Spa treatments, including aromatherapy massages and facials, are limited to one per day per guest (and strictly scheduled), but you can put in as many hours as you can muster on the nine-hole pitch-and-putt course, the tennis courts, and the watersports toys. For my money, the luxury oceanfront suites, with corner rooms with sitting areas and lovely little balconies, are worth the splurge — you can cuddle all night to the crashing of the waves beneath your window and wake up to unobstructed views of the ocean, all in absolute privacy. 100 rooms and suites. Doubles $440–$690. *La Source, P.O. Box 852, St. George's, Grenada, West Indies. Telephone: 888/527-0044 or 473/444-2556; fax: 473/444-2561; e-mail: tropichol@aol.com; Web: www.la sourcegrenada.com.*

RENDEZVOUS, ST. LUCIA Subtitled "The escape for romantics," Rendezvous is the antithesis of the early all-inclusives like Hedonism — this one is strictly for couples in search of low-key privacy. With just 100 rooms and suites, Rendezvous is an oasis of serenity with landscaped gardens set beside the beach and sea. The range of lodgings includes seaside lanais, ocean-front cottages, veranda suites, luxury rooms with ocean views, and 36 rooms with garden views — something for everyone, in other words. Four-poster beds, dimmer lights, and body showers for two set the right romantic tone. Quiet the place may be, but not dull — the two restaurants, offering indoor and outdoor dining, are augmented with live music for barbecue and Caribbean nights, and the piano bar keeps things humming until 2am. By day, guests are pampered with a swim-up bar, a beachside bar, and fruit icicles delivered to sun worshippers every afternoon. Active lovers have access to two pools, watersports, a fitness center, tennis, golf, biking, archery, spa treatments in open-air gazebos — even dance classes. With so much to enjoy, you'll probably find the rates among the resort's biggest attractions. 100 rooms and suites. Doubles $416–$600. *Rendezvous, Malabar Beach, P.O. Box 190, Castries, St. Lucia, West Indies. Telephone: 800/544-2883; fax: 758/452-7419; e-mail: tropcihol@aol.com; Web: www.rendezvous.com.lc.*

TURTLE BEACH, BARBADOS Opened in January 1998 on the south coast of Barbados, Turtle Beach Resort tucks just 166 rooms and suites in a quiet plot fronting 1,500 feet of beach. A coral-and-white, three-story struc-ture with a big open lobby that leads to a three-story restaurant, this is one of the most stylish all-inclusive resorts in the islands. The tasteful, tile-floored guest rooms are unusually spacious — the smallest measure around 160 square feet, with an additional 12×12-foot terrace, partly in the shade and partly in the open for sunning. The resort has three eating spots, but the Chalonia Dining Room can hold its own, for service and cuisine, with the finest restaurants on the island (for example, my young waiter asked me if I wanted my cappuccino with dessert or after — a courtesy you don't always find even in top restaurants in Manhattan). Sports facilities include two ten-nis courts, gym, three pools, sailing, boogie-boarding, windsurfing, and scuba (the latter costs extra). 166 rooms and suites. Doubles $593–$916. *Turtle Beach Resort, Christ Church, Barbados. Telephone: 800/326-6898 or 246/428-7131; fax: 246/428-6089; e-mail: turtlebeach@eleganthotels.com.bb; Web: www.eleganthotels. com/turtle/turtle.htm.*

Reservations & Tourist Information

THE REPS

Hotel representatives keep tabs on the availability of rooms in the hotels they represent and handle reservations and confirmations at no extra charge to you (unless you wait until the last minute and they have to send faxes or make phone calls back and forth, in which case you'll be charged). The reps who have appeared most frequently in these pages are listed below; in the interest of simplicity, only the main offices are listed for each one. They're useful people to know: If you're trying to make a reservation for a peak period or at the last minute, and your first choice is not available, chances are they can find you something similar — saving you the trouble of phoning and faxing half a dozen hotels.

American Wolfe International
1890 Palmer Ave.
Larchmont, NY 10543
800/223-5695 or 914/833-3303
Fax: 914/833-3308

Caribbean Inns, Ltd.
P.O. Box 7411
Hilton Head Island, SC 29938
800/633-7411 or 803/785-7411
Fax: 803/686-7411
site@caribbeaninns.com
www.caribbeaninns.com

Design Hotels
323 B Pine St.
Sausalito, CA 94965
800/337-4685
www.designhotels.com

Elegant Resorts International
Box 800
Montego Bay, Jamaica
West Indies
800/237-3237

International Travel & Resorts
300 E. 40th St.
New York, NY 10016
800/223-9815 or 212/476-9444
Fax: 212/476-9452

Island Destinations
1875 Palmer Ave., Suite 209
Larchmont, NY 10538
800/729-9599 or 914/833-3300
Fax: 914/833-3318

JDB Associates
P.O. Box 16086
Alexandria, VA 22302-6086
800/346-5358
Fax: 703/548-5825

Karen Bull & Associates
3355 Lenox Road NE, Suite 750
Atlanta, GA 30326
800/250-8017
karenbull@mindspring.com

Leading Hotels of the World
747 Third Ave.
New York, NY 10017
800/223-6800 or 212/838-3110
Fax: 212/758-7367
info@lhw.com
www.lhw.com

Ralph Locke Islands
P.O. Box 492477
Los Angeles, CA 90049
800/223-1108
Fax: 310/440-4220
caribisles@aol.com
www.caribisles.com

Robert Reid Associates
810 N. 96th St.
Omaha, NE 68114-2594
800/223-6510 or 402/398-3218
Fax: 402/398-5484

Small Luxury Hotels of the World
800/525-4800
www.slh.com

WIMCO
Box 1461
Newport, RI 02840
800/932-3222 or 401/849-8012
Fax: 401/847-6290
www.wimco.com
www.wimco.com/email/geninquiry.asp

TOURIST INFORMATION

The function of this guide is to give you facts and tips on where to stay, rather than what to see; there just isn't space to cover both. In any case, with the exceptions of islands like Puerto Rico, Jamaica, and a few others, there really isn't much to see — a fort, a volcano, a native market or two. Many of the major sightseeing attractions (and a few offbeat sights) are mentioned in these pages; if you want more information on topics like shopping and sightseeing, I suggest you get in touch with the tourist office of the islands that interest you.

The other possibility is to contact the Caribbean Tourism Organization (80 Broad St., 32nd floor, New York, NY 10004; 212/635-9530 or www.DoIt Caribbean.com) for basic, sometimes biased, information on most of the islands.

Index

Accommodations. *See also*
specific destinations
air-conditioning, xvi
double beds, xxvii
doubling up, xxiii
kitchens, xxiii
money-saving tips, xxii–xxiv
in "Other Choices" sections, xxvii
package deals, xxiii–xxiv, xxxviii
rates, xxxv–xxxviii
ratings, xxiv–xxvii
rebates on meals, xxxvi–xxxvii
reservations, xx–xxi
service charges, xxxvii
signing in, xix–xx
taxes, xxxvii
The Admiral's Inn (Antigua),
160–162
Air Canada, xxx, 16, 22, 124, 208, 250
Air Caraïbes, xxxii–xxxiii, 174
Air-conditioning, xvi
Airfares, xxiv
Air Jamaica, xxx, xxxi, 2, 16, 22, 124,
208, 209, 250, 280
Air Jamaica Express, 35, 36, 38
Air travel, xxx–xxxiv. *See also*
specific destinations
within the Caribbean, xxxi
All-inclusive resorts, 295–298
Altos de Chavon (Dominican
Republic), 52

American Airlines, xxx, xxxi, 2, 16, 22,
50, 56, 108, 124, 208, 209, 250, 280
American Eagle, xxxi, 56, 86, 124,
125, 174, 209, 250, 280
American Wolfe International, 299
Anacaona Restaurant (Turks &
Caicos), 8
Anegada Reef Hotel, 103–104
Anguilla, 124
Cap Juluca, 129–131
CoveCastles Villa Resort, 133–134
CuisinArt Resort & Spa, 134–136
La Sirena Hotel, 131–133
Malliouhana Hotel, 125–129
map, 126–127
traveling to, 125
Anse Chastanet Beach Hotel
(St. Lucia), 214–216
Antigua, 123–124
The Admiral's Inn, 160–162
Blue Waters, 165–166
Cocobay, 172
The Copper & Lumber Store
Hotel, 171
Curtain Bluff, 157–159
Galley Bay, 163–165
Harmony Hall, 172
The Inn at English Harbour,
159–160
Jumby Bay Resort, 154–156

Antigua *(continued)*
　map, 155
　St. James's Club, 296
　Siboney Beach Club, 162–163
　tourist information, 125
　traveling to, 124–125
Aruba, 280
　tourist information, 280
　traveling to, 280
Auberge Les Petits Saints (Terre de Haut), 204–205
Aveda Concept Spa (Jamaica), 40
Avila Beach Hotel (Curaçao), 284–286

Bamboo Beach Bar, The (Jamaica), 48
Barbados, 207, 208
　Cobblers Cove, 228–229
　Coral Reef Club, 221–224
　Fairmont Glitter Bay, 224–226
　Fairmont Royal Pavilion, 226–227
　Hotel Little Good Harbour, 238–239
　The House, 233–235
　Lone Star, 246
　map, 223
　The Sandpiper, 230–231
　Sandy Lane, 231–233
　The Savannah, 245–246
　tourist information, 209
　traveling to, 208
　Turtle Beach, 298
　Villa Nova Hotel, 235–237
Barbuda
　K Club, 166–169
　map, 167
　tourist information, 125
Bartoloméo Restaurant (St. Barths), 190
Basse-Terre, 174, 194
Beach Café (Tortola), 88
Beach Grill (Peter Island), 92
Bellafonte Chateau de la Mer (Bonaire), 293
Belle Terrace Restaurant (Curaçao), 285
Bequia, 248
　The Frangipani, 257–258
　Plantation House Hotel, 256–257
　Spring on Bequia, 254–255

Biras Creek Resort (Virgin Gorda), 98–101
The Bitter End Yacht Club (Virgin Gorda), 101–103
Blue Haven Hotel (Tobago), 241–243
Blue Horizons Cottage Hotel (Grenada), 276
Blue Waters (Antigua), 165–166
Boat travel, xxxiv
The Body Holiday at Lesport (St. Lucia), 297
Bomba Charger, M/V, xxxiv
Bonaire, 280
　Bellafonte Chateau de la Mer, 293
　Captain Don's Habitat, 292–293
　Harbour Village Beach Resort, 289–290
　map, 290–291
　tourist information, 280
　traveling to, 280
Britannia (Cayman Islands), 18
Britannia Golf Club & Grille (Cayman Islands), 18
British Virgin Islands, 58, 85–105. *See also* **Tortola; Virgin Gorda**
　Anegada Reef Hotel, 103–104
　Guana Island, 94–96
　map, 87
　tourist information, 86
The Buccaneer (St. Croix), 81–82, 84
BWIA (British West Indies Airways), xxx, xxxi, 124, 208, 209, 250

Café, The (St. Thomas), 80
Cafe Bohemio (Puerto Rico), 66
Cafe del Nispero (Puerto Rico), 66
Café Taboras (Barbados), 227
The Calabash Hotel (Grenada), 269–270
Caneel Bay (St. John), 71–72, 74–75
Canouan, 248, 276–277
Canouan Beach Hotel (St. Vincent-Grenadines), 276–277
Cape Air, xxxii, 56, 86
Cap Juluca (Anguilla), 129–131
Captain Don's Habitat (Bonaire), 292–293
Caribbean Express, xxxiv
Caribbean Inns, Ltd., 299

Caribbean Paradise Inn (Turks & Caicos), 11–12
Caribbean Star, xxxii, 209, 250
Caribbean Sun, xxxii, 86
Caribbean Tourism Organization, 301
Casa de Campo (Dominican Republic), 50, 52–53
Casinos, Wyndham Martineau Bay Resort & Spa (Puerto Rico), 69
Catalina Island (Dominican Republic), 53
The Caves (Jamaica), 43–45
Cayman Ball, 18
Cayman Islands, 15–19
  Hyatt Regency Grand Cayman, 16, 18–19
  map, 17
  tourist information, 16
  traveling to, 16
Cellular phones, xviii–xix
Charlotte Amalie, 56
Children, xix
Christiansted, 56
The Clubhouse (Virgin Gorda), 102
Cobblers Cove (Barbados), 228–229
Cockburn Town (Grand Turk), 2
Cocobay (Antigua), 172
Continental Airlines, xxx, 16, 22, 56, 108, 124, 280
Conventions, xix
Cooperage Dining Room (Nevis), 153
The Copper & Lumber Store Hotel (Antigua), 171
Coral Reef Club (Barbados), 221–224
The Cottage Club (Saba), 122
The Cotton House Hotel (Mustique), 259–261
Couples Swept Away (Jamaica), 296–297
CoveCastles Villa Resort (Anguilla), 133–134
Coyaba Beach Resort & Club (Jamaica), 46
CP (Continental Plan), xxxvi
Crime, xxviii–xxix
Cruise ship passengers, xvi–xvii
Cruz Bay (St. John), 56
CuisinArt Resort & Spa (Anguilla), 134–136

Curaçao, 280
  Avila Beach Hotel, 284–286
  Curaçao Marriott Beach Resort Emerald Casino, 287–289
  Floris Suite Hotel, 286
  Hotel Kurá Hulanda, 281–283
  map, 281
  tourist information, 280
  traveling to, 280
Curaçao Marriott Beach Resort & Emerald Casino, 287–289
Curtain Bluff (Antigua), 157–159

Daphne's Barbados, 234
Deadman's Bay (Peter Island), 91
Delta Airlines, xxx, 2, 16, 22, 56, 108, 280
Deposits, with reservations, xxi–xxii
Design Hotels, 300
The Dining Room (St. Thomas), 80
Dollar signs, in rating system, xxvi
Dominica, 207
  Exotica, 243
  Fort Young, 244
  map, 245
  tourist information, 209
Dominican Republic, 49–53
  Casa de Campo, 50, 52–53
  map, 51
  tourist information, 50
Dorado (Puerto Rico), Hyatt Dorado Beach Resort & Country Club, 58–60
Double beds, xxvii
Dress code, for restaurants, xxv–xxvi
The Dutch Leewards, 279–293
The Dutch Windwards, 107–122. *See also* Saba; St. Martin
  map, 109
  traveling to, 108

East Winds Inn (St. Lucia), 211–213
Elegant Resorts International, 300
El Picetao (Puerto Rico), 66
English Harbour (Antigua), 124
EP (European Plan), xxxvi
Esperanza (Vieques, Puerto Rico), 70
Exotica (Dominica), 243

Fairmont Glitter Bay (Barbados), 224–226

Fairmont Royal Pavilion (Barbados), 226–227

FAP (Full American Plan), xxxvi

FAP+ (Full American Plan with extras), xxxvi

Ferries, xxxiv
Bequia, 250
British Virgin Islands, 86

Filao Beach Hotel (St. Barths), 184–186

Firefly (Mustique), 262–263

Florentine Room (St. Thomas), 80

Floris Suite Hotel (Curaçao), 286–287

Fort-de-France, 174

Fort Young (Dominica), 244

Four Seasons Nevis Resort, 144–148

François Plantation (St. Barths), 175

The Frangipani (Bequia), 257–258

Frégate Bleue Inn (Martinique), 203

Frenchman's Cay Resort Hotel (Tortola), 105

Frenchman's Cove Beach (Jamaica), 38

French West Indies, 173–205. *See also* Guadeloupe; St. Barthélemy (St. Barts)
Hotel La Cohoba (Marie Galante), 196–197

Fungi's (St. Thomas), 76

Galley Bay (Antigua), 163–165

Garden Loggia (Cayman Islands), 18

Garden Restaurant (Tortola), 88

Gauguin Restaurant (Antigua), 164

Goblets, in rating system, xxv

Golden Door Spa (Puerto Rico), 67

Goldeneye (Jamaica), 33–35

The Golden Lemon (St. Kitts), 136–139

Golden Rock (Nevis), 150–151

Golf
Britannia (Cayman Islands), 18
Casa de Campo (Dominican Republic), 50
Half Moon Golf, Tennis & Beach Club (Jamaica), 29
Hyatt Dorado Beach Resort & Country Club (Puerto Rico), 59
The Tryall Club (Jamaica), 27

Grace Bay Beach (Turks & Caicos), 12

Grace Bay Club (Turks & Caicos), 7–9

Grace's Cottage (Turks & Caicos), 10

Grand Cayman, Hyatt Regency Grand Cayman, 16, 18–19

Grand Cul-de-Sac Bay (St. Barths), 189

Grande-Terre, 174

Grand Lido Negril (Jamaica), 296

Grand Lido Sans Souci (Jamaica), 297

Grand View Beach Hotel (St. Vincent), 253–254

Grantley Adams International Airport (Barbados), 208

Grenada, 247, 248
Blue Horizons Cottage Hotel, 276
The Calabash Hotel, 269–270
Laluna, 273–275
La Source, 297–298
map, 249
Secret Harbour Resort, 270–271
Spice Island Beach Resort, 271–273
tourist information, 250
traveling to, 250
Twelve Degrees North, 275

The Grenadines. *See* St. Vincent-Grenadines

Grenadines Air, 250

Guadeloupe, 174
Hôtel Saint-Georges, 195–196
map, 192–193
tourist information, 175
traveling to, 174–175

Guana Island, 94–96

Gustavia, 174

Habitation Lagrange (Martinique), 197–198, 200

Half Moon Golf, Tennis & Beach Club (near Montego Bay), 28–31

Half Moon Shopping Village (Jamaica), 29

Hamilton, Alexander, 124, 151

Harbour Village Beach Resort (Bonaire), 289–290

Harmony Hall (Antigua), 172

Hemingways (Cayman Islands), 18

Hermitage Plantation Inn (Nevis), 151–153

Hibiscus Beach Hotel (St. Croix), 84
Honeymoon packages, xxiii
The Horned Dorset Primavera
(Puerto Rico), 60–63
Horseshoe Reef, 102
Hôtel Cap Est Lagoon Resort
(Martinique), 203
Hôtel Carl Gustaf (St. Barths), 177–179
Hôtel Eden Rock (St. Barths), 186–187
Hotel El Convento (Puerto Rico),
65–67
Hôtel Emeraude Plage (St. Barts), 202
Hôtel Guanahani (St. Barths), 189–190
Hotel Kurá Hulanda (Curaçao),
281–283
Hôtel La Cohoba (Marie Galante),
196–197
Hotel La Plantation (St. Martin),
115–116
Hotel L'Esplanade Caraïbe
(St. Martin), 121
Hôtel Le Toiny (St. Barths), 181–183
Hotel Little Good Harbour
(Barbados), 238–239
Hôtel Manapany Cottages
(St. Barths), 183–184
Hotel Mocking Bird Hill (Jamaica),
37–39
Hoôtel Plantation Leyritz
(Martinique), 204
Hotels. *See* Accommodations
Hôtel St. Barth Isle de France
(St. Barths), 179–181
Hôtel Saint-Georges (Guadeloupe),
195–196
The House (Barbados), 233–235
Hurricane Cove Bungalows (Nevis),
169–170
Hyatt Regency Cerromar Beach
Resort & Casino (Puerto Rico), 58
Hyatt Regency Grand Cayman
(Cayman Islands), 16, 18–19

Idle Awhile (Jamaica), 48
Il Giardino (Jamaica), 30
IN Cafe (Anguilla), 132
Indigo Beach Restaurant
(St. Barths), 190

The Inn at English Harbour
(Antigua), 159–160
Insect repellent, xxvii
Inter-Island Airways, Salt Cay, 13
International Travel & Resorts, 300
Irish Town (Jamaica), Stawberry Hill,
39–41
Island Destinations, 300

Jake's (Jamaica), 42–43
Jalousie Hilton Resort & Spa
(St. Lucia), 219–221
Jamaica, 21–48. *See also* Montego Bay;
Negril; Ocho Rios; Port Antonio
Goldeneye (Oracabessa), 33–35
Jake's (Treasure Beach), 42–43
map, 23
Stawberry Hill (Irish Town), 39–41
tourist information, 22
traveling to, xxxi, 22
Jamaica Inn (Jamaica), 31–33
The Jamaica Palace Hotel
(Port Antonio), 45–46
JDB Associates, 300
JetBlue, xxx, 56
Jost Van Dyke, Sandcastle Hotel,
104–105
Jumby Bay Resort (Antigua), 154–156

Kai M'jame (St. Lucia), 213–214
Karen Bull & Associates, 300
K Club (Barbuda), 166–169
KiYara Ocean Spa (Jamaica), 32
Krizia, 166–168
Kurland, David, 63

La Baguette (Jamaica), 30
La Belle Créole (Grenada), 276
La Belle France (St. Martin), 113
Ladera Resort (St. Lucia), 217–218
La Gaiac (St. Barths), 182
Laluna (Grenada), 273–275
La Romana (Dominican Republic),
Casa de Campo, 50, 52–53
La Samanna (St. Martin), 110–112
Las Casitas Village (Puerto Rico),
67–68

Las Croabas (Puerto Rico), Las
   Casitas Village, 67–68
La Sirena Hotel (Anguilla), 131–133
La Source (Grenada), 297–298
La Veranda restaurant (St.
   Martin), 113
Leading Hotels of the World, 300
Le Bistro (Puerto Rico), 62
Leeward Islands Air Transport, xxxii
Le Jardin Malanga (Guadeloupe),
   192–195
Le Meridien (St. Martin), 112–114
Le Mississippi (St. Martin), 114–115

Mille Fleurs Restaurant (Jamaica), 38
Money-saving tips, xxii–xxiv
Montego Bay (Jamaica)
   Coyaba Beach Resort & Club, 46
   Half Moon Golf, Tennis & Beach
      Club, 28–31
   Round Hill Hotel & Villas, 22, 24–26
   The Tryall Club, 26–28
Montpelier Plantation Inn (Nevis),
   148–150
Montserrat, 124, 125
Morgan, Jeff and Jinx, 89
Mosquitoes, xxvii
Mount Irvine Bay Hotel & Golf Club
   (Tobago), 239–240
The Mount Nevis Hotel & Beach
   Club (Nevis), 170
Music, xvii–xviii
Mustique, 248
   The Cotton House Hotel, 259–261
   Firefly, 262–263
Mustique Airways, xxxiii, 250

Negril (Jamaica)
   The Caves, 43–45
   Couples Swept Away, 296–297
   Grand Lido Negril, 296
   Idle Awhile, 48
   Rockhouse, 47–48
   Tensing Pen Village, 46–47
Nevis, 124
   Four Seasons Nevis Resort, 144–148
   Golden Rock, 150–151
   Hermitage Plantation Inn, 151–153
   Hurricane Cove Bungalows, 169–170

Montpelier Plantation Inn, 148–150
The Mount Nevis Hotel & Beach
   Club, 170
Nisbet Plantation Beach Club,
   143–144
Old Manor Estate & Hotel, 153–154
   tourist information, 125
   traveling to, 125
Nevis Express, xxxii
Nisbet Plantation Beach Club
   (Nevis), 143–144
North American Airlines, 174

Ocean Terrace Inn (St. Kitts), 170–171
Ocho Rios (Jamaica)
   Grand Lido Sans Souci, 297
   Jamaica Inn, 31
Off-season, xxxviii
Old Manor Estate & Hotel (Nevis),
   153–154
Old San Juan (Puerto Rico), 56
   Hotel El Convento, 65–67
Oracabessa (Jamaica), Goldeneye,
   33–35
Orient Bay (St. Martin), 116
"Other Choices" sections, xxvii
Ottley's Plantation Inn (St. Kitts),
   141–142
Outdoor activities, xxvi

Package deals, xxiii–xxiv, xxxviii
Paging systems, xviii–xix
Palm Island (St. Vincent-Grenadines),
   248, 277–278
Parrot Cay (Turks & Caicos), 5–7
Paso Fino (Puerto Rico), 70
Pavilions & Pools (St. Thomas),
   78–79
Peak season, xxii, xxxviii
Peter Island Resort, 91–93
Petit St. Vincent area, 248
Petit St. Vincent Resort, 266–268
Pine Cay (Turks & Caicos), The
   Meridian Club, 2, 4–5
Plantation House Hotel (Bequia),
   256–257
Pointe-à-Pitre, 174

Point Grace (Turks & Caicos), 9–11
Point Pleasant Resort (St. Thomas),
  75–76
Port Antonio (Jamaica)
  Hotel Mocking Bird Hill, 37–39
  The Jamaica Palace Hotel, 45–46
  Trident Villas & Hotel, 36–37
  ratings, xxv

Richardson, Haze, 266, 267
Rincón (Puerto Rico), The Horned
  Dorset Primavera, 60–63
Ristorante Fellini (St. Barths), 183
The Ritz-Carlton, St. Thomas, 79–81
Robert, 300
Robert Reid Associates, 301
Roberts, Mark, 148
Rockhouse (Jamaica), 47–48
Rostang, Jo, 127
Rostang, Michel, 127
Round Hill Hotel & Villas (Jamaica),
  22, 24–26
Royal Palm (St. Kitts), 142
The Royal St. Lucian Hotel, 244
Roydon, Leon, 126–128
Rudolf family, 255
Rum, xxii–xxiii

Saba, 107, 108
  The Cottage Club, 122
  map, 117
  Queen's Gardens Resort, 119–120
  tourist information, 109
  Willard's of Saba, 117–119
Safety, xxviii–xxix
Sailing, Nick Trotter Sailing School
  (Virgin Gorda), 102
St. Barthélemy (St. Barts), 174
  Filao Beach Hotel, 184–186
  François Plantation, 175
  Hôtel Carl Gustaf, 177–179
  Hôtel Eden Rock, 186–187
  Hôtel Emeraude Plage, 202
  Hôtel Guanahani, 189–190
  Hôtel Le Toiny, 181–183
  Hôtel Manapany Cottages, 183–184
  Hôtel St. Barth Isle de France,
    179–181
  map, 177

Residence les Lataniers, 202
  Tom Beach Hotel, 188–189
  tourist information, 175
  Tropical Hotel, 201–202
  Village St. Jean Hotel Cottages,
    191–192
St. Croix, 56
  The Buccaneer, 81–82, 84
  Hibiscus Beach Hotel, 84
  map, 83
  tourist information, 58
  traveling to, 56
St. Eustatius (Statia), 108
  tourist information, 109
St. James's Club (Antigua), 296
St. John (Antigua), 124
St. John (U.S. Virgin Islands), 56
  Caneel Bay, 71–72, 74–75
  map, 73
  tourist information, 58
  traveling to, 58
St. Kitts, 124
  The Golden Lemon, 136–139
  map, 137
  Ocean Terrace Inn, 170–171
  Ottley's Plantation Inn, 141–142
  Rawlins Plantation, 139–141
  tourist information, 125
  traveling to, 125
St. Lucia, 208
  Anse Chastanet Beach Hotel,
    214–216
  The Body Holiday at Lesport, 297
  East Winds Inn, 211–213
  Jalousie Hilton Resort & Spa,
    219–221
  Ladera Resort, 217–218
  map, 211
  Rendezvous, 298
  The Royal St. Lucian Hotel, 244
  Ti Kaye Village, 213–214
  tourist information, 209
  traveling to, 208
  Windjammer Landing Beach Resort,
    209–210
St. Martin, 107–108
  Hotel La Plantation, 115–116
  Hotel L'Esplanade Caraïbe, 121
  La Samanna, 110–112

St. Martin *(continued)*
    Le Meridien, 112–114
    Le Mississippi, 114–115
    Le Petit Hotel, 121–122
    tourist information, 109
St. Pierre, 174
St. Thomas, 56
    map, 77
    Pavilions & Pools, 78–79
    Point Pleasant Resort, 75–76
    The Ritz-Carlton, 79–81
    tourist information, 58
    traveling to, 56
St. Vincent, 248
    Grand View Beach Hotel, 253–254
    Young Island, 251–252
St. Vincent-Grenadines. *See also*
    Bequia; Mustique
    Canouan Beach Hotel, 276–277
    map, 249
    Palm Island, 277–278
    Petit St. Vincent Resort, 266–268
    Saltwhistle Bay Club (Mayreau),
        263–266
    Tamarind Beach Hotel
        (Canouan), 277
    tourist information, 250
    traveling to, 250
Salt Cay, Windmills Plantation
    (Turks & Caicos), 13
Saltwhistle Bay Club (Mayreau),
    263–266
Sandcastle Hotel (Jost Van Dyke),
    104–105
The Sandpiper (Barbados), 230–231
Sandy Lane (Barbados), 231–233
San Juan (Puerto Rico), 56
    The Water Club, 63–65
Sapphire Beach (St. Thomas), 78
The Savannah (Barbados), 245–246
Scenery, Mount (Saba), 117, 118, 122
Seabourne Seaplanes, 56
Seagrape Terrace (Jamaica), 30
Sea urchins, xxvii–xxviii
Secret Harbour Resort (Grenada),
    270–271
The Serenity Spa (Providenciales), 8
Service charges, xxxvii

Sevestre, Oliver, 260
Shambhala (Parrot Cay), 6
Showers, xxx
Shutters by the Bay Restaurant
    (Tobago), 242
Siboney Beach Club (Antigua),
    162–163
Sibonné Boutique Hotel (Turks &
    Caicos), 12–13
Signing in, xix–xx
Simonitsch, Heinz, 29
Small Luxury Hotels of the World, 301
Snook, Kevin, 262
The Spa (Vieques, Puerto Rico), 69
Spa del Sol (Puerto Rico), 59
Spas
    Aveda Concept Spa (Jamaica), 40
    Golden Door Spa (Puerto Rico), 67
    Hotel Eden Rock (St. Barths), 187
    Jalousie Hilton Resort & Spa
        (St. Lucia), 220
    KiYara Ocean Spa (Jamaica), 32
    Manioukani (Guadeloupe), 194
    Round Hill Hotel & Villas
        (Jamaica), 25
    Sandy Lane (Barbados), 231–232
    The Serenity Spa (Turks & Caicos), 8
    Shambhala (Turks & Caicos), 6
    The Spa (Vieques, Puerto Rico), 69
    Spa del Sol (Puerto Rico), 59
    Spa Suite (Virgin Gorda), 97
    Thalasso Spa (Turks & Caicos), 10
    Venus Spa (Anguilla), 135
Spa Suite (Virgin Gorda), 97
Speedy's Fantasy, M/V, xxxiv
Spice Island Beach Resort (Grenada),
    271–273
Spindler, Didier, 205
Sports packages, xxiii
Spring on Bequia, 254–255
Stars, in rating system, xxiv
Statia (St. Eustatius), 108
    tourist information, 109
Stawberry Hill (Jamaica), 39–41
Stevenson, Ross, 229
Stewart, Don, 292
Su Casa (Puerto Rico), 59
Sugar Mill (Jamaica), 29, 30

The Sugar Mill (Tortola), 89
Sugar Mill Restaurant (Tobago), 239
Sun exposure, xxviii
Superman II, 217
The Surf Room (Puerto Rico), 59
SVG Air/Grenadine Express, xxxiii, 250
Swept Away (Jamaica), 48

Tamarind Beach Hotel (Canouan), 277
Tangerine (Puerto Rico), 64
Taxes, xxii, xxxvii
    Cayman Islands, 16
Taxis, xxix
Taylor, Michael, 228–229
Television, xviii
Tensing Pen Village (Jamaica), 46–47
Terre de Haut, Auberge Les Petits
    Saints, 204–205
Thalasso Spa (Turks & Caicos), 10
Thevenet, Dominique, 134
Ti Kaye Village (St. Lucia), 213–214
Tipping, service charges and, xxxvii
Tobago, 208
    Blue Haven Hotel, 241–243
    map, 240–241
    Mount Irvine Bay Hotel & Golf
        Club, 239–240
    tourist information, 209
    traveling to, 209
Tom Beach Hotel (St. Barths), 188–189
Tortola
    Frenchman's Cay Resort Hotel, 105
    Long Bay Beach Resort, 86, 88–89
    Peter Island Resort, 91–93
    The Sugar Mill, 89–91
Total Gym (Turks & Caicos), 13
Tourist information, 301
    Antigua, 125
    Aruba, 280
    Barbados, 209
    Bonaire, 280
    British Virgin Islands, 86
    Cayman Islands, 16
    Curaçao, 280
    Dominica, 209
    Dominican Republic, 50
    Grenada, 250
    Guadeloupe, 175

Jamaica, 22
Martinique, 175
Montserrat, 125
Nevis, 125
Puerto Rico, 58
Saba, 109
St. Barths, 175
St. Eustatius, 109
St. Kitts, 125
St. Lucia, 209
St. Maarten/St. Martin, 109
St. Vincent-Grenadines, 250
Trinidad and Tobago, 209
Turks & Caicos, 2
Tour packages, xxiii–xxiv
Trans Air, xxxiii
Travel agents, xx
Treasure Beach (Jamaica), Jake's, 42–43
Trident Villas & Hotel (Jamaica), 36–37
Trinidad, 208
    tourist information, 209
    traveling to, 209
Tropical Hotel (St. Barts), 201–202
Troubetzkoy, Nick and Karolin, 215
The Tryall Club (Jamaica), 26–28
Turks & Caicos Islands (TCI), 1–13
    Caribbean Paradise Inn
        (Providenciales), 11–12
    Grace Bay Club (Providenciales), 7–9
    map, 3
    The Meridian Club (Pine Cay), 2, 4–5
    Parrot Cay, 5–7
    Point Grace (Providenciales), 9–11
    Sibonné Boutique Hotel, 12–13
    tourist information, 2
    traveling to, 2
    Windmills Plantation (Salt Cay), 13
Turtle Beach (Barbados), 298
Twelve Degrees North (Grenada), 275

United Airlines, xxx
US Airways, xxx, 16, 22, 56, 108, 124,
    208, 209, 280
U.S. Virgin Islands. *See also* St. Croix;
    St. John; St. Thomas
    maps, 57, 73, 77, 83
    tourist information, 58

Venus Spa (Anguilla), 135
Vieques (Puerto Rico), Wyndham
  Martineau Bay Resort & Spa, 68–71
Village St. Jean Hotel Cottages
  (St. Barths), 191–192
Villa Nova Hotel (Barbados), 235–237
Virgin Gorda
    Biras Creek Resort, 98–101
    The Bitter End Yacht Club, 101–103
    Little Dix Bay, 96–98

Walker, Barbara, 37
Water
    conservation, xxx
    drinking, xxviii
The Water Club (Puerto Rico), 63–65
Watersports
    Hyatt Regency Grand Cayman
      (Cayman Islands), 18
    Long Bay Beach Resort (Tortola), 88

Whitfield, Richard, 29
Willard's of Saba, 117–119
Willemstad (Curaçao), 282
WIMCO, 300, 301
Windjammer Landing Beach Resort
  (St. Lucia), 209–210
Windmills Plantation (Turks &
  Caicos), 13
Windward Airways (Winair), xxxii,
  108, 117, 124, 125, 174
Wratten, Aaron, 62
Wratten, Kingsley, 60
Wyndham Martineau Bay Resort &
  Spa (Puerto Rico), 68–71

Young Island (St. Vincent), 251–252

FROMMER'S® COMPLETE TRAVEL GUIDES

Alaska
Alaska Cruises & Ports of Call
Amsterdam
Argentina & Chile
Arizona
Atlanta
Australia
Austria
Bahamas
Barcelona, Madrid & Seville
Beijing
Belgium, Holland & Luxembourg
Bermuda
Boston
Brazil
British Columbia & the Canadian
  Rockies
Brussels & Bruges
Budapest & the Best of Hungary
California
Canada
Cancún, Cozumel & the Yucatán
Cape Cod, Nantucket & Martha's
  Vineyard
Caribbean
Caribbean Cruises & Ports of Call
Caribbean Ports of Call
Carolinas & Georgia
Chicago
China
Colorado
Costa Rica
Cuba
Denmark
Denver, Boulder & Colorado Springs
England
Europe
European Cruises & Ports of Call

Florida
France
Germany
Great Britain
Greece
Greek Islands
Hawaii
Hong Kong
Honolulu, Waikiki & Oahu
Ireland
Israel
Italy
Jamaica
Japan
Las Vegas
London
Los Angeles
Maryland & Delaware
Maui
Mexico
Montana & Wyoming
Montréal & Québec City
Munich & the Bavarian Alps
Nashville & Memphis
New England
New Mexico
New Orleans
New York City
New Zealand
Northern Italy
Norway
Nova Scotia, New Brunswick &
  Prince Edward Island
Oregon
Paris
Peru
Philadelphia & the Amish Country
Portugal

Prague & the Best of the Czech
  Republic
Provence & the Riviera
Puerto Rico
Rome
San Antonio & Austin
San Diego
San Francisco
Santa Fe, Taos & Albuquerque
Scandinavia
Scotland
Seattle & Portland
Shanghai
Sicily
Singapore & Malaysia
South Africa
South America
South Florida
South Pacific
Southeast Asia
Spain
Sweden
Switzerland
Texas
Thailand
Tokyo
Toronto
Tuscany & Umbria
USA
Utah
Vancouver & Victoria
Vermont, New Hampshire & Maine
Vienna & the Danube Valley
Virgin Islands
Virginia
Walt Disney World® & Orlando
Washington, D.C.
Washington State

FROMMER'S® DOLLAR-A-DAY GUIDES

Australia from $50 a Day
California from $70 a Day
England from $75 a Day
Europe from $70 a Day
Florida from $70 a Day
Hawaii from $80 a Day

Ireland from $60 a Day
Italy from $70 a Day
London from $85 a Day
New York from $90 a Day
Paris from $80 a Day

San Francisco from $70 a Day
Washington, D.C. from $80 a Day
Portable London from $85 a Day
Portable New York City from $90
  a Day

FROMMER'S® PORTABLE GUIDES

Acapulco, Ixtapa & Zihuatanejo
Amsterdam
Aruba
Australia's Great Barrier Reef
Bahamas
Berlin
Big Island of Hawaii
Boston
California Wine Country
Cancún
Cayman Islands
Charleston
Chicago
Disneyland®
Dublin
Florence

Frankfurt
Hong Kong
Houston
Las Vegas
Las Vegas for Non-Gamblers
London
Los Angeles
Los Cabos & Baja
Maine Coast
Maui
Miami
Nantucket & Martha's Vineyard
New Orleans
New York City
Paris
Phoenix & Scottsdale

Portland
Puerto Rico
Puerto Vallarta, Manzanillo &
  Guadalajara
Rio de Janeiro
San Diego
San Francisco
Savannah
Seattle
Sydney
Tampa & St. Petersburg
Vancouver
Venice
Virgin Islands
Washington, D.C.

FROMMER'S® NATIONAL PARK GUIDES

Banff & Jasper
Family Vacations in the National
  Parks

Grand Canyon
National Parks of the American West
Rocky Mountain

Yellowstone & Grand Teton
Yosemite & Sequoia/Kings Canyon
Zion & Bryce Canyon

FROMMER'S® MEMORABLE WALKS

Chicago
London

New York
Paris

San Francisco

FROMMER'S® WITH KIDS GUIDES

Chicago
Las Vegas
New York City

Ottawa
San Francisco
Toronto

Vancouver
Washington, D.C.

SUZY GERSHMAN'S BORN TO SHOP GUIDES

Born to Shop: France
Born to Shop: Hong Kong,
    Shanghai & Beijing

Born to Shop: Italy
Born to Shop: London

Born to Shop: New York
Born to Shop: Paris

FROMMER'S® IRREVERENT GUIDES

Amsterdam
Boston
Chicago
Las Vegas
London

Los Angeles
Manhattan
New Orleans
Paris
Rome

San Francisco
Seattle & Portland
Vancouver
Walt Disney World®
Washington, D.C.

FROMMER'S® BEST-LOVED DRIVING TOURS

Britain
California
Florida
France

Germany
Ireland
Italy
New England

Northern Italy
Scotland
Spain
Tuscany & Umbria

HANGING OUT™ GUIDES

Hanging Out in England
Hanging Out in Europe

Hanging Out in France
Hanging Out in Ireland

Hanging Out in Italy
Hanging Out in Spain

THE UNOFFICIAL GUIDES®

Bed & Breakfasts and Country
    Inns in:
    California
    Great Lakes States
    Mid-Atlantic
    New England
    Northwest
    Rockies
    Southeast
    Southwest
Best RV & Tent Campgrounds in:
    California & the West
    Florida & the Southeast
    Great Lakes States
    Mid-Atlantic
    Northeast
    Northwest & Central Plains

Southwest & South Central
    Plains
    U.S.A.
Beyond Disney
Branson, Missouri
California with Kids
Central Italy
Chicago
Cruises
Disneyland®
Florida with Kids
Golf Vacations in the Eastern U.S.
Great Smoky & Blue Ridge Region
Inside Disney
Hawaii
Las Vegas
London
Maui

Mexio's Best Beach Resorts
Mid-Atlantic with Kids
Mini Las Vegas
Mini-Mickey
New England & New York with
    Kids
New Orleans
New York City
Paris
San Francisco
Skiing & Snowboarding in the West
Southeast with Kids
Walt Disney World®
Walt Disney World® for
    Grown-ups
Walt Disney World® with Kids
Washington, D.C.
World's Best Diving Vacations

SPECIAL-INTEREST TITLES

Frommer's Adventure Guide to Australia &
    New Zealand
Frommer's Adventure Guide to Central America
Frommer's Adventure Guide to India & Pakistan
Frommer's Adventure Guide to South America
Frommer's Adventure Guide to Southeast Asia
Frommer's Adventure Guide to Southern Africa
Frommer's Britain's Best Bed & Breakfasts and
    Country Inns
Frommer's Caribbean Hideaways
Frommer's Exploring America by RV
Frommer's Fly Safe, Fly Smart

Frommer's France's Best Bed & Breakfasts and
    Country Inns
Frommer's Gay & Lesbian Europe
Frommer's Italy's Best Bed & Breakfasts and
    Country Inns
Frommer's Road Atlas Britain
Frommer's Road Atlas Europe
Frommer's Road Atlas France
The New York Times' Guide to Unforgettable
    Weekends
Places Rated Almanac
Retirement Places Rated
Rome Past & Present